# MIND, LANGUAGE, AND MI

This volume presents a selection of the philosophical essays which Richard Rorty wrote during the first decade of his career, and complements four previous volumes of his papers published by Cambridge University Press. In this long neglected body of work, which many leading philosophers still consider to be his best, Rorty develops his views on the nature and scope of philosophy in a manner which supplements and elucidates his definitive statement on these matters in *Philosophy and the Mirror of Nature*. He also develops his ground-breaking version of eliminative materialism and sets out original views on various central topics in the philosophy of language, concerning private language, indeterminacy, and verificationalism. A substantial introduction examines Rorty's philosophical development from 1961 to 1972. The volume completes our understanding of Rorty's intellectual trajectory and offers lucid statements of positions which retain their relevance to current debates.

RICHARD RORTY (1931–2007) was Professor of Comparative Literature and Philosophy at Stanford University.

STEPHEN LEACH is an Honorary Fellow of the Research Institute for Law, Politics and Justice at Keele University. He is the author of *The Foundations of History* (2009), and co-author, with James Connelly and Peter Johnson, of *R. G. Collingwood: A Research Companion* (2014).

JAMES TARTAGLIA is Senior Lecturer in Philosophy at Keele University. He is the author of *Rorty and the Mirror of Nature* (2007) and *Philosophy in a Meaningless Life* (forthcoming), and editor of *Richard Rorty: Critical Assessments of Leading Philosophers* (2009).

# MIND, LANGUAGE, AND METAPHILOSOPHY

## Early Philosophical Papers

RICHARD RORTY

EDITED BY

STEPHEN LEACH AND JAMES TARTAGLIA

# CAMBRIDGE
## UNIVERSITY PRESS

University Printing House, Cambridge CB2 8BS, United Kingdom

Published in the United States of America by Cambridge University Press, New York

Cambridge University Press is part of the University of Cambridge.

It furthers the University's mission by disseminating knowledge in the pursuit of education, learning and research at the highest international levels of excellence.

www.cambridge.org
Information on this title: www.cambridge.org/9781107039780

© Stephen Leach and James Tartaglia, 2014

First published 2014

Printed in the United Kingdom by Clays, St Ives plc

*A catalogue record for this publication is available from the British Library*

*Library of Congress Cataloguing in Publication data*
Rorty, Richard.
Mind, language, and metaphilosophy : early philosophical papers / Richard Rorty ; edited by Stephen Leach and James Tartaglia.
pages    cm
Includes index.
ISBN 978-1-107-03978-0 (Hardback) – ISBN 978-1-107-61229-7 (Paperback)
1. Philosophy, American–20th century.    2. Philosophy, Modern–20th century.    I. Title.
B945.R521L43 2013
191–dc23    2013026803

ISBN 978-1-107-03978-0 Hardback
ISBN 978-1-107-61229-7 Paperback

# Contents

# Contents

# *Foreword*

The acclaim and controversy that has surrounded Richard Rorty's later work, starting with *Philosophy and the Mirror of Nature* in 1979, has tended to eclipse the influence of his major contributions to analytic philosophy of mind in the 1960s and 1970s. Like Hilary Putnam, whose papers from that era remain classics in spite of their author's abandonment of them, Rorty shaped the field for subsequent decades with a series of insightful, constructive, imaginative papers harnessing the insights of Sellars and Quine, and developing his own distinctive varieties of pragmatism and naturalism. Rorty's version of eliminative materialism was both the first and the subtlest, and anybody interested in defending any variation today would be well advised to mine his work for insights. The same can be said for his delicate and undoctrinaire treatment of functionalism.

I would venture to say that today's combatants in the skirmishes over property dualism, supervenience, mental causation, and their subsidiary issues would find that most of their moves and countermoves were anticipated and preempted by Rorty's discussions more than forty years ago. "Mind-Body Identity, Privacy, and Categories" (1965), "Incorrigibility as the Mark of the Mental" (1970), "In Defense of Eliminative Materialism" (1972), and "Functionalism, Machines, and Incorrigibility" (1972) ought to be required reading for all aspiring philosophers of mind today, as they were for us when they first appeared, and they are only the best known of his works from that period. Fortunately, Rorty wrote admirably clear and vivid philosophy which holds up well at this remove in time, so this volume will be a joy to read, both for those who remember the impact these essays had when they were published and for those who know Rorty only as the lightning rod of the later culture wars.

DANIEL C. DENNETT

# Acknowledgments

The editors would like to thank Mary Varney Rorty and Alan Mala-chowski for making this volume possible, as well as Matthew Festenstein for some useful suggestions, and they would also like to thank Hilary Gaskin, Anna Lowe, Gaia Poggiogalli, and Linda Randall at Cambridge University Press, all of whom made invaluable contributions to the pro-duction of this volume. The articles have, wherever practicable, been formatted to conform with the layout of the four previous volumes of Rorty's papers published by Cambridge University Press, but otherwise they are reproduced in their original form except for the correction of a few typographical errors.

"Pragmatism, categories, and language" was published in *Philosophical Review*, 70: 197–223 (1961).

"The limits of reductionism" was published in *Experience, Existence, and the Good: Essays in honour of Paul Weiss*, 100–16, edited by Irwin C. Lieb (Carbondale: Southern Illinois University Press 1961).

"Realism, categories, and the "linguistic turn"" was published in *International Philosophical Quarterly*, Volume 2, Issue 2: 307–22 (1962); DOI: 10.5840/ipq19622214

"The subjectivist principle and the linguistic turn" was published in *Alfred North Whitehead: Essays on his philosophy*, 134–57, edited by George L. Kline (New Jersey: Prentice-Hall, 1963). While every effort has been made, it has not been possible to identify the current copyright holder for this chapter. If any omissions are brought to our notice, we will be happy to include the appropriate acknowledgements on reprinting.

'Empiricism, extensionalism, and reductionism' was published in *Mind*, 72: 176–86 (1963).

'Mind-body identity, privacy, and categories' was published in *Review of Metaphysics*, 19: 24–54 (1965).

'Do analysts and metaphysicians disagree?' was published in *Proceedings of the American Catholic Philosophical Association*, Volume 41: 39–53 (1967).

'Incorrigibility as the mark of the mental' was published in *Journal of Philosophy*, 67, issue no. 3: 399–429 (1970).

'Wittgenstein, privileged access, and incommunicability' was published by *American Philosophical Quartely*, 7: 192–205 (1970).

'In defence of eliminative materialism' was published in *Review of Metaphysics*, 24: 112–21 (1970).

'Cartesian epistemology and changes in ontology' was published in *Contemporary American Philosophy*, 273–92, edited by John E. Smith (London: Allen and Unwin / New York: Humanities Press, 1970). While every effort has been made, it has not been possible to identify the current copyright holder for this chapter. If any omissions are brought to our notice, we will be happy to include the appropriate acknowledgements on reprinting.

'Strawson's objectivity argument' was published in *Review of Metaphysics*, 24: 207–44 (1970).

'Verificationism and transcendental arguments' was published in *Nous*, 5: 3–14 (1971).

'Indeterminacy of translation and of truth' was published in *Synthese*, 23: 443–62 (1972).

'Dennett on awareness' was published in *Philosophical Studies*, 23, issue no. 3: 153–62 (1972).

'Functionalism, machines, and incorrigibility' was published in *Journal of Philosophy*, 69: 203–20 (1972).

# Introduction

## Stephen Leach and James Tartaglia

Richard Rorty published six volumes of his own selections from the papers he wrote between 1972 and 2006. Together with his two monographs, these now provide the main source for his views, and scholars may debate at leisure whether some of the papers Rorty did not select have been unjustly neglected as a consequence. However, it seems clear to us that there is a large body of Rorty's work which has most certainly been unjustly neglected: the early work. For before he wrote "The World Well Lost," the 1972 paper that opens *Consequences of Pragmatism*, Rorty was already an influential philosopher. Many still fondly recall this first phase of his career, and we have often heard say that Rorty was an excellent analytic philosopher back in the 1960s and early 1970s before he read some continental philosophy, became a postmodernist, and consequently went off the rails. Almost everything about this latter view is wrong, but there is nevertheless a kernel of truth to it.[1] This is that Rorty wrote some classic papers in the 1960s and early 1970s which, for better or worse, would probably be of more interest to the average contemporary philosopher working on mind or language than his mature manifesto of replacing objectivity with solidarity and metaphysics with literature. But given that Rorty's thinking never did radically change direction, there is also plenty to be found here for those interested in the mature Rorty. To neglect the papers in this volume is, in short, to neglect innovative ideas which retain their interest and relevance, as well as a significant part of the career of a highly significant thinker – the part you might well find you like best. The early Rorty has been languishing in old journals, obscure collections and faded memories for too long!

---

[1] Rorty's MA supervisor Charles Hartshorne studied under Husserl and Heidegger in the 1920s, and Rorty taught a course on Heidegger during his first appointment at Wellesley College. Any philosopher who thinks that mistrusting the notion of objective truth amounts to being off the rails will find little reason in this volume for believing Rorty was ever on them.

Despite our enthusiasm for early Rorty, however, we must admit that Rorty himself had no interest in seeing his early papers reprinted; he thought they had passed their sell-by date.[2] On this matter, we shall simply have to disagree, noting that his assessment of his earlier work was typically harsh, even allowing for the admirable trait of modesty.[3] We also suspect Rorty's dismissal of these early works was influenced by his pragmatic concern to produce a positive effect upon intellectual life; he was reluctant to risk mixing his message. But if that was indeed his concern, he need not have worried. For although Rorty changed his mind about some of the issues discussed in this volume, the things that really mattered to him, namely his pragmatism, his desire to metaphilosophically get behind technical philosophical debates, his unflagging ambition to reconcile apparently divergent strands of thought, his conviction in the importance of the history of philosophy – all these characteristically Rortyan traits are abundantly in evidence here. The more complete picture of Rorty that emerges with these papers is of a thinker with a particularly single-minded vision, in the light of which it becomes easier to believe, and be impressed by, his 1992 statement that, "I have spent 40 years looking for a coherent and convincing way of formulating my worries about what, if anything, philosophy is good for."[4]

As regards our selection, we have only included papers published before "The World Well Lost" since Rorty made his own selections after that, and we have tried to select pieces that still stand up on their own, retaining more philosophical than historical interest. We have not included any reviews, even though some are of interest in understanding the genesis of his thought, and we have also missed out some minor occasional pieces, his encyclopedia entries, a paper on Whitehead, and the introduction to his philosophy of language anthology, *The Linguistic Turn*. The latter, we think, is the only really significant omission, but it remains best read in the context for which it was intended: at the start of the anthology.

Rorty used the introductions to his collections to draw out the moral of his work, marshaling diverse discussions in support of a common

---

[2] We have this on the authority of Alan Malachowski (personal correspondence); Rorty also suggests as much in his 2007 "Intellectual Biography" (in R. Auxier and L. Hahn, eds., *The Philosophy of Richard Rorty* [Chicago, 2010]).

[3] See, for example, the later assessment he made of his 1965 introduction to *The Linguistic Turn* ("Twenty-Five Years Later", in R. Rorty, ed., *The Linguistic Turn* [Chicago, 1992]); or some of his later comments on *Philosophy and the Mirror of Nature* ("Response to Michael Williams", in R. Brandom, ed., *Rorty and his Critics* [Oxford, 2000]).

[4] *Philosophy and Social Hope* (London, 1999), p. 11.

pragmatist cause. Obviously, we cannot do this for him, so we have instead supplied what we think most readers would most appreciate: discussion of the papers in chronological order of publication.[5] We will not critically evaluate Rorty's arguments, since this would not be an appropriate place to do so; this is a collection of papers by Rorty, not about him.[6] Rather, we will restrict ourselves to providing overviews, making connections, and highlighting points of interest, whether from the perspective of on-going debates or of Rorty's wider projects. We will also provide some bibliographical information. Rorty once said that "[a]ttempts to link up a thinker's ideas with his or her politics or personal life are not irrational, and they may produce truths. But they are optional."[7] Thus, he thought Heidegger was "a pretty nasty character," but this was irrelevant to his work: he could have written the same books if he had been a hero.[8] However, the fact that Rorty, unlike Heidegger, was not entirely dismissive of biography presumably explains why he wrote two autobiographical essays, gave sociologist Neil Gross access to his papers to write his biography, and why he increasingly added autobiographical notes to his later writings.[9] Gross argued for a strong connection between Rorty's thought and biography, but we have no such commitment: we simply include biographical information whenever it seems interesting, and especially when it helps explain how ideas entered Rorty's work in support of his on-going aims.

The collection starts in 1961 with Rorty's first published article "Pragmatism, Categories, and Language." Appearing in the *Philosophical Review*, this was certainly an auspicious start for a twenty-nine-year-old

---

[5] There was too much overlap for a useful thematic organization, and chronological order of composition, to the extent we were able to determine this, provided no revelations.

[6] It does not follow that we accept all his views. One of us has argued that Rorty's thinking ultimately hits a brick wall, since he cannot provide good reasons to accept his pragmatism; he seems to offer plenty but on closer inspection they disintegrate (J. Tartaglia, "Did Rorty's Pragmatism Have Foundations?," *International Journal of Philosophical Studies*, 18 [2010], pp. 607–27; for an earlier evaluation, see J. Tartaglia, *Rorty and the Mirror of Nature* [London, 2007], pp. 224–30). The other has argued that were Rorty's criticisms of philosophy as a mirror of nature to be made from the viewpoint of the Pyrrhonian skeptic, philosophy might yet retain its autonomy; as an autonomous discipline philosophy does not necessarily stand or fall with a mirroring role (S. Leach, "Pyrrhonian Skepticism and the Mirror of Nature," *Journal of Speculative Philosophy*, 27, 4 [2013], pp. 308–401).

[7] E. Mendieta, ed., *Take care of freedom and truth will take care of itself: interviews with Richard Rorty* (Stanford, 2005), p. 108.

[8] *Contingency, Irony, and Solidarity* (Cambridge, 1989), p. 111. Rorty imagines an alternative, better Heidegger in *Philosophy and Social Hope*, pp. 190–7.

[9] For Heidegger's notorious attitude, see R. Safranski, *Ein Meister aus Deutschland: Heidegger und seine Zeit* (Munich, 1994), p. 15. Rorty's autobiographical essays are in *Philosophy and Social Hope* and Auxier and Hahn *op. cit.*; Gross's biography is *Richard Rorty: The Making of an American Philosopher* (Chicago, 2008).

philosopher. But Rorty already had a reputation as someone to watch; the paper was written at Wellesley College, where Rorty had his first teaching post from 1958, but by the time it was published he was already set to move to Princeton in the fall, having turned down offers from Harvard, Yale, John Hopkins, Connecticut, and Texas. At Wellesley, Rorty felt he was "behind the times," for he had done his Ph.D. at Yale, which was then "entirely pre-analytic … the most reactionary of U.S. philosophy departments." Consequently, now that "[a]nalytic philosophy was taking over," he thought his expertise in metaphysics and history of philosophy would no longer stand him in good stead, so he immersed himself in Quine, Wittgenstein, and Austin; he "retooled" himself to become an analytic philosopher.[10] This paper finds him trying to reconcile these new-found interests with pragmatism.

The paper begins: "Pragmatism is getting respectable again." As a patriotic fifteen-year-old arriving at the University of Chicago, Rorty had been shocked to discover that pragmatism, America's only home-grown philosophy, was looked down upon by the establishment. This was because the establishment was dominated by European émigrés like Carnap, who had "simply [taken] over American philosophy departments,"[11] and who stood for the "hard" discipline of logic and analysis, not "soft" concerns with historical understanding and social benefits. But Rorty was never a believer in irreconcilable dichotomies, so he sets out in this paper, just as later in *Philosophy and the Mirror of Nature*, to show that analytic philosophy can lead to pragmatist conclusions. At the time, he was encouraged by Morton White's recent *Toward Reunion in Philosophy*, which had argued that Quinean holism supported the pragmatist view that inquiry should have prior ends in view. But nevertheless, back in the early 1960s there was considerable wishful thinking behind this memorable opener.[12] Did Rorty succeed in making pragmatism respectable? Not really, for by the time he was associated with it he was no longer a respectable figure in the eyes of the establishment, given his later adoption

---

[10] Rorty in D. Nystrom and K. Puckett, *Against Bosses, Against Oligarchies: A Conversation with Richard Rorty* (Chicago, 2002), pp. 53–4.

[11] Rorty in G. Borradori, ed., *The American Philosopher: Interviews* (Chicago, 1994), p. 109.

[12] For the institutional status of pragmatism at the time, see N. Gross "Becoming a Pragmatist Philosopher: Status, Self-Concept, and Intellectual Choice," *American Sociological Review*, 67 (2002), pp. 52–76 (pp. 56–7), and N. Gross "Richard Rorty's Pragmatism: A Case Study in the Sociology of Ideas," *Theory and Society*, 32 (2003), pp. 93–148 (p. 127).

of a rather less conciliatory stance than he takes here, namely that analytic philosophy self-destructs after leading us to pragmatism.[13]

To try to rehabilitate pragmatism, Rorty discusses Peirce because unlike Dewey and James, Peirce was a logician, and thus the most liable to be viewed as respectable in analytic eyes. However, Peirce was the classical pragmatist for whom the mature Rorty had least sympathy owing to the former's lack of concern for moral and social issues, a worry foreshadowed here in an ambivalent footnote.[14] The paper tries to show that Peirce's doctrine of the reality and irreducibility of "thirdness" shows the way beyond the reductionism of logical positivism towards the more enlightened stance of the later Wittgenstein. Crucially, the latter stance recognizes that "language cannot be transcended" (p. 26), or, in other words, as Rorty would later formulate this most typical of Rortyan claims, that we cannot "step outside our skins."[15] With this first paper clearly in mind, Rorty later recalled in withering tones that he "wast-e[d]" his "27th and 28th years trying to discover the secret of Charles Saunders Peirce's esoteric doctrine of 'the reality of Thirdness' and thus of his fantastically elaborate semiotico-metaphysical 'System'."[16] However, even if he did eventually find less circuitous ways to unite Wittgensteinian philosophy of language with pragmatism, his direction of travel was clear from the outset, and there is still plenty that remains of interest in this dense and rich paper, particularly the reflections on vagueness (another concern he later considered a waste of time).[17]

When "The Limits of Reductionism" came out later in the year, Rorty had just started at Princeton and become a new father with his first wife, the philosopher Amélie Oksenberg Rorty. The paper is set on the "ethereal plane of metaphilosophy" (p. 43), and finds Rorty concerned with the problem of self-referential consistency for reductionist programs in philosophy. The best-known example of this problem arose for the logical positivist claim that all linguistic expressions are tautologies, empirical hypotheses, or nonsense; the problem was that the claim itself did not seem to fit these categories. Faced with this problem, the reductionist urge

---

[13] In *Philosophy and the Mirror of Nature* (Princeton, 1979), Rorty says "epistemological behaviorism" rather than "pragmatism", but he adopted the latter label for his position soon afterwards.

[14] Rorty ultimately decided that Peirce's views were incoherent; see Auxier and Hahn *op. cit.*, p. 8. For an interesting imagined dialogue between Rorty and Peirce, see Susan Haack's "'We pragmatists...': Peirce and Rorty in conversation,' reprinted from the *Partisan Review* (1997) in vol. III of J. Tartaglia, ed., *Richard Rorty: Critical Assessments of Leading Philosophers* (London, 2009).

[15] R. Rorty, *Consequences of Pragmatism* (Minneapolis, 1982), p. xix.

[16] *Philosophy and Social Hope*, p. 134.

[17] R. Rorty, "How many grains make a heap?," *London Review of Books*, January 20, 2005.

to explain the bewildering diversity of the world in terms of a more manageable number of elements is blocked. To unblock it a "distinction of level" must be made (p. 46), such as Carnap's distinction between internal and external questions, or Kant's distinction between empirical reality and the things-in-themselves, since then the reductionist claim need no longer be subject to its own strictures. The task of metaphilosophy, Rorty thinks, is to determine the utility of such distinctions of level; philosophy requires metaphilosophy to make these distinctions and keep itself self-consistent, for reductionism reaches its limit when it can no longer provide a metaphilosophical account of itself.[18]

Metaphilosophy is also the subject of "Realism, Categories, and the 'Linguistic Turn'," published in 1962. This was a troubled year for Rorty, since his father suffered a nervous breakdown and became psychotic, remaining so until his death in 1973, while Rorty himself began treatment for obsessional neurosis which continued until 1968.[19] It was also the year Rorty started approaching publishers with his idea for *The Linguistic Turn*, and just as in the introduction to that anthology, this paper defends analytic philosophy's preoccupation with language, while setting the distinction between ideal and ordinary language philosophy within a metaphilosophical framework. Rorty begins by trying to allay the suspicions of Aristotelian realists that the linguistic turn was a misguided product of Cartesian subjectivist premises. Rather, he argues, it was justified by two key ideas we have already encountered: the impossibility of transcending language and the need to avoid self-referential inconsistency. There are good reasons for taking the linguistic turn, then; moreover, doing so does not require realism to be abandoned, for although ideal-language philosophy does indeed lead in that direction, ordinary-language philosophy offers realism new and powerful support.

In 1963, Rorty published two papers on A. N. Whitehead, a philosopher of great significance to him as a graduate student; his MA dissertation at Chicago was about Whitehead, and was supervised by Charles Hartshorne, one of Whitehead's students, while his Ph.D. at Yale was supervised by Paul Weiss, also one of Whitehead's students. The paper we have included, "The Subjectivist Principle and the Linguistic Turn," finds Rorty pointing out affinities between Whitehead's metaphysics and

---

[18] It is interesting that Rorty always saw the importance of avoiding self-referential inconsistency, and even tried to develop a general framework to understand how it could be avoided, given that the problem plagued his career in the eyes of some of his critics. For the definitive statement of this criticism, see Hilary Putnam, *Realism with a Human Face* (Cambridge, MA, 1992), pp. 18–29; and for an assessment of Rorty's response, see Tartaglia, "Did Rorty's Pragmatism have Foundations?".

[19] Gross, *Richard Rorty*, p. 216.

Wilfrid Sellars's analytic philosophy.[20] In 2007, he remembered this as one of only two papers from the 1960s, along with "Pragmatism, Categories, and Language," that he still liked; both attempted to "fuse the horizons of seemingly opposed philosophers." And this fusion was particularly significant to Rorty, since Sellars was his new hero: while immersing himself in analytic philosophy he had soon found that "the one analytic philosopher I really cared for was Wilfrid Sellars" and he later recalled that "for the next twenty years most of what I published was an attempt to capitalize on his achievements."[21] This paper, then, announces Rorty's new affiliation with Sellars and analytic philosophy. He still sympathized with Whitehead's aim of overcoming the substance–property framework of traditional metaphysics, for he saw both Whitehead and Sellars as grappling with the "central task of contemporary philosophy" (p. 95), namely to show that we can have knowledge of an independent reality despite our inability to "step outside our skins." But Rorty now thought Whitehead's metaphysical approach had been superseded. The personal significance that this had for him can be gauged by the fact that the previous year he had proposed, to the outrage of his old teacher Hartshorne, to give a lecture entitled, "Why Whitehead is Good but Wilfrid Sellars is Better."[22] The  key Sellarsian claim in the paper, namely that knowledge relates to facts, not substances or properties, was later to play a prominent role in *Philosophy and the Mirror of Nature*.

"Empiricism, Extensionalism, and Reductionism" also appeared in 1963. Its aim is to show that empiricism and extensionalism have been unjustly tarred with the same brush as reductionism, but when suitably disentangled, we see that only reductionism should be rejected. Rorty begins by arguing that the empiricist view that distinct ideas can be traced back to distinct sensory impressions, and hence that "there is no real indefiniteness in our thought" (p. 98), naturally leads to the extensionalist view that the world can be described in exclusively extensional language, that is, language in which co-referring terms can be freely interchanged without changing the truth-values of its statements. Typical examples of nonextensional language involve mental states. For example, it is true that "Danglars believed the Count of Monte Cristo was rich" but, until he discovered that they were one and the same, Danglars did not believe this of Edmond Dantès;

[20] The other paper, "Matter and Event," is more narrowly focused on the interpretation of Whitehead's philosophy. We judged that one paper about Whitehead would probably suffice.

[21] Auxier and Hahn *op. cit.*, p. 11; Nystrom and Puckett *op. cit.*, p. 53; Auxier and Hahn *op. cit.*, p. 8.

[22] Gross, *Richard Rorty*, p. 166.

thus the sentence is not extensional. This suggests an indefiniteness in language, on the grounds that since the terms for Dantès cannot be freely substituted, they cannot simply be being used to discriminate features in the world. However, Rorty provides two alternative strategies he thinks will always allow us to "fix it so that each difference in words can be correlated with a difference in the world" (p. 100). The possibility of such extensionalist reconstructions is all empiricism requires, he thinks, and although they might lead to the *ad hoc* positing of new entities, or perhaps even "a new language to suit the occasion" (p. 103), this will not be perceived as a problem except by those held captive by Sellars's "Myth of the Given," who think experience provides the means to construct a unitary, reductionist language adequate to the timeless nature of the world. But "this world is well lost" (p. 105) says Rorty, just as he would nine years later.

The year 1965 signalled a breakthrough in Rorty's career, since he received tenure at Princeton and published "Mind-Body Identity, Privacy, and Categories," a landmark paper in the history of the philosophy of mind, and the only one in this collection to have been regularly reprinted.[23] He later described it as "an attempt to please [Gregory] Vlastos, and my Harvard- or Oxford-trained colleagues, by contributing to an ongoing debate in the philosophical journals, eschewing historical retrospection."[24] The debate in question concerned U. T. Place and J. J. C. Smart's "Identity Theory," which claims that sensations are brain-processes, and hence are compatible with a physicalist understanding of the world. Rorty proposed radicalizing the theory with a "Disappearance Form of the Identity Theory" which aimed to "impugn the existence of sensations" (p. 114). During the debate that ensued, the label "eliminative materialism" was coined to describe Rorty's position. A similar position had earlier been defended by Paul Feyerabend, but Rorty's paper remained the *locus classicus* of eliminative materialism, even after Rorty himself abandoned it, until Paul Churchland's 1981 "Eliminative Materialism and the Propositional Attitudes" changed the target of elimination from conscious sensations to beliefs and other propositional attitudes.[25]

---

[23] Rorty must have written the paper long before 1965, since he submitted it in 1963 for a collection edited by Max Black; Black rejected it (*ibid.*, p. 186).

[24] Auxier and Hahn *op. cit.*, p. 11.

[25] James Cornman coined it in "On the Elimination of 'Sensations' and Sensations," *Review of Metaphysics*, 22 (1968), pp. 15–35. For highlights of the ensuing debate, see vol. 1 of Tartaglia, ed., *Richard Rorty*. Feyerabend's eliminativism is presented in "Materialism and the Mind-Body

In 1967, Rorty finally saw *The Linguistic Turn* published, together with two entries in Paul Edward's high-profile *Encyclopedia of Philosophy*, and the long-forgotten but fascinating paper we reproduce here, "Do Analysts and Metaphysicians Disagree?" The topic is again metaphilosophy, and Rorty spends most of the paper trying to show that a principled distinction between analytic philosophers and metaphysicians cannot be drawn. Both deal with the same problems, he thinks, and the only significance to the analyst's focus on second-order questions about language rather than first-order questions about the world is that "there are no methods except attending to actual or possible linguistic behavior to decide questions about the nature of *x*" (pp. 137–8). Unless metaphysicians have "an alternative method of inquiry at hand" (p. 138), then, and Rorty does not think they do, this apparently key difference is just presentational, since analysts are free to follow metaphysicians in claiming to have made discoveries about the world rather than language. Rorty's conclusion is that a "vague" but "less misleading" way of drawing the distinction is through their differing attitudes to wisdom (p. 9). Thus, the metaphysician does, and the analyst does not, believe that finding answers to the traditional problems of philosophy will make us wise; only the metaphysician retains "Platonic faith that argument can bring us to truth" (p. 146). The analytic philosopher, by contrast, looks for wisdom in science, art, and the kind of "speculative philosophy" which aims not at discovering truths, but at "finding new ways of seeing things through finding new ways of saying things" (p. 133); Rorty's "edifying philosophy" was later to play this role.[26] Thus, ultimately, the analyst realises that the philosophical tradition leads "either to speculative philosophy or to a postphilosophical culture" (p. 146). Rorty was to draw much the same conclusion in the introduction to *Consequences of Pragmatism*, but by then it is the pragmatist who ushers in a "post-Philosophical culture";[27] in this paper the analyst was still the hero.

There were no publications from Rorty in 1968–9. During this time, he suffered from clinical depression, but he still managed to remain productive, writing drafts of at least two of his 1970 papers and beginning work on the plot to *Philosophy and the Mirror of Nature*, the leading idea of which had already been announced in *The Linguistic Turn*, where Rorty says "the most important thing that has happened in philosophy during the last

---

Problem," *Review of Metaphysics*, 17 (1963), pp. 49–66. For Rorty's ambivalent rejection of eliminative materialism, see *Philosophy and the Mirror of Nature*, pp. 118–27.
[26] *Philosophy and the Mirror of Nature*, p. 360.
[27] *Consequences of Pragmatism*, p. xl.

thirty years" was not the linguistic turn itself, but rather "the beginning of a thoroughgoing rethinking of certain epistemological difficulties" which stemmed from "the traditional 'spectatorial' account of knowledge."[28]

Then in 1970, five papers were published, all reproduced here. The first, "Incorrigibility as the Mark of the Mental," is one of the all-time great Rorty papers; it influenced Daniel Dennett and remains fully relevant to contemporary debates in the philosophy of mind, where intentionality and phenomenal consciousness still dominate the field as putative "marks of the mental." Rorty considers many more options than this, but concludes that strictly speaking there is no mark of the mental, although there is nevertheless a family resemblance based on incorrigibility "that ties the various things called 'mental' together and makes it possible to contrast them all with the physical" (p. 168). Following Sellars in *Empiricism and the Philosophy of Mind*, Rorty understands incorrigibility as the linguistic practice of allowing first-person reports of sensations and thoughts to trump third-person judgments. But since this practice might one day cease, it could transpire that there are no mental entities; thus Rorty neatly ties this view in with his eliminative materialism.[29]

"Wittgenstein, Privileged Access, and Incommunicability" is stylistically atypical for Rorty, a trenchantly analytical piece overflowing with fine distinctions and numbered claims. In it, Rorty disputes interpretations of Wittgenstein's private-language argument by both George Pitcher and John Cook, arguing that the emphasis they place on Wittgenstein's "hostility to privacy" (p. 197) obscures his real insight. Rorty argues that there is no good reason to deny that sensations and thoughts are private, nameable and knowable, once it is grasped that "privileged access" to them is fully accounted for by the linguistic practice of incorrigibility. The reason Wittgenstein targeted privacy was that he wanted to "cut Cartesian skepticism off at the roots" (pp. 196–7), but this aim is already achieved by the realization that there is no prelinguistic awareness, and hence that

---

[28] *The Linguistic Turn*, p. 39. For Rorty's illness, see J. Knobe, "A Talent for Bricolage: An Interview with Richard Rorty," *The Dualist*, 2 (1995), pp. 56–71. The two papers Rorty drafted were "Cartesian Epistemology and Changes in Ontology" (Gross, *Richard Rorty*, pp. 203–4) and "In Defense of Eliminative Materialism" (there is a 1969 draft of the latter in the Rorty archives: Box 8, Folder 9). He says he began *Philosophy and the Mirror of Nature* during this period in the preface to the book.

[29] Dennett acknowledges Rorty's influence in "The Case for Rorts" (R. Brandom, ed., *Rorty and his Critics* [Oxford, 2000]). For intentionality as the mark of the mental, see, e.g., M. Tye, *Ten Problems of Consciousness* (Cambridge, MA, 1995); for phenomenal consciousness as the mark of the mental, see, e.g., J. Searle, *The Rediscovery of the Mind* (Cambridge, MA, 1992). For the relevance of Rorty's views on the mark of the mental to on-going debates, see J. Tartaglia, "Consciousness, Intentionality, and the Mark of the Mental: Rorty's Challenge," *The Monist*, 91 (2008), pp. 324–46.

privileged access to mental states cannot be a matter of a linguistically unmediated conscious presence; the latter point, summed up in Sellars's slogan "all awareness is a linguistic affair,"[30] was Wittgenstein's real insight.

"In Defense of Eliminative Materialism" finds Rorty responding to critics of his 1965 paper. The objection is that reports of brain states cannot replace reports of sensations without descriptive loss unless the former entail the latter, which they do not. Rorty's response is that this entailment is only insisted upon because his critics are held captive by Sellars's "Myth of the Given," and hence think we have a prelinguistic awareness of sensations to which our descriptions must be adequate. But the notion of linguistic adequacy to something of which we are nonlinguistically aware is an illusion, an attempt to "step outside our skins," and to illustrate this Rorty gives his "Antipodeans" thought-experiment a first outing, arguing that we would be unable to isolate any "same thing" referred to by both ordinary speakers reporting their mental states and speakers who report only neural states.[31]

"Cartesian Epistemology and Changes in Ontology" is, in effect, a prolegomenon to *Philosophy and the Mirror of Nature*, offering an elegant overview of one major thread of argument in his later attempt to historically deconstruct Western philosophy, while also showing where his earlier concerns with reductionism, the linguistic turn, and eliminative materialism fit in. Ontology, and thus the problems of metaphysics, Rorty argues, is rooted in Cartesian skepticism; it is an attempt to redescribe the world which only seemed necessary because philosophers bought into the Cartesian notion of mind as an inner repository of representations about which we are incorrigible. The task of ontology became that of doing "enough reducing so that the universe looked reasonably neat, but not so much that one had to say such *outré* things as 'Numbers are really inscriptions'" (p. 214). This came to seem unnecessary, however, when philosophers took the linguistic turn and realized that incorrigibility is a contingent linguistic practice, a realization Rorty identifies with rejecting the Myth of the Given (p. 216). Rejecting this myth undermines Cartesian skepticism, allowing us to acquiesce in an exclusively social conception of justification, and thereby obviating any need for ontology.

Although the central argument of "Strawson's Objectivity Argument" was later repeated,[32] this paper remains Rorty's most sustained engagement

---

[30] *Empiricism and the Philosophy of Mind* (Cambridge, MA, 1997: orig. publ. 1956), p. 63.
[31] The definitive version of the thought-experiment is in *Philosophy and the Mirror of Nature*, ch. 2.
[32] In *Philosophy and the Mirror of Nature*, pp. 148–55.

with Kant. Rorty thinks P. F. Strawson was right to want an analytical reconstruction of Kant's transcendental deduction, purged of idealist metaphysics but preserving the insight that the possibility of experience presupposes a world of objects. However, Strawson fails to get the job done since his argument remains wedded to the Kantian notion of intuition. Rorty's preferred reconstruction finds in the transcendental deduction a challenge to the skeptic to imagine a language which does not allow us to make judgments by subsuming particulars under kinds, or which does so without containing names for objects; the aim is simply to shift the burden of proof onto the skeptic. Then, in the final and most interesting section of the paper (pp. 252–9), Rorty turns to a historical diagnosis of Kant as a "half-way point between Descartes and Wittgenstein." Kant advanced beyond the Cartesian notion of experience as "self-luminescent," an automatic kind of knowledge, by showing that knowledge is "discursive rather than intuitive." However, he did this by introducing two kinds of unconscious representation, "unsynthesized intuitions" and "unsynthesizing concepts," thereby remaining wedded to representationalism and creating the "pseudo-discipline" of transcendental philosophy whose job it was to work out how these ineffable representations unite. Wittgenstein, however, takes the final step beyond Cartesianism by realising that concepts and intuitions are dispositions to linguistic behavior abstracted from judgments, and that judgment is the "indecomposable unit of epistemological analysis" (p. 257).

The year 1971 was another turbulent one for Rorty; on the positive side, he met his second wife, the bioethicist Mary Varney Rorty, but he also became involved in an acrimonious divorce with his first. The latter accentuated tensions with his Princeton colleagues that had already been brewing, and as the decade progressed, he became both increasingly isolated at Princeton and increasingly prepared to pit himself against the analytic establishment.[33] But there was no accompanying shift in his position; the Wittgensteinian views he had been developing for years remained in place, they were just no longer credited to "analytic philosophy" and "the linguistic turn."[34] The paper he published that year, "Verificationism and Transcendental Arguments,"

---

[33] Gross, *Richard Rorty*, p. 200.
[34] For one of Rorty's later attempts to put some distance between himself and analytic philosophy, see "Twenty-Five Years Later" in the 1992 edition of *The Linguistic Turn*. It seems to us, however, that most of the reasons he provides there for downplaying the analyst's focus on language are reasons he gave back in the 1960s, and that "analyst," "epistemological behaviorist," and "pragmatist" were little more than different labels he used for the same view at different points of his career.

continues Rorty's interest in the antiskeptical force of Wittgenstein's private-language argument and Strawson's analytical reconstructions of transcendental arguments, an interest soon to be usurped by the more radical position he developed in "The World Well Lost" out of Donald Davidson's rejection of conceptual schemes. In this earlier paper, Rorty accepts the criticism that linguistic antiskeptical arguments only show that to talk about experiences we must accept that it seems there is a world of objects, not that there actually is, and that to secure the stronger conclusion would require an implausible verificationism, namely that our commitment to objects cannot be mistaken since it cannot be verified to be mistaken. However, Rorty thinks the arguments only require a milder form of intravocabulary verificationism, which says that the skeptic cannot show that our commitment to objects is mistaken unless he or she can show that we already accept a way of verifying that it is mistaken.

"Indeterminacy of Translation and of Truth," one of three papers from 1972 reproduced here, is Rorty's first critical engagement with Quine. Rorty adopts a similar line against Quine's thesis of the indeterminacy of translation to that of Chomsky's famous critique,[35] arguing that Quine cannot maintain a principled distinction between the indeterminacy of translation and the general phenomenon of underdetermination of theory by data, and as such cannot consistently reject realism about meaning on the grounds of the former while remaining a realist about physics in spite of the latter. According to Rorty's "mild 'epistemological' interpretation" (p. 282), Quinean indeterminacy is just a consequence of correct translation being underdetermined by all the available evidence, distinguished from scientific cases of underdetermination only by its unexpectedness, given that knowledge of meaning seems, on the face of it, intuitive rather than "the result of applying a *theory*" (p. 278). Rorty is not misinterpretating Quine, since he knows Quine's intentions were ontological rather than epistemological.[36] Rather, he is trying to show that Quine is not entitled to his ontological commitments, and concludes by presenting him with a dilemma: either give up on all objective matters of fact, physics included, or else allow them in linguistics. The former, which would emphasize

---

[35] N. Chomsky, "Quine's Empirical Assumptions," in D. Davidson and J. Hintikka, eds., *Words and Objections* (Dordrecht, 1969).

[36] *Pace* C. Hookway, *Quine* (Cambridge, 1988), p. 137.

"the revolutionary character of the Hegelianism which Quine picked up from Dewey" (p. 280), is of course the paradigmatically Rortyan choice.

Daniel Dennett, along with Donald Davidson and Thomas Kuhn, was one of a select group of Rorty's contemporaries whose work he tirelessly promoted, albeit far from uncritically. In "Dennett on Awareness," Rorty argues that Dennett is mistaken in thinking that insight in philosophy of mind is to be gained by empirically investigating internal functional organization; by finding out what is going on "beneath the skin" rather than treating a person as a sealed "black box," as Dennett thinks previous philosophers had done. The problem, Rorty thinks, is that any functional division of the physical processes inside a human is inevitably metaphorical and arbitrary, and those Dennett defends are motivated by the Cartesian picture of thoughts and feelings as inner causes of behavior; Dennett is looking for scientifically respectable inner causes to take the place of immaterial Cartesian ones. Rather than attributing the capacities of persons to sub-personal states, Rorty thinks we should explain those capacities socially in terms of linguistic practice.

"Functionalism, Machines, and Incorrigibility" continues in a similar vein, but here the criticism of functionalism is more expansive and the target is Hilary Putnam. Rorty argues that functionalism should not be considered a new theory of mind comparable to dualism, and that analogies with machines will not shed light on mental states. The basic problem, as before, is that functional states generally, and those qualifying as "logical states" by reference to a program, are too cheap, given that "anything you like is at any time in as many logical states as there are distinct programs you have the patience to write" (p. 302). Thus, there is no natural analogy between the internal states of machines such as computers and the human mind. Rather, the "animism" that leads us to apply psychological language to these machines, and which pays off because they have been designed to act in characteristically human ways, is what *creates* the analogy by leading us to functionally describe the machine at the same level of abstraction as the psychological language, even though in principle we could use any level of abstraction at all. It is a mistake, then, to think we might discover that mental states are really functional states. Rather, our ascription of mental states on the basis of behavior, whether of a human or a machine, simply makes us interested in functional descriptions of the internal states of the human or machine at a particular level of abstraction.

The fourth paper Rorty published in 1972 was "The World Well Lost," named, we presume, from the subtitle of Dryden's *All for Love*. It definitely does mark a transition of sorts, because the style is now noticeably bolder, the rhetoric has been ratcheted up a few notches, and Rorty's Wittgensteinian skepticism about philosophical problems is center stage for the first time. But otherwise it just reads like a natural outgrowth from the papers in this volume.

# CHAPTER I

# Pragmatism, categories, and language

Pragmatism is getting respectable again. Some philosophers are still content to think of it as a sort of muddle-headed first approximation to logical positivism – which they think of in turn as a prelude to our own enlightened epoch. But those who have taken a closer look have realized that the movement of thought involved here is more like a pendulum than like an arrow.[1] This renewed interest in pragmatism has led to a new interest in Peirce, who somehow seems the most "up-to-date" of the pragmatists,[2] and whose work in logic permits one to call him muddle-headed only if one is also willing to call him schizophrenic. But students of Peirce, even the most sympathetic, have had trouble digesting what he called his "Scotistic realism" and his categories of Firstness, Secondness, and Thirdness. These are obviously central features of his thought, yet they do not seem to sit well with his pragmatism. Still, Peirce insists over and over again that "the validity of the pragmatic maxim" and "Scotistic realism" mutually entail each other, and he suggests that they are both expressions of "the irreducibility of Thirdness."[3]

My purpose in this chapter is to try to show that the point Peirce is making in this identification is sound and important. Focusing on this point shows how far Peirce was in advance of the positivism of his day and how close his views are to the present trends in philosophy which have arisen in reaction to the more sophisticated positivism of Wittgenstein's *Tractatus* and of the Vienna Circle. I want to suggest that Peirce's thought

---

[1] Cf. Morton White, *Toward Reunion in Philosophy* (Cambridge, MA, 1956), pp. 268ff, and Alan Pasch, *Experience and the Analytic* (Chicago, 1958).

[2] Perhaps because he was neither as concerned with religion and morality as James, nor as interested in social and political issues as Dewey.

[3] Cf. *Collected Papers of C. S. Peirce*, ed. Charles Hartshorne and Paul Weiss, 8 vols. (Cambridge, MA, 1931–58), v, p. 453, v, p. 470, v, p. 527, v, p. 503, v, p. 4 (on pragmatism and synechism), v, p. 469 (on pragmatism as an outcome of the logical derivation of Peirce's categories), I, p. 26. Hereafter references to the *Collected Papers* (by volume and paragraph number) will be inserted in the text.

envisaged, and repudiated in advance, the stages in the development of empiricism which logical positivism represented, and that it came to rest in a group of insights and a philosophical mood much like those we find in the *Philosophical Investigations* and in the writings of philosophers influenced by the later Wittgenstein. A little empiricism, plus a passion for rigor, will make a man a nominalist. Thinking about the antinomies created by the mutual repugnance of experience and rigor will drive him, if he thinks as long and as hard as Peirce and Wittgenstein did, to something quite different. In trying to show that this "something different" was pretty much the same for both men, I shall argue for the following points:

(1)   What Peirce called "nominalism" and what present-day philosophers call "reductionism" are forms of a single error.

(2)   The error in both cases goes back to "the Protean meta-physical urge to transcend language."[4]

(3)   Peirce's attempt to give sense to the notion of *universalia ante rem* is not a result of succumbing to this urge, but is rather his device for repudiating it as strongly as possible.

(4)   When Peirce says that "vagueness is real" and when Wittgenstein points to the difference between causal and logical determination, the only differences between what they are saying are verbal (or, to give the cash value of this overworked word, uninteresting).

(5)   The similarity of their insights about language reflects the fact that the slogans "Don't look for the meaning, look for the use" and "The meaning of a concept is the sum of its possible effects upon conduct" reciprocally support each other.

Before proceeding to these points, however, it may be useful to remark that I am trying to show neither that Peirce saw through a glass darkly what Wittgenstein saw face to face, nor the reverse. One can take the first slogan mentioned in (5) as a special case of the second, or vice versa; which way one sees it depends, and should depend, on the purposes of one's inquiry at a given moment. What I *am* trying to show is that the closer one brings pragmatism to the writings of the later Wittgenstein and of those influenced by him, the more light they shed on each other.[5]

---

[4] The phrase is taken from D. F. Pears's article "Universals," reprinted in *Logic and Language*, Second Series, ed. A. N. Flew (Oxford, 1955). More will be heard of this article in section II below.

[5] In particular, Peirce and Wittgenstein complement each other especially well; one presents you with a bewildering and wonderfully abstract apparatus of categories; the other shoves you into very particular puzzles. Peirce's odd numerological categories, just because they are so abstract and so

# I

Peirce liked to refer to any doctrine he disagreed with as "nominalistic." One of the dozens of different ways in which he tried to formulate the common error of all nominalists was by calling nominalism the doctrine that vagueness is not real.[6] Nominalists thought, that is, that whatever was real had sharp edges (like a sense datum or an atomic fact), and that whatever did not have sharp edges could be "reduced" to things that did. Most of Peirce's work was devoted to showing that this reduction could not be performed. Among the vague things which, he thought, nominalists could not reduce (and hence could not account for consistently with their assumptions) were Intelligence, Intention, Signs, Continuity, Potentiality, Meaning, Rules, and Habits. All these he blithely baptized – to the perpetual delight of neo-Pythagorean hedgehogs among his readers and the confusion of all foxes – "Thirds." The point of the baptism was his claim that phenomena which exhibit features referred to by some or all of these capitalized terms have in common a certain peculiarity: their adequate characterization requires a language which contains, as primitive predicates, the names of triadic relations.[7]

This claim involves two theses: (1) that triadic relations cannot be built up out of monadic, or dyadic ones and still retain their original significance, and (2) that the phenomena in question cannot be made intelligible in language which lacks names for triadic relationships. I shall not be concerned with deciding whether he was right about either of these points. This is because I do not think (and here I differ from Peirce, who believed that there *were* decision-procedures for these theses[8]) that either (1) or (2) is the kind of thesis that can be decided. They cannot be decided because

---

far from the clichés of the history of philosophy, are perhaps the best handles for grasping what one learns from Wittgenstein. Conversely, Wittgenstein's riddles and aphorisms, just because they are so fresh and fragmentary, let one see the point of some of Peirce's darker sayings.

[6] On the reality of vagueness as the thesis of scholastic realism, cf. v, p. 453. On the opposition between nominalism and scholastic realism, cf. I, pp. 15ff. On nominalism as the thesis that all vagueness is due to a defect of cognition, cf. IV, p. 344.

[7] Thus, the translation of the metaphysical thesis that "Thirds are real" into the "formal mode of speech" is: "No language will be adequate to reconstruct the meaning of sentences referring to 'Intelligence,' 'Signs,' etc., unless it contains as primitives the names of $n$-adic relations with $n \geq 3$." Peirce claimed that tetradic, pentadic, etc., relations could all be analyzed into triadic ones, but that no triadic relation could be built up out of monadic and dyadic relations. Cf. I, pp. 345ff, I, p. 363.

[8] He would have said that (1) was a matter of formal logic (cf. v, p. 469, I, p. 345) and (2) of empirical fact (I, p. 345). I should want to argue that in attempting *a priori* deductions of the categories (cf. IV, pp. 2ff) Peirce was unfaithful to his own better insight when (in such passages as v, p. 36) he says that logic must be founded upon aesthetics.

both of them have built-in escape clauses which permit one to reply to the offer of a counterexample: "but that does not retain the original significance" or "but that does not make it intelligible." The presence of such escape clauses is not a defect in Peirce's thinking, but a characteristic of all utterances which are intended simply to point to similarities and yet find themselves forced into sentences about which the unanswerable riddle "analytic or synthetic?" can be raised. To free either thesis from these escape clauses, one would have to find a criterion for knowing when the "same" significance is preserved.[9]

But even though it would be useless to try to prove either thesis, it is useful to show how Peirce gave them plausibility. His clearest example, perhaps, was the act *of giving*.[10] If I give you a book, can you describe my action "adequately" in terms which avoid the *prima facie* triadic character of the situation? Can you replace the three-place predicate "giving" with a set of two-place or one-place predicates? The obvious move is to try some such pair of dyads as "You shoved it toward me and I picked it up." But something is missing. What? Well, roughly the same sort of thing that is missing when I analyze "I lifted my arm" into "First I had kinaesthetic sense datum *a*, and then I had visual sense datum *b*, and so forth." It is probably also the same sort of thing that is missing when one substitutes causes for motives or tries to reduce "ascribing" to "describing."[11] What is missing is, in short, the kind of thing people mean when they talk of the "meaning" of the action or of the "intention" behind it. Now Peirce's way of describing the loss is that "Seconds" have been substituted for "Thirds." To put it loosely, if something passes from my hand to yours we are, in so far forth, just two things bumping into one another in a somewhat complicated way. The situation thus does not differ in any essential way from the collision of two billiard balls (which is one of Peirce's examples of

---

[9] That one cannot get such a criterion is a corollary of Peirce's claim that vagueness (Thirdness) is irreducible. If one notes that rules are Thirds, it can also be seen as a corollary of Wittgenstein's remark that "The use of the word 'rule' and the use of the word 'same' are interwoven." (*Philosophical Investigations* [Oxford, 1953], No. 225.) All future references to Wittgenstein will be to Part 1 of the *Philosophical Investigations*, will be made by paragraph number, and will usually be inserted in the text.

[10] Cf. 1, p. 345, and compare Wittgenstein, No. 268, where he discusses why your right hand cannot give something to your left hand.

[11] Cf. H. L. A. Hart, "The Ascription of Responsibility and Rights," reprinted in *Logic and Language*, First Series (Oxford, 1951), pp. 145ff. Peirce would have noted with delight the triadic character of ascription (I ascribe *x* to you) and its difference from a simple description (I saw *y*). Notice that "I saw you do that" is a true triad for Peirce only if it means "I saw *you* ('you responsible person' or 'you swine') do that"; if, on the other hand, it is replaceable by "I saw the following sense data" then it is a pseudo-triad.

pure Secondness). Putting it another way, the action can be described in the same "language-stratum"[12] as can the billiard balls.

This example perhaps makes clearer what Peirce meant by describing nominalists as people who try to reduce Thirds to Seconds. It should also suggest that these "nominalists" – who for Peirce included just about everyone from Descartes to J. S. Mill, with the possible exception of Kant – are the intellectual ancestors of the "reductionists" whose downfall Mr. Urmson takes to be the prelude to "the beginnings of contemporary philosophy."[13] These latter philosophers, best exemplified perhaps by the *Aufbau* phase of logical positivism, did most of their reducing in two main areas. One was the cluster of notions which center around "intention." We have just seen how Peirce's apparatus of categories is applied to a member of this cluster. The other was the epistemology of perception, where they restated phenomenalism as the doctrine that anything sayable in the language of material objects could be said equally well in the language of sense data. Here too Peirce is antireductionist, despite the *prima facie* phenomenalist character of pragmatism.[14] His explanation of the failure of phenomenalism is, once again, that Thirds (in this case material objects[15]) cannot be built up out of Firsts (unsensed *sensibilia*) or Seconds (acts of sensing). Material objects are permanent *possibilities* of sensation, and, as such, they have the character of *laws* (I, p. 487). Looked at from the side of the knower, this point is made in the doctrines (1) that a percept is always "excessively vague" (IV, p. 539) and therefore requires a "logical" as well as an "emotional" (First) and an "energetic" (Second) interpretant (V, pp. 475ff); and (2) that the logical interpretant will, if it is simply some determinate image or other mental state (or set of states), always require further interpretation, and that therefore it must be something as indeterminate in its application as a law, namely, a *habit* (V, p. 486).[16]

---

[12] I shall be using this term in the sense given it by Dr. Waismann in "Language-Strata," *Logic and Language*, Second Series, pp. 11ff.

[13] J. O. Urmson, *Philosophical Analysis* (Oxford, 1956), ch. 10.

[14] Cf. Peirce's contrast between reductionist Humean phenomenalism and Kantian or pragmatist phenomenalism (VIII, p. 15). The latter, which Peirce calls "phenomenalism *aufgehoben*" (VIII, p. 186) turns out to be the sort of perspectival realism which Roderick Firth puts forward in "Sense-Data and the Percept Theory, Part II," *Mind*, 59 (1950), pp. 34–55. Cf. especially pp. 48ff of this article on the "sign function" of the ostensible physical object, a topic which Peirce developed at great length and which is at the heart of his epistemology. The relations between pragmatism and perspectival realism are brilliantly exhibited by Pasch (*op. cit.*, esp. chs. iv, vi).

[15] On matter as Third, and as such opposed to mere quality or mere action, cf. I, p. 420.

[16] The doctrine of the "ultimate" logical interpretant, and Peirce's semiotic generally, contain many puzzles which we cannot touch on here. The difference between an infinite series of determinates and an infinitely determinable indetermination will be discussed in section III below. Peirce's use of

In plainer language, one might explain what makes a batch of sense data a cat by saying either that it *means* a cat to somebody, or that somebody *intends* to take it to be a cat, or that somebody follows a *rule* in terms of which it represents a cat, or that somebody has a *habit* of saying "cat" when he encounters it, or that somebody expects the usual *laws* describing the behavior of such sense data to hold. Peirce's point is that all these italicized terms are names for Thirdness, and that consequently any of them may be analyzed in terms of another, but that none of them can be reduced either to the sense data themselves (Firsts) or to the merely dyadic relations which hold among sense data (for example, such Seconds as spatiotemporal nextness and sheer similarity[17]). Any "reduction" of cats to patches will, therefore, miss the reference to a logical interpretant which makes the cat a cat. It will lose the same kind of thing that gets lost when we "reduce" giving to handing over and taking.

In applying the name "Thirdness" to all the things which reductionists mislay, Peirce is trying to do in a wholesale way what current antireductionist writers have been doing case by case. The most fashionable antireductionist argument at the moment runs as follows: reductionism represents a confusion of the meaning of something (for example, a word) with the reasons which we give for applying it in a given case. The cash value of this argument is: certain statements which the unreduced item entails or otherwise licenses are not entailed or otherwise licensed by the reduced form of this item. Now the obvious come-back for the reductionist is: tell me just what these statements are, and I shall fix my reduction up to take care of them. And the clinching reply to this is: we *cannot* tell you what they are, because there are an indefinite number of them.[18] Now this clincher is, as we shall see in more detail later on, just what Peirce is insisting on when he says that "there is no exception to the law that every thought-sign is translated or interpreted in a subsequent one" (v, p. 284) or that "no collection of facts can constitute a law" (1, p. 420) or that "there is no absolute third,

---

this distinction is well treated by George Gentry in "Habit and the Logical Interpretant" (*Studies in the Philosophy of Charles Sanders Peirce* [Cambridge, MA, 1952], pp. 75ff; this collection of essays will be referred to hereafter as *Studies*).

[17] Not similarity in some given *respect*, for this would be triadic ("*x* resembles *y* in being a *z*"). If sheer similarity seems unintelligible, Peirce would rejoin that this unintelligibility just shows you that it *is* Second, and therefore brute and unmediated.

[18] Cf. Urmson on the difficulties of analyzing propositions such as "Britain declared war on Germany" and his conclusion (*op. cit.*, p. 161) that "the ancient doctrine of British empiricism that all non-simple concepts must be reduced to complexes of simple concepts must finally go."

for the third is of its own nature relative" (1, p. 362).[19] All these dicta amount to saying to the reductionist: language is incurably vague, but perfectly real and utterly inescapable.

# II

Here, then, we see the way in which the two Peircian definitions of "nominalism" coincide: to assert that Thirds can be reduced to Seconds and Firsts is to deny that vagueness is real. Further, we see how the denial of the reality of vagueness leads to reductionism. Having now suggested that Peirce and "postpositivistic" analytic philosophy have common enemies, I want in this section to compare and contrast their approaches to a particular problem: that of *naming*. In doing so, we shall see what Peirce meant by "Scotistic realism." Further, we shall see how Peirce's old-fashioned solutions of philosophic problems with the help of an array of ontological categories resemble, when looked at closely, contemporary "dissolutions" of these problems. As an example of the modern dissolution of the problem of naming, I shall use D. F. Pears's article, "Universals," whose concluding remark I partially quoted above: "The desire to go on explaining naming . . . is the result of the Protean metaphysical urge to transcend language."[20]

One achievement of Pears's masterly discussion is to show that the same *Sehnsucht* impels the Platonist and the nominalist. The one thinks "Nature but a spume that plays / Upon a ghostly paradigm of things." The other thinks of language as a haze drifting among sharp-edged sense data, or neural sparkings, or Democritean atoms; if it does not actually hamper our vision of these divinely actual and determinate realities, it at least needs to be crystallized into equally sharp-edged units before it can represent them properly. Both look toward a day when thought will, in Pears's terms, "exit from the maze of words" (p. 53) and will know just where and why it exited, and just what it found. In this self-conscious exiting, man will differ from the beasts of the field (and from the user of C. I. Lewis's "expressive language") in that he will somehow be able not only to exit but to return and drag others up (if he is a Platonist) or down (if he is a nominalist) to the same exit. Men will thus "transcend language" either by finding the color-patches behind the use of "cat" or by finding *"Die schönen*

---

[19]  One may find these phrases reminiscent of some key idealist arguments. But Peirce is no idealist; for him, its error lies in ignoring Secondness and Firstness (cf. the description of "Hegelianism of all shades" in v, p. 77n). In other words, idealists reasoned illegitimately from "there is a sign (Third) behind every sign" to "there are nothing but signs (Thirds)."

[20]  *Loc. cit.*, p. 64. Hereafter, references to Pears's article will be inserted in the text.

*regionen / Wo die reinen Formen wohnen"* beyond both patches and cats. In either case, as Pears says, we could "combine the concreteness of ostensive definition with the clarity of verbal definition" (p. 63). As Hegel saw, when thought strives for self-consciousness it strives for a concrete universal.

By taking "naming" as the datum which theories about universals are intended to explain, Pears is able to put his critique of all such theories – nominalist, conceptualist, and realist – in the following two theses: (1) "any comprehensive explanation of naming is necessarily circular" and (2) "all other processes [to which naming might be analogized by philosophers] either already contain the very feature of naming which was puzzling, or else are too natural or too artificial really to be analogous" (p. 53). "The possible analogies," Pears says, "can be mapped in this simple way": either the many things related to some single thing (in the way in which instances of a name's application are related to the name) are related to this single thing naturally (independently of what we do about it) or they are related just because we choose that they shall be related (purely artificially) or else we choose to relate them because of some feature which makes it "convenient but not necessary" so to relate them.[21] Now only the latter, obviously, will do if we are to have a satisfactory analogy. But, Pears says, "This compromise between the two extremes introduces into the analogy the very feature which it was intended to explain. For just how something works in influencing usage was what was to be explained. Nor is there a fourth alternative" (pp. 60–1).

Taken positively, what Pears's article shows us is roughly this: (1) we now know as well as we ever will why it is "convenient but not necessary" to give certain batches of things a common name; (2) the hunt for an insight into batchiness will either fail or else simply send us back to this original knowledge. "Naming cannot be explained by anything which goes beyond a reasoned choice of usage" (p. 62). So the puzzling thing is not so much naming as the existence of theories about naming, the dialectic of which Pears exhibits as follows:

> Thus moderate nominalists maintain that similarity is a better explanation of the unity of a class than the presence of a universal. (But why should people not *just* recognize the presence of universals?) And moderate realists retort that this admits the existence of at least one universal, similarity. (But why should the presence of a universal explain the recognition of similarity if it cannot explain the recognition of anything else? Why should we not *just* recognize similarity?) Really these are not two arguments but two bare

---

[21] This is a paraphrase of Pears's "map" as given on p. 60.

assertions of superiority . . . Yet these theories do seem to be striving toward something. And they are. Their goal is the unattainable completely satisfactory explanation of naming. And, as so often happens in metaphysics, progress is measured by distance from the starting-point and not by proximity to the goal whose unattainability each uses against its rivals without allowing it to deter itself. (p. 62)

Peirce's solution to the problem of naming, realigned and restated so as to form a commentary on Pears's dissolution, involves the following points:

(1) What is wrong with most theories about naming (nominalism and conceptualism, and also realism as it is usually stated) is not that they strive after an unattainable goal. (This, roughly speaking, is not a specific vice of metaphysics, but a generic one of all inquiry.) Rather, what is wrong is that they block the way of inquiry by appealing to one form or another of "just seeing."

(2) Properly understood, realism is not the postulation of a new breed of entity combined with the claim that we somehow intuit these entities but is, on the contrary, a way of asserting that no such postulation will do.

(3) Such an assertion is contained in the doctrine that Thirdness is real, for this doctrine has a corollary that the "convenience without absolute necessity" involved in naming is not collapsible into absolute necessity nor into sheer arbitrariness.

(4) Saying that "vagueness" (or any of the other sobriquets of Thirdness) is real is preferable to saying that "naming is *sui generis*" – and thus closing off the possibility of "explaining" naming in any sense – because it points the way to an indefinitely long series of things which are like naming. To say that these analogies do not explain is true only if one means by "explanation" something like a Cartesian "clear and distinct apprehension."

Thus, when Peirce says that naming is possible because Thirds are real he is saying something like this: "It is true that nothing which is not a Third is sufficiently like naming to be used as an explanation of naming, and also true that all other Thirds are, as such, like naming merely in being triadic. But by exhibiting more and more of the ways in which Thirdness appears we gain understanding of any given Third." Peirce can agree when Pears says that no theory of naming "goes deep enough to satisfy the true metaphysician who is in all of us, since though they take us to the bottom of naming, we were in a simpler way already there, and they do not succeed in showing us how naming is founded on something else which lies even deeper" (p. 62). But Peirce points out that explanations can succeed by being broad as well as by being deep. *Any* analogy, no matter how illuminating at first glance, can be made to look ridiculous by asking "and in just what *respect* are these purported analogues analogous?"[22] But the illumination one gets from an analogy may be nonetheless real, even though it is gained not by going deeper but by looking about and noticing that the object of one's previous puzzlement is no more and no less puzzling than a lot of other things. After all, we have to take our illumination where we find it, and we cannot know that we are no closer to our goal of complete illumination unless we somehow know the criteria for such completeness in advance. The naming-theorist's myth of a complete noncircular explanation of naming is, in Peirce's eyes, simply turned upside down to produce Pears's myth of a simple understanding of naming possessed prior to all analogies and explanations. For Peirce, both are myths because both "admit something to be absolutely inexplicable" (v, p. 318), thereby succumbing to the Cartesian yearning for the intuitive. To say that we "just know what naming is" is no more of an advance, and is no less immodest a claim, than to say that we "just recognize" similarities or Similarity or Catness.

But what illumination does Peirce's Thirdness offer us? And why must he call his doctrine of the reality of Thirdness "Scotistic realism"? The answer to these questions must begin by distinguishing the intent behind realism from what Peirce thinks of as a parody of realism – the notion that universals are "things." The parody consists in holding that realists believe in two independent sets of sharp-edged, fully determinate entities – particular universals and particular particulars. This reduplication of the world, like all parodies of philosophic theories, is easily refuted; in this case, the job is done by one variant or another of the "third man" argument. But for Peirce, this notion of what realism is could only have occurred to a mind so imbued with nominalism as to give a nominalistic twist to anything it encounters.[23] The intent of realism is the

---

[22] Think how easily one could "expose" the *Philosophical Investigations* if one insisted on pressing this question, and how pointless it would be to do so.
[23] This is why "the doctrine of Platonic ideas has been held by the extremest nominalists" (v, 470), and is why Leibniz, with his utterly determinate *possibilia*, is "the modern nominalist *par excellence*" (v, p. 62). For an amusing exhibition of the central difficulty of Leibniz's theory of possible worlds – a difficulty Peirce would say was involved, *mutatis mutandis*, in all nonpragmatic theories – see N. P. Stallknecht, "Decision and Existence," *Review of Metaphysics*, 6 (1952), pp. 31ff.

opposite: rather than adding new determinate entities to the world, it was intended precisely to get rid of

> the Ockhamistic prejudice ... that in thought, in being, and in development the indefinite is due to a degeneration from a primary state of perfect definiteness ... The truth is rather on the side of the scholastic realists that the unsettled is the primal state, and that definiteness and determinateness ... are, in the large, approximations, developmentally, epistemologically, and metaphysically. (vi, p. 348).

Now whether or not Peirce was right in construing medieval realists to mean what he meant,[24] his own doctrine of the reality of Thirdness is no more and no less than this insistence on the irreducibility of the indefinite and the indeterminate.[25] For Peirce, it is the nominalist and the reductionist who succumb to belief in metaphysical figments – namely the belief that beneath all the evident fuzziness, vagueness, and generality which we encounter in language (and, therefore, in all thought[26]) there are nonfuzzy, particular, clearly intuitable reals. (Compare vi, p. 492, v, p. 312.) To repeat an earlier point, Peirce's realism is simply the phrasing in metaphysical language of the unrestricted form of the doctrine that language cannot be transcended. And the illumination given by this way of phrasing the point is simply that such phrasing lights up, and points to similarities between, the Protean attempts at such transcendence which have occurred in the history of thought. In particular, Peirce uses it to expose the parallelism between the movements of reductionist explanation charted by means of Pears's map of analogies about naming and the movements of reductionist explanation of such topics as induction, mind, intention, value, and freedom. In the various phenomena grouped under these headings, we encounter indefiniteness becoming definite or indetermination calling on us to determine it; just in so far as we are reductionists or nominalists, we assume that the progress toward definiteness and determinacy is not only completable but that the fully definite and determinate

---

[24] Cf. I, p. 27n: "It must not be imagined that any notable realist of the 13th or 14th century took the ground that any 'universal' was what we in English should call a 'thing'." For a discussion of the historical question, cf. Charles K. McKeon, "Peirce's Scotistic Realism" in *Studies*, pp. 238ff.

[25] The difference between these two notions is the difference between vagueness (indefiniteness) and generality (indeterminacy) – a distinction which is of great importance in Peirce's system but which space prevents being employed here. Cf. v, pp. 447ff, for the distinction between the two, and v, p. 450, and v, p. 506, for their formal identity (as Thirds). In what follows, I shall continue to use the terms interchangeably.

[26] Cf. v, pp. 250ff, and vol. v, bk II, ch. i of the *Collected Papers*, *passim*.

is somehow there already; just in so far as we are "realists" in Peirce's sense, we do not assume this.

To show how this general map of philosophical issues works in all these areas, or even to give the details of Peirce's application of it to naming and the use of language, is beyond the scope of this chapter. But we can sketch its use in regard to naming by focusing on two of the most important sobriquets of Thirdness: "Sign" and "Habit." The reality of Thirdness is sometimes put by Peirce as the claim that "The entire universe . . . is perfused with signs" (v, p. 448n). Combined with the doctrine that no sign is fully determinate (iii, p. 93, v, p. 506),[27] and that "everything indeterminate is in the nature of a sign" (v, p. 448n), this gives us the corollary notions of a man's mind being itself a sign (v, p. 313) and "nature" (the sum of objects of knowledge) being an utterer of signs which we interpret. But no sign – neither a thought nor a natural event – is *completely* indeterminate. If it were, it would be unrecognizable and thus could not be this sign rather than that one. A sign is thus always a determinate indetermination. The act of signifying, of meaning something, is thus analogous to the act of naming (that is, the act of assigning a single sign to represent a batch of things). For as Pears reminds us, naming is neither simply artificial (indeterminate) nor simply natural (determinate), neither forced on us nor performed by us in a spirit of pure whimsy. To signify or to name such-and-such by so-and-so is "convenient but not absolutely necessary." Now this is just what one would expect if the "things" that are batched under a given name are what Peirce says they are – neither physical, logical, nor psychological atoms, but rather signs which, while giving us latitude for interpretation, resist some interpretations more than others. Thus, the picture of a universe perfused by signs is a picture of a universe in which indeterminacy is neither an illusion nor a peculiar property of a human artifact called "language." A Peircian realist thus "explains" naming not by claiming to "recognize the presence of a universal" as one would recognize the presence of a bird in a bush – as one would recognize the presence of a bird in a bush – as one determinate entity among others – but by taking the peculiar thing about naming (the peculiar determinate compresence of nature and art, force and passivity, determinacy and indeterminacy) to be a feature of the named as well as the namer. From the point of view of the nominalist, of course, this

---

[27] See iii, p. 93, for Peirce's refutation of logical atomism, taken as the claim that there are fully determinate signs: "The logical atom . . . must be one of which every predicate may be universally affirmed or denied . . . But an absolutely determinate term cannot be realized, because, not being given by sense, such a concept would have to be formed by synthesis, and there would be no end to the synthesis because there is no limit to the number of possible predicates."

merely amounts to reading back into nature and "hypostatizing" a peculiarity of our mind; Peirce's reply is that this charge of hypostatization can be made only by one who has himself hypostatized the results of analysis in some form of atomism, logical or otherwise.

This explanation of naming can be put in terms of the notion of "Habit" as well as that of "Sign." Pears's description of a "reasoned choice of usage" in terms of "convenience without absolute necessity" is clearly reminiscent of Hume's remark on "custom or habit": "the uniting principle among ideas is not to be considered as an inseparable connexion" but as a "gentle force, which commonly prevails, and is the cause why, among other things, languages so nearly correspond to each other."[28] Even apart from the triadic character which Peirce attributes to them both, it is not hard to see how signs and habits can be thought of as two ways of looking at the same phenomenon. Both are vague; both are neither natural nor altogether conventional; a sign can have many interpretations (while resisting some more than others) and a habit can express itself at various times in various manners (but not in any and every manner). The cash value of my giving a name to a batch of things is my establishing a habit of correlating tokens of a given sign with tokens of other signs. For nominalists, reductionists, and atomists, this habit is either a confused way of thinking about a set of reflexes, or else a *sui generis* phenomenon occurring in human beings (which is more or less what it was for Hume). But Peirce, looking at the universe as perfused with habits as well as with signs, explains the convenience of naming certain batches – of slicing up nature in certain ways, and thereby developing certain habits of expectation – by reference to the fact that nature has already sliced itself up by developing habits on its own.[29] Thus, his realism can be seen as the thesis that the

---

[28] *Treatise*, ed. L. A. Selby-Bigge (Oxford, 1951), p. 10.

[29] The fact that assigning a name creates a habit of expectation (which, for Peirce, was the definition of a "belief") is basic to Peirce's thought. The essential thesis in question has been exhibited with great elegance in Wilfrid Sellars's "Concepts as Involving Laws and Inconceivable Without Them" (*Philosophy of Science*, 15 [1948], pp. 287–315). The point expressed by the title of this article is clearly seen by Wittgenstein when he says, "If language is to be a means of communication, there must be agreement not only in definitions but also (queer as this may sound) in judgments" (No. 242).

The thesis that nature has habits (which in modern jargon is the thesis that dispositional predicates are irreducible) is the starting point of Peirce's solution to the problem of induction (cf. v, p. 170, v, p. 457). This is unfortunately too large a topic to enter on here; suffice it to say that he is here putting in metaphysical language the conclusion at which present-day inquiry is now gradually arriving: that the control which nature exercises over our inductive inferences appears not only in the results of experiment and observation but in the construction of frameworks within which we observe and experiment, and that this latter sort of control is not reducible to the former. Cf. Nelson Goodman, *Fact, Fiction, and Forecast* (Cambridge, MA, 1955), p. 117, and ch. iv, *passim*. When this conclusion is more broadly stated, it appears as Professor Polanyi's view that *all* inquiry "reasoned choice of usage" which is naming *is* rational, in part, because of its respect for the rationality which it encounters in nature. But for nature to be rational in this sense does not mean that it "recognizes the same universals" as does the mind, but simply that it contains the sort of determinate indeterminations that our mind does.

Thus, the real difference between Pears's view of naming as *sui generis* and Peirce's "explanation" of it as one more appearance of that pervasive feature of nature and thought which he calls Thirdness is indeed, if one likes to call it so, verbal. To say that nature has habits or utters signs is not to take us any deeper into our own expecting and talking than we were already. If we ask for an explanation of the "possibility" of any given instance of naming we shall still have to look at the details of the particular situation (although if we are Peircians we shall look at these details through different spectacles). Peirce's application of his categorial scheme to the act of naming can be seen as simply an elaboration of Pears's (crucial) remark that "No description of any item of mental furniture which included only its momentary properties and not its habitual use could possibly explain the generality of thought" (p. 56n). But equally, both this remark and the whole of Pears's discussion can be seen as an illustration of Peirce's key heuristic principle – that Thirdness is not reducible to Secondness and Firstness. In applying Peirce's categories to the act of naming, no new exit has been found from the maze of words; but perhaps something has happened to the man who feels caught in the maze analogous to what happens to a prisoner who takes to heart the realization that all men are, in one sense or another, prisoners. All that has happened is that the maze of words has been enlarged by more words, but what more can we reasonably hope for, once we are convinced that language cannot be transcended?

## III

In this final section, I want to press one step further the analogy between some manifestations of Peirce's doctrine of the irreducibility of Thirdness and some of the insights that underlie the antireductionist revolt in contemporary empiricism. A whole range of distinctions which Wittgenstein makes in the *Philosophical Investigations* can be seen as clustering around the distinction between "causal" and "logical" determin-ation (No. 220). Causal determination is what using language would be

(not merely bad science or metaphysics) is "circular" and has an "epicyclical character"; cf. his *Personal Knowledge* (Chicago, 1958), pp. 288ff and chs. ix and x, *passim*.

like if it were a matter of being "inspired" by an "intuition" (Nos. 213, 232). Logical determination, on the other hand, is what goes on when we *follow a rule*.[30]

The program of enforcing this distinction covers a great deal of what Wittgenstein accomplishes in the *Philosophical Investigations* (especially in the first half of Part I). In his analysis of meaning and understanding he spends much of his time exhibiting how useless it is to look for "some item of mental furniture" which will "guide" or "compel" or "influence" one to, for example, utter a certain sound when one sees a certain letter (Nos. 169, 170). Reductionism as applied to the activities of meaning and understanding appears as the attempt to find an "intermediary between the sign and the fact" (No. 94) which will supply a "lever," the felt pressure of which *causes* us (No. 170) to mean or understand just so-and-so in just such-and-such a way. Wittgenstein's critique of the notion of "mental states," centering on the fact that we cannot find any particular experience which is "an experience of being influenced" (No. 176), provides the answer to those who think it a flaw in Hume not to have produced somehow an impression of the "gentle force" of habit. The answer consists in pointing up the categorial gap between any given here-and-now "state" and the temporal *stretch* which is a *use* (No. 138) or the application of a *rule* (No. 140), or the having of a *habit* (all the time, whether it is being exhibited or not). But in destroying the myth that we sense a certain "psychological" compulsion which we can distinguish from the "logical" compulsion which it purportedly underlies (No. 140), Wittgenstein shows that we can and must distinguish logical from causal determination (No. 220). This distinction, I now want to show, is tied up with Peirce's central distinction between the indeterminate and the determinate.

In its most general form, Wittgenstein's "master argument" against all forms of reductionism is that they generate infinite regresses, and this is also Peirce's master argument against Cartesian intuitionism. Wittgenstein's use of this form of argument is clearest in his insistence on the vagueness of rules (and, *a fortiori*, of concepts). If a rule were perfectly definite and nonvague – if it left nothing to the discretion of its applier – then the applier would need a rule to determine the application of this rule, and so *ad infinitum*: "What does a game look like that is everywhere bounded by rules? ... whose rules never let a doubt creep in, but stop up all the cracks where it might? Cannot we imagine a rule

---

[30] Cf. Nos. 169–76, 198–220, and especially No. 198, where Wittgenstein explicitly contrasts causal connection with *custom*.

determining the operation of a rule, and a doubt which it removes – and so on?"[31] If we admit that the application of a rule requires something to mediate between the rule and its instances, we are at once caught in the "third man" regress – for the mediator can only be another rule.[32] But if the rule is something as sharp-edged and definite as a mental state – if it comes like a flash (Nos. 139, 191, 197) and "intimates" (Nos. 222, 232) to me what I am to do – then it *will* require a mediator:

> "But this initial segment of a series obviously admitted of various interpret-ations (e.g., by means of algebraic expressions) and so you must first have chosen *one* such interpretation." Not at all ... A doubt was possible in certain circumstances. But that is not to say that I did doubt, or even could doubt ...
>
> So it must have been intuition that removed this doubt? If intuition is an inner voice – how do I know how I am to obey it? And how do I know that it doesn't mislead me? For if it can guide me right, it can also guide me wrong.
>
> ((Intuition an unnecessary shuffle.))
>
> If you have to have an intuition in order to develop the series 1234 ... you must also have one in order to develop the series 2222. [Nos. 213–14]

Whenever we try to resolve the indeterminacy which is in doubt by an appeal to intuition, we let ourselves in for being forced to postulate a superintuition which will let us know whether this intuition is the appro-priate one for the occasion (compare Nos. 190–2). As Peirce puts it:

> Now it is plainly one thing to have an intuition and another to know intuitively that it is an intuition, and the question is whether these two things, distinguishable in thought, are invariably connected, so that we can always intuitively distinguish between an intuition and a cognition deter-mined by another ... There is no evidence that we have this faculty, except that we seem to *feel* we have it. But the weight of the testimony depends entirely on our being supposed to have the power of distinguishing in this feeling whether the feeling be the result of education, old associations, etc., or whether it is an intuitive cognition; or, in other words, it depends on presupposing the very matter testified to. (v, p. 214)[33]

---

[31] The remainder of the paragraph (No. 84) from which this is quoted goes on to point out that leaving room for doubt does not paralyze action; cf. No. 87. This should be compared with Peirce's discussion of "make-believe doubt" (e.g., at v, p. 265).

[32] See Wittgenstein's discussion at No. 86 of the notion that we need a schema to tell us how to use a table, another schema to tell us how to use the first, etc. This should be compared with Kant's notion of "schemata" (*K. d. r. V.*, A 137-B 176ff) and Peirce's critique thereof (v, p. 531).

[33] On not being able to find in ourselves a faculty which we feel is there, cf. Wittgenstein, No. 176.

What Peirce calls "knowing that it is an intuition" is pragmatically equivalent to "knowing that it does not mislead me." In still more general phrasing, both men are saying that the kind of indetermination involved in understanding or following a rule is not removed by postulating any determinate entity to eliminate it, for the original indefiniteness reappears at the level of this new entity.[34] Whether one postulates mental states, or formation rules of an ideal language, or Leibnizian essences, the vagueness which one is trying to expel will turn up again in the instrument of expulsion (for example, in criteria for detecting a given mental state, or in the metalanguage used to state formation rules).

Now "causal determination" (as Wittgenstein uses the term) is among relations what "bare particulars" or Leibnizian monads are among the terms of relations – that is, it is the archetype of determinacy. The paradigm case of causal determination, in this distinctive sense, is Hume's rebound of billiard balls (Peirce's Secondness *qua* Efficient Causality), to which (reverting to Pears's terms) absolute necessity is central and "convenience" is quite irrelevant: βία rather than ανάγκη. The temptation which mechanism held out to the empiricists of the nineteenth century was to "reduce" the ανάγκη of Hume's "gentle force" to the βία of corpuscles or electric charges. Peirce, in the metaphysical application of his categories, was reacting against this attempt, and Wittgenstein was reacting against its successor – the attempt to perform the same reduction "epistemologically" (or *logisch-philosophisch*) rather than psychologically. Their language is therefore different, but the patterns of arguments they use, and the kinds of similarities and dissimilarities to which they point, are as similar as are their enemies. Both are fighting against the "Ockhamistic" prejudice that the determinate always lurks – actually, and not merely potentially – behind the indeterminate. Both recognize the sense in which we cannot break out of the cluster of things which Peirce calls Thirds and whose workings Wittgenstein calls "logical determination" (for example, signs, words, habits, rules, meanings, games, understanding) to something more definite which will somehow replace these things. The general thesis that reductionism, nominalism, and intuitionism are at one in trying to transcend language is, so to speak, the methodological way of putting what Peirce put metaphysically when he said that they were at one in trying to avoid admitting the reality of Thirdness.

[34] The argument sketched on p. 21 above can easily be seen to be a special case of this general line of argument.

We should now be able to see the problem of naming as a special case of a more general problem. One of the forms in which the distinction between causal and logical determination appears in the *Philosophical Investigations* is the replacement of the dyadic "mirroring" relationship of sign and fact in the *Tractatus* by the triad "$X$ means $Y$ to $Z$," where $Z$ is something (for example, a human being) which is not sharp-edged, is not fully determinate (like an atomic fact or a picture of one), but is quite fuzzy around the edges. Broadly speaking, the reason for this fuzziness is that even this triad is incomplete, because it contains implicit reference to a context which is indefinite in extent. If we regard this context as grouping itself around the language user rather than around his signs or their referents, we can see it as the fact that behind the use of every rule in a language-game there are the rest of the rules of the game.[35] Beyond these rules, in turn, one glimpses the rules of still another game, in terms of which the first one has meaning. And so on. Now a reductionist, invoking the "cannot get started" argument[36] to avoid this creeping contextualism, will usually retreat to the topic of learning rules rather than using them – and, in particular, to the putatively primitive process of *learning names*, a process whose context, in so far as it has one, is presumably exclusively causal rather than logical in character. But here we are met by the opening argument of the *Investigations*, against the usual notion of how this learning works. Now in the light of our description of the Wittgensteinian "master argument," we can see that Pears's exhibition of the *sui generis* character of naming is equivalent to this opening argument. For the central thesis of both is that, granting that in ostensive definition we do exit from the maze of words, this exit does not give us a touchstone to which we can recur and on which we can rest our understanding of learning and using language. As Wittgenstein points out: one of the differences between obeying an inspiration and following a rule is that in the former case we cannot teach somebody else our technique (No. 232). The appeal to ostensive definition in any of its forms ("just recognizing" color samples, or similarities, or universals) is simply a special case of intuitionism, and is to be met with the same set of arguments as any other such case – namely, that such an appeal is either a confession of failure or else the generator of an infinite regress. Specifically, the sort of infinite regress generated is

---

[35] Cf. No. 31 on separating the character of being a king from the rest of the game of chess and, generally, the critique of ostensive definition which stretches roughly from No. 26 to No. 38.

[36] The term is due to Alan Pasch (*op. cit.*, pp. 162–3). Pasch's counterargument, to which Wittgenstein would certainly have been sympathetic, is, "After all, what cannot get started without a lowest-level language is not language but analysis."

indicated by Pears when he says that the answer offered by realism to the question, "Why are we able to name things as we do?"

> ... could not be informative even if it were detailed; since there could be a non-circular answer to the question, "What universal?" only if the exit from the maze of words were made at some different point, which would merely put off the moment of embarrassment from which in the end neither speech nor thought can be saved. (p. 54)

The infinite regress is generated by successive puttings off of the moment of embarrassment, performed by successive requests to "just recognize" something.[37]

Given this view of the negative dialectic which Pears's article exhibits as a special case of the general antireductionist and anti-intuitionist dialectic exhibited by Peirce and Wittgenstein, we can now compare the "positive" sides of their doctrines. Without attempting to turn the *Philosophical Investigations* into a work on ontology, it is perhaps not unduly distorting to say that Wittgenstein, like Peirce, is insisting on the reality of vagueness. When he argues against Frege and "Ockhamists" generally that a concept's having vague boundaries does not prevent it from being a concept, precisely because it does not prevent it from being *used* (No. 71), he is articulating the germ of Peirce's thesis that realism (in the sense of the irreducibility of the indeterminate) and pragmatism reciprocally entail each other. The character and the importance of the pragmatism of both men becomes evident if we remark that both, despite their use of the antireductionist master argument sketched above, insist on the unavoidability of certain "harmless" infinite regresses. For Peirce there is potentially a sign behind every sign, and for Wittgenstein there is potentially a language-game behind every language-game; but both consider these regresses harmless on the pragmatic ground that practice does not require the actualization of these potentialities.

The difference between harmful and harmless infinite regresses will be clearer if we revert to a metaphor of section II and talk about the difference between the depth and the breadth of an explanation. The intuitionist

---

[37] It is perhaps worth noting that an accusation that one's opponent is caught in a vicious circle is almost always answered by his attempt to break the circle by moving up to a higher logical type – e.g., by appealing to an intuition of the intuitional character of the experience which was originally presented as itself a complete explanation. The counterploy is then to chase one's opponent up a ladder of types (converting the vicious circle into a vicious helix) until you get tired, at which point you accuse him of generating an infinite regress. Thus, the "vicious circle" and the "infinite regress" ploys form the two horns of a destructive dilemma and each is, in a sense, incomplete without the other. A fuller statement of Peirce's and Wittgenstein's antireductionist master argument would bring this point out.

and the reductionist look for something determinate underlying the indeterminate – something of which the indeterminate is an epiphenomenon. In the antireductionist master argument, this determinate thing is shown to be itself indeterminate and to require the postulation of a still deeper-lying determinate, and so on. Whether one thinks of this regress as going down in search of the Deepest or up the ladder of logical types in search of the Highest is less important than what I shall call the *vertical* character of both searches. This character consists in the fact that one looks at each new step as a transition to a new level – a level which is a necessary condition for the existence of the previous step(s). That is, at level $n$ one looks at the existence of level $n$-1 as possible only by virtue of $n$, which itself exists *a se*. Such a regress can be contrasted with what I shall call a *horizontal* one, in which each new step gives us something which is of essentially the same kind as what we had at the last, but something which renders the last step more determinate than it was. The relation between step $n$ and step $n$-1 is thus not like the relation between creator and created, but like that between a mystifying book and a brilliant commentary on it; the book was there already, even though perhaps nobody could make much of it until the commentary came along. Nor would there be anything surprising in somebody writing a commentary on the commentary, and so *ad infinitum*. Movement along a horizontal regress lacks the sort of jolts we feel whenever we are forced to a new level in a vertical regress (the sort of jolt felt by the child when the question "Who made God?" first occurs to him) and it also lacks the sense of utter futility which grips us when we realize that we can always be forced to move on from any level of a vertical regress. The reason a vertical regress can be condemned to futility by the antireductionist master argument is that it attempts the impossible task of making determinate the relationship between the purely determinate and the purely indeterminate (resembling in this the task of explaining *creatio ex nihilo*, or the Concrete Universal). The reason why a horizontal regress cannot be destroyed by the same argument is that it takes the datum as it finds it, as a determinate indetermination, and realizes that all further steps will also produce determinate indeterminations which, while they can render the original datum more determinate, cannot, because of their own indetermination, render it *perfectly* determinate.[38]

---

[38] The horizontal vs. vertical metaphor can be pressed a bit further, as follows: a horizontal regress exhibits a process which actually takes place in time. It is thus stretched out along time's arrow, whereas the steps of a vertical regress are connected by atemporal relations of "presupposition." Vertical regresses are, in fact, horizontal ones turned on end by people with unpragmatical minds and a preference for eternity over time.

The relation of this notion of a horizontal regress to pragmatism will perhaps be clearer if we glance at the example of religious explanation used in the last paragraph. Does it harm our relation to God if we realize the futility of understanding his relation to the world? To some men, this is indeed harmful; they may, for instance, cease to be able to pray. Such men are analogous to those who commit the classic reductionist error of expecting the results of analysis to exist prior to the analysis, and who take the ill success of an analysis to entail the irreality of the datum. But, as "existentialist" as well as pragmatist theologians tell us, such a realization need not be harmful (and may well be therapeutic). When Tillich, for instance, tells us that the task of theology is no more and no less than to "correlate" revelation with the culture of the times, and that revelation prior to such correlation is, in so far forth, indeterminate, he is saying that theological explanation takes a horizontal rather than a vertical form. But since theology is, after all, not the religious life but simply one (more or less optional) expression of it, this eternally indeterminate character of theological explanation is harmless. Just so, the fact that our understanding of how we follow a rule or give a name will be permanently vague does not interfere with our actually obeying rules and naming things. This resolution of the indeterminacy of interpretation is put by Wittgenstein as follows:

> This was our paradox: no course of action could be determined by a rule, because every course of action can be made out to accord with the rule. The answer was: if everything can be made out to accord with a rule, then it can also be made out to conflict with it. And so there would be neither accord nor conflict here.
>
> It can be seen that there is a misunderstanding here from the mere fact that in the course of our argument we give one interpretation after another; as if each one contented us at least for a moment, until we thought of yet another standing behind it. What this shows is that there is a way of grasping a rule which is *not* an *interpretation*, but which is exhibited in what we call "obeying the rule" and "going against it" in actual cases.
>
> Hence there is an inclination to say: every action according to the rule is an interpretation. But we ought to restrict the term "interpretation" to the substitution of one expression of the rule for another.
>
> And hence also "obeying a rule" is a practice. And to *think* one is obeying a rule is not to obey a rule. (Nos. 201–2)

The permanent possibility of *practice* is what renders harmless the indefinite horizontal regress of interpretations, oscillating as they do between the purely determinate ("nothing accords with the rule") and the purely indeterminate ("everything accords with it").

Finally, if we turn from the theory of meaning to the theory of knowledge, we can see how this pragmatism ties in with the more familiar notion of pragmatism as mediating between realism and idealism. Both realism and idealism are forms of intuitionism: the former attributes a lot of little, completely determinate intuitions to us; the latter attributes one great big, completely determinate intuition to the Absolute. The permanent truth of idealism is that every state of knowledge is indeterminate and incomplete, whereas the permanent truth of realism is that each state of knowing is what it is and no other thing. The recognition that a series of knowings is a series of determinate indeterminations does justice to both sides of this putative dilemma, but this recognition is possible only if we grant that indeterminacy is inescapable.[39] Now the cash value of the distinction between an appeal to practice and an appeal to intuition is just that an intuition cannot be vague and still be an intuition, whereas an action is neither vague nor nonvague. Your thought of obeying a rule can be made as sharp-edged as you please, but the question of the determinacy or indeterminacy of the *act* of obedience simply does not arise.[40] The regress of incomplete interpretations – a regress of rules, habits, and signs standing behind rules, habits, and signs – which we find in Peirce's and Wittgenstein's horizontal regresses gives idealism its due. But reference to action, which (because degree of determinacy is irrelevant to it) can take place at any step in the eternally incomplete series of interpretations, preserves the down-to-earth character of realism.

---

[39] The reader who is bothered by my free-and-easy use of "indeterminacy" will find support for his suspicions in D. C. Williams's critique of "a confusion which affects much of contemporary philosophy, the confusion between the idea of the *determinate* and the idea of the *determined*. The new word 'determinacy' or 'indeterminacy' seems expressly invented to elide and conceal the distinction." ("The Sea-Fight Tomorrow," in Paul Henle, Horace M. Kallen, and Susanne L. Langer, eds., *Structure, Method and Meaning* [New York, 1951], pp. 292–3.) The point cannot be argued in this space, but I should want to say that what pragmatism invites us to see is precisely what the tradition which Professor Williams calls "the extensionalistic view of things" never saw: that the determinate is such only because it is determined by something. This general critique of extensionalism and related strands of thought is put forward very clearly in W. D. Oliver's *Theory of Order* (Yellow Springs, 1951), especially ch. 3.

[40] As Wittgenstein suggests (No. 176), the inability to find an item of mental furniture which is the experience of being influenced by a rule is the "germ of the idea that the will is not a phenomenon." In Peircian language, this Kantian point is expressed by saying that Secondness is not Thirdness. In the language of language-strata, we can say that terms like "vague" and "indefinite" occur in the stratum in which we talk about interpretations (in Wittgenstein's restricted sense of the "substitution of one *expression* of a rule for another"), but not in the stratum in which we talk about actions *qua* actions (if there is such a stratum).

In this chapter, I have been emphasizing similarities between Peirce and Wittgenstein, and I have played down the differences between them. These differences are real and important – and I have hinted at them in section II, in discussing Pears's appeal to a direct acquaintance with the naming process. There is obviously no room here for a systematic exposition of these differences, but I should like to suggest that such an exposition will be most fruitful if it is given against the background of the similarities which I have attempted to sketch. The lesson which Wittgenstein's later writings taught us about the nature of philosophy loses much of its value when it is construed as an attack on systematic theory construction and technical vocabularies. Such a reading of Wittgenstein confuses the real enemy – reductionism – with the use of a tactic which is available to the reductionist and the antireductionist alike. It uses the accidents of Wittgenstein's thought to criticize the accidents of previous philosophizing. The followers of a great philosopher often confuse the tactics he used in criticizing his predecessors with the master strategy of his approach to philosophic problems. This happened to Peirce in his own day, and there is evidence that it is happening to Wittgenstein in ours. Drawing historical parallels, in the fashion illustrated by this chapter, can be mischievous if done in a "reductionist" spirit – treating one mode of philosophizing as merely a confused approach to what some other mode has made plain. But if this spirit is avoided (and I have done my best to avoid it here), historical comparisons can help free us from preoccupation with accidents of tactics and can direct us toward the crucial insights which generate master strategies.

# CHAPTER 2

# *The limits of reductionism*

## I

One criticism which philosophers often make of their opponents is that they are "reductionists." One gathers that a typical philosophic error is to infer from "X has the property Y" to "X is nothing but Y," or to infer from "X is analogous to Y in respect to Z" that "X and Y are indistinguishable." Another form of the same criticism is that philosophers take some feature of experience or reality or language to be paradigmatic, and are not then able to account for features which depart from this paradigm. Yet no such criticism can, without absurdity, object to the general procedure which these inferences illustrate. All rational inquiry is reductionist; all abstract thought takes selected aspects of a subject-matter as paradigmatic and ignores other aspects. Thought is reductionist or nothing, and the criticism only makes sense if it is narrowed down. When it *is* narrowed down, it usually turns out to be the claim that a reduction of X to Y is illegitimate because the very process of reducing presupposes some X that is not reduced. This claim, which we shall call "the appeal to self-referential consistency," is the topic of this chapter. Our aim is to see what can be done to specify a point of diminishing returns in the reductive process, and thus to locate the limits of reductionism.

In its narrower form, the antireductionist criticism is one of three great patterns of argument which philosophers often use. The other two are the appeal to fact, and the appeal to simplicity (crystallized in the phrase "Occam's Razor"). The appeal to simplicity was the first to manifest itself in the history of Western philosophizing, in the sweeping reductions of the pre-Socratics. An initial zest for the reductive possibilities which abstraction presents led to philosophies which recognized only one kind of thing. In later history, each new triumph of abstraction in extraphilosophic disciplines has induced a resurgence of thoroughgoing reductionism among philosophers, and each resurgence has been spear-headed by the appeal that entities (or concepts, or terms) not be multiplied without necessity. But just as in the dawn of philosophy the charming simplicity of Thales and Democritus was countered by the down-to-earth realistic pluralism of Aristotle, resting on an appeal to inspect things as they are, each resurgence has been countered by the hard-headed insistence that the subject-matter isn't as simple as all that. Most of the later history of philosophy is a battle between the reductionist's appeal to simplicity and the pluralist's appeal to facts.[1] Although in the absolute sense, all philosophy is reductionist – it wants to reduce, if not the Many to the One, at least the Too Many to the Fewer – at any given moment in the history of philosophy, one can easily detect a struggle between those who think that the reductive process has gone too far and those who think that it hasn't yet gone far enough.

Neither the appeal to simplicity nor to fact, by itself, permits much fruitful controversy. The appeal to Occam's Razor hinges on the clause "without necessity," and as soon as this is realized, the quarrel between reductionist and pluralist moves to a metaphilosophical level and becomes the question "Necessary for what?" Conversely, the appeal to fact is always met by the claim that the pluralist's putative "fact" is an artificial construct created by an over-blown vocabulary. When the difficulty of telling the difference between something actually present in the subject-matter and an illusion created by the use of a particular set of spectacles is realized, the quarrel moves once again to a metaphilosophical level. If one takes the aim of philosophizing to be "saving the appearances," then one can say that testing whether this aim has been fulfilled is inevitably obscured by the ambiguity of "saving," on the one hand, and of "appearances," on the other. Any pluralistic philosophy's theory of explanation will give a meaning to "saving" which makes the reductionist's explanation illegitimate. Any reductionist will give a meaning to "appearances" which makes the pluralist's appearances illusory.

---

[1] "Pluralism," as I shall he using the term, should not be contrasted with "monism," nor thought of as the name for a particular metaphysical doctrine. Rather, it should be taken as meaning simply "antireductionism," a term which, but for its clumsiness, Í could have used instead. Thus, when I speak of a pluralist, I do not necessarily mean a philosopher whose general tenor of thought is pluralistic in the traditional sense, but rather a philosopher of any sort who sees some cherished entity or concept or term being down-graded by another philospher. The appeal to self-referential inconsistency can, of course, be used against any kind of philosopher. The "pluralist" who insists on the richness and the diversity of things will usually be a reductionist when it comes to dealing with those particular things which his "reductionist" opponent has tried to turn into ultimates. Similarly, when I speak of a reductionist, it should be borne in mind that the philosopher may be pluralistic on the whole and reductionist only in some particular area – as is the case below, in the example of the debate between Royce and the Epistemological Realist.

It is at this point that the third great argument enters philososophic controversy. It is the argument that some given reduction is self-referentially inconsistent, in the sense that the result of the reduction does not permit an account of the reduction itself. The argument hopes for mutual agreement on what is to be taken as an explanation, and on what is to be taken as a fact. In employing it, the pluralist is saying: "As an example of 'fact,' I take the actual process of explaining in which you are engaged, and as criteria of explanation, I use the criteria which you yourself apply in this process. Now, explain your explanation in terms of these criteria." This treatment of philosophizing as itself a fact in need of explanation is the metaphilosophical attitude *par excellence*. It is the rhetorical device which moves discussion up to the level on which the questions "Necessary for what?" and "When is a fact not *really* a fact?" must be raised explicitly. The acceptance of this gambit might indeed be taken as the defining characteristic of that species of discourse which we call "philosophy." For it is precisely when the gambit is *refused*, and the reductionist replies that his concern is with a certain delimited subject-matter which does *not* include his own activity of inquiry, that a given type of inquiry is liable to separate itself from philosophy and to set up shop as science. Having refused the gambit, the reductionist can defend himself by saying that the things which the pluralist wants him to recognize are not necessary for doing the job which he has set himself, and that he couldn't care less whether they are necessary for an account of the doing of the job. Similarly, he can reply that, for his job, the "facts" are exhausted by, for example, the pointer readings on his instruments. Refusing to go beyond these defenses cuts him off, little by little, from the continuing dialogue which is the history of philosophy. It is in this fashion that "physics without metaphysics," "psychology without epistemology," and "logic without psychology" (phrases which began as rallying cries and ended as redundant platitudes) came into being.[2] In what follows, however, we shall

---

[2] In addition to these examples of inquiries which have won the status of autonomous disciplines (either by the spectacular character of their results or the blind workings of Parkinson's Law), there is another product of the rejection of this gambit. This is the sort of philosophy which frowns on metaphilosophical questions, delimits a set of data and a set of criteria of explanation (although usually leaving the latter rather obscure), and calls inquiry about these data according to these criteria "philosophy." The most interesting contemporary example of this "Philosophy-is-what-*I*-do" ploy is on the pluralist side of the debate within contemporary empiricism, and is best represented by the work of certain disciples of the late Professor J. L. Austin. (Austin himself did not pretend that his sort of philosophy was the only proper denotations of the word "philosophy"; his disciples have often been less sensible.) But there are recent examples on the reductionist side, such as Nelson Goodman's attempts to revitalize logical reconstructionism by discarding "epistemological primacy" or "utility for the sciences" as criteria for the value of constructions and substituting "the

be primarily concerned with the dialogue which ensues if the reductionist *accepts* this gambit.

We may begin by reminding ourselves of the ubiquity and power of the appeal to self-referential consistency. It can be employed both microscopically and macroscopically – in the details of carrying out some particular philosophic program, as a criticism of the program as a whole, and in all the stages that mediate between these two extremes. Let us consider some sample cases. (1) When positivism puts forward its trichotomous division of linguistic expressions (either a tautology, or an empirical hypothesis, or cognitively meaningless), critics immediately ask which pigeonhole the statement of this trichotomy goes in. (2) When logical reconstructionism tries to solve paradoxes by invoking a hierarchy of metalanguages, the critic asks for a language in which the theory of this hierarchy can be stated without giving rise to new paradoxes. (3) When realism insists that beings are absolutely independent of thought, idealists reply that the thinking of this very assertion will then be absolutely independent of, and irrelevant to, the world it purports to think. (4) When idealists try to reduce external relations to illusions, realists reply that this entails that the external relation between the world as unreduced illusion and the world as reduced to reality must itself be a mere illusion. (5) When Marxists or Freudians tell us that all philosophical explanations are rationalizations, we reply that their own explanation of philosophy must then itself be a mere rationalization. (6) When an all-embracing classification of possible philosophies is offered (by, for example, Pepper or McKeon), we are curious to know on what ground the philosopher who announces this classification stands. And so it goes. In each case, the critic employs the appeal to self-referential consistency to suggest that even if all *other* appearances can be saved by the reductionist theory under attack, the appearance of saving them can't be.

We can try to clarify the common logical structure involved in such varied instances of this appeal by noting how invoking it complicates the rules for philosophizing. If one attends solely to the pluralisms appeal to fact, one has as a rule "Classify the facts according to distinctions present in the facts themselves." If one attends to the reductionist appeal to simplicity, one has: "Impose the most perspicacious and efficient possible order upon the facts" (with the implicit addition: "and don't worry too much about where the parameters you use in this ordering come from"). The appeal to self-referential consistency produces some such rule as: "In your

satisfaction of curiosity." Cf. "The Revision of Philosophy," in S. Hook, ed., *American Philosophers at Work* (New York, 1956), p. 83.

descriptive classifications, or in your impositions of order, don't neglect to leave a place for the criterion of classification, or the choice of ordering principles." If, like most philosophers, we pay our respects to all three appeals, we get a three-fold rule of roughly this form: "(1) Explain every-thing, but (2) don't say more than you have to, and (3) don't deny anything presupposed by what you've already said." This rule is reasonable enough, and philosophers of all persuasions could perhaps join in taking it as a charter. But the attempt to use it as a criterion for deciding between competing philosophies will usually founder on the notion of "presuppos-ing." To get clear about the force of the appeal to self-referential consist-ency, we need to get clear about the meaning of this term.

Now the evident vagueness of the notion of presupposing might seem to show that our present inquiry, and any other inquiry on the ethereal plane of metaphilosophy, is bound to be unfruitful. For either a presupposition relation is something that is available for inspection *in natura rerum*, antecedent to philosophizing, or else it is the kind of thing which comes into being in and through the activity of philosophic theory construction. In the first case, its presence can presumably be detected only by an inspection of the actual use of language (as in Strawson's philosophy of logic, where one finds out whether one statement presupposes another by asking oneself, or someone else, whether the question of the truth of the first would arise if the second were false).[3] But in metaphilosophy we are concerned not with well-formed linguistic communities, but with idiosyn-cratic and technical vocabularies. If the putative inspection is something more subtle than this, then it will probably be a special kind of activity which makes sense only to philosophers of a certain stripe.[4] In the second case – if a presupposition is something one makes, rather than finds – the implication that metaphilosophy can employ the notion of presupposing only at the cost of abandoning neutrality and adopting a full-fledged set of ontological and other commitments seems still more obvious. The only way out of this dilemma, I think, is to adopt a modification of Strawson's technique and to look for some common features in the kinds of dialogues which take place when a philosopher is faced with the challenge that his explanation has denied one of its presuppositions. By seeing what moves

---

[3] Cf. *Introduction to Logical Theory* (London, 1952), pp. 18, 213.
[4] Cf. David Harrah's "Theses on Presuppositions," *Review of Metaphysics*, 9 (1955–6), p. 117: "To discern a presupposition relationship we need general criteria for 'being a property of the entity' in question and for ontological status. Because to have these criteria is to have a comprehensive philosophical theory, to assert that a presupposition relation holds is to assert such a theory."

are made in response to such a challenge, we may get an understanding of what the challenge amounts to.

To make our inspection of dialogues more manageable, we shall confine ourselves to cases where the quarrel is explicitly about the exhaustiveness of a distinction, and where the claim that a theory denies one of its own presuppositions takes the form of the claim that the *ratio divisionis* doesn't itself fall within one of the divisions which it itself creates.[5] Carnap's treatment of the logical status of the verifiability criterion of cognitive significance gives us a good example of a reply to such a challenge. Once it becomes clear that the criterion isn't itself an empirical hypothesis, the positivist is tempted to suggest that it is an analytic truth. But when this alternative is also seen to be inadequate, resort is made to a new distinction, formulated by Carnap as the distinction between questions internal and external to conceptual frameworks.[6] The verifiability criterion, and the trichotomy it produces, is now seen as an answer to an external question: "Which are the cognitively meaningful utterances for framework F?" Whereas the question "Is this utterance a cognitively meaningful one?" is a question which can be posed only *within* some given framework. We thus have a distinction which creates a new set of pigeonholes, in one of which the old, putatively objectionable distinction may he placed. The charge that the original distinction presupposed, and yet made impossible, its own cognitive significance is taken care of by the claim that the question of cognitive significance can't be raised about it. Notice the parallel here with Strawson's notion of the presupposition relation as holding between a statement and another statement B such that if B is false the question of A's truth or falsity does not arise. In Carnap's metatheory about criteria, the falsity of the statement "Q is a question raised internally to a framework F " means that the question of the cognitive significance of answers to Q doesn't arise, just as, within the framework created by the original criterion, the falsity of "A is either verifiable by inspection of the meanings of words or conformable by empirical observation" means that the question of A's truth or falsity doesn't arise.[7] What we wind up with is a

---

[5] A case could be made, for saying that *all* arguments brought on by an appeal to self-referential consistency can be resolved into arguments about the exhaustiveness of distinctions, but I shan't try to make it here.

[6] Cf. Carnap, "Empiricism, Semantics and Ontology," reprinted in Leonard Linsky, ed., *Semantics and the Philosophy of Language* (Urbana, 1952).

[7] Strawson's and Carnap's choice of the kind of statements which must be true if the question of the truth or falsity of another statement is to arise are, of course, radically different. But the difference is irrelevant to the point I want to make here.

triple-decker structure of distinctions: (1) truth vs. falsity, (2) meaningful vs. meaningless, (3) internal vs. external. The second and third levels of this structure contain both the *ratio divisionis* of the distinction immediately beneath it and the vocabulary for formulating the conditions of applicability of this subordinate distinction.

We can find a parallel pattern in another of the examples cited above. Consider a dialogue between realist and idealist as presented by Royce.[8] The realist wants to make an exhaustive distinction between Being and Thought by saying that Beings are absolutely independent of the acts of thought which refer to them. Royce replies that, if this is so, then the converse relation must also hold, and that therefore the very thought which expresses the difference between Being and Thought must be absolutely independent of the nature of Being. Yet the realist's assertion of the validity of this thought would seem to presuppose that it is an accurate picture of reality. The realist, weakening his thesis a bit, tries to make a distinction of kind between aspects of tables and chairs which are mind-dependent and aspects which aren't. Royce replies by asking for the *ratio divisionis*, and puts forward Berkeley-like arguments against all those which the realist tries to propound. So, at length, the realist takes the plunge; instead of making a distinction of kind between different aspects of tables and chairs, he becomes a Kantian and makes a distinction of level between the phenomenal world which contains the tables and chairs, and the thing-in-itself. He then invokes the right of the transcendental idealist to be an empirical realist, employs the distinction between appearance and illusion, insists on the independence of spatial substance from mind (along the lines of Kant's "Refutation of Idealism"), and explains that this is what he meant all the time. Now Royce, of course, is not yet finished with the hapless realist; but it will be useful to stop the debate here and to point out the parallels between Carnap's relativizing of the meaningful–meaningless distinction and the Kantian's relativizing of the distinction between Being and Thought. Both the naive positivist and the naive realist start out with what they unselfconsciously take to be an empirically given classification: some utterances have a property called "cognitive significance" and some don't, and some entities (such as tables) have a property called "mind-independence" and others (such as my sensations of tables) don't. The charge is then made to both that although the ascription of such properties

---

[8] See *The World and the Individual* (New York, 1901), 1, pp. 132ff. Royce is distinguished both for his persistent use of the appeal to self-referential consistency and his conviction that such arguments are the only hope for an end to philosophic controversy.

presupposes that this ascription itself fits into the favored pigeonhole (i.e., that it's cognitively significant in the one case, and mind-independent in the other), the criterion given for classifying utterances or entities neverthe-less doesn't allow it to be put in these pigeonholes. The first, and clearly inadequate, reply to this charge is to erect a new distinction which further subdivides the favored side of the original distinction; in the case of the realist this is some form of the distinction between primary and secondary qualities, whereas in the case of the positivist it's the distinction between empirical hypotheses and analytic statements. The realist would like to say, *à la* Locke, that his distinction is simply a report on the status of various aspects of tables and chairs; the positivist would like to say that his distinction is a report on the meaning of terms like "cognitively meaning-ful." But, for Berkelean reasons in the one case and Quinean reasons in the other, this is disallowed. What we need, and what we eventually get, is not a distinction which further subdivides a member of the original distinc-tion, but a distinction which embraces the original distinction as one of its members. In the case of the realist-turned-Kantian, the analogue of the distinction between the inside and the outside of conceptual frameworks is the distinction between the empirical and the transcendental standpoints. From the latter standpoint, we can explain the criteria for subjectivity and mind-dependence ("illusion" as opposed to "appearance") without treating the question as to the subjectivity of these criteria themselves, for the question "subjective or objective?" arises only within a phenomenal world. For Kant, as for Carnap, we have a three-decker structure of distinctions: (1) empirically real vs. illusory, (2) appearance vs. thing-in-itself, (3) empir-ical standpoint vs. transcendental standpoint. Here again the second and third levels contain both the *ratio divisionis* for the distinction beneath and the vocabulary for formulating the conditions under which this lower distinction applies.

## II

On the basis of these examples, to the charge that a formulation of an exhaustive distinction denies one of its own presuppositions, the decisive *riposte* seems to be the assertion of a *distinction of level*, and not a distinc-tion of kind. A distinction of level relegates what was originally divided into kinds into a subdivision of a larger universe of discourse. As such, it permits one to insist upon the exhaustiveness of the original distinction of kind, but to say that the exhaustiveness intended was a limited one. It permits one to reply that the critic's charge of self-referential inconsistency confuses levels, for the presuppositions of a distinction do not belong within the range of things which it distinguishes.

This counterreply seems foolproof; it is never very hard to find a distinction of level to suit one's needs. But, of course, the dialogue isn't over yet. In resuming it, a critic may complain that the distinction of level is *ad hoc*, and merely verbal. Despite the vagueness of such a charge, one can certainly distinguish cases in which it has plausibility, and cases where it has none. An instance of the latter is Ryle's well-known example of category-confusion in common-sense discourse.[9] We tell a visitor that the buildings he's just seen (the various colleges, etc.) exhaust the University of Oxford: "That's all there is to it." The visitor replies that the assertion of the exhaustiveness of the distinction is incompatible with the statement of the distinction, since the term "University of Oxford" which appears in this statement isn't itself one of the entities distinguished. We make a distinction of level by explaining to him that the relationship between the University and the Colleges isn't a physical one, but one of another type ("functional" or "legal" or the like), and that our exhaustive division wasn't meant to be a complete analysis of the University of Oxford, but only an analysis of it *qua* physical object. If he then charges that this distinction between the physical and the nonphysical is an *ad hoc* and verbalistic dodge, and demands that we either bring him face to face with the University or else retract our original claim to exhaustiveness, we can safely give him up as hopeless. But in other cases we can see a point to such a charge.

These are the cases where we're inclined to say that an alternative distinguished in a distinction of level is too much like one of the kinds distinguished in the original distinctions of kind. In the case of Carnap, we detect a certain resemblance between the emotive utterances which are distinguished as one kind of thing which occurs within a conceptual framework and the formulations of "pragmatic" considerations about what conceptual frameworks are to construct. In the case of the realist-turned-Kantian, the notion of a world of appearance existing independently of the Ego, despite its having been structured by the Ego, seems too much like the notion of a permanent illusion for comfort. We may be tempted to suggest that "pragmatic considerations dictating one's choice of a

---

[9] Ryle's "categories" – what a thing must fall in if a certain range of questions is to be sensibly raised about it – are produced by distinctions of level. Each member of such a distinction creates a category which determines the applicability of some lower-level distinction of kind. Ryle tends to think of these categories as given by inspecting usage of non-technical language; here, however, we're emphasizing their deliberate construction by philosophers under critical pressure.

conceptual framework" are simply the kind of emotive utterances which positivists happen to like, and that the world constituted by the Categories is just the kind of illusion which Kantians happen to like. Even if we happen to share their likes and dislikes, we may be troubled by the apparent disingenuousness involved in their putative distinctions of level, and we may feel that problems are being baptized rather than solved.

Our attempt to evaluate the force of the appeal to self-referential consistency now appears to have saddled us with the job of stating criteria for *ad hoc*ness, for "verbal" distinctions as opposed to nonverbal ones. But it seems clear that this job can't be done alone wholesale, and that each new distinction advanced must be analyzed in its own terms and on its own merits. Still, we can, I think, formulate some useful heuristic principles for particular analyses by noting the connection of the charge that a distinction of level is *ad hoc* with the charge that it generates a vicious circle and/or an infinite regress. These latter charges have a slightly more solid ring, and we may have some hope of arriving at criteria for determining whether they are justified. Notice first that to say that a distinction of level is verbal because it merely gives a new (and more respectable name) to one of the kinds distinguished on a lower level is equivalent to saying that its attempt to explain the presuppositions of the lower-level distinction is circular. The variation is only in phrasing. But the charge of generating an infinite regress is a somewhat more complicated affair. When one isn't sure whether a given circle is real or apparent, one requests a new distinction of level which will provide, if it can successfully be made, a nonverbal distinction between the two elements which appear to be related circularly. In the example of the positivist, the request will be "Within what conceptual framework do you make this distinction between internal and external questions?" In the case of the Kantian, it will be some form of the question, "From what standpoint do you make this distinction between the transcendental and the empirical standpoints?" If one's opponent undertakes to provide such a new distinction, however – creating, in our examples, a four-decker structure of distinctions – one will often have the same suspicion of verbalism and circularity about the relation between levels three and four as one did about the relations between pairs of lower levels. By urging this suspicion, one moves one's opponent up one level more. This process generates an *n*-decker structure of distinctions (with each level coming to look more like the last, as one exhausts one's opponent's ingenuity). If no terminal value for *n* is in sight, one now charges the opponent with having generated an infinite regress.

This sketch of the moves and countermoves which ensue once a suspicion of verbalism has been voiced suggests that the charge of *ad hoc*ness (or verbalism) and the charge of circularity are both, so to speak, primitive forms of the charge of generating an infinite regress. The latter is the sophisticated (and the only really useful) form of the first two, because it takes into account the opponent's countermoves. To say that an explanation is verbal or circular, and leave it at that, is a form of the pluralist's appeal to fact; it amounts to saying that (a) a given universe of discourse is the only relevant one, (b) there are just so-and-so many sorts of things in this universe of discourse, and (c) the original distinction of kind exhausted them. One therefore claims to know in advance that one isn't going to be able to see more kinds of things, or to enter other universes of discourse, and that any postulation of more kinds or of other universes is bound to be a mere verbal maneuver. When this sort of advance knowledge is claimed, of course, dialogue is no longer possible. The charge that an infinite regress has been generated, however, can only be made if one is first willing to listen to the successive distinctions of level which are put forward, and to phrase one's successive criticisms within the successive new universes of discourse whose existence is suggested by these distinctions of level. One may indeed conclude, after going through a good many such steps, that one just can't see any difference between the new universes and the old, but this is not the same thing as the claim to antecedent knowledge of all possible relevant universes of discourse which is involved in the simple, plonking accusation of circularity or of verbalism.[10]

## III

We're now at last in a position to call a halt to our inspection of dialogues, and to our classification of typical moves and countermoves. We started from the notion of the appeal to self-referential consistency against putatively overstringent reductionisms, and we isolated the notion of presupposition as crucial to this appeal. In order to provide a context in which

[10] It is perhaps worth noting that the really complete impasses in communication between philosophic schools are usually marked by reciprocal accusations of verbalism. The two most obvious cases are the relations between Thomists and the general run of philosophers since Kant, and, within the latter, the relations between philosophers who have made "the linguistic turn" and those who haven't. In the second case, the linguistic philosophers see their colleagues' work as verbal manipulation stupidly taken to be inquiry, whereas the nonlinguistic philosophers see the work of linguistic philosophers as verbal manipulation wickedly and deliberately put forward as a substitute for inquiry. (A third impasse, now rapidly developing, between linguistic philosophizing in the manner of Vienna and in the manner of Oxford is marked by precisely similar interchanges.)

that notion would be meaningful, we proceeded to a distinction between distinctions of kind and distinctions of level. We then moved on to the charge of *ad hoc*ness or verbalism made against distinctions of level, and came finally to the charge of an infinite regress. Gathering together these threads, wispy as they are, gives us some material with which to start answering our original question about the limits of reductionism: can the argument that a reduction of X to Y must not presuppose an unreduced X be generalized so as to produce an *a priori* designation of the point of diminishing returns for reductive thought?

If the prospects for getting an affirmative answer to this question seem faint, this is because asking it reminds us of the central paradox of metaphilosophy: metaphilosophy aims at neutrality among philosophic systems, and yet each system can and does create its own private metaphilosophical criteria, designed to authenticate itself and to disallow competitors. The presence of this paradox shows us that the quest for absolute neutrality, and for a categorical imperative which would bind all philosophers equally, is hopeless. We have already admitted this, indeed, by the earlier remark that any program in philosophy can split itself off from the sort of dialogue we've been analyzing by an appeal to pragmatic justification. In other words, it can exhibit success at getting a certain job done, and refuse to discuss the relation of this job to other jobs. The permanent possibility of an appeal to practice makes an unqualifiedly affirmative answer to our question impossible – for this appeal, just in so far as it is distinct from the three kinds of appeals previously considered, is a request for the appreciation of new values. It calls in question the value of remaining within the dialogue which we call "philosophy," and suggests that other values take precedence. The appeal to practice transfers the question of the acceptability of a philosophical program out of metaphilosophy and into the realm of moral choice.[11] The paradox of metaphilosophy is, indeed, merely a special case of the general paradox involved in attempts to give grounds for such a choice: any reasons which support the claim that an imperative applies categorically serve to render that imperative hypothetical (by serving as a protasis to it). Thus, if metaphilosophy can offer an answer to our question about the limits of reductionism, it will have to be done in the restricted form of advice about what has to be done

---

[11] The perception of the need for such a transference underlies (and has been made familiar by) both Dewey's and Kierkegaard's criticisms of "objectivity" as the goal of philosophizing. The first self-conscious recognition of the dependence of criteriology upon ethical norms is found in Hegel; Dewey and Kierkegaard borrow this insight from Hegel, and employ it to good effect when, in the name of their own ethical interests, they turn and rend him.

to stay in the dialogue. In this form, I believe, our question *can* be answered.

One can escape the paradox of metaphilosophy by making a virtue of necessity: the requirement which a philosophy must fulfill to stay in the dialogue is precisely that it *should* develop its own metaphilosophy. Granted that every philosophy will contrive to present a self-justificatory account of the criteria for choice between philosophies, it is nevertheless by and through such contrivance that philosophical controversy is made possible, and the dialogue permitted to continue. There is, indeed, an important sense in which all philosophical controversy which is not *Sprachstreit* is metaphilosophy; for in terms of our previous classifications, all controversy which is not a simple (and quite undecidable) disagreement about facts is a disagreement about the utility of a distinction of level, and it is precisely this latter kind of disagreement which constitutes metaphilosophy. To say that a philosophical system must equip itself with a metaphilosophy if it is to stay in the dialogue is simply to say over again that a philosophy must be prepared to place its original distinctions of kind within distinctions of level in order to reply to charges of self-referential inconsistency.

This last point makes us see that the answer to our original question about the limits of reductionism is simply this: reduction goes too far when it makes the construction of distinctions of level impossible. The point of diminishing returns for reductionism comes when it is no longer able to construct a metaphilosophical account of itself. The kind of neutral metaphilosophy which we're essaying here cannot specify a criterion for determining whether some given distinction of level (or some given potential infinite regress of such distinctions) is fruitful; but it can insist, as a condition of remaining in the dialogue, that such distinctions be possible.

But this requirement may seem trivial and empty. Is *any* philosophy so impoverished that it cannot rig up, if need be, some metaphilosophic self-justification? What reductionist program is so narrow but that it cannot construct a distinction of level, when and as needed? Here we reach the central question of the present inquiry: even granted the soundness of the metaphilosophical analyses advanced so far, can we infer anything from them that is relevant to the actual workaday issues of, e.g., metaphysics, logic, and epistemology? Can we get anything out of them which tells us what distinctions of kind to make, down on the ground-floor level of philosophical explanation? I think we can, but in the present space I shall only be able to suggest an answer. The answer is: a philosophy which excludes from its initial, putatively exhaustive, distinction of kind the notion of *rules* as distinct from *data* will be unable to fulfill the requirements for staying in the dialogue. In other words, I want to suggest that without the notion of "rule" as an unreduced and irreducible element of the initial conceptual framework of a philosophical program, the construction of distinctions of level will not be possible.

This suggestion may he given some initial plausibility by going back to a broader and vaguer characterization of the charge of self-referential inconsistency. When we bring such a charge, we're saying that the reductionist has somehow excluded himself from the universe which he's analyzing or describing, while yet maintaining that this universe is in some important sense all-inclusive. And when we say *this*, we're saying, among other things, that he can't account for the fact that his analysis or description is one among many – that his activity of inquiry is *fallible*. A philosopher who announces an exhaustive distinction of kind, and from then on relies solely upon the appeal to fact ("But can't you see . . . ?"), greeting suggested alternative distinctions with a simple refusal to understand the terms used unless they're translated into his own, has effectively taken himself out of the dialogue. The only way to get him back into it is to explain to him that these alternatives are suggestions that he conduct his analyzing or describing according to different rules. (Another game is being played, as it were – one which cannot be learned through translation of its rules, but only by being played.) But if he doesn't understand what *rules* are, we can *never* get him back in, because we can never have even that minimum dialogue which is required to explain why we're objecting to his claimed infallibility.[12]

We can put this point more precisely by recurring to the difference between level and kind. To understand the difference between distinctions of kind and distinctions which include distinctions as members (which was our definition of "distinction of level") one has to understand the difference between the kind of force which intuitions have and the kind of force which rules have. To distinguish distinctions from what they distinguish is to abandon the notion of a method of pure description (of passive reception of intuited differences), and to introduce the sort of relativity, indeterminacy, and fallibility which characterize rule-governed behavior. It is only in terms of the kind of force which rules have that the phrase "the applicability of the distinction (of kind) to itself is a question that doesn't

---

[12] I owe my understanding of the connection between self-referential consistency and the problem of error, as well as the argument of this and the following paragraph to my wife, Dr. Amélie O. Rorty.

arise" makes sense, and this is the key phrase in the construction of a distinction of level. For a philosophy which bases itself squarely, and exclusively, on the appeal to fact (one in which the act of distinguishing is taken to be a matter of directly reporting the intuitable "joints" in the subject-matter), the difference between the intuition of difference and the difference intuited is invisible. Therefore, the notions of the applicability or inapplicability of the classificatory scheme to the act of classification are unintelligible. Where the difference between the intuiting and the intuited is invisible, the question of fallibility cannot be understood, and, in particular, the charge of self-referential inconsistency cannot be understood. Nor, *a fortiori*, can a distinction between the level on which acts of distinguishing are performed and the level on which the things distinguished exist be formulated. To make any of these notions intelligible, one has to be able to envisage a compulsion different from that exerted by an intuited difference: the kind of compulsion exerted by a rule. A rule, as Wittgenstein has argued,[13] is always subject to interpretation: to follow a rule is to be perpetually susceptible to doubt (though not necessarily to be gripped by it at any given moment) as to whether the ride is being interpreted aright.[14] This leeway for interpretation is a phenomenon which cannot be reconstructed out of, not stated in terms of, the quite different phenomenon of receiving intuitions of data. To be given a datum is to be saddled with something; to be given a rule is to be given a chance to do something. A distinction of kind which includes the notion of rule can, so to speak, turn around and look at itself as a rule, as offering a chance to see the subject-matter in a new way. A distinction of kind which does not include this notion cannot consistently look at itself at all, because it cannot be conscious of itself *as* a distinction. The intertwined notions of "distinction," "interpretation," and "fallibility" are all unintelligible to, and unformulatable by, a reductionism whose ground-floor distinction of kind does not leave a place for the notion of "rule."

## IV

My thesis, then, is that without an understanding of what rules are, there can be neither understanding of the charge of self-referential inconsistency nor effective defense against it. But is there, in real life, anyone who doesn't know what rules are, and how they differ from intuitions? Certainly not,

---

[13] *Philosophical Investigations* (Oxford, 1953), pp. 84–6.    [14] *Ibid.*, pp. 20, 213, 230–7.

but there are philosophies which don't. The reason for their existence is not far to seek. As long as one stays clear of the notion of "rule" (and the cluster of notions associated with it), one still can think of philosophizing as a finite task – something which might get done, and done right, once and for all. As long as one takes the goal of philosophic inquiry to be the correct apprehension of some antecedently existing set of data, one can regard the questions posed to one by competing philosophers as *Scheinprobleme*, arising out of these competitors' confused apprehensions of this reality. But as soon as one sees one's self as *making* rather than *finding* – as proposer of rules rather than as a discoverer of facts – one realizes the possibility of alternative rules, and of a plurality of interpretations of any proposed rule. This realization permits one to engage, for the first time, in genuine dialogue; but a dialogue is not always a comfortable environment. The attempt to think of rules and rule-governed behavior as local, epiphenomenal features of the subject-matter at hand (and thus capable either of being reduced away, or of simply being shoved aside as unimportant) is thus a natural and predictable move for philosophers to make, and one which has in fact been made by the vast majority.[15] But it is the brunt of my argument in this chapter that making this attempt condemns one, eventually, either to the sort of incoherent stammering which goes on when philosophers trade accusations of verbalism, or to an inconsistent, covert, and shame-faced employment of an unreduced notion of "rule" as a defense against critical attack.

---

[15] Some horrible examples, I should argue, are: Hobbes, Leibniz, Hume, and the early Wittgenstein. Some honorable exceptions are: Kant, Hegel, Peirce, and the later Wittgenstein.

# CHAPTER 3

# *Realism, categories, and the "linguistic turn"*

## Realist criticism of linguistic philosophy[1]

Among contemporary realistic philosophers there is a tendency to see the history of philosophy from Descartes to Wittgenstein as one continuous process of garnering the wages of sin. One can identify the original sin as the representative theory of perception, as the confusion of noetic being with being as such, or in various other ways. In any case, the dialectical progression which in the course of three centuries has led philosophers away from things to ideas, and away from ideas to words, presents itself as the enactment of an agonizing drama of self-destruction.

Given the initial Cartesian sundering of cognition from the object of cognition, it was only to be expected that epistemology should claim priority over metaphysics. Once this happened, it was only a matter of time before metaphysics shriveled away and died. In due course, epistemology, finding itself unable to function as an autonomous discipline when deprived of metaphysical support, was pushed aside by its ungrateful child, linguistic analysis. The ultimate, foredoomed, result of this development is, according to such neo-Thomist descriptions of recent philosophy as that of Oliver Martin,[2] the total confusion of the theoretic and instrumental orders, and the consequent replacement of philosophic controversy by ideological conflict. Linguistic analysis, Martin says, though not itself an ideology, is at the service of ideology through being "one of the many non-philosophical forms of anti-philosophy."[3] Probably, Martin continues, "It would not exist were it not for the fact that professors of philosophy who no longer believe in philosophy must do something if they are to continue to receive a salary for doing that which they profess to be impossible."

---

[1] This paper was read at a meeting of the Association for Realistic Philosophy on October 22, 1960.
[2] See his *Metaphysics and Ideology* (Milwaukee, 1959).     [3] *Ibid.*, p. 68.

This way of thinking about the present fortunes of philosophy suggests that there can be no real controversy between realists and linguistic analysts until the latter are willing to retrace the steps of the dialectic, get back to asking questions about things rather than about words, and thus put themselves in a position to consider Aristotelianism and Thomism on their merits, rather than dismissing them as sets of verbal answers to verbal questions. If they are willing to do this, they may discover that the Cartesian assumptions which they have been taking for granted all their lives are simply false. In any case, it would seem impossible, given such a view as Martin's, that linguistic analysis should arrive at a rediscovery of realism in its own way, using its own methods, and working out its own internal dialectic.

### Needed: revised map of philosophical battle-lines

Now the funny thing is that something very much like a rediscovery of realism *has* taken place among linguistic analysts. Further, this has taken place precisely among those analysts who, *prima facie*, might seem most alienated from the traditional aims and methods of philosophic inquiry – namely, among the so-called "ordinary-language" analysts. If certain writings of this school look, at first glance, more like lexicography than philosophy, a second glance will show that they are filled with devastating critiques of phenomenalism,[4] disdainful dismissals of Humean skepticism (both in epistemology[5] and in ethics[6]), violent rejections of Cartesian dualism,[7] and even (in some cases) wholesale borrowings of Thomistic distinctions and maxims.[8] Somehow, a movement of thought which led philosophers to rephrase all traditional philosophic problems in linguistic terms, and to discard problems which were not amenable to such phrasing, has now led them to give answers to these problems which are almost indistinguishable from the answers offered by writers in the realistic tradition. It is as if a set of methodological assumptions which seemed to lead to nothing except the suicide of philosophic inquiry had all along

---

[4] See, for example, G. J. Warnock, *Berkeley* (London, 1953), pp. 236–47.
[5] Cf. Peter Strawson, *Individuals* (London, 1959), p. 35; Stephen Toulmin, *The Uses of Argument* (Cambridge, 1958), pp. 299ff.
[6] See Kurt Baier, *The Moral Point of View* (Ithaca, 1958).
[7] See Ryle's *The Concept of Mind* (London, 1949), *passim*, and also Ryle's early expressions of sympathy with Husserl's revivification of the realistic thesis of the intentionality of consciousness, in a symposium on "Phenomenology," *Proceedings of the Aristotelian Society*, suppl. vol. 11 (1932), 68ff.
[8] See Peter Geach, *Mental Acts* (New York, 1957).

contained within themselves potentialities for their own transformation, and for the revivification of realistic thought.

In this chapter, I shall not try to offer a detailed comparison and contrast between this ordinary-language brand of realism and more familiar realisms. Nor shall I offer any critical judgments about realism in general nor about the comparative merits of the various brands. What I want to do is simply to sketch a revised map of present-day philosophical battle-lines – one which will take into account this new and rather startling *volte-face* in the ranks of the traditional enemies of realism. I think that it is important for these new battle-lines to be recognized if any fruitful conversation is going to take place between traditional realists and analytic philosophers. In particular, realists are, I suspect, soon going to find themselves in the peculiar position of heartily agreeing with ordinary-language philosophers on most substantive epistemological and metaphysical doctrines, while disagreeing equally heartily about the nature of metaphysics and epistemology themselves. To deal with this situation, realists need to recognize that there are *two* directions in which one may proceed after having taken the so-called "linguistic turn" and that the second of these directions leads to a position which is almost indistinguishable from Aristotelianism.

## Two linguistic theories of ultimate categories

To show that these two directions are radically distinct, I shall distinguish between two theories about the nature of ultimate categories. One of these I shall call the "ideal-language" theory, or, indifferently, the "pragmatist" theory about categories. This theory was, I think, common to most analytic philosophers in America up until the Second World War, although it was not always explicitly acknowledged. It rests upon the following three theses:

(1) One cannot transcend language; that is, one cannot find a point of view outside of all linguistic frameworks from which the world will appear "as it is." One can't think without thinking in a language.
(2) Philosophical problems are problems about what language to speak in order best to suit our purposes. Philosophical categories are the primitive predicates of this ideal language.
(3) The philosophically perfect language, once found, may not be suitable for everyday use, but this is not a defect in it. We can and should "think with the learned and speak with the vulgar." Therefore what

philosophers decide to be ultimate categorial distinctions need bear no resemblance to the distinctions which the man-in-the-street is in the habit of making.

The *ordinary*-language theory of categories, on the other hand, starts by accepting the first thesis – that we cannot transcend language[9] – but diverges immediately thereafter. Instead of inferring the second and third theses from the first, and thus moving toward a program of logical reconstructionism, this school asks us to take the claim that language cannot be transcended with redoubled seriousness. So taken, one realizes that one cannot even think about what language it would be well to think in without using some antecedently given language in which to do this thinking. Having realized this, one then looks about for this language. It turns out, unsurprisingly, to be ordinary English. The thought then dawns that if philosophic problems are indeed problems about which language works best, then one might do well to look to the language which has been given the longest and hardest work-out. At this point in one's reflections, one proceeds to develop a theory of categories based on theses which look something like this:

(1)  Language cannot be transcended, and therefore the philosopher should refrain not only from trying to discover extralinguistic facts, but from trying to discover extraordinary languages which, *per impossibile*, could take the place of the ordinary language which he finds himself speaking.

(2)  Philosophical problems are indeed problems about what language works best, but the assumption that our ordinary one doesn't work well is unjustified. What we need to do is not to construct an ideal language, and thus *make* a set of categories, but to *find* the categories which we've been using all the while.

(3)  The traditional problems of philosophy are generated not by inconsistencies or over-simplifications built into the language of the vulgar, but by the artificial distortions of this language which have been committed by philosophers who claim to be correcting the language of the vulgar.[10] The oddity, in the ear of the man-in-the-street, of a putatively ultimate category is *prima facie* evidence of its non-ultimacy.

---

[9] On the thesis that we cannot transcend language, and its relation to anti-Cartesian currents in contemporary philosophy, see the present writer's "Pragmatism, Categories, and Language," *Philosophical Review*, 70 (1961), pp. 197–223 [Chapter 1 in the present volume].

[10] Cf. Warnock, *loc. cit.*, and also his *English Philosophy since 1900* (Oxford, 1958), ch. 12.

These two parallel triplets of metaphilosophical theses about categories suffice for an initial indication of the contrast I want to exhibit. In the remainder of this chapter, I intend to develop this contrast in somewhat more detail. I shall do this in four stages. First, I shall discuss the status of the thesis which is common ground to both theories of categories – the thesis that language cannot be transcended. Then, I shall proceed to sketch the way in which the pragmatist theory of categories leads one to adopt a distinctly nonrealistic set of categories, using Peirce as an example. Then, I shall return to the ordinary-language theory and suggest why, if one starts off from this theory, one is inevitably going to wind up with a realistic set of categories. Finally, I shall try to formulate the central questions which the return to realism by way of linguistic analysis raises for philosophers who have come to realism by more traditional routes.

## Common ground: language cannot be transcended

Both these sets of theses about categories take as common ground that we can't penetrate through language to nonlinguistic data which will guide our choice of languages. This assumption can easily be construed as rephrasing, in the idiom of the Way of Words, the Kantian conclusion that we cannot penetrate behind a battery of epistemological categories to the thing-in-itself. But it would be misleading to take it as simply such a rephrasing, and to assume that it stands or falls with a Kantian epistemology. There are *two* routes by which one may reach a conception of philosophy as something that lives, moves, and has its being within language. One is, indeed, the familiar route that leads from Kant's transcendental idealism through, say, C. I. Lewis's conceptual pragmatism, to Carnap's restatement of Lewis's pragmatism in terms of a choice between languages. This progression from the Way of Ideas to the Way of Words is the one usually explained, in the terms of traditional realism, by saying that once the intentional character of mental acts is no longer recognized, then nominalism is the inevitable result.

But this oft-told tale does not, by itself, account for the "linguistic turn" in philosophy. The thesis that language cannot be transcended is also reached by starting from the practical problem of how to avoid an impasse in dialectical controversy, rather than from the Cartesian or Kantian versions of the problem of cognition. I want now to sketch this second route, and to emphasize that it is independent of the first.

A central dialectical device in philosophic controversy has always been the appeal to self-referential consistency. It counts as a decisive argument against a philosophical opponent if one can show that a set of categories which he takes as ultimate is, in some sense, inadequate to cover the case of his own arguments for the ultimacy of this set. Yet, it sometimes seems that one can avoid self-referential inconsistency only at the cost of circularity. For if a philosopher can show that his categories do in fact extend far enough to cover his arguments for these very categories, then he will usually be accused of having begged the question, and having formulated a criterion for the ultimacy of categories which presupposes the ultimacy of the very set of categories which he wants to propose as satisfying this criterion.

The traditional way out of this familiar dialectical dilemma has been to look for categories about whose ultimacy argument would be superfluous – to invoke, in short, some sort of appeal to self-evidence. The traditional come-back to such an appeal is to protest that one does not understand the formula in which the putatively self-evident category is expressed, and to demand that it be translated into a formula of a language which one does understand. But since adopting a new philosophical vocabulary is half-way toward adopting a new set of categories,[11] the dialectical opponent who offers such a translation usually finds that he's lost his case.

Noticing the frequency with which this impasse has been reached in the history of philosophy, one may, as Hegel did, turn away from the attempt to find criteria for the success of the dialectical process *outside* of that process. One then takes dialectical controversy to be an autonomous realm. Now the thesis that language cannot be transcended is simply a purification of the Hegelian thesis that the progress of dialectical controversy cannot be judged from a standpoint outside of that controversy itself. It strips Hegel's theory of philosophic method of the pretense of being a conclusion drawn from a set of (rather dubious) metaphysical premises,[12] and reveals it as a practical solution to a practical problem. The problem is: how can we maintain a philosophic thesis about the ultimacy of some given set of categories without falling into the dilemma of self-referential inconsistency on the one hand and circularity on the other? The answer is:

---

[11] I cannot here attempt to argue for the thesis that a choice of terms in which to discuss philosophical issues can, and usually will, irretrievably prejudice the outcome of the discussion. Support for such a view can be found in the writings of Benjamin Whorf on the conceptual structures of exotic languages, in studies by Richard McKeon of the history of philosophical controversy, and in such recent metaphilosophic studies as Henry Johnstone, *Philosophy and Argument* (University Park, PA, 1959), and Everett Hall, *Philosophical Systems* (Chicago, 1960).

[12] The deduction of the validity of the dialectic method from idealistic metaphysical premises is not really Hegelian. But it is characteristic of Hegel's interpreters. See Walter Stace, *The Philosophy of Hegel* (New York, 1955), pp. 88ff.

by recognizing that to propose a set of categories is not to offer a description of a nonlinguistic fact, but to offer a tool for getting a job done. The cash-value of the claim that a given category is ultimate thus becomes, simply, the claim that a language built around a given set of primitive predicates will work better than any other.

This second account of the reasons for taking the linguistic turn is often described, from the standpoint of traditional realism, as the dissolution of the theoretic order in favor of the instrumental order. What is important to note, however, is that this dissolution is deliberately and self-consciously chosen – not on theoretic grounds, but as a practical answer to a practical problem. Thus, questions about the epistemological justification for such a dissolution are not in point here (as they are in regard to the first route, discussed above). Those who have taken this second route toward the linguistic turn have done so *precisely to avoid* the dialectical circle involved in grounding one's metaphilosophy upon one's epistemology. From their point of view, Aristotle, Descartes, Hume, and Kant are *all* caught in this circle; the difference between realistic epistemology and nonrealistic epistemology becomes negligible when metaphilosophical problems are posed in this purely practical context.

## Ideal-language theory of categories

I have spent some time sketching these two routes toward the linguistic turn because I want to emphasize that one is free, after taking the linguistic turn, to move either towards or away from realism. Some realists think that however linguistic analysts may twist and turn, they cannot rid themselves of their inheritance from Kant,[13] and of the paradoxes involved in Kant's transcendental idealism. I think that this opinion is mistaken, and therefore I have tried to sketch the argument which linguistic analysts would use to show that the linguistic turn has not committed them one way or the other. Having done this, I can now turn to my second point: the antirealistic character of the categories to which one is led if, having taken the linguistic turn, one adopts the pragmatist or "ideal-language" theory of categories.

This theory can best be described by reference to Waismann's notion of "language-strata."[14] Waismann formulates this notion as follows. It is a

---

[13] Or from Descartes: cf. D. J. B. Hawkins, *Wittgenstein and the Cult of Language*, Aquinas Society of London: Aquinas Paper No. 27 (London, 1957), p. 4.
[14] Cf. F. Waismann, "Language-Strata," in *Logic and Language*, Second Series, ed. A. N. Flew (Oxford, 1955), pp. 11–31.

commonplace that different kinds of things require different sorts of language for their description: sensations, physical objects, numbers, and philosophic systems cannot all be treated of in the same terms. There is a systematic equivocity in such terms as "true," "real," "entails," and so on, depending upon what strata they are being used in. If we keep this equivocity in mind, we shall not be tempted to fall into such simple-minded reductionisms as sense-data empiricism and logical atomism. So far, Waismann's line of thought is in perfect accordance with the anti-reductionist character of traditional realism. The switch comes when Waismann suggests that we should cease to describe a given language-stratum in terms of the kind of thing we use it to talk about, and instead start describing this kind of thing in terms of the structure of the language-stratum. Thus Waismann says:

> It was hitherto the custom to refer to what I have called "strata" by indicating their subject-matter, using terms such as "material-object state-ments," "descriptions of vague impressions," . . . and the like. What I now suggest we do is to reverse the whole situation by saying: "The formal motifs which we have been considering (e.g., the different ways in which statements in different strata are verified) all combine to impress a certain stamp upon a stratum; they give us the means to characterize each stratum 'from within,' that is, with no reference to the subject." We may say, for instance: a material object is something that is describable in a language of such-and-such a structure, a sense impression is something which can be described in such-and-such a language . . . and so on.[15]

This suggestion of Waismann's supplies us with a particularly neat way of replacing the metaphysical question, "What is there?," with the question, "What language do we (or should we) speak?" It expresses, in terms of a practical program, the cash-value of the thesis that language can't be transcended. To the critic who attempts to transcend it by insisting that these language-strata are, after all, merely human artifacts,[16] one replies: the stratum which you, the critic, use for formulating and defending this remark is itself but one of many possible language-strata. It is, namely, the one which permits us to talk about languages in the way in which we talk about axs and microscopes. When considered in this light, the polemical force of the remark that languages are mere artifacts tends to vanish, since it is hard to see why speaking of languages in *that* way should claim any sort of priority over all the other ways of speaking of them.

---

[15] *Ibid.*, pp. 29–30.     [16] Cf. Hawkins, *op. cit.*, p. 13.

Given this reversal of the traditional notion of the relation between language and reality, then, the search for ultimate categories naturally takes the form of a search for an "ultimate" language-stratum. The primitive predicates of this stratum will then be ultimate categories. Now what this comes down to is that we must find, or make, a language-stratum which will have such a structure that the thing that is describable in it is: a language-stratum. In other words, the ultimate language-stratum will be the one in which we shall be able to describe the structure of all other language-strata, present and future, and, self-referentially, the structure of this ultimate language-stratum itself. Unsurprisingly, in a philosophy which reverses the usual relationships between sign and signification, distinctions which are relevant to characterizing signs will become ultimate distinctions. This language-stratum about language-strata will be the "ideal" language because it will form a permanent neutral matrix for the interpretation of all other strata and for the construction, as needed, of new strata. It will be, so to speak, language *qua* language, and inquiry about it will be first philosophy for the same reason that, in the Aristotelian tradition, inquiry about being *qua* being is first philosophy.

The "ideal-language" theory of categories thus eventuates in a search for the fundamental classifications necessary to give an account of language. The best example of a set of categories arrived at by this method is, I think, Peirce's categories of Firstness, Secondness, and Thirdness. More consistently and candidly than any other systematic philosopher, Peirce carried out the program of reversing the usual relationship between signs and what they signify, and of shaping categorial distinctions around the requirements of the process of signification, rather than around a putative intuition of what it is that needs to be signified. Indeed, Peirce may, I think, properly be taken as the purest case of "ideal-language" philosophy. The ideal-language theorists who come later (such as Russell, Carnap, and Bergmann) work with a much less comprehensive semiotic than Peirce's – a semiotic which seems tailor-made to suit an antecedently chosen epistemology. It is important to see that the intimate historical association of "ideal-language" philosophy with reductionist empiricism is no more than an historical accident, and in no way a consequence of adopting a pragmatist theory of categories. Peirce's own system was, of course, thoroughly antireductionist and antinominalist.

But, although Peirce was an enemy of the enemies of Aristotelian realism, he was hardly its friend. On the contrary, Peirce's semiotic categories lay the foundations of an epistemology in which the phrase "knowledge of things as they are in themselves" can only mean "what we shall call 'knowledge' at the indefinitely far off end of inquiry."[17] Veridical knowledge is never a starting point of inquiry for Peirce, but only its ideal end. Further, this antirealistic account of knowledge is intrinsically related to Peirce's "ideal-language" account of the nature of philosophy. For if one holds that (a) what one claims to know veridically will depend upon the structure of the language in which the terms "knowledge" and "veridically" are used, and (b) there are a potential infinity of such languages from which to choose, then it does follow that to know what is veridically known we must wait until we have chosen a "last" language, and *that* will only be at the "end of inquiry." If one asks what, on this view of things, can save inquiry from anarchy, then I think Peirce's answer is the only possible one. His answer was "self-control": a moral virtue rather than a theoretical insight.[18] Such an ethically centered epistemology is, I think, the only one which can emerge once one has assented to the metaphilosophical theses which make up the "ideal-language" theory of the nature of categories.

### Ordinary-language theory of categories

So much, then, for the results of adopting the ideal-language theory. I now want to show how the internal dialectic of linguistic philosophy leads away from this theory toward the ordinary-language theory of categories, and why the adoption of this latter theory leads to the adoption of a realistic epistemology.

The basic insight that has, in recent years, led linguistic analysts away from ideal-language theorizing is the recognition that there simply *isn't* a potential infinity of languages from which to choose. Previously, it had seemed obvious that we had vast horizons of choice. The profusion of proposals for new formalized languages which filled Carnap's books, for instance, gave the impression that alternative languages were as plentiful as blackberries. But in the course of time, philosophers began to notice that these were "languages" only by courtesy, and to recognize that one does not create a language simply by listing some primitive predicates and some syntactical and semantical rules. For if a language is, in Wittgenstein's phrase, "a form of life," then one has to confess that there has only been *one* form of life exhibited in the whole ideal-language movement – namely

---

[17] Cf. *Collected Papers of C. S. Peirce*, ed. Charles Hartshorne and Paul Weiss, 8 vols. (Cambridge, MA, 1931–5), v, p. 407.

[18] *Ibid.*, I, pp. 575–611, and also v, pp. 34–6.

that exhibited by the ordinary English, or, indifferently, the ordinary German or Polish, in which the writings of the school are presented. As I remarked before, ordinary-language philosophers take the slogan that language cannot be transcended with redoubled seriousness. They see projects for ideal languages as a particularly sneaky sort of attempt to transcend language. In their eyes, such projected languages are merely, so to speak, epiphenomena of the underlying reality which is the ordinary language in which these projects are formulated, and it is simply a disingenuous device to present them as *alternatives* to this ordinary language.

This suspicion about ideal-language theorizing is expressed by such questions as the following, addressed to these theorists: granted the desirability of the reversal of the usual relationship between signs and what they signify, why should you start looking for an *ultimate* language-stratum? Granted that there is a stratum which permits the characterization of all other strata, so what? What problems will be solved by discovering this stratum? The initial answer to these questions, from the side of ideal-language theorists, is that the problems solved will be all the traditional problems of philosophy – that these problems will simply not be capable of being formulated in the ideal language.

The ordinary-language philosopher's come-back to this is: no problem can be raised in ordinary language which ordinary language cannot handle, and, in fact, no philosophic problems ever *are* formulated in ordinary language, but only in the jargonesque pseudo-languages constructed by philosophers out of ill-assorted fragments of ordinary speech. This come-back says, in other words, that the job of dissolving philosophic problems can be accomplished by simply refusing to accept questions posed in philosophic jargon, and insisting that those who pose such questions restate them. They are to be restated in such a way that each word is used, in Wittgenstein's phrase, as it is "in the language-game which is its original home."[19] Once this is done, it is assumed, the answer to such questions will become ordinary, obvious, and trivial. If this assumption is verified, then it may plausibly be claimed that projects for dissolving philosophical problems by constructing extraordinary languages are, in the first place, superfluous, and, in the second place, liable to create new philosophic perplexities to take the place of the old.

Now the substantive philosophical inquiry of ordinary-language philosophers consists precisely in verifying this assumption. They try to remind us of the distinctions which are present in our ordinary speech,

---

[19] Wittgenstein, *Philosophical Investigations* (Oxford, 1953), § 116.

and to show us that these distinctions suffice to answer all philosophic questions, once these questions are properly rephrased. These distinctions are those which Ryle has referred to as "category-differences." For Ryle, philosophical problems are generated by asking questions which are appropriate only to items falling under, say, Category A, about items which in fact fall under Category B. In other words, questions are raised in Language-Stratum A about items which can only be discussed in Language-Stratum B. The ill success one finds in trying to answer such questions is then taken to indicate a mystery lying in the nature of things, rather than what it really is: a mistake in grammar.[20]

On this view, the ultimate categories are not the primitive predicates of any particular language-stratum, but are instead the primitive predicates of *all* the language-strata which are actually used in ordinary speech. There are quite a lot of these strata, and thus there is no prospect of our getting our categories down to a nice, neat list of half-a-dozen or so. But why, after all, should we want to, once we've realized that the way to solve philosophic problems is by distinctions rather than by reductions?

### Drift towards realism

This line of attack on philosophic problems is, I think, pretty clearly reminiscent of the kinds of criticisms which realists make of reductionist epistemologies, and of metaphysics written within the Cartesian tradition. Realists, like ordinary-language philosophers, see their opponents as making *a priori* decisions about what needs to be reduced to what, and then landing themselves in insoluble dilemmas when the reduction doesn't proceed according to schedule.

More important than this similarity of strategy, however, is that what takes the place of the reductionisms attacked is, for Ryle and many other ordinary-language philosophers, an epistemology and a metaphysics which sound remarkably like Aristotle's. These are, of course, not usually presented *as* epistemology and metaphysics, but rather as expositions of the grammatical structure of ordinary English. However, the opposition involved between the two kinds of disciplines becomes obscure once one notices philosophers of this school praising Aristotle for his admirable expositions of the grammatical structures of ordinary Greek.[21] The fact

---

[20] See Ryle's "Categories," in *Logic and Language*, Second Series, ed. A. N. Flew pp. 65–81.
[21] Cf. A. N. Flew, "Philosophy and Language," in Flew, ed., *Essays in Conceptual Analysis* (London, 1956), pp. 1–20, esp. p. 2.

is, of course, that the language-strata which are ordinarily used for talking about things, and for talking about knowing things, have pretty much the same structure in Greek as they have in English, and these structures have, ever since Aristotle, provided the guidelines of realistic philosophizing.

I shall not enlarge this chapter by offering concrete examples of the realistic conclusions about particular philosophic questions which one finds in the writings of the ordinary-language school. I do not wish to exaggerate the degree to which these philosophers agree among themselves, and I certainly do not intend to say that *all* their conclusions are ones with which Aristotelian realists would sympathize. But I think it *is* clear that the literature of this movement shows just as decided a drift toward the theses which are usually taken as hallmarks of classical realism[22] as the literature of ideal-language philosophizing showed in the other direction. Within ordinary-language philosophy, the first reductionist assumption to be discarded was the Cartesian copy theory of ideas. A rejection of this theory (particularly in the form of the notion of "sense datum"), combined with a recognition of the intentional character of acts of cognition, is now pretty much taken for granted by these philosophers.

Quite apart from the empirical evidence offered by recent publications, one might predict *a priori* that this repudiation of the crucial premise of three centuries' worth of antirealistic arguments was inevitably going to be followed by a repudiation of a good many of the conclusions of these arguments, and a drift toward contrary conclusions. I have tried to suggest that, given the metaphilosophical assumptions with which this school begins, this drift is inevitable. Realism is, after all, the instinctive philosophy of the vulgar. This has, for three centuries, been taken as a count against it. Realism's central distinctions show a remarkable similarity to ordinary grammatical distinctions. This fact has been taken, by everybody from Spinoza to Russell, as an indication of the realists' childlike naiveté (especially in the heyday of ideal-language philosophizing, when it was fashionable to say that the distinction between substance and attribute was one that could only occur to someone who was hypnotized by the subject-predicate sentence-form). But once we adopt the ordinary-language theory of categories, all these purported vices of realism are automatically transmuted into virtues.

---

[22] Such as, for example, the theses contained in the "Platform of the Association for Realistic Philosophy," in J. Wild, ed., *The Return to Reason* (Chicago, 1953), pp. 357–63.

### New alternatives for realists

I shall conclude by offering a summary of the dialectical situation in which, as I see it, realists now find themselves, *vis-à-vis* philosophers who have taken the linguistic turn. When, in the past, realists have criticized such philosophers, they have usually used one or the other of two strategies. On the one hand, they have assumed that the thesis that language can't be transcended rests on Kantian epistemological grounds, and have contented themselves with attacking these grounds. On the other hand, they have mocked at linguistic philosophers for producing, after much labor, conclusions which were either trivial or unfruitfully paradoxical, and for having trivialized philosophic inquiry itself by making it into mere word-play.

I have argued in this chapter that neither of these strategies are effective. The first ignores the metaphilosophical arguments for taking the linguistic turn – arguments which are independent of Kantian assumptions. The second is effective, if it is effective at all, only against the ideal-language theorists, and only against some of them. (I should want to argue, in particular, that it is not effective against Peirce.) If this second strategy is applied against ordinary-language philosophers, it boomerangs. A realist cannot call the conclusions reached by, for instance, Ryle, Austin, and Strawson trivial or paradoxical without being forced to apply the same epithets to the conclusions reached by Aristotle.

If he is going to criticize the ordinary-language philosophers at all, he is going to have to do it on metaphilosophic grounds. That is, the realist is going to have to explain what difference it makes whether the questions to which realistic answers are given are posed in terms of how words are used instead of how things are, and whether this difference *makes* any difference. He is going to have to stop assuming that linguistic philosophy is intrinsically and inevitably reductionistic in spirit, and begin to ask what the difference is between the traditional antireductionist arguments and antireductionist arguments which base themselves upon grammatical distinctions. He will then have to ask himself whether the difference is worth fighting for. He will have to suppress his instinctive inclination to insist that language is as it is because the world is as *it* is, and ask himself whether, if we agree on how the world is, it makes any difference how we come to recognize it as being that way. Finally, he will have to take seriously the central metaphilosophical argument which is common ground to both ideal-language and ordinary-language theorists: the argument that traditional methods of posing and resolving philosophical questions inevitably lead to dialectical impasses between competing schools, and that only by taking the linguistic turn can we escape from such impasses.

# CHAPTER 4

# The subjectivist principle and the linguistic turn

## I

To understand the needs which *Process and Reality* was intended to satisfy, one must understand Whitehead's diagnosis of the state of modern philosophy: "The difficulties of all schools of modern philosophy lie in the fact that, having accepted the subjectivist principle, they continue to use philosophical categories derived from another point of view" (PR, p. 253). The plausibility of this diagnosis is brought out by the following considerations. The substance–property framework, which philosophical thought has taken over from ordinary language, leads us to think of everything to which we refer as either a substance or a property of a substance. The distinction between a substance and a property is the distinction between what is in principle unrepeatable and what is in principle repeatable, for substances are the referents of proper names, and properties the referents of predicates. Now when we think about knowing, we are led to the conception of the experiencing subject as a substance having, among its properties, mental states. When we ask for the relation of these states to that which is known, it appears natural to say that what we know are other substances. But these mental states are not substances. They must, then, be representations of substances. But our mental states, being properties of a substance, are in principle repeatable. So if they are representations, it seems that they can represent nothing but what is itself repeatable. Thus, it seems that our mental states cannot represent other substances, but only the properties of other substances.

This is an unwelcome conclusion. It becomes doubly unwelcome after the Cartesian turn is taken. As Whitehead says:

> [Descartes] laid down the principle, that those substances which are the subjects enjoying conscious experiences, provide the primary data for philosophy, namely, themselves as in the enjoyment of such experience. This is the famous subjectivist bias which entered into modern philosophy

through Descartes. In this doctrine, Descartes undoubtedly made the greatest philosophical discovery since the age of Plato and Aristotle. For his doctrine directly traversed the notion that the proposition, "This stone is grey," expresses a primary form of known fact from which metaphysics can start its generalizations . . . But . . . Descartes . . . continued to construe the functioning of the subjective enjoyment of experience according to the substance–quality categories. Yet if the enjoyment of experience be the constitutive subjective fact, these categories have lost all claim to any fundamental character in metaphysics. (PR, p. 241)

Specifically, the attempt to combine the principle that "the whole universe consists of elements disclosed in the analysis of the experience of subjects" (which Whitehead calls "the subjectivist principle") with the substance–quality framework led straight to Lockeian paradox. For if the experience of substances discloses only repeatables, then substances, since they are unrepeatables, are not disclosed in experience. So, by the subjectivist principle, they do not exist. But if substances do not exist, what does? Not merely properties, one would think, for properties are properties of substances. But then *what?* The history of attempts to answer this question is a history of attempts to fall back on The Unknowable (Locke's "I know not what," Kant's Noumenon, Bradley's Absolute, and the like), and thus to tacitly betray Descartes – alternating with attempts to envisage a world of properties-without-substances (phenomenalism, radical empiricism).

Neither sort of attempt can succeed. The former runs afoul of our conviction that, despite all the inconveniences of subjectivism, the Cartesian quest for clear and distinct ideas, with which to replace the pseudo-explanations of Aristotelianism, was a Good Thing. Aristotelian philosophical explanations depended for their plausibility on the distinction between what is more knowable to us and what is more knowable in itself – a distinction which permits one to shrug off the patent obscurity and indistinctness of such expressions as "pure actuality" and "form without matter." These expressions are obscure and indistinct because they employ contrastive terms in a context in which these terms are prohibited from playing a contrastive role. (We know, e.g., what the difference between a potential house and an actual house is, but we do not know what pure actuality is.) The assumption that in such cases we are nevertheless entitled to postulate the existence of entities described by such expressions, and to use statements about such entities as explanations, is the assumption against which Descartes rebelled. Acceptance of the methodological form of the subjectivist principle – *viz.*, that nothing may be used as a philosophical explanation which is not, in some sense, an object of possible experience – is what binds post-Cartesian philosophers together. (What separates them, as we shall see, is their interpretations of the phrase "object of possible experience.")

But the latter sort of attempt – the attempt to construct a world consisting entirely of repeatables, and thus to treat the substance–property distinction as an eliminable pragmatic convenience – has always run afoul of our conviction that if we once let go of the distinction between the sort of thing which is unrepeatable (the sort of thing, which we ourselves exemplify, of which it is senseless to say that there are two of them) and the repeatable properties of these things, we shall have lost all contact with common sense. In recent years, this conviction has been strengthened by arguments designed to show that the notion of a language which does not contain singular terms is a fake – that such a language cannot serve the purposes which are served by ordinary language.[1] Those arguments suggest that the distinction between unrepeatable and repeatable entities is so firmly built into the structure of our language that proposals to abandon it must necessarily be abortive.

The challenge to modern philosophy, as Whitehead saw it, was to slip between the horns of this dilemma – a dilemma which seems to force us either to betray the Cartesian quest for clarity and distinctness or to betray common sense. His attempt to do so involved a reinterpretation of the notion of "unrepeatable particular." He held that almost everyone since Aristotle had assumed that "this round ball" was a paradigm of such an unrepeatable particular (cf. PR, p. 253). He attempted to find another paradigm – an entity which, though unrepeatable, could nonetheless be experienced, and could be described in terms which would meet the requirements of the subjectivist principle. In other words, he wanted to hold on to the common-sense contrast between the unrepeatable and the repeatable which is embodied in the substance–property categoreal frame (a contrast which his principal rivals – the logical empiricists – were prepared to do away with altogether), while defining "unrepeatable entity" in a way which would conform to "the subjectivist bias of modern philosophy."

The "actual entities" of *Process and Reality* were tailor-made to fit these requirements. To see this, it is helpful to consider the following Lockeian line of argument:

---

[1] Cf., for example, Strawson's "Singular Terms, Ontology and Identity," *Mind*, 65 (1956), pp. 433–54.

(1)   Only the sort of concrete entity which we experience is the sort of concrete entity which we can know about – where "concrete" has a meaning such that "$K_1$, $K_2$ ... $K_n$ are the only sorts of concrete entity" entails "all statements containing expressions denoting an entity of any other sort are equivalent to statements which contain only expressions which denote entities of sorts $K_1$, $K_2$ ... $K_n$."

(2)   Substances (defined as unrepeatable entities, uniquely locatable in spatiotemporal regions) and their properties (defined as repeatable entities, locatable in spatiotemporal regions) are the only candidates for the title of *concrete* entities.

(3)   All substances are entities which can endure through time and which thus can be substrates of contrary determinations.

(4)   Every experience is in principle repeatable – that is, it is (logically) possible that the same experience be had at different times by the same subject, or be had by two different subjects.

(5)   An experience which is repeatable must be the experience of a repeatable entity.

Now (2), taken together with (4) and (5) entails

(6)   We do not experience substances, but only their properties.

And (6) and (1) entail

(7)   We can only know about properties of substances, never about substances.

This conclusion leads straight to the traditional dilemma: either unrepeatable entities do not exist, or nothing can be known about them. The conclusion may be attacked by attacking any of the premises. Whitehead's challenge is to (4), and takes the form of asserting that only the misleading abstractions built into ordinary language could have persuaded us that the same experience can be had twice. In particular, the assumption that the experiencing subject is a perduring substrate of contrary determinations – premise (3) above – lets us think of experiences as properties of a substance (as colors are properties of a ball). Just as this ball can be now red, now green, and now red again, so I can have the experience A, the experience B, and then the experience A again. But, Whitehead points out, the same facts which impel us to make the experiencing subject a paradigm case of unrepeatability prevent us from thinking of the self as such a perduring substrate – for if we do so think of ourselves, then we shall have to apply the Lockeian argument sketched above to ourselves, and wind up with the conclusion that we never know anything about ourselves – not even, therefore, that we *are* unrepeatable entities. In other words, (4) is plausible only if we adopt a conception of the self which is destroyed by an argument which uses (4) as a premise. So, Whitehead argued, what was needed was a new conception of substance – one which would make it possible to deny (3), and would thus make it possible to deny (4).

Whitehead (and here he was at one with the idealists) thought that the notion that there were unrepeatable and knowable entities could be saved from Lockeian lines of argument only by disentangling the notion of "being unrepeatable" from that of "being a substrate of repeatables," identifying the former notion with that of "being an experience," and conceiving of the latter as an abstraction from the former. But in order to abide (as the idealists did not) by the insistence of common sense that, in every experience, there is a difference between the experience itself and the object of this experience, and that the latter can exist independently of the former, Whitehead had to find a new model of the relation between experience and the object of experience.

For the previous model – which involved the same repeatable entity being attached to two unrepeatable entities – was precisely the model which had brought us to the conclusion that unrepeatables could not, after all, be experienced. To find a new model, he had to find a way in which two unrepeatables could be brought into relation with one another without the mediation of repeatables – "properties" (on the side of the object of experience) and "ideas" (on the side of the subject).

His solution to this problem contained two steps. The first was to model the general relationship *experiencing* on the relationship of "feeling another's feeling of" (cf. PR, p. 216) or *prehending*. The relationship of "prehending" cannot, for Whitehead, be modeled on any relationship which holds among (what his system takes to be) *abstracta;* it therefore cannot be modeled on any familiar relation holding between entities mentioned in ordinary language. For "there is a togetherness of the component elements in individual experience. This 'togetherness' has that special peculiar meaning of 'togetherness in experience.' It is a togetherness of its own kind, explicable by reference to nothing else" (PR, p. 288). Whitehead held that the assumption that there was *another* sort of togetherness (*viz.*, that which united a perduring self with its experiences, or, more generally, a perduring substance with its "accidental" properties) in terms of which "togetherness in experience" needed to be analyzed, created "the insurmountable difficulty for epistemology" (PR, p. 289). He held further that if the Lockeian line of argument was to be gotten around, then it was necessary that *all* other relationships be conceived as abstractions from this fundamental relationship.

In this first step, Whitehead is, of course, quite unoriginal. This step had already been taken by idealists – the only difference being that for metaphors with which to shadow forth the character of this ultimate and irreducible relationship the idealists (other than Bradley) tended to look toward "higher" syntheses (such as scientific theories), whereas Whitehead looked toward "lower" syntheses – examples of "simple feeling." But this difference is of interest only in so far as it is relevant to the *second* step which Whitehead took in order to provide a new model of the subject–object relationship.

This second step consisted in remodeling the *terms* of the relationship which is expressed by the phrase "togetherness in experience." This remodeling was dictated by the following requirements: if the realism of common sense is to be maintained, then both the experiencing subject and the object which we experience must be unrepeatable entities (a requirement satisfied by idealism, since the Absolute, which is both the only object and the only subject of experience, is indeed unrepeatable – though not spatiotemporally locatable). But they must be distinct from each other (a requirement which idealism was unable to satisfy, since "distinctness" in this sense is intelligible only as long as spatiotemporality is applicable, and it is therefore impossible to conceive of an unrepeatable entity distinct from the Absolute). Now there is a difficulty in satisfying this second requirement once one adopts "feeling another's feeling of" as the primitive relation which unites subject and object. For "A's feeling B's feeling of C" always needs to be expanded into "A's feeling of B's feeling of C's feeling of D's," and so on *ad indefinitum*. We seem to be confronted by the dissolution of every unrepeatable entity into an indefinitely large, seamless web of relationships – the same dissolution which is so familiar a feature of idealism.[2] Given this regress, how are we to find a plurality of distinct entities in it? Whitehead's answer is: "By noticing that 'A feeling the feelings of B' is always an ellipsis for 'A *now* feeling the feelings *felt* by B in the past.'" *The distinction between unrepeatable entities and repeatable entities is simply, for Whitehead, a distinction between present actual entities and past actual entities* – between actual entities (feelings of past feelings bound together in "experienced togetherness") now feeling (i.e., "concrescing")

---

[2] For the view that Whitehead never satisfactorily escapes from this dissolution, and thus is driven to monism, cf. William Alston, "Internal Relatedness and Pluralism in Whitehead," *Review of Metaphysics*, 5 (1951–2), pp. 535–58.

and actual occasions felt.[3] Thus, instead of drawing a line between the unrepeatable and the repeatable in such a way that there are two sorts of perduring entities (e.g., unrepeatable balls, and their repeatable colors), Whitehead draws it in such a way that entities switch from one class to the other, simply by ceasing to be. By "taking time seriously," and, specifically, by equating "actuality" with "presentness" (thus entailing that "actual world" is a token-reflexive term – cf. PR, p. 102 and n. 4 below), Whitehead tries to make the notion of unrepeatable entity unmysterious and unobjectionable. For it is not mysterious that "time *t*" is unrepeatable, nor that an entity which (logically) can exist only at time *t* should be unrepeatable.

However, it may be objected that to explain the notion of "unrepeatable entity" in this way is hopeless. For to make sense of "entity which *logically* can exist only at time *t*," one needs to give a sense to the notion of an entity whose temporal location is not a mere "accident" of it, but is essential to it – so that the statement "A is at time *t*" is a necessary truth about A. Now it may be thought that this notion is just unintelligible. It does seem that our grammar is such that if we say "A is at time $t_i$" we may also say "It is a logical possibility that A could have been at time $t_j$." The contingency of statements about temporal locations seems to be part of the very fabric of temporal discourse. But there *is* one sort of expression which is a necessary truth about the temporal location of a concrete entity: "I am here now" *is* a necessary truth about me. The one sort of statement which can attribute a temporal location to an entity as a necessary feature of that entity is a statement which connects one token-reflexive expression with another token-reflexive expression. More generally, the only referring expressions in ordinary speech which, given a relativistic interpretation of time, can never be used to refer twice to the same entity, are such token-reflexive expressions as "that ... now," "this ... now," "my ... now," "your ... now," and the like.

Now Whitehead's unrepeatable (i.e., present) actual entities, if they are characterizable in terms of ordinary speech at all, must be characterized as entities which can only be referred to by expressions of the form "my ... now," where " ... " is replaced by expressions of the form "experienced togetherness of – , – , – , etc." These latter blanks, it must be noted, are filled in *not* with token-reflexive expressions, but with names of past, and

---

[3] Strictly, this is the distinction between unrepeatable *concrete* entities and repeatable *concrete* entities. Eternal objects are, of course, repeatable, but they are not *concrete* entities in the sense of "concrete" given by (2) above.

therefore repeatable, actual entities. That is, they are filled in with expressions which stand to "my . . . now" as "Smith was at spot *s* at time *t* "stands to "I am here now" (uttered by Smith at *s* at *t*).

The difference between entities referred to in the first way and entities referred to in the second way is, for Whitehead, the difference between repeatable and unrepeatable entities. The sense in which it is (timelessly) the "same" entity which once was unrepeatable and is now repeat-able is the same sense in which "I am here now" and "Smith was at spot *s* at time *t* " report the "same" occurrence. Whitehead's use of the doctrine of relativity to show that every actual entity has its own space-time scheme – that it atomizes the extensive continuum (cf. PR, p. 104) in a unique way, so that "no two actual entities define the same actual world" (PR, p. 102) – amounts to a claim that present entities can only be referred to by token-reflexive expressions.[4] The difference between Whiteheadian actual entities ("present actual entities" – a phrase which, strictly, is pleonastic for Whitehead) and episodes in the history of persons (or of things, mythically endowed with the ability to say "I") is the difference between entities referable to only in the first way and entities referable to in both ways. (The fact that it is essential to our ordinary ways of speaking that anything referable to in the one way is referable to in the other is the fundamental reason why Whitehead thought ordinary language hopeless for metaphysical purposes, and is the fundamental reason why it is so extraordinarily difficult to translate sentences in Whiteheadian jargon into sentences in ordinary discourse.)

---

[4] This point expresses, I believe, the cash value of the claim that Whitehead, by "taking time seriously," substituted "process" for "being" as "the inclusive category." This formulation is misleading in various ways – particularly in that, except for the special case of God, Whitehead held firmly to the truth of (2). The proper way of contrasting Whitehead's "process philosophy" with "philosophies of being" is Hartshorne's: "any word, such as 'reality,' or 'being,' can be used as the inclusive term, the point at issue remaining this: does the term indicate a unique, final totality that does not become, or else rather, in each case of the employment of the term, a new totality which has just become as it is referred to? The question, as Whitehead suggests, is whether the inclusive term is, or is not, a 'demonstrative pronoun' (a token-reflexive term)" ("Process as Inclusive Category: A Reply," *Journal of Philosophy*, 52 [1955], p. 95). Whitehead's attempt to give an intelligible affirmative answer to this latter question about the totality referred to by the inclusive category leads him to say that some of the concrete particular entities which go to make up this totality must themselves be describable only in token-reflexive terms – namely, the present ones. (The expression "token-reflexive term," incidentally, is not used by Whitehead himself; like Hartshorne, however, I find it most useful in giving an account of his doctrines. A definition may be helpful: a term is "token-reflexive" if its essential occurrence in a sentence makes that sentence capable of being used to make statements of different truth-values depending upon the circumstances in which the statements are made. "I," "this," and "now" are perhaps the most common such terms.)

To state this point more formally, let us call "token-reflexive statements" statements in which token-reflexive terms are either the subject of the sentence used to make the statement or in which token-reflexive terms occur essentially in its predicate. We can now say that a basic Whiteheadian thesis is that *the only sort of statement which can describe a nonrepeatable entity is a token-reflexive statement, and that the only entities which non-token-reflexive discourse can describe are repeatable entities.* Now this thesis explains why we naturally make a distinction between repeatable and unrepeatable entities, despite the *prima facie* repeatability of all our experiences, and thus the *prima facie* mysterious-ness of the notion of "unrepeatable entity." The root of the notion of "substance" (unrepeatable spatiotemporally locatable entity) is the notion of *self.*[5] We think of some entities as unrepeatable because we think of them as like ourselves – as quasi-people and thus quasi-users of token-reflexive discourse. This thesis also explains why traditional philosophical accounts of the relation between subject and object have never been able to make sense of the notion of "knowledge of an unrepeatable entity." We are unable to make sense of the notion of knowing unrepeatables because when we describe past entities we do not (and cannot) use "their" (token-reflexive) terms, but only our own non-token-reflexive descriptive statements about them. In describing them, as Whitehead says, we objectify them. The principal mark of this objectification is that the "now" of a present actual entity A becomes, for the later actual entities which prehend A, a mere "time *t.*" When so objectified, these entities become repeatable entities.[6]

---

[5] This is why *persons* were, for Aristotle, the paradigm cases of substances. It was only under the influence of the Cartesian reinterpretation of "matter" as "vacuous actuality" (rather than "potentiality for form") that the question "Is the self a substance?" began to take on the appearance of sense. I have tried to describe the motives for this reinterpretation, and the parallels between Aristotelian and Whiteheadian dissents from Cartesian principles, in "Matter and Event" (in E. McMullin (ed.), *The Concept of Matter* [Notre Dame, IN, 1963]).

[6] But they are not repeatable *because* they have been objectified; they are objectifiable because they are repeatable – that is, past. It is essential to understanding Whitehead to avoid the assumption that when an actual entity becomes past, and is objectified by its successors, it somehow *changes*. No property is added to or taken away from the unrepeatable actual entity of the present when it becomes past – it simply ceases to be. To raise the question of what property is added to an actual entity when it goes from being present and unrepeatable to being past and repeatable is to ask as meaningless a question as the question of what is added to or subtracted from a human being when he dies. Death is not the addition of a property, any more than it is the subtraction of a property called "life" – it is simply ceasing to be.

## II

I now turn to what seems to me the most fundamental criticism which has been made of Whitehead's attempt to develop a new model of "unrepeatable entity." I have tried to show how, by reinterpreting "experience" so that it refers not to episodes in the history of a human being but rather to entities describable only in the way outlined above ("my experienced togetherness of – , – , – , etc. now," where "now" is pleonastic) Whitehead believes himself to have found a way of denying (4).[7] This reinterpretation is not, Whitehead thought, a mere verbal maneuver. To mediate between the two meanings of "experience," he attempts to provide an account of (4)'s plausibility by interpreting the vocabulary used in describing the experiences of human beings as composed of high abstractions from the concrete experiences of the actual entities which are components of the societies which are human beings. Further, he holds that his use of "experienced togetherness," and similar terms, in characterizing actual entities is a legitimate metaphorical extension of their ordinary uses.

Now most criticism of the adequacy of Whitehead's system (as opposed to its coherence) consists in questioning his ability to make the connection between his technical meaning of "experience" (in which "experience" is synonymous with "present experienced togetherness" and both are synonymous with "unrepeatable concrete entity") and the ordinary meaning of the term. Such questioning can be of two different sorts. One may grant to Whitehead that one understands, and can work with, the metaphorically extended meanings of ordinary terms which he uses in formulating his categoreal scheme, but claim that the materials provided are insufficient to construct adequate theories of, e.g., consciousness, personality, language, or moral responsibility. Or one may refuse to grant this, and claim that these meanings are not intelligible and that there is no point in trying to work with them until they are made intelligible.

---

[7] It may be objected that Whitehead thought that (4) was false even if "experience" were interpreted in the *normal* way. This may be the case; it is rendered plausible by Whitehead's evident conviction that language was inadequate to express certain features of experience. But if he did think this, he at least recognized the hopelessness of trying to rebut, within the framework of ordinary language, the usual defenses of (4). Proponents of (4) – such as the idealists – ask for an example of an unrepeatable experience. But this demand cannot be met if (a) it is required that this experience be reported in ordinary language, and (b) the ordinary assumption that any episode reportable in token-reflexive language can also be reported in non-token-reflexive language is granted.

It is this latter, more radical and more Philistine, criticism of Whitehead which I wish to discuss (and, in the end, defend) in this chapter. This line of criticism bases itself on the view that the Cartesian methodological requirement that "nothing may be used as a philosophical explanation which is not, in some sense, an object of possible experience" requires a stronger interpretation than Whitehead gives it. Whitehead thinks that this requirement is satisfied if no unknowables are postulated. But he interprets "unknowable" as "vacuous actuality, void of subjective experience" (cf. PR, p. 253). He thinks that if an entity is described as an "experienced togetherness," then, whatever the difficulties of saying anything *more* about it, it is absurd to call it an "unknowable." (For "experienced togetherness" is what we know if we know anything.) In other words, he construes "use nothing as a principle of explanation which is not an object of possible experience" in such a way that "being an object of possible experience" does not entail "being describable in a language used for communicating between human beings." If, however, one construes the former phrase in such a way that it entails the latter (as "analytic" philosophers do) then one will hold that Whitehead produces mere pseudo-explanations. The "linguistic turn" in philosophy has, in respect to the methodological requirements set for philosophical explanation, consisted in adopting the view that the cash value of the rather unclear Cartesian dictum that we should use none but "clear and distinct ideas" is as follows: (a) we should, in offering explanations, use no terms but those which have a nonphilosophical use, and then we should use them in their nonphilosophical senses; or, (b) when we do use other terms (or use terms which have a nonphilosophical use in an abnormal, peculiarly philosophical sense) then we should explicitly endow them with a use (or a new use).

This reformulated dictum will appear weak and platitudinous only until one begins to reflect upon the variations in meaning between apparent near-synonyms in ordinary speech, and upon the complicated presuppositions which are made in quite ordinary and unassuming nonphilosophical statements.[8] If one does so reflect, one will see that Whitehead, no less than Aristotle, is employing terms whose ordinary use presupposes certain standard contrasts – and whose ordinary meaning is determined by the possibility of such contrasts – in new, noncontrastive ways. (Compare the relation between "actual (as contrasted with potential) house" and "pure actuality" with the relation between, e.g., "the form of the argument" and

---

[8]  The work of Austin and his followers on such variations, and of Wittgenstein and his followers on such presuppositions, have made the force of the dictum increasingly evident.

"the subjective form of an actual entity," or between "an efficacious remedy" and "prehension in the mode of causal efficacy.") Every present Whiteheadian actual entity must be thought of as the sort of thing which can only be described *by itself* – in such phrases as "my . . . now." But most actual entities, to put it bluntly, can't talk. At best, only the very high-grade ones (the conscious ones) can (and it is not clear whether their use of "I" or "my" refers to themselves or rather to the society of which they are a part). In the case of the lower-grade actual entities, we are asked to envisage a sort of entity which (a) it is absurd to think of as talking, but which (b) belongs to a category which is delimited by the condition that entities of this category, if they could talk, would only be able to talk in a certain way.

It is of no real help to be told, as Whitehead tells us, that "actual entity" is clearer than, e.g., "pure actuality," because an actual entity is an experienced togetherness of feeling, and we understand what *that* is. For to understand what "experienced togetherness" means is to understand how to use this term in discourse about the way in which we ourselves, and other human beings, grasp the features of more or less enduring objects. (It cannot, as Wittgenstein has shown, be thought of as the ability to recognize a peculiar introspectible content.) When the term is used, as Whitehead uses it, as a primitive predicate applying to entities which are not people, and have in common with people only the very fact that they are said to be instances of "experienced togetherness," then it is clear that (as Whitehead himself admits) we are dealing with a "metaphor mutely appealing for an imaginative leap" (PR, p. 6). But the same mute appeal is made (in the form of the "appeal to analogy") by the vocabulary of Aristotelian substantialist metaphysics, and it may well seem that what is being pleaded for is the same in both cases – *viz.*, that we should retain just so much of the ordinary meaning of a term as is required to attribute desirable features (i.e., features which do not raise philosophical problems) to the entities to which the term is applied, while discarding just so much of it as would permit the attribution of undesirable features (i.e., features which raise philosophical problems) to those entities. When confronted with such an appeal, therefore, it seems reasonable to reply that it is the job of the philosopher who transmits it to show that enough of the original meaning of the metaphorical term remains to make its use more than a mere baptism of the problem at hand. In particular, where the terms in question are used to characterize entities, the philosopher needs to show that there is enough meaning left in them so that these entities may actually be *identified* by criteria formulated in these terms. To assert that a theoretical entity is described by certain novel terms, it is not sufficient merely to deduce consequences from the rules governing the use of these novel terms (or the abnormal use of conventional terms). One must also show that hypotheses about the entities so described can be inductively verified by inspection (though, perhaps, indirect inspection) of samples of such entities. If this cannot be done, then the requirements of Cartesian subjectivism remain unfulfilled.

This line of criticism of Whitehead is familiar. It amounts to saying that one cannot satisfy the methodological form of the subjectivist principle simply by borrowing the primitive predicates of the vocabulary in which one will phrase one's philosophical explanations from the ordinary vocabulary of reports of mental states (rather than from the ordinary vocabulary of reports of events in the physical world), unless one can supply criteria for applying these terms, in their extended meanings, to particular cases – instructions which have the same degree of specificity as the criteria which we use in applying these terms to particular cases in their unextended meanings. Now Whitehead admits that nothing approaching this degree of specificity can be obtained. In the first place, the fact that Whiteheadian unrepeatable entities can only be described in token-reflexive statements means that we shall never, ever, be able to describe any such entity other than, perhaps, ourselves. But in fact we shall never even be able to describe *ourselves*, for even the finest discriminations which could conceivably be expressed in symbols used for communication between human beings would be discriminations on a level of abstraction far above the level at which, e.g., the individual entity which is the "I" of this moment prehends another in the mode of causal efficacy. "Language almost exclusively refers to presentational immediacy as interpreted by symbolic reference" (PR, p. 263).

If this criticism is familiar, so is the Whiteheadian answer to it. The answer is that the demand for criteria of such specificity is self-defeating. For, when strictly applied, it would forbid the philosopher to postulate the existence of entities other than those for which criteria of indentification can be provided with the aid of the apparatus available in ordinary language. Now since the philosopher's problems are created precisely by the structure of ordinary language, to subject him to the proposed requirement is to forbid him to solve his problems by transcending the categories built into that structure. Granted that the scientist should be bound by this requirement (roughly, the requirement that there be rules which correlate statements about the existence of particular theoretical entities with statements about the existence of particular observed entities[9]), the philosopher should not be.[10] The attempt to impose "verificationism" on scientists is a natural consequence of conceiving of the aim of scientific inquiry as the discovery of practically useful abstractions, and abstractions are of little practical use unless there is a road back and forth between the abstract and the concrete, and, in particular, unless there are criteria for the identification of theoretical entities. But since philosophical problems are not problems about how to deal with observed phenomena, but about how to find nonparadoxical characterizations of these phenomena, this requirement need not apply.[11] To suggest that we think of our perception of a table on the model of feeling the feelings of another person, rather than on the model of taking pictures of the table and studying them, may be a useful suggestion, even though we may never be able to isolate a single prehension among those which constitute one of the actual occasions which make up the society which is the table.

The general Whiteheadian reply to the charge that Whitehead's method betrays the Cartesian quest for clarity and distinctness is, therefore, this: if clarity is defined in terms of fidelity to the basic structures of ordinary language, no "clear" explanation can be given which will dissolve the problems which are built into those structures. For let us suppose that Whitehead is right in saying that the subject-property categoreal frame is the cause of our inability to give a coherent statement of our knowledge of unrepeatable entities. Since so many of the terms of our language have meanings which are determined by the roles which these terms play in asking and answering questions about the possession of qualities by substances, it seems clear that we shall never make any progress if we try to stick to the unextended meanings of this cluster of terms. Further, we shall never extend their meaning far enough unless we can imaginatively leap right out of "the language-game which is their original home." To assume that methodological subjectivism requires us to stay within the language-game in which we find ourselves is to claim, implausibly, that every sort of experience which we have can be expressed in the language

---

[9] Or, at least, correlate statements about the statistical behavior of batches of theoretical entities with statements about the existence of particular observed entities.

[10] There are, however, grounds for holding that this requirement should not even be applied to scientific explanations. Cf., e.g., Feyerabend's defense of the view that "introducing a new [scientific] theory involves changes of outlook both with respect to the observable and with respect to the unobservable features of the world, and corresponding changes in the meaning of even the most 'fundamental' terms of the language employed" ("Explanation, Reduction, and Empiricism," *Minnesota Studies in the Philosophy of Science*, 3 [1962], p. 29).

[11] "Philosophy is explanatory of abstraction, and not of concreteness" (PR, 30).

currently available to us, and to fail to realize that "a precise language must await a complete metaphysical knowledge" (PR, p. 18). It is an assumption which would make sense only if one held that (a) there is really no "problem of knowledge" to be solved at all, or (b) that the resources of ordinary language are adequate to solve whatever problem there is.

In the preceding paragraphs I have tried to sketch both sides of the somewhat hackneyed quarrel about the value of doing the sort of "speculative philosophy" which *Process and Reality* typifies. This is a quarrel which has never, I think, been satisfactorily resolved. During the reign of phenomenalistically oriented "ideal-language" philosophizing it was fiercely waged; on the whole, the Whiteheadians came out ahead. For they had two very strong *ad hominem* arguments to present. First, the phenomenalistic ideal-language philosophers were failing to do any better at solving traditional epistemological problems than their predecessors. Their phenomenalism drove them to a behavioristic interpretation of mental acts, and such an interpretation proved inadequate for an analysis of intentional statements. Whiteheadians hastened to attribute this failure to the same unwillingness to desert the level of abstraction characteristic of ordinary language which had vitiated previous empiricisms. They took this new failure to be one more demonstration of the need to look beneath this level for the "truly concrete elements in experience."[12] Second, the ideal-language philosophers were in no position to complain about the metaphysicians' habit of postulating entities without being able to supply criteria for picking out instances of such entities. For these philosophers were compelled to admit that the "sense-contents" of their own theory were incapable of being individuated by such criteria, and could only be described in an unspeakable "expressive language."[13]

The triumph of "metaphysics" over "positivism" in which this quarrel seemed to eventuate has made Whiteheadians still more confident that no philosophical explanation which renounces the appeal to "experience too concrete to be expressed in language" can be adequate. Specifically, no such explanation can straighten out the confusions about knowledge

---

[12] Intentionality – the reference of every conscious judgment to an entity capable of existing independently of that judgment – is, on a Whiteheadian view, to be thought of as grounded upon, and explicable only in terms of, the "presence" of one actual entity "in" another. "The philosophy of organism is mainly devoted to the task of making clear the notion of 'being present in another entity'" (PR, pp. 79–80). For if this notion is not admitted, Whitehead thinks, we shall be driven, like Locke, to some form of the doctrine of representative perception (cf. PR, pp. 84–5), and then it will be all up with realism.

[13] Cf. C. I. Lewis, *An Analysis of Knowledge and Valuation* (La Salle, IL, 1946), p. 204.

which the clash between Cartesian subjectivism and the substance–property framework had made inevitable. This confidence has led to a complacent assurance that the recrudescence of common-sense realism which has marked more recent "linguistic" philosophy is merely a transitory reaction to a transitory delusion. This revived realism has led analytic philosophers to agree with Whiteheadians that Ayer and Russell are just as much "metaphysicians" as the Whiteheadians themselves, and to agree that the metaphysics which they produced was simply "the old Berkeleian, Kantian ontology of the 'sensible manifold'"[14] all over again. But the strategy of postphenomenalistic linguistic philosophy – a return to the realism of common sense, centering on an insistence on the irreducibility of (of all things) the substance–property distinction – strikes Whiteheadians as equally hopeless. "Every new Aristotle," as Hartshorne said in attacking neo-Thomist critics of Whitehead, "can only usher in a new Berkeley."[15] This new sort of linguistic-philosophy explicitly adopts the slogan that the resources of ordinary language are adequate to solve every philosophical problem which they are adequate to state – a slogan which provides precisely the dialectical weapon against Whiteheadian appeals to "experiences inexpressible in language" which the phenomenalists had, perforce, abjured. But this slogan strikes Whiteheadians as patently false, and as having been demonstrated to be false by the history of philosophy.

## III

In the preceding section of this chapter I have been trying to get the following question into focus: is Whitehead right in saying that an account of knowledge which preserves the realism of common sense must postulate the existence of entities which are describable neither in ordinary language nor in an extension of ordinary language?[16] An answer to this question is a necessary part of the grounds needed for decisions about what is living and

---

[14] The phrase is taken from Austin's characterization of Ayer (*Sense and Sensibilia* [Oxford, 1962], p. 61).

[15] "The Compound Individual," in *Philosophical Essays for Alfred North Whitehead* (New York, 1936), p. 200. On some parallels between "ordinary-language philosophy" and Aristotelian realism, cf. the present writer's "Realism, Categories, and the Linguistic Turn," *International Philosophical Quarterly*, 2 (1962), pp. 307–22.

[16] By "an extension of ordinary language" I mean a systematic use of ordinary terms in non-normal ways, together with an account of these deviant uses – an account which itself *is* phrased in terms used in normal ways. By "describable" I mean (as above) not simply "capable of being spoken of" but "capable of being spoken of in such a way that hypotheses about these entities are capable of being confirmed by inspection of individual (or statistical) samples of them."

what is dead in Whitehead's thought. If he *is* right, and can be shown to be right, then most of contemporary analytic philosophy is heading straight for a dead end – the same dead end in which neo-Thomists have been backing and filling for half a century. But if he is wrong, and can be shown to be wrong, then a step will have been taken toward showing the plausibility of the reinterpretation of Cartesian subjectivism which has been a consequence of the "linguistic turn." For if Whitehead is wrong on this point, then the interlocked claims that to be a clear and distinct idea is to be spoken of in terms which are used in their normal meanings, that to be an "object of possible experience" is to be describable in terms so used, and that no philosophical explanation need go beyond terms so used, are at least not obviously wrong.

I think that Whitehead *is* wrong on this point, and that because he is wrong there is little use in trying to polish up either his theory of actual entities or any other theory which postulates the existence of undescribable unrepeatables as the concrete entities from which the entities describable in ordinary language are "abstractions." However, I cannot here make even a start at *showing* that he was wrong. What I shall do is merely to point to the existence of an alternative way of reconciling the realism of common sense with Cartesian subjectivism, a way which renounces the appeal to undescribable entities and to "experiences inexpressible in ordinary language." If this alternative is successful, then Whitehead is wrong. In my exposition of this alternative, however, I hope to show that it is a development of the same insight which guided Whitehead in his search for the "right" sort of unrepeatable entity. This insight is that each experiencing subject has a perspective upon the world, and that any picture of the world which does not include explicit reference to such a perspective is a picture of an abstraction – an abstraction which, if taken (through a "fallacy of misplaced concreteness") to be the primary sort of picture of the world, will lead to paradox.[17] Whitehead's exploration of the consequences of this

---

[17] My phrasing of this point is borrowed from Wilfrid Sellars, who has presented the most comprehensive argument for it with which I am familiar in his "Time and the World Order" (*Minnesota Studies in the Philosophy of Science*, 3 [1962], pp. 527–616, esp. p. 593). More will be heard of this article, and of other articles by Sellars, in what follows. The "alternative way of reconciling realism and subjectivism" which I shall be describing is, in its essentials, a vulgarized version of a view which Sellars has presented in a series of articles over the past fifteen years. The heart of this defense, as will become clear, is an analysis of knowledge based on "the doctrine of the mental word" (cf. Sellars's "Being and Being Known," *Proceedings of the American Catholic Philosophical Association* [1960], p. 30). Sellars's articles give the most complete statement of the presuppositions and ramifications of this doctrine which is available. However, this doctrine, and the defense of realism which is made possible thereby, is not peculiar to Sellars. Some other exponents of the same approach are Geach (in *Mental Acts* [New York, 1957]) and Bergmann (cf., particularly,

insight is an extraordinary intellectual achievement. But if he is wrong in his assumption that there are experiences which may be appealed to in support of philosophical explanations, but which are nonetheless not expressible in ordinary language, then we may have to conclude that his system was the wrong vehicle for the expression of this insight.

The view taken by "ordinary-language" philosophers is that the dilemma sketched at the beginning of this chapter – the choice between betraying Descartes by resorting to an Unknowable or betraying common sense by postulating a world of repeatables, devoid of unrepeatable par- ticulars – can be evaded simply by a more careful deployment of our ordinary resources for describing mental acts. Although these philosophers cheerfully agree with Whitehead that the attempt to conceive selves as substances and "mental states" as their properties is, in large measure, responsible for the traditional "problem of knowledge," they deny that ordinary language is committed to such a conception.[18] Whitehead has assumed too quickly that, so to speak, there is really one language-game which is played in ordinary language – that of describing substances by reporting their properties – and that all ordinary uses of language somehow "reduce" to this. He has thus made precisely the same mistake as his idealist and phenomenalist rivals – he has assumed that a person's know- ledge about a thing is to be analyzed into relations between the thing, the person, and their respective properties. This assumption is based on the assumption that these are the only concrete entities concerned, an assump- tion which is made explicit in (2) above.[19]

---

*Meaning and Existence* [Madison, 1959], pp. 1–38, especially the claim at pp. 29f that the inclusion of "the intentional 'means' and the quoting operator" in the ideal language will render it able "to bear the burden of the philosophy of mind"). If there is a single point of departure common to the various forms which this approach has taken in the recent literature, it is probably Wittgenstein's *Tractatus.*

[18] Cf., e.g., Ryle, *The Concept of Mind* (London, 1949), p. 120.

[19] If one grants this assumption, then, as long as one holds to the truth of

(1) Only the sort of concrete entity which we experience is the sort of concrete entity which we can know about, and as long as one wants to assert that we know about things, one will be obliged to argue that the macroscopic things of common sense are not really unrepeatable entities.

(For if they *were* unrepeatable, they couldn't be experienced – only their properties could.) One is driven to saying either that these things are repeatable congeries of repeatable sense-contents (as the phenomenalists did) or that they are repeatable abstractions from the *really* unrepeatable entities (as Whitehead did). One will thus be driven to "reduce" the unrepeatable perduring bodies of common sense to entities of a quite different sort. But these perduring bodies are, as Strawson has argued, "basic" to our ordinary language, in the sense that if we were not able to make identifying references to such bodies, we should not be able to make identifying references to anything else, and thus should not be able to use the language we do. (Cf. *Individuals* [London, 1959], ch. 1, esp. pp. 38–9.) Consequently, it is not surprising that both phenomenalist and Whiteheadian "reductions" of these common-sense "basic particulars" must resort to "experiences inexpressible in (ordinary) language"

This latter assumption has caused traditional analyses of knowledge to pass over the principal form in which, in ordinary language, we report and discuss our knowledge: the form "S knows —— ," where the blank is filled by the name of a *fact* rather than the name of either a substance or a property of a substance. One standard completion of the form "S knows —— " is a clause made up of the word "that" and a declarative sentence – e.g., "that X is Y." Let us call a *fact* that which is named by such a that-clause. Now the assumption that facts are "abstract" entities in the sense defined above follows naturally from (2). The cash value of this assumption is that statements containing that-clauses – of which the two principal varieties are epistemic statements ("S knows that . . . ," "S believes that . . . ," "S hopes that . . . ") and semantic statements (e.g., " ' . . .' means that ——") – must have the same meaning as statements which do *not* contain that-clauses. This assumption entails, in other words, that the relation between, e.g., S and the fact which S knows is analyzable into a relation between S and the entities denoted by the referring expressions contained in the that-clause which names the fact in question.

Now if S's knowing that X is Y is decomposable into relations between S and X, between S and Y, and between S and entities of the same categoreal type(s) as X or Y, and if we assume the truth of (2), then it follows that S's knowing that X is Y must be decomposable into a set of relations whose terms are persons, substances, and their properties. What relations are appropriate? Clearly, only those relations which relate persons *qua* conscious subjects (rather than *qua* bodies) to things and their properties – *viz.*, the relations which are usually lumped together under the heading of *experiencing* and have their paradigm in *sensing*. This chain of reasoning is the source of "intuitionist" theories of knowing – theories which hold that all acts of cognition break down into complex intuitions, and which are dominated by the metaphor of the "mental eye." Such theories find it natural to grant the truth of (1), for on their view we cannot *know about* any concrete entity which we do not *know, simpliciter* – "know," in other

and to the assurance that if only we were able to speak a different sort of language (one, unfortunately, untranslatable into our own) in which identifying references to entities of novel categoreal types *could* be made, everything would be all right.

(Strawson's line of argument is supplemented and expanded by Sellars in "Time and the World Order." Here, Sellars argues that the notion of an "event" whose spatiotemporal location is specified topologically is a notion which is parasitical upon our ordinary notion of "episodes occurring in changeable things." He argues, in other words, that the "event" framework of description is not an alternative to the usual substance–property framework of description, but is conceivable only as an abstraction from the latter. The importance of this claim for an analysis of the Whiteheadian categoreal framework is obvious, but the point cannot be followed up here.)

words, in the way in which we are said to "know" people to whom we've been introduced.[20] Such theories must insist that entities which are knowable-about without being experienceable are one and all *abstracta*. Such theories, therefore, insist on the truth of (1) above.

We thus see how (1) follows naturally from (2), taken together with some fairly plausible additional premises. The view which I shall now sketch sets itself the problem of showing that relations between a person and a fact (the sort of relation exemplified by "S knows that X is Y") are irreducible. If this can be shown, then (2) will have been shown to be false and the way will be open to denying (1). The view in question comprises the following claims:

(I)   The fundamental flaw in previous attempts to discuss knowing has been the confusion of *facts* with *objects*.[21] We do not know unrepeat-able objects, but we do know facts *about* such objects. Our know-ledge of these facts is grounded upon, but is not identical with, our acquaintance with the repeatable entities proffered by sensory experi-ence. The world which is symbolized in true statements, and which is composed of "what we know," is in Wittgenstein's phrase, "a totality of facts, not of things." (This is the kernel of truth in the "subjectivist bias" of modern philosophy – and, in particular, in Kant's claim that we do not know "things-in-themselves" but only entities which are already "infected with subjectivity.")

(II)  A fact is not to be thought of as a complex of objects.[22] Rather, it is to be thought of either (a) as what is named by that-clauses, or (b) as the sort of thing which we know. There is thus no more sense to the question "What is the ontological status of facts?" than, for Kant, there was sense to the question "What is the ontological status of phenomena?" Both questions presuppose that we possess knowledge of nonfacts (or nonphenomena) by reference to which we can allot such a status.

---

[20] The cases in which "I know ... " is not completed by a that-clause but by a name or a description of a non-fact (e.g., "the Ambassador," "Brussels," "the Lombard dialect") require a taxonomic treatment which cannot be attempted here, nor can the question of the reducibility of these cases to "knowing that" be discussed. It suffices to note that intuitionist theories of knowing have traditionally tried to isolate a species of "acquaintance" common to all such cases and have insisted that sentences referring to such "acquaintance" be a part of any analysis of "knowing that." Cf. Sellars, "Empiricism and the Philosophy of Mind," *Minnesota Studies in the Philosophy of Science*, 1 (1956), p. 256.

[21] Cf. Ryle, *op. cit.*, pp. 161f.

[22] Cf. Sellars, "Truth and 'Correspondence,'" *Journal of Philosophy*, 59 (1962), pp. 44ff.

(III)  Of the two possible ways of thinking of what a fact is, it is obvious that only the former ("what is named by that-clauses") can be of any use to us in *explicating* the knowledge-relation. But thinking of a fact in this way *does* so help us. For if we can disabuse ourselves of the notion that because language is an expression of knowledge, it is somehow a mere epiphenomenon which cannot be used to explain that of which it is the expression, we shall see that "*S* knows that . . ." can be explicated in terms of " '. . .' means that ——."

(IV)  Metalinguistic (semantical) discourse may be used to analyze discourse about knowledge as follows:

(a)  We start by recognizing that, in Sellars's words, " ' ". . ." means ——' is the core of a unique mode of discourse which is as distinct from the description and explanation of empirical facts as is the language of prescription and justification."[23]

(b)  We confine the term "thoughts" to matters which are reported in such expressions as "he believes that . . . ," "he knows that . . . ," "he guesses that . . . "; we thus exclude from the category of thoughts *sensations* (i.e., such "mental states" as pains and tickles which are not naturally reported in that-clauses, but rather in such locutions as "I feel a . . . "). This distinction expresses the fact that we *know* facts but *sense* particulars – and thus that, if "experience" is construed, as we have been construing it here, as "intuition" (where sensing is the paradigm case of intuiting), it is false that we know the same sort of things which we experience.[24]

(c)  We view thoughts as entities which have a relation of "aboutness" to entities which are (normally) not thoughts – a relation which is "intentional" in the sense that it can hold between thoughts and entities which do not exist, and perhaps could not exist. The problem for an analysis of knowing is to

---

[23] "Intentionality and the Mental," *Minnesota Studies in the Philosophy of Science*, 2 (1958), p. 527.

[24] Note that the distinction between the intentional notion "having knowledge about" and the non-intentional notion "being aware of" has, as Sellars says, always been characteristic of Physical Realism, and is basic to the account of knowledge being sketched here. ("Physical Realism," *Philosophy and Phenomenological Research*, 15 (1954–1955). pp. 13–32, esp. p. 20. In this article Sellars explains why the confusion of these two notions was "the root error of the positivistic-phenomenalistic tradition," and sketches the similarities between his own criticisms of this error and those made in the course of R. W. Sellars's exposition of Physical Realism. The broad outlines of the difference between the methods used by both Sellarses in defending realism and those used by Whitehead are presented in R. W. Sellars's "Philosophy of Organism and Physical Realism," in Paul Arthur Schilpp, ed., *The Philosophy of A. N. Whitehead* (New York, 1941), pp. 405–33, esp. pp. 416ff).

provide a satisfactory account of this relation. For if we can find an analysis of this relation which will allow for the fact that thoughts can be about entities which (logically) cannot be experienced (e.g., unrepeatable entities), then we shall be in a position to deny the key premise of the Lockeian argument above – *viz.*,

(1)   Only the sort of concrete entity which we can experience is the sort of concrete entity which we can know about.

(d)  Thoughts may, *prima facie*, be analyzed as dispositions to act, and, in particular, dispositions to utter.[25] But such analyses will work only if the utterances the thinker is disposed to utter are meaningful utterances – that is, if we can say something specific about what they do mean.[26] Now it has usually been thought that to describe the meaning of an utterance, since it is clearly not simply to describe the sign-vehicle, must be to describe the thoughts (and, specifically, the intentions) of the utterer. Specifically, it is usually assumed that the "aboutness" which characterizes thoughts cannot be analyzed in terms of the relation of "meaning" which linguistic entities bear to nonlinguistic entities without circularity – for the latter relation is itself unintelligible without understanding the way in which thoughts endow sign-vehicles with a special feature called "meaning" – and thus without understanding the "aboutness" of thoughts.[27]

(e)  But this assumption is incorrect. It confuses statements about the meaning of utterances (tokening activities) with statements about the meaning of types of utterances (e.g., words, sentences). (Contrast answers to "What did he mean by saying 'It's cold' [when it was actually sizzling]?" with answers to "What does the English sentence 'It's cold' mean?") The latter sort of statement is confirmable in ordinary, unproblematic, intersubjective ways – by noting "semantical regularities," and

---

[25] They may also, in a more sophisticated version of the view being presented here, be regarded not as dispositions but as introspectible *episodes*. Cf. "Empiricism and the Philosophy of Mind," pp. 317–21. But this important refinement must be passed over.

[26] Cf. R. Chisholm, *Perceiving* (Ithaca, 1957), ch. 11; also Chisholm, "Sentences about Believing," *Minnesota Studies in the Philosophy of Science*, 2 (1958), pp. 510–19, and W. Sellars, "A Semantical Solution to the Mind-Body Problem," *Methodos*, 5 (1953), pp. 61ff.

[27] The picture involved is that meaning is a sort of subtle electric current which flows from minds into sound waves or inkspots and makes them "glow."

reporting them in such formulae as "When '...' is uttered, then in general such-and-such is the case."[28]

(f)  The analysis of "S is thinking that ...," therefore, can be built around "S is disposed to utter '...' under appropriate conditions, and '...' means that——." Such an analysis is able to provide the explication of the intentional "about" demanded in (c) above, for we can now analyze "S is thinking about E" as "S is disposed to utter '...' under appropriate conditions and '...' is about E" (and analyze "S has knowledge about E" in a similar way). To ascertain what '...' is about we merely invoke the principle that statements in which referring expressions occur essentially are normally *about* the entities to which these expressions refer. The sense of aboutness invoked here is "intentional" in the way required. The suggested analyses amount, therefore, to the claim that (a) there is no mystery to *this* sort of aboutness, and that (b) thoughts are about entities in exactly the way in which statements are.

(g)  But once aboutness is analyzed in this way, it is clear that no force remains to (1). For on this analysis to say that

> Only the sort of concrete entity which we can experience is the sort of concrete entity which we can know about.

is to say something obviously false. It is to say that, for example, if the value of X in any true statement of the form "S knows that X is Y" is the name of a concrete entity, then it is the name of an entity which can be the content of an experience. This is just as obviously false as the suggestion that it must be the name of a nonfictional entity, or the name of a present entity. The traditional problems of how one can have knowledge of the past, the fictional, and the (logically) inexperienceable are at bottom the same problem. All forms of the problem are resolved by interpreting knowledge as knowledge of facts, rather than objects, and interpreting "knowledge about" as knowledge about entities referred to in the statements which are the names of the facts known. For such an interpretation permits one to see that although our

---

[28] For this use of the term "semantical regularity," and for a general account of how an empirical inquiry into the meaning of words may be conducted without reference to the "intentions" of utterers, see Paul Ziff's *Semantic Analysis* (Ithaca, 1961).

knowledge about the past, the fictional, and the (logically) inexperienceable may be based entirely on experiences of present nonfictional experienceables, we need not view the former as an abstraction from, a logical construction out of, or in any other way "reducible to" the latter. This interpretation, in other words, disentangles $S$'s relation to what he knows about from his relation to what he experiences – or, in other words, disentangles his relation to the "intentional object" of his knowledge from his relation to the experiences which form the ground of his knowledge.

## IV

Given this final claim – IV(g) – we are now in a position to say that the substances of common sense are both unrepeatable entities and are known about, without fear of Lockeian attack. We are thus free of the need either to find a new model of "unrepeatable entity" (like Whitehead) or to eliminate unrepeatable entities from our world view and singular terms from our ideal language (like the phenomenalists). Further, we have remained faithful to the linguistic version of the methodological form of Cartesian subjectivism – the elements which go into our explication of ordinary discourse about knowing are drawn from other regions of ordinary discourse, and no appeal is made to the existence of entities for which no criteria of identification can be supplied. The only entities whose existence is presupposed are utterances – which are as readily describable and identifiable as anything could be.

Such are the advantages of this view – if it comes off. To show that it *does* come off is not the purpose of this chapter. I shall conclude, rather, with a brief comparison between this method of defending realism and Whitehead's method. The basic strategy of the view just outlined is to explicate problematic features of knowing by reference to unproblematic features of *talking*. The basic strategy which Whitehead employed was to explicate problematic features of knowing by reference to unproblematic features of *feeling*. As we have seen, Whitehead's construal of intentional aboutness in terms of the feeling of past entities by present entities requires him, in order to save realism, to construct a new category of entities – entities which can only be described in token-reflexive terms. We may now note that the strategy employed in the Sellarsian analysis outlined above leads to a similar result. Here too we are led to give central importance to token-reflexive terms.

The reader will have perceived that the crucial claim made in the previous section is IV(a) – the claim that semantical discourse is distinct from, and irreducible to, empirical discourse. If it were not, there would be no point in the claim that it can supply an analysis of epistemic discourse which empirical (and, specifically, "behavioristic") discourse cannot. Unless " '. . .' means ———" is indeed "the core of a unique mode of discourse," it is implausible that the schema " '. . .' means that———" should be both "intentional" enough for the purposes of IV(d) and "behavioristic" enough for those of IV(e). But what is unique about it? The answer to this question is that the assertion of statements of this form, unlike the assertion of empirical statements, *presupposes* the truth of certain token-reflexive statements. For, as Sellars says, "The basic role of significa- tion statements is to say that two expressions, *at least one of which is in our own vocabulary*, have the same use."[29] Thus, although statements of this form do not themselves normally contain token-reflexive terms, they will not be true unless statements of the form "Users of the language in which this statement is phrased use '. . .' under the following circumstances: . . ." are true. The truth of the latter sort of statements is presupposed by the assertion of the former sort. The occurrence of such a token-reflexive term as 'the language in which this statement is phrased' is, furthermore, ineliminable. (If one replaces this term by, e.g., "English," one will then have to say that the truth of the original signification statements presup- poses the further condition that "this statement is in English" is true – a presupposition which is, once more, formulated in a token-reflexive statement.)[30]

---

[29] "Being and Being Known," p. 46. Cf. *ibid.*, p. 45: "There is an obvious difference between
"'Mensch' signifies *man*'
and
"'Mensch' has the same use as "man"'
This difference is that the former won't achieve its purpose of explaining the word 'Mensch' unless the hearer knows the use of the word 'man,' whereas the latter can be fully appreciated by one who doesn't know this use. Thus, these two statements are not equivalent. This, however, can be remedied by interpreting the former statement as presupposing that the word 'man' is in the hearer's vocabulary, and hence as equivalent (roughly) to
"'Mensch' (in German) has the same use as your word "man."'

[30] Note that the truth of these latter statements is presupposed by reports of meanings not simply in the sense that such reports would be *unintelligible* to the auditor if the presuppositions were false, but in the sense that these reports would be *false* if these presuppositions were false. If the user of " 'Der Mond is blau' means that the moon is blue" does not use "the moon is blue" in the same way in which Germans use "Der Mond ist blau," then the statement is false. Nonsemantical statements, however, including such empirical reports of semantical regularities as "When 'Der Mond ist blau' is uttered, then generally the moon is blue," may be unintelligible if their user does not use terms used in the statements in certain ways – but they will still be true. The truth of the empirical statements which verify reports of meaning are themselves language-independent, in the sense that they may be

We see, then, that semantical statements are always, when made in fully explicit form, token-reflexive statements – statements which involve explicit reference to the language *we* speak *now*. Let us now recall that a crucial step in the analysis of knowing which we have sketched was to insist that what we know are *facts*, and that the only principle for differentiating among facts is that a distinct fact is named by every that-clause which has a distinct meaning. A fact is, in short, an entity which can only be identified in semantical, as opposed to empirical, discourse.[31] A fact is, therefore, an entity which can only be identified with the aid of criteria which, when made fully explicit, involve explicit reference to the language we are now speaking. But this means that the only entities which we can know are entities which we can describe only with the aid of token-reflexive terms. Let us now recall that the same conclusion was reached, along a very different route, by Whitehead. Is there anything more than coincidence in the fact that these two strategies converge at this point?

I think that there is, and that it consists in the fact that both strategies realize that the "subjectivist bias of modern philosophy" can only be reconciled with realism if we can find a way of reconciling the fact that all knowledge is *perspectival* with the fact that knowledge is about objects distinct from and independent of the experiencing subject. For to show that the objects of knowledge are characterizable only in token-reflexive terms is to show that all knowledge is perspectival, and it is also to show, as Michael Dummett has recently pointed out, that there can be no such thing as "the complete description of reality."[32] ("Reality" here means simply "the totality of what is known about.") Both strategies accept this consequence, and both insist that this consequence – the fact that it is logically impossible that there should be a description of reality which is not a description from a perspective which is one among alternative perspectives – does not involve a surrender to idealism. To grant this consequence is to take the wind out of the idealist's sails; to show that it is compatible with the claim that reality remains distinct from, and independent of, our knowledge about it is to defeat him. This thesis – that our

---

true even if the expressions *used* in them do not have the same use as any of the expressions *mentioned* in them, but this is not the case for statements of the form " '. . .' means that – ." Such statements are language-dependent, in the sense that if they are true then the semantical-statement-user must use " – " in the way in which ". . ." is used. Cf. Sellars, "A Semantical Solution to the Mind-Body Problem," esp. pp. 64–8, 78–9.

[31] See Sellars's claim that "that-clauses are metalinguistic in character": "Time and the World Order," p. 542; also "Truth and 'Correspondence,'" p. 45.

[32] "A Defense of McTaggart's Proof of the Unreality of Time," *Philosophical Review*, 69 (1960), pp. 497–504, esp. pp. 503–4.

knowledge may be about an independent reality without its being the case that it is even logically possible that this reality should be described independently of the observer's perspective – is the common ground shared by both strategies. The relative overall success of the two strategies may, I believe, best be judged on the basis of their success in making this thesis explicit and convincing. For I should hold that the presentation and defense of this thesis has been, and continues to be, the central task of contemporary philosophy. Whitehead's attempt to break free from the substance–property framework and thereby show that temporal perspectives are internal to the nature of concrete actualities was the last, and the most important, attempt to perform this task prior to the "linguistic turn." But once this turn is taken, new methods of carrying out this task become available.

# CHAPTER 5

# Empiricism, extensionalism, and reductionism

There was a time when the slogan "Let us construct an extensional language which is adequate to say everything!" stirred the hearts of empiricists. It seemed evident that all that was required to accomplish the project was energy and discrimination, for surely to deny that the job *could* be done would be somehow tantamount to doubting the cardinal tenets of empiricism. In the course of some twenty or thirty years, however, extensionalism has fallen into disrepute. On the one hand, there is a history of failure in the attempts actually to get the job done. On the other, there is the suggestion that empiricism was led astray by its delight in a new toy, and that the use of an extensional calculus has nothing in particular to do with the tradition of Locke and Hume. American philosophers have been told by their British colleagues that they have picked a quite arbitrary straight-jacket in which to confine language, and have thereby created for themselves a host of pseudo-problems about areas where the straight-jacket pinches. The artificiality of suggested extensionalistic reconstructions of these areas of discourse has made many philosophers receptive to suggestions that they can be *bona fide* empiricists without being "reductionists."

The purpose of this chapter is to show that there are indeed internal relationships between empiricism and extensionalism, to explain what these relationships are, and to show that neither empiricism nor extensionalism is internally related to reductionism, in the sense in which this term is usually understood. In other words, I want to disentangle three theses which empiricists have tried to establish and discuss what the history of recent empiricism teaches us about the hopes for establishing them. These three theses are:

(1)  What I shall call the *thesis of empiricism*, enshrined in a formula which I am borrowing from Sellars: "the fundamental concepts pertaining to observable fact are logically independent of each other."[1]

---

[1] W. Sellars, "Empiricism and the Philosophy of Mind," in *Minnesota Studies in the Philosophy of Science*, 1 (Minneapolis, 1956), p. 275.

(2)   The *thesis of extensionalism*: One can construct a language (*a*) which is adequate to express any given body of knowledge about observable fact, and (*b*) in which predicates which apply to all and only the same things can be everywhere substituted for each other *salva veritate*.

(3)   The *thesis of reductionism*: One can construct a language which will form a *permanent* neutral matrix for stating the results of *all future* empirical inquiry – that is, a language which will require no additions to, or subtractions from, its list of undefined predicates in order to handle any such result.

In what follows, I shall argue that the theses of empiricism and of extensionalism, as stated, are linked to each other by being both immediate corollaries of Hume's pregnant remark that "whatever is distinguishable is distinct." I shall argue further that neither of them entails or is entailed by the thesis of reductionism. I shall conclude by suggesting that the confusion between the theses of extensionalism and of reductionism is responsible for most of the contemporary distrust of extensionalism.

I should hold, for reasons which I shall suggest at the conclusion of this chapter but which I shall not have space to defend, that the thesis of reductionism is, indeed, untenable. But I should also hold that in their flight from reductionism, and their eagerness to avoid the seemingly fruitless artificiality to which the joint defense of these three theses has been found to lead, empiricists are in danger of throwing out insight along with artificiality. The program of simultaneously defending these three theses gave rise to a movement almost unique in the history of philosophy: a sharply focused co-operative inquiry extending over many years. A great many lessons were learned in the course of this inquiry about what empiricism was and what it was not, and about what can be safely "reduced" and what cannot. This chapter is an attempt to sketch some of these lessons.

Hume's claim that whatever is distinct is distinguishable, and vice versa, occurs at various places in the *Treatise*. It is perhaps most fully stated in the *locus classicus* of reductionist empiricism: the section "Of Abstract Ideas":

> We have observ'd that whatever objects are different are distinguishable, and that whatever objects are distinguishable are separable by the thought and imagination. And we may here add, that these propositions are equally true in the *inverse*, and that whatever objects are separable are also distinguishable, and that whatever objects are distinguishable are also different.

There are four assertions here, each of which appears more trivial and verbal than the last. And so they are. Yet they are quite enough to show what Hume wants to show: that there is no real indefiniteness in our thought, and that the apparent counter-instance of an abstract idea (one which applies to indefinitely many things) is not a real one. It is not a real counter-instance because every mental act can be broken up into its least parts, and because they *are* least, they will be perfectly definite. The linguistic counterpart of this gambit is to claim that there need be no real indefiniteness in language, because everything that one says can be broken up into perfectly definite bits. The gambit is foolproof, because given any proposed irreducible indefiniteness, one can always ask the proposer to spell out just what the indefiniteness is indefinite *about*. When he has spelled it out, one tells him that he has just reduced what he claimed was irreducible. If he claims that he cannot build up the initial datum out of the bits, one need only reply that since all he can present for inspection *are* the bits, he obviously did manage it. To put it another way, the gambit consists in saying that one will not understand expressions in a given vocabulary about which a series of questions of the form "P or non-P" remain unanswered, choosing one's "P's" from another vocabulary. When one gets answers to these questions, one has "reduced" the initial expressions about one sort of thing to expressions about another sort of thing. Hume can get a quasi-factual thesis out of a series of verbalisms for the same reason that one can get the quasi-factual thesis that "irrational numbers exist" out of a similar set of verbalisms. All one needs is an appropriate choice of "P's." Given them, one can argue that P-ish X's are distinguishable from non-P-ish X's (as of course they are, because one has just distinguished them), and that therefore there are two distinct things in place of the one "irreducible" thing which one started with.

When these verbalisms are applied to language a bit more carefully, the thesis of extensionalism emerges. The thesis that there is no context in which two predicates denoting all and only the same things cannot be substituted for one another *salva veritate* is tantamount to the claim that for any context which appears to be a counter-example one can find a distinguishable which, when erected into a distinct entity, will be denoted by one predicate and not by the other. In other words, if one can find a difference, *any* difference, between contexts in which the first predicate applies and the second does not, other than this simple fact of asymmetry, one can fashion this difference into a denotatum of one of these two predicates, which will thereby cease to be extensionally equivalent to the other. The process is parallel to that of proving that every two distinct ideas go back to distinct sets of impressions: you ask why one calls them "distinct" and then you call the respect in which they are said to differ the name of an impression. Whatever is distinguishable, no matter how, is, in some easily constructable language-stratum, the name of a distinct entity.

This may seem an oddly artificial way of going about proving the truth of extensionalism. Further, one suspects that creating all these odd denotata is sooner or later going to get the extensionalist in trouble. On this latter point, I shall be arguing later on that the extensionalist need not be troubled, *qua* extensionalist, by these odd denotata; they will cause him trouble only in so far as he is also a reductionist. As to artificiality, I shall now try to show that the strategies used by ideal-language empiricists do, in fact, exemplify the Humean pattern of argument I have been describing.

These strategies can be uncovered most readily if we look at some sample cases of areas of discourse which impede the development of an extensional language. Quine's "Notes on Existence and Necessity" gives us a good compendium of cases where substitutability of extensional equivalents *salva veritate* fails.[2] Let us take the case of "Philip believed Cicero denounced Cataline," where substitutability of "Tully" for "Cicero" fails because Philip does not know that Tully and Cicero are the same man. We are tempted to say that the fault lies in the peculiar character of "believes," "knows," "thinks," etc. When we see that quotation marks and modal operators create the same "referential opacity" as "believes," we are tempted to generalize and to say, with Quine, that such contexts are ones in which "the statement depends not only on the object but on the form of the name" (p. 140). Now we say: these failures of extensionality can be taken care of if, in our reconstruction of discourse, we distinguish carefully enough between things, their names, names of these names, and so forth. For they all seem to occur at places where, as it were, the linguistic and the factual truth-conditions for statements get tangled with one another.

Another way of looking at the problem appears, however, if we consider another batch of failures of substitutability. Bergmann has pointed out that if we happen to have two undefined predicates which apply to all and only the same things, and some "higher-order" predicates which apply to the undefined predicates, then substitutability *salva veritate*

---

[2] Cf. W. V. O. Quine, *From a Logical Point of View* (Cambridge, MA, 1953), c. 8.

will fail.[3] His example is as follows: suppose we have undefined predicates which name pitches and loudnesses, and suppose that "$p_I$" applies to all and only the things which "$I_I$" applies to. If we have a predicate "Pitch," we shall want to say "$p_I$ is a pitch," but we shall not want to say "$I_I$ is a pitch," and thus substitutability fails. Our reaction to this is not to say that we have a superfluity of names, but rather that we have too few. There is no particular reason why Marcus has to be called both "Tully" and "Cicero," but we ought to be able to distinguish that part (or "aspect," or "relation") of a tone which is its pitch from the part which is its loudness; if we did, then "$p_I$" and "$I_I$" would not name the same things, but would name different things related by constant conjunction.

Both batches of failures illustrate the fact that talking about the words which we use to talk about things will, if two of the latter words name the same thing(s), produce differences in words which are not differences in the world, and thereby failures of substitutability. To get an extensional language, we have to fix it so that each difference in words can be correlated with a difference in the world. But we have a choice as to which of the two series shall be expanded or contracted to produce this correlation. Sometimes we are inclined to think that our language is overgrown, and sometimes that it is not rich enough to catch non-linguistic differences. Depending on which diagnosis we adopt, we shall attempt an extensionalistic reconstruction along one or the other of the following lines:

(1)   Segregate the names of names of things from the names of things themselves, and restrict the range of the "intensional" predicates ("knows," "necessarily," etc.) to the former. As needed, we can also segregate names of names of names of things, and restrict certain predicates to them, and so on. The basis of this strategy is the notion that language is, indeed, overgrown (at least in regard to higher-order predicates), but that it can be made manageable by splitting it up into distinct levels. I shall call this first method the "metalanguage strategy."

(2)   Whenever one finds that a pair of first-level predicates refer to all and only the same things, replace them by a new set of first-level predicates which divide the world more finely. That is, assign a name to that feature in which the two things denoted by the old first-level predicates agree, and make this a second-level predicate definable in terms of new first-level predicates which express the features in which the things

---

[3]   G. Bergman, *The Metaphysics of Logical Positivism* (New York, 1954), pp. 232–7.

denoted differ. If, for example, one actually found that a tone of pitch $p_1$ was always of loudness $1_1$, one could christen it "The Abnormal Tone," and define it in terms of the compresence of $p_1$ and $1_1$ where the latter are construed not as naming experiences of hearing a tone *en gros*, but rather as naming two different experiences. The basis of this strategy is the notion that when we have two words for the "same thing," we are probably using too broad a criterion of "sameness." I shall call this second technique the "linguistic behaviourism strategy."

These two strategies illustrate two ways of getting rid of putatively "objective" ambiguity. A thoroughly naive spectator of the language-game might find it baffling that the same thing could be somehow two things – e.g., that the same man could be both Tully and Cicero, and that the same tone could be both $p_1$ and $1_1$. His bafflement can be cleared up either by telling him that the same thing can have two names, or by telling him that there are in fact two things which always appear, as it were, side-by-side. The first strategy seems more natural in the case of Tully and Cicero, but we can apply the second easily enough by distinguishing the Tully-phenomena and the Cicero-phenomena, as we might distinguish the Jekyll-phenomena and the Hyde-phenomena. The second strategy might seem more natural in the case of the Abnormal Tone, but we can apply the first by restricting the predicate "Pitch" to the "p's" – a gambit whose *ad hoc* character is diminished by distinguishing the language in which we talk about tones from the language in which we talk about this talk, and saying that the $p_1$ in "That's $p_1$!" names a feature of auditory experience, whereas the "$p_1$" in "$P_1$ is a pitch" names the name of this feature.

Both these strategies have the guarantee of success which is given by the adoption of the principle that every distinguishable is distinct. They vary only in that one of them finds distinguishability, and thereby distinctness, in linguistic events, and the other in non-linguistic events. Confronted by the failure of a set of symbols and a set of objects to mesh with each other, one can either pin the failure on the confusion of two symbols or on the confusion of two objects. Either strategy will suffice to eradicate any given violation of extensionality. To show that the thesis of extensionalism is true, therefore, one needs to consider only the question of whether the language which is developed out of ordinary discourse by successive applications of either strategy will be "adequate."

I shall not try to answer this latter question in this chapter; I think that it cannot be answered until one has a clear notion of what one means by "adequate," and that to get clear on this point one must first eliminate certain confusions about what we mean by empiricism, and about the relations between empiricism and reductionism. In what follows, I shall try to indicate what these confusions are. I shall do this by answering a possible objection to what I have said so far.

This objection runs as follows: one can hardly call "empiricist" a program which indulges in the kind of *ad hoc* hypostatization which you have been describing. For what becomes of the control which the given exerts over our thought and our language if we allow such free-and-easy construction of new entities? Does not everything you have said merely show that extensionalism is a piece of dogmatic metaphysics which pays no heed to the empirically given?

In answer to this objection, I need to begin by distinguishing two things that empiricists have often asserted. One is expressed by the slogan which I referred to above as "the thesis of empiricism": "The fundamental concepts pertaining to observable fact are logically independent of one another." The other is perhaps most simply expressed by the slogan: "One can tell an observable fact when one sees one." The lesson of recent empiricism is, I believe, that the latter slogan is false. It enshrines what Sellars has called the "Myth of the Given" (*op. cit.* p. 267, *passim*) and it is this polymorphous myth which pragmatists, contextualists, and ordinary-language philosophers have jointly, and, I think, successfully, demolished. So my answer to the objection is simply that the strategies for defending extensionalism which I have outlined are indeed incompatible with empiricism as defined by this Myth, but that the destruction of this Myth does not destroy empiricism, as defined by the *first* slogan. It is this *first* slogan – that the fundamental concepts pertaining to observable facts are logically independent of one another – which, I believe, expresses what empiricists have always been fighting for, even though they may not have known it. This slogan epitomizes such varied dicta as "All internal relations are made rather than found," and "No synthetic statement can be known to be true *a priori.*" All such dicta express the the doctrine that, although experience and discourse are shot through with both internal and external relations, the internal ones are there only because we created them for our convenience, and can be eliminated at no greater cost than inconvenience. The confusion between this doctrine and the Myth of the Given has arisen through a confusion between the notion of "being a property whose givenness to the senses is *itself* given" and the notion of "being a property which may vary independently of all other properties."

To undo this confusion we must realize that a philosopher who has adopted the slogan that "Whatever is distinguishable is distinct" has lost the right to think of the given-*versus*-constructed distinction as itself "given." For this slogan says that whatever we "make," by a process of distinguishing in thought or imagination, is indeed a distinct thing, as distinct as the things that are "found." This slogan licenses the use of any vocabulary to supply parameters for a reductive analysis of any putative "given," and thus licenses the creation of new "givens." To stop such a regress, we should need a "last" or "basic" vocabulary. We can always give, by fiat, such a preferred status to *any* vocabulary. But it must be noticed that the only way in which we can do even *this* is by an enumeration of such a vocabulary. For the only other alternatives are (1) that "given" is an unanalyzable notion or (2) that it is a "theoretical" term to be explicated in terms of nontheoretical terms. If it is unanalyzable, then the "control" which the found was to exert over the made disappears, for we are left free to indulge in Hegelian, Aristotelian, or Cartesian assumptions about "where thought begins" as well as Lockean ones. But it cannot be a "theoretical" term to be explicated in terms of nontheoretical ones, because we don't know which terms *are* non-theoretical until we have explicated "theoretical." (As Sellars has pointed out, trying to define "given" is like trying to define "good"; both are cases of the attempt to define an ultimate methodological notion by the use of the very method which depends on an understanding of that notion [*op. cit.*, p. 257].)

Returning now to extensionalism, I think one can see that the confusion between the thesis of empiricism and the Myth of the Given is reflected in the confusion between extensionalism and reductionism. The linguistic counterpart of the Myth of the Given is the Myth of the Permanent Neutral Matrix – the myth that we are somehow going to get a vocabulary which will be adequate to formulate the results of any future inquiry about anything: that some given enumeration of primitive predicates will suffice to permit us to formulate rules for the use of any new predicate that one might some day wish to employ. I wish to suggest, although I cannot here argue, that most of the grounds for pessimism about our ability to construct an adequate extensional language which have been voiced in recent years are grounds for pessimism only if "adequate" is interpreted as meaning "adequate to provide such a matrix." At the beginning of this chapter, I distinguished the theses of extensionalism and reductionism in terms of the distinction between the ability to provide an extensionalist reconstruction of any given piece of discourse *ad hoc* (by, if necessary, creating a new language to suit the occasion), and the ability to find a *single* language within which such a reconstruction will be possible in any future contingency. The stumbling blocks which have been encountered, for example, by philosophers attempting an extensionalistic reconstruction of the confirmation-relation seem to me to show decisively that we will never have this latter ability. We cannot find a way of reconstructing this relationship, and thus giving an account of nomologicality, unless we pay attention to what Goodman has called the "entrenchment" of predicates[4] – unless, that is, we realize that we have to consider what vocabulary has been successfully used for formulating nomological generalizations in the past before we can tell whether any suggested generalization will be confirmed by its positive instances. But if we do do this, then our criteria of nomologicality will have to be made relative to scientific epochs, since we hardly want to say that science is henceforth forbidden to formulate its theories in any vocabulary except one which can be constructed out of the primitive predicates in use at some arbitrary point in its history. In general, once we abandon the Myth of the Given, and with it the temptation to think in terms of some presently available enumeration of predicates as somehow known intuitively to be an adequate base for all future discourse, then the rejection of reductionism is only a matter of time. But we should observe that our inability to carry out the program of reductionism tells us nothing about out ability to carry out an extensionalist reconstruction of any given piece of discourse. As Bergman's example shows, it may be impossible to formulate a language which is both rich enough to describe empirical inquiry and such that we can know in advance that no violation of extensionality will occur within it. But this says nothing about whether we can construct *ad hoc* an extensional language which will meet any given emergency. It seems to me that, by employing one or the other of the extensionalist strategies sketched earlier in this chapter, we always can.

I shall conclude by restating the distinctions I have been trying to draw in terms of the Kantian distinction between the regulative and the constitutive use of principles. I have suggested that the theses of both empiricism and extensionalism, as I have construed them, are corollaries of the Humean principle that whatever is separable in thought or imagination is distinct. When these theses are thought of as *regulative* principles for the analysis either of knowledge or of language, we recognize that they are simply ways of saying the following: *given any two series of things which we wish to correlate one-to-one, we can do so, provided we are permitted to insert a*

[4] Cf. N. Goodman, *Fact, Fiction, and Forecast* (Cambridge, MA, 1955), pp. 95ff.

*new member at will.* That we are so permitted is precisely the force of Hume's principle. When, however, we add to Hume's principle the further assumption that we can know in advance of future inquiry just what we shall be able to distinguish and what we shall not, then we are tempted to construe these two theses as *constitutive* principles, as telling us something about the nature of knowledge and of language, and thus to engender the twin myths of the Given and of the Permanent Neutral Matrix. Holding to this latter assumption, and thus to these myths, has seemed to many philosophers an essential feature of the tough-mindedness which made empiricism so attractive. But this is a mistake. What takes a tough mind is just the opposite – the willingness to concede that any putative set of indubitables or ultimates may, in Peirce's phrase, be "blocking the road of inquiry." To adopt the Humean principle *without* the addition of this further assumption is (as neo-Thomists never tire of pointing out) to lose the feeling of a solid world underfoot. But this world is well lost, for its loss gives us new worlds to conquer. This is why extensionalistic reconstructions of language, although stemming from Hume's trivial remark, are not themselves trivial, any more than arithmetic is trivial because it stems, or can be seen to stem, from the trivialities which form the axioms of set theory. To call them "artificial" is, again, like calling the counterintuitive parts of mathematics "artificial" To quote Sellars again, "empirical knowledge, like its sophisticated extension, science, is rational, not because it has a foundation, but because it is a self-correcting enterprise, which can put *any* claim in jeopardy, although not *all* at once" (*op. cit.*, p. 300). This distinction between "any given claim" and "all claims at once" is parallel to the distinction between the regulative and the constitutive uses of the theses of empiricism and extensionalism. If we bear these distinctions in mind, we may be able to dissolve the antinomies created by empiricist metaphysics in the same way in which Kant dissolved those created by rationalist metaphysics.

# CHAPTER 6

# Mind-body identity, privacy, and categories

## I Introductory

Current controversies about the Mind-Body Identity Theory form a case-study for the investigation of the methods practiced by linguistic philosophers. Recent criticisms of these methods question that philosophers can discern lines of demarcation between "categories" of entities, and thereby diagnose "conceptual confusions" in "reductionist" philosophical theories. Such doubts arise once we see that it is very difficult, and perhaps impossible, to draw a firm line between the "conceptual" and the "empirical," and thus to differentiate between a statement embodying a conceptual confusion and one that expresses a surprising empirical result. The proponent of the Identity Theory (by which I mean one who thinks it sensible to assert that empirical inquiry will discover that *sensations* (not thoughts) are identical with certain brain-processes)[1] holds that his opponents' arguments to the effect that empirical inquiry *could* not identify brain-processes and sensations are admirable illustrations of this difficulty. For, he argues, the classifications of linguistic expressions that are the ground of his opponents' criticism are classifications of a language which is as it is because it is the language spoken at a given stage of empirical inquiry. But the sort of empirical results that would show brain-processes and sensations to be identical would also bring about changes in our ways of speaking. These changes would make these classifications out of date. To argue against the Identity Theory on the basis of the way we talk now is

---

[1] A proponent of the Identity Theory is usually thought of as one who predicts that empirical inquiry *will* reach this result – but few philosophers in fact stick their necks out in this way. The issue is not the truth of the prediction, but whether such a prediction makes sense. Consequently, by "Identity Theory" I shall mean the assertion that it does make sense. I include only sensations within the scope of the theory because the inclusion of thoughts would raise a host of separate problems (about the reducibility of intentional and semantic discourse to statements about linguistic behavior), and because the form of the Identity Theory which has been most discussed in the recent literature restricts itself to a consideration of sensations.

like arguing against an assertion that supernatural phenomena are identical with certain natural phenomena on the basis of the way in which super-stitious people talk. There is simply no such thing as a method of classifying linguistic expressions that has results guaranteed to remain intact despite the results of future empirical inquiry. Thus, in this area (and perhaps in all areas) there is no method which will have the sort of magisterial neutrality of which linguistic philosophers fondly dream.

In this chapter, I wish to support this general line of argument. I shall begin by pressing the claims of the analogy between mental events and supernatural events. Then I shall try to rebut the objection which seems generally regarded as fatal to the claims of the Identity Theory – the objection that "privacy" is of the essence of mental events, and thus that a theory which holds that mental events might *not* be "private" is *ipso facto* confused. I shall conclude with some brief remarks on the implications of my arguments for the more general metaphilosophical issues at stake.

## II   The two forms of the Identity Theory

The obvious objection to the Identity Theory is that "identical" either means a relation such that

$$(x) \ (y) \left[ (x = y) \supset (F) \ (Fx \equiv Fy) \right]$$

(the relation of "strict identity") or it does not. If it does, then we find ourselves forced into "saying truthfully that physical processes such as brain processes are dim or fading or nagging or false, and that mental phenomena such as after-images are publicly observable or physical or spatially located or swift,"[2] and thus using meaningless expressions, for "we may say that the above expressions are meaningless in the sense that they commit a category mistake; i.e., in forming these expressions we have predicated predicates, appropriate to one logical category, of expressions that belong to a different logical category. This is surely a conceptual mistake."[3] But if by "identical" the Identity Theory does *not* mean a relation of strict identity, then what relation *is* intended? How does it differ from the mere relation of "correlation" which, it is admitted on all sides, might without confusion be said to hold between sensations and brain processes?

[2] James Cornman, "The Identity of Mind and Body," *Journal of Philosophy*, 59 (1962), p. 490.
[3] *Ibid.*, p. 491.

Given this dilemma, two forms of the Identity Theory may be distinguished. The first, which I shall call the *translation* form, grasps the first horn, and attempts to show that the odd-sounding expressions mentioned above do not involve category-mistakes, and that this can be shown by suitable translations into "topic-neutral" language of the sentences in which these terms are originally used.[4] The second, which I shall call the *disappearance* form, grasps the second horn, and holds that the relation in question is not strict identity, but rather the sort of relation which obtains between, to put it crudely, existent entities and nonexistent entities when reference to the latter once served (some of) the purposes presently served by reference to the former – the sort of relation that holds, e.g., between "quantity of caloric fluid" and "mean kinetic energy of molecules." There is an obvious sense of "same" in which what used to be called "a quantity of caloric fluid" is *the same thing* as what is now called a certain mean kinetic energy of molecules, but there is no reason to think that all features truly predicated of the one may be sensibly predicated of the other.[5] The translation term of the theory holds that if we really understood what we were saying when we said things like "I am having a stabbing pain" we should see that since we are talking about "topic-neutral" matters, we might, for all we know, be talking about brain-processes. The disappearance form holds that it is unnecessary to show that suitable translations (into "topic-neutral" language) of our talk about sensations can be given – as unnecessary as to show that statements about quantities of caloric fluid, when properly understood, may be seen to be topic-neutral statements.[6]

---

[4] Cf. J. J. C. Smart, "Sensations and Brain Processes," reprinted in V. C. Chappell, ed., *The Philosophy of Mind* (Englewood Cliffs, 1962), pp. 160–72, esp. pp. 166–8, and especially the claim that "When a person says 'I see a yellowish-orange after-image' he is saying something like this: 'There is something going on which is like what is going on when I have my eyes open, am awake, and there is an orange illuminated in good light in front of me, that is, when I really see an orange'" (p. 167). For criticisms of Smart's program of translation, see Cornman, *op. cit.*; Jerome Shaffer, "Could Mental States Be Brain Processes?," *Journal of Philosophy*, 58 (1961), pp. 812–22; Shaffer, "Mental Events and the Brain," *Journal of Philosophy*, 60 (1963), pp. 160–6. See also the articles cited in the first footnote to Smart's own article.

[5] No statement of the disappearance form of the theory with which I am acquainted is as clear and explicit as Smart's statement of the translation form. See, however, Paul Feyerabend, "Mental Events and the Brain," *Journal of Philosophy*, 60 (1963), pp. 295–6, and "Materialism and the Mind-Body Problem," *Review of Metaphysics*, 17 (1963), pp. 49–67. See also Wilfrid Sellars, "The Identity Approach to the Mind-Body Problem," *ibid.*, 18 (1965), pp. 430–51. My indebtedness to this and other writings of Sellars will be obvious in what follows.

[6] Both forms agree, however, on the requirements which would have to be satisfied if we are to claim that the empirical discovery in question has been made. Roughly, they are (1) that one-one or one-many correlations could be established between every type of sensation and some clearly demarcated kind(s) of brain-processes; (2) that every known law which refers to sensations would be subsumed

From the point of view of this second form of the theory, it is a mistake to assume that "X's are nothing but Y's" entails "All attributes meaningfully predicable of X's are meaningfully predicated of Y's," for this assumption would forbid us ever to express the results of scientific inquiry in terms of (in Cornman's useful phrase) "cross-category identity."[7] It would seem that the verb in such statements as "Zeus's thunderbolts are discharges of static electricity" and "Demoniacal possession is a form of hallucinatory psychosis" is the "is" of identity, yet it can hardly express *strict* identity. The disappearance form of the Identity Theory suggests that we view such statements as elliptical for, e.g., "What people used to call 'demoniacal possession' is a form of hallucinatory psychosis," where the relation in question *is* strict identity. Since there is no reason why "what people call 'X'" should be in the same "category" (in the Rylean sense) as "X," there is no need to claim, as the translation form of the theory must, that topic-neutral translations of statements using "X" are possible.

In what follows, I shall confine myself to a discussion and defense of the disappearance form of the theory. My first reason for this is that I believe that the analysis of "Sensations are identical with certain brain-processes" proposed by the disappearance form (*viz.*, "What people now call 'sensations' are identical with certain brain-processes") accomplishes the same end as the translation form's program of topic-neutral translation – namely, avoiding the charge of "category-mistake," while preserving the full force of the traditional materialist position. My second reason is that I believe that an attempt to defend the translation form will inevitably get bogged down in controversy about the adequacy of proposed topic-neutral translations of statements about sensations. There is obviously a sense of "adequate translation" in which the topic-neutrality of the purported translations *ipso facto* makes them inadequate. So the proponent of the translation form of the theory will have to fall back on a weaker sense of "adequate translation." But the weaker this sense becomes, the less impressive is the claim being made, and the less difference between the Identity Theory and the noncontroversial thesis that certain brain-processes may be constantly correlated with certain sensations.

---

under laws about brain-processes; (3) that new laws about sensations be discovered by deduction from laws about brain-processes.

[7] Cornman, p. 492.

### III   The analogy between demons and sensations

At first glance, there seems to be a fatal weakness in the disappearance form of the Identity Theory. For normally when we say "What people call 'X's' are nothing but Y's" we are prepared to add that "There are no X's." Thus, when, e.g., we say that "What people call 'caloric fluid' is nothing but the motion of molecules" or "What people call 'witches' are nothing but psychotic women" we are prepared to say that there are no witches, and no such thing as caloric fluid. But it seems absurd to say that there might turn out to be no such things as sensations.

To see that this disanalogy is not fatal to the Identity Theory, let us consider the following situation. A certain primitive tribe holds the view that illnesses are caused by demons – a different demon for each sort of illness. When asked what more is known about these demons than that they cause illness, they reply that certain members of the tribe – the witch-doctors – can see, after a meal of sacred mushrooms, various (intangible) humanoid forms on or near the bodies of patients. The witch-doctors have noted, for example, that a blue demon with a long nose accompanies epileptics, a fat red one accompanies sufferers from pneumonia, etc., etc. They know such further facts as that the fat red demon dislikes a certain sort of mold which the witch-doctors give people who have pneumonia. (There are various competing theories about what demons do when not causing diseases, but serious witch-doctors regard such speculations as unverifiable and profitless.)

If we encountered such a tribe, we would be inclined to tell them that there are no demons. We would tell them that diseases were caused by germs, viruses, and the like. We would add that the witch-doctors were not seeing demons, but merely having hallucinations. We would be quite right, but would we be right on *empirical* grounds? What empirical criteria, built into the demon-talk of the tribe, go unsatisfied? What predictions which the tribesmen make fail to come true? If there are none, a sophisti-cated witch-doctor may reply that all modern science can do is to show (1) that the presence of demons is constantly correlated with that of germs, viruses, and the like, and (2) that eating certain mushrooms sometimes makes people think they see things that aren't really there. This is hardly sufficient to show that there are no demons. At best, it shows that if we forget about demons, then (a) a simpler account of the cause and cure of disease and (b) a simpler account of why people make the perceptual reports they do, may be given.

What do we reply to such a sophisticated witch-doctor? I think that all that we would have left to say is that the simplicity of the accounts which can be offered if we forget about demons *is* an excellent reason for saying that there are no demons. Demon-discourse is one way of describing and predicting phenomena, but there are better ways. We *could* (as the witch-doctor urges) tack demon-discourse on to modern science by saying, first, that diseases are caused by the compresence of demons and germs (each being a necessary, but neither a sufficient, condition) and, second, that the witch-doctors (unlike drunkards and psychotics) really do see intangible beings (about whom, alas, nothing is known save their visual appearances). If we did so, we would retain all the predictive and explanatory advantages of modern science. We would know as much about the cause and cure of disease, and about hallucinations, as we did before. We would, however, be burdened with problems which we did not have before: the problem of why demons are visible only to witch-doctors, and the problem of why germs cannot cause diseases all by themselves. We avoid both problems by saying that demons do not exist. The witch-doctor may remark that this use of Occam's Razor has the same advantage as that of theft over honest toil. To such a remark, the only reply could be an account of the practical advantages gained by the use of the Razor in the past.

Now the Identity Theorist's claim is that sensations may be to the future progress of psychophysiology as demons are to modern science. Just as we now want to deny that there are demons, future science may want to deny that there are sensations. The only obstacle to replacing sensation-discourse with brain-discourse seems to be that sensation-statements have a reporting as well as an explanatory function. But the demon case makes clear that the discovery of a new way of explaining the phenomena previously explained by reference to a certain sort of entity, *combined with a new account of what is being reported by observation-statements about that sort of entity*, may give good reason for saying that there are no entities of that sort. The absurdity of saying "Nobody has ever felt a pain" is no greater than that of saying "Nobody has ever seen a demon," *if* we have a suitable answer to the question "What *was* I reporting when I said I felt a pain?" To this question, the science of the future may reply "You were reporting the occurrence of a certain brain-process, and it would make life simpler for us if you would, in the future, *say* 'My C-fibers are firing' instead of saying 'I'm in pain'." In so saying, he has as good a *prima facie* case as the scientist who answers the witch-doctor's question "What *was* I reporting when I reported a demon?" by saying "You were reporting the content of your hallucination, and it would make life simpler if, in the future, you would describe your experiences in those terms."

Given this *prima facie* analogy between demons and sensations, we can now attend to some disanalogies. We may note, first, that there is no simple way of filling in the blank in "What people called 'demons' are nothing but ———." For neither "hallucinatory contents" nor "germs" will do. The observational and the explanatory roles of "demon" must be distinguished. We need to say something like "What people who reported seeing demons were reporting was simply the content of their hallucinations," and *also* something like "What people explained by reference to demons can be explained better by reference to germs, viruses, etc." Because of the need for a relatively complex account of how we are to get along without reference to demons, we cannot *identify* "What we called 'demons'" with anything. So, instead, we simply deny their existence. In the case of sensations, however, we can give a relatively simple account of how to get along in the future. Both the explanatory *and* the reporting functions of statements about sensations can be taken over by statements about brain-processes. Therefore, we are prepared to identify "What we called 'sensations'" with brain-processes, and to say "What we called 'sensations' turn out to be nothing but brain-processes."

Thus, this disanalogy does not have the importance which it appears to have at first. In both the demon case and the sensation case, the proposed reduction has the same pragmatic consequences: namely, that we should stop asking questions about the causal and/or spatio-temporal relationships holding between the "reduced" entities (demons, sensations) and the rest of the universe, and replace these with questions about the relationships holding between certain other entities (germs, hallucinatory experiences, brain-processes) and the rest of the universe. It happens, for the reasons just sketched, that the proposed reduction is put in the form of a denial of existence in one case, and of an identification in another case. But "There are no demons" and "What people call 'sensations' are nothing but brain-processes" can both equally well be paraphrased as "Elimination of the referring use of the expression in question ('demon,' 'sensation') from our language would leave our ability to describe and predict undiminished."

Nevertheless, the claim that there might turn out to be no such thing as a "sensation" seems scandalous. The fact that a witch-doctor might be scandalized by a similar claim about demons does not, in itself, do much to diminish our sense of shock. In what follows, I wish to account for this intuitive implausibility. I shall argue that it rests *solely* upon the fact that elimination of the referring use of "sensation" from our language would be in the highest degree *impractical.* If this can be shown, then I think that the Identity Theorist will be cleared of the charge of "conceptual confusion" usually leveled against him. Rather than proceeding directly to this argument, however, I shall first consider a line of argument which has often been used to show that he *is* guilty of this charge. Examining this line of argument will permit me to sketch in greater detail what the Identity Theorist is and is not saying.

## IV   The eliminability of observation-terms

The usual move made by the opponents of the Identity Theory is to compare suggested reduction of sensations to brain-processes to certain other cases in which we say that "X's turn out to be nothing but Y's." There are two significantly different classes of cases and it might seem that the Identity Theorist confuses them. First, there is the sort of case in which both "X" and "Y" are used to refer to observable entities, and the claim that "What people called 'X's' are nothing but Y's" backed up by pointing out that the statement "This is an X" commits one to an empirically false proposition. For example, we say that "What people called 'unicorn horns' are nothing but narwhal horns," and urge that we cease to respond to a perceptual situation with "This is a unicorn horn." We do this because "This is a unicorn horn" commits one to the existence of unicorns, and there are, it turns out, no unicorns. Let us call this sort of case *identification of observables with other observables.* Second, there is the sort of case in which "X" is used to refer to an observable entity and "Y" is used to refer to an unobservable entity. Here we do not (typically) back up the claim that "What people called 'X's' are nothing but Y's" by citing an empirically false proposition presupposed by "This is an X." For example, the statement that "What people call 'tables' are nothing but clouds of molecules" does not suggest, or require as a ground, that people who say "This is a table" hold false beliefs. Rather, we are suggesting that something *more* has been found out about the sort of situation reported by "This is a table." Let us call this second sort of case *identification of observables with theoretical entities.*

It seems that we cannot assimilate the identification of sensations with brain-processes to either of these cases. For, unlike the typical case of identification of observables with other observables, we do not wish to say that people who have reported sensations in the past have (necessarily) any empirically disconfirmed beliefs. People are not wrong about sensations in the way in which they were wrong about "unicorn horns."

Again, unlike the typical case of the identification of observables with theoretical entities, we do not want to say that brain-processes are "theoretical" or unobservable. Furthermore, in cases in which we identify an observable X with an unobservable Y, we are usually willing to accept the remark that "That does not show that there are no X's." The existence of tables is not (it would seem) impugned by their identification with clouds of electrons, as the existence of unicorn horns is impugned by their identification with narwhal horns. But a defender of the disappearance form of the Identity Theory *does* want to impugn the existence of sensations.

Because the claim that "What people call 'sensations' may turn out to be nothing but brain-processes" cannot be assimilated to either of these cases, it has been attacked as trivial or incoherent. The following dilemma is posed by those who attack it: either the Identity Theorist claims that talk about sensations presupposes some empirically disconfirmed belief (and what could it be?) or the "identity" which he has in mind is the uninteresting sort of identity which holds between tables and clouds of molecules (mere "theoretical replacability").

The point at which the Identity Theorist should attack this dilemma is the premise invoked in stating the second horn – the premise that the identification of tables with clouds of molecules does not permit us to infer to the non-existence of tables. This premise is true, but *why* is it true? That there is room for reflection here is apparent when we place the case of tables side-by-side with the case of demons. If there is any point to saying that tables are nothing but clouds of molecules it is presumably to say that, in principle, we could stop making a referring use of "table," and of any extensionally equivalent term, and still leave our ability to describe and predict undiminished. But this would seem just the point of (and the justification for) saying that there are no demons. Why does the realization that nothing would be lost by the dropping of "table" from our vocabulary still leave us with the conviction that there are tables, whereas the same realization about demons leave us with the conviction that there are no demons? I suggest that the only answer to this question which will stand examination is that although we could *in principle* drop "table," it would be monstruously inconvenient to do so, whereas it is both possible in principle and convenient in practice to drop "demon." The reason "But there still are tables" sounds so plausible is that nobody would dream of suggesting that we stop reporting our experiences in table-talk and start reporting them in molecule-talk. The reason "There are no demons" sounds so plausible is that we are quite willing to suggest that the witch-doctors stop reporting their experiences in demon-talk and start reporting them in hallucination-talk.

A conclusive argument that this practical difference is the *only* relevant difference would, obviously, canvass all the other differences which might be noted. I shall not attempt this. Instead, I shall try to make my claim plausible by sketching a general theory of the conditions under which a term may cease to have a referring use without those who made such a use being convicted of having held false beliefs.

Given the same sorts of correlations between X's and Y's, we are more likely to say "X's are nothing but Y's" when reference to X's is habitually made in noninferential reports, and more likely to say "There are no X's" when such reference is never or rarely made. (By "non-inferential report" I mean a statement in response to which questions like "How did you know?" "On what evidence do you say … ?" and "What leads you to think … ?" are normally considered misplaced and unanswerable, but which is nonetheless capable of empirical confirmation.) Thus, we do not say that the identification of temperature with the kinetic energy of molecules shows that there is no such thing as temperature, since "temperature" originally (i.e., before the invention of thermometers) stood for something which was always reported noninferentially, and still is frequently so reported. Similarly for all identifications of familiar macroobjects with unfamiliar microobjects. But since in our culture-circle we do not *habitually* report noninferentially the presence of caloric fluid, demons, etc., we do not feel unhappy at the bald suggestion that there are no such things.

Roughly speaking, then, the more accustomed we are to "X" serving as an observation-term (by which I mean a term habitually used in noninferential reports) the more we prefer, when inquiry shows the possibility of accounting for the phenomena explained by reference to X's without such reference, to "identify" X's with some sort of Y's, rather than to deny existence to X's *tout court. But the more grounds we have for such identification, the more chance there is that we shall stop using "X" in non-inferential reports*, and thus the greater chance of our eventually coming to accept the claim that "there are no X's" with equanimity. This is why we find borderline cases, and gradual shifts from assimilations of X's to Y's to an assertion that X's do not exist. For example, most people do not report the presence of pink rats non-inferentially (nor inferentially, for that matter), but some do. The recognition that they are in the minority helps those who do so to admit that there are no pink rats. But suppose that the vast majority of us had always seen (intangible and uncatchable) pink rats;

would it not then be likely that we should resist the bald assertion that there are no pink rats and insist on something of the form "pink rats are nothing but . . . "? It might be a very long time before we came to drop the habit of reporting pink rats and began reporting hallucinations instead.

The typical case-history of an observation-term ceasing to have a referring use runs the following course: (1) X's are the subjects of both inferential and noninferential reports;[8] (2) empirical discoveries are made which enable us to subsume X-laws under Y-laws and to produce new X-laws by studying Y's; (3) inferential reports of X's cease to be made; (4) noninferential reports of X's are reinterpreted either (4a) as reports of Y's, *or* (4b) as reports of mental entities (thoughts that one is seeing an X, hallucinatory images, etc.); (5) noninferential reports of X's cease to be made (because their place is taken by noninferential reports either of Y's or of thoughts, hallucinatory images, etc.); (6) we conclude that there simply are no such things as X's.

This breakdown of stages lets us pick out two crucial conditions that must be satisfied if we are to move from "X's are nothing but Y's" (stage 2) to "there are no X's" (stage 6). These conditions are;

(A)   The Y-laws must be *better* at explaining the kinds of phenomena explained by the X-laws (not just equally good). Indeed, they must be sufficiently better so that *the inconvenience of changing one's linguistic habits by ceasing to make reports about Xs is less than the inconvenience of going through the routine of translating one's X-reports into Y-reports in order to get satisfactory explanations of the phenomena in question.* If this condition is not satisfied, the move from stage (2) to stage (3) will not be made, and thus no later move will be made.

(B)   Either Y-reports may themselves be made noninferentially, or X-reports may be treated as reports of mental entities. For we must be able to have some answer to the question "What *am* I reporting when I noninferentially report about an X?," and the only answers available are "you're reporting on a Y" or "you're reporting on some merely mental entity." If neither answer is available, we can move neither to (4a) nor to (4b), nor, therefore, on to (5) and (6).

Now the reason we move from stage (2) to stage (3) in the case of demons is that (A) is obviously satisfied. The phenomena which we explained by

---

[8]  Note that if X's are *only* referred to in inferential reports – as in the case of "neutrons" and "epicycles," no philosophically interesting reduction takes place. For in such cases there is no hope of getting rid of an explanandum; all we get rid of is a putative explanation.

reference to the activity of demons are so much better explained in other ways that it is simpler to stop inferring to the existence of demons altogether than to continue making such inferences, and then turning to laws about germs and the like for an explanation of the behavior of the demons. The reason why we do *not* move from (2) to (3) – much less to (6) – in the case of temperature or tables is that explanations formulated in terms of temperatures are so good, on the ground which they were originally intended to cover, that we feel no temptation to stop talking about temperatures and tables merely because we can, in some cases, get more precise predictions by going up a level to laws about molecules. The reason why we move on from (3) to (4) in the case of demons is that the alternative labeled (4b) is readily available – we can easily consign experiences of demons to that great dumping-ground of out-dated entities, the Mind. There were no experiences of demons, we say, but only experiences of mental images.

Now it seems obvious that, in the case of sensations, (A) will not be satisfied. The inconvenience of ceasing to talk about sensations would be so great that only a fanatical materialist would think it worth the trouble to cease referring to sensations. If the Identity Theorist is taken to be predicting that some day "sensation," "pain," "mental image," and the like will drop out of our vocabulary, he is almost certainly wrong. But if he is saying simply that, at no greater cost than an inconvenient linguistic reform, we *could* drop such terms, he is entirely justified. And I take this latter claim to be all that traditional materialism has ever desired.

Before leaving the analogy between demons and sensations, I wish to note one further disanalogy which an opponent of the Identity Theory might pounce upon. Even if we set aside the fact that (A) would not be satisfied in the case of sensations, such an opponent might say, we should note the difficulty in satisfying (B). It would seem that there is no satisfactory answer to the question "What *was* I noninferentially reporting when I reported on my sensations?" For neither (4a) nor (4b) seems an available option. The first does not seem to be available because it is counter-intuitive to think of, e.g., "I am having my C-fibers stimulated," as capable of being used to make a non-inferential report. The second alternative is simply silly – there is no point in saying that when we report a sensation we are reporting some "merely mental" event. For sensations are *already* mental events. The last point is important for an understanding of the *prima facie* absurdity of the disappearance form of the Identity Theory. The reason why most statements of the form "there might turn out to be no X's at all" can be accepted with more or less equanimity in the context of forecasts of scientific results is that we are confident we shall always be able to "save the phenomena" by answering the question "But what about all those X's we've been accustomed to observe?" with some reference to thoughts-of X's, images-of X's, and the like. Reference to mental entities provides noninferential reports of X's with something to have been about. But when we want to say "There might turn out to be no mental entities at all," we cannot use this device. This result makes clear that if the analogy between the past disappearance of supernatural beings and the possible future disappearance of sensations is to be pressed, we must claim that alternative (4a) is, appearances to the contrary, still open. That is, we must hold that the question "What *was* I noninferentially reporting when I noninferentially reported a stabbing pain?" can be sensibly answered "You were reporting a stimulation of your C-fibers."

Now why should this *not* be a sensible answer? Let us begin by getting a bad objection to it out of the way. One can imagine someone arguing that this answer can only be given if a stimulation of C-fibers is strictly identical with a stabbing pain, and that such strict identification involves category-mistakes. But this objection presupposes that "A report of an X is a report of a Y" entails that "X's are Y's." If we grant this presupposition we shall not be able to say that the question "What was I reporting when I reported a demon?" is properly answered by "You were reporting the content of an hallucination which you were having." However, if we ask why this objection is plausible, we can see the grain of truth which it embodies and conceals. We are usually unwilling to accept "You were reporting a Y" as an answer to the question "What *was* I noninferentially reporting when I noninferentially reported an X?" unless (a) Y's are themselves the kind of thing we habitually report on noninferentially, and (b) there does not exist already an habitual practice of reporting Y's non-inferentially. Thus, we accept "the content of an hallucination" as a sensible answer because we know that such contents, being "mental images," are just the sort of thing which do get noninferentially reported (once they are recognized for what they are) and because we are not accustomed to making noninferential reports in the form "I am having an hallucinatory image of . . . "[9] To take an example of answers to this sort of question that are *not* sensible, we reject the claim that when we report on a table we are reporting on a mass

[9] Note that people who *become* accustomed to making the latter sort of reports may no longer accept explanations of their erroneous non-inferential reports by reference to hallucinations. For they know what mental images are like, and they know that *this* pink rat was not an hallucinatory content. The more frequent case, fortunately, is that they just cease to report pink rats and begin reporting hallucinations, for their hallucinations no longer deceive them.

of whirling particles, for either we think we know under what circumstances we should make such a report, and know that these circumstances do not obtain, or we believe that the presence of such particles can only be inferred and never observed.

The oddity of saying that when I think I am reporting on a stabbing pain I am actually reporting on a stimulation of my C-fibers is similar to these last two cases. We either imagine a situation in which we can envisage ourselves non-inferentially reporting such stimulation (periscope hitched up to a microscope so as to give us a view of our trepanned skull, overlying fibers folded out of the way, stimulation evident by change in color, etc., etc.), or else we regard "stimulation of C-fibers" as not the sort of thing which *could* be the subject of a noninferential report (but inherently a "theoretical" state of affairs whose existence can only be inferred, and not observed). In either case, the assertion that we have been noninferentially reporting on a brain-process all our lives seems absurd. So the proponent of the disappearance form of the Identity Theory must show that reports of brain-processes are neither incapable of being non-inferential nor, if non-inferential, necessarily made in the way just imagined (with the periscope-microscope gadget) or in some other peculiar way. But now we must ask who bears the burden of proof. Why, after all, should we think that brain-processes are *not* a fit subject-matter for non-inferential reports? And why should it not be the case that the circumstances in which we make non-inferential reports about brain-processes are just those circumstances in which we make non-inferential reports about sensations? For this will in fact be the case if, when we were trained to say, e.g., "I'm in pain" we were in fact being trained to respond to the occurrence within ourselves of a stimulation of C-fibers. If this is the case, the situation will be perfectly parallel to the case of demons and hallucinations. We *will*, indeed, have been making non-inferential reports about brain-processes all our lives *sans le savoir*.

This latter suggestion can hardly be rejected *a priori*, unless we hold that we can only be taught to respond to the occurrence of A's with the utterance "A!" if we were able, prior to this teaching, to be aware, when an A was present, that it was present. But this latter claim is plausible only if we assume that there is an activity which can reasonably be called "awareness" prior to the learning of language. I do not wish to fight once again the battle which has been fought by Wittgenstein and many of his followers against such a notion of awareness. I wish rather to take it as having been won, and to take for granted that there is no *a priori* reason why a brain-process is inherently unsuited to be the subject of a non-inferential report. The distinction between observation-terms and nonobservation-terms is relative to linguistic practices (practices which may change as inquiry progresses), rather than capable of being marked out once and for all by distinguishing between the "found" and the "made" elements in our experience. I think that the recognition of this relativity is the first of the steps necessary for a proper appreciation of the claims of the Identity Theory. In what follows, I want to show that this first step leads naturally to a second: the recognition that the distinction between *private* and *public* subject-matters is as relative as that between items signified by observation-terms and items not so signified.

The importance of this second step is clear. For even if we grant that reports of brain-processes may be non-inferential, we still need to get around the facts that reports of sensations have an epistemological peculiarity that leads us to call them reports of *private* entities, and that brain-processes are intrinsically *public* entities. Unless we can overcome our intuitive conviction that a report of a private matter (with its attendent infallibility) cannot be identified with a report of a public matter (with its attendent fallibility), we shall not be able to take seriously the claim of the proponents of the disappearance form of the Identity Theory that alternative (4a) is open, and hence that nothing prevents sensations from disappearing from discourse in the same manner, and for the same reasons, as supernatural beings have disappeared from discourse. So far in this chapter I have deliberately avoided the problem of the "privacy" of sensations, because I wished to show that if this problem *can* be surmounted, the Identity Theorist may fairly throw the burden of proof onto his opponent by asking whether a criterion can be produced which would show that the identification of sensations and brain-processes involves a conceptual confusion, while absolving the claim that demons do not exist because of such a confusion. Since I doubt that such a criterion *can* be produced, I am inclined to say that if the problem about "privacy" is overcome, then the Identity Theorist has made out his case.

## V    The "privacy" objection

The problem that the privacy of first-person sensation reports presents for the Identity Theory has recently been formulated in considerable detail by Baier.[10] In this section, I shall confine myself to a discussion of his criticism of Smart's initial reply to this argument. Smart holds that the fact that "the

---

[10] Kurt Baier, "Smart on Sensations," *Australasian Journal of Philosophy*, 40 (1962), pp. 57–68.

language of introspective reports has a different logic from the logic of material processes" is no objection to the Identity Theory, since we may expect that empirical inquiry can and will change this logic: "It is obvious that until the brain-process theory is much improved and widely accepted there will be no *criteria* for saying 'Smith has an experience of such-and-such a sort' except Smith's introspective reports. So we have adopted a rule of language that (normally) what Smith says goes."[11] Baier thinks that this reply "is simply a confusion of the privacy of the subject-matter and the availability of external evidence."[12] Baier's intuition is that the difference between a language-stratum in which the fact that a report is sincerely made is sufficient warrant for its truth, and one in which this situation does not obtain, seems so great as to call for an explanation – and that the only explanation is that the two strata concern different subject-matters. Indeed, Baier is content to let the mental–physical distinction stand or fall with the distinction between "private" subject-matters and "public" subject-matters, and he therefore assumes that to show that "introspective reports are necessarily about something private, and that being about something private is *incompatible with being* about something public"[13] is to show, once and for all, that the Identity Theory involves a conceptual confusion. Baier, in short, is undertaking to show that "once private, always private."

He argues for his view as follows:

> To say that one day our physiological knowledge will increase to such an extent that we shall be able to make absolutely reliable encephalograph-based claims about people's experiences, is only to say that, if carefully checked, our encephalograph-based claims about "experiences" will always be *correct*, i.e., will make the *same claims* as a *truthful* introspective reports. If correct encephalograph-based claims about Smith's experiences contradict Smith's introspective reports, we shall be entitled to infer that he is *lying*. In that sense, what Smith says will no longer go. But we cannot of course infer that he is making a mistake, for that is nonsense … *However good the evidence may be, such a physiological theory can never be used to show to the sufferer that he was mistaken in thinking that he had a pain, for such a mistake is inconceivable.* The sufferer's epistemological authority must therefore be better than the best physiological theory can ever be. Physiology can therefore never provide a person with more than *evidence* that someone else is having an experience of one sort or another. It can never lay down *criteria* for saying that someone is having an experience of a certain sort. Talk about brain-processes therefore must be about something other than talk about

---

[11] Smart, "Sensations and Brain Processes," p. 169.    [12] Baier, p. 63.    [13] Baier, p. 59.

experiences. Hence, introspective reports and brain process talk cannot be merely different ways of talking about the same thing.[14]

Smart's own reply to this line of argument is to admit that

> No physiological evidence, say from a gadget attached to my skull, could make me withdraw the statement that I have a pain when as a matter of fact I feel a pain. For example, the gadget might show no suitable similarities of cerebral processes on the various occasions on which I felt a pain . . . I must, I think, agree with Baier that if the sort of situation which we have just envisaged did in fact come about, then I should have to reject the brain process thesis, and would perhaps espouse dualism.[15]

But this is not the interesting case. The interesting case is the one in which suitable similarities are in fact found to occur – the same similarities in all subjects – until one day (long after all empirical generalizations about sensations *qua* sensations have been subsumed under physiological laws, and long after direct manipulation of the brain has become the exclusive method of relieving pain) somebody (call him Jones) thinks he has no pain, but the encephalograph says that the brain-process correlated with pain did occur. (Let us imagine that Jones himself is observing the gadget, and that the problem about whether he might have made a mistake is a problem for Jones; this eliminates the possibility of lying.) Now in most cases in which one's observation throws doubt on a correlation which is so central to current scientific explanations, one tries to eliminate the possibility of observational error. But in Baier's view it would be absurd for Jones to do this, for "a mistake is inconceivable." Actually, however, it is fairly clear what Jones's first move would be – he will begin to suspect that he does not know what pain is – i.e., that he is not using the word "pain" in the way in which his fellows use it.[16]

So now Jones looks about for independent verification of the hypothesis that he does not use "I am in pain" incorrectly. But here he runs up against the familiar difficulty about the vocabulary used in making introspective reports – the difficulty of distinguishing between "misuse of language" and "mistake in judgment," between (a) recognizing the state of affairs which obtains for what it is, but describing it wrongly because the words used in the description are not the right words, and (b) being able to describe it

---

[14] Baier, pp. 64–5; italics added.

[15] Smart, "Brain Processes and Incorrigibility – a Reply to Professor Baier," *Australasian Journal of Philosophy*, 40 (1962), p. 68.

[16] This problem will remain, of course, even if Jones merely *thinks* about whether he is in pain, but does not say anything.

rightly once it is recognized for what it is, but not in fact recognizing it for what it is (in the way in which one deceived by an illusion does not recognize the situation for what it is). If we do not have a way of determining which of these situations obtains, we do not have a genuine contrast between misnaming and misjudging. To see that there is no genuine contrast in this case, suppose that Jones was not burned prior to the time that he hitches on the encephalograph, but now he is. When he is, the encephalograph says that the brain-process constantly correlated with pain-reports occurs in Jones's brain. However, although he exhibits pain-behavior, Jones thinks that he does not feel pain. (But, now as in the past, he both exhibits pain-behavior and thinks that he feels pain when he is frozen, stuck, struck, racked, etc.) Now is it that he does not know that *pain* covers what you feel when you are burned as well as what you feel when you are stuck, struck, etc.? Or is it that he really does not feel pain when he is burned? Suppose we tell Jones that what he feels when he is burned is *also* called "pain." Suppose he then admits that he does feel *something*, but insists that what he feels is quite *different* from what he feels when he is stuck, struck, etc. Where does Jones go from here? Has he failed to learn the language properly, or is he correctly (indeed infallibly) reporting that he has different sensations than those normally had in the situation in question? (Compare the parallel question in the case of a man who uses "blue" in all the usual ways except that he refuses to grant that blue is a color – on the ground that it is so different from red, yellow, orange, violet, etc.)

The only device which would decide this question would be to establish a convention that anyone who sincerely denied that he felt a pain while exhibiting pain-behavior and being burned *ipso facto* did not understand how to use "pain." This denial would *prove* that he lacked such an understanding. But this would be a dangerous path to follow. For not to understand when to use the word "pain" in non-inferential reports is presumably to be unable to know which of one's sensations to call a "pain." And the denial that one felt pain in the circumstances mentioned would only prove such inability if one indeed *had* the sensation normally called a pain. So now we would have a public criterion, satisfaction of which would count as showing that the subject had such a sensation – i.e., that he felt a pain even though he did not think that he did. But if such a criterion exists, its application overrides any contradictory report that he may make – for such a report will be automatically disallowed by the fact that it constitutes a demonstration that he does not know what he is talking about. The dilemma is that either a report about one's sensations which violates a certain public criterion is a sufficient condition for saying that the reporter does not know how to use "pain" in the correct way, or there is no such criterion. If there is, the fact that one cannot be mistaken about pains does not entail that sincere reports of pain cannot be overridden. If there is not, then there is no way to answer the question formulated at the end of the last paragraph, and hence no way to eliminate the possibility that Jones may not know what pain is. Now since the *a priori* probability that he does not is a good deal higher than the *a priori* probability that the psychophysiological theory of Jones's era is mistaken, this theory has little to fear from Jones. (Although it would have a great deal to fear from a sizable accumulation of cases like Jones's.)

To sum up this point, we may look back at the italicized sentence in the above quotation from Baier. We now see that the claim that "such a mistake is inconceivable" is an ellipsis for the claim that a mistake, made *by one who knows what pain is*, is inconceivable, for only this expanded form will entail that when Jones and the encephalograph disagree, Jones is always right. But when formulated in this way our infallibility about our pains can be seen to be empty. Being infallible about something would be useful only if we could draw the usual distinction between misnaming and misjudging, and, having ascertained that we were not misnaming, know that we were not misjudging. But where there are no criteria for misjudging (or to put it more accurately, where in the crucial cases the criteria for misjudging turn out to be the same as the criteria for misnaming) than to say that we are infallible is to pay ourselves an empty compliment. Our neighbors will not hesitate to ride roughshod over our reports of our sensations unless they are assured that we know our way around among them, and we cannot satisfy them on this point unless, up to a certain point, we tell the same sort of story about them as they do. The limits of permissible stories are flexible enough for us to be able to convince them occasionally that we have odd sensations, but not flexible enough for us to use these surprising sensations to break down, at one blow, well-confirmed scientific theories. As in the case of other infallible pronouncements, the price of retaining one's epistemological authority is a decent respect for the opinions of mankind.

Thus, the common-sense remark that first-person reports always will be a better source of information about the occurrence of pains than any other source borrows its plausibility from the fact that we normally do not raise questions about a man's ability to use the word "pain" correctly. Once we *do* raise such questions seriously (as in the case of Jones), we realize that the question (1) "Does he know which sensations are called 'pains'?" and (2) "Is he a good judge of whether he is in pain or not?" are simply two ways of asking the same question: *viz.*, "Can we fit his pain-reports into our scheme for explaining and predicting pains?" or, more bluntly, "Shall we disregard his pain-reports or not?" And once we see this we realize that if "always be a better source of information" means "will never be overridden on the sort of grounds on which presumed observational errors are overridden elsewhere in science," then our common-sensical remark is probably false. If "always be a better source of information" means merely "can only be overridden on the basis of a charge of misnaming, and never on the basis of a charge of misjudging," then our common-sensical remark turns out to depend upon a distinction that is not there.

This Wittgensteinian point that sensation-reports must conform to public criteria or else be disallowed may also be brought out in the following way. We determine whether to take a surprising first-person report of pain or its absence seriously (that is, whether to say that the sensation reported is something that science must try to explain) by seeing whether the reporter's overall pattern of pain-reporting is, by the usual behavioral and environmental criteria, normal. Now suppose that these public criteria (for "knowing how to use 'pain' ") change as physiology and technology progress. Suppose, in particular, that we find it convenient to speed up the learning of contrastive observation predicates (such as "painful," "tickling," etc.) by supplying children with portable encephalographs-cum-teaching-machines which, whenever the appropriate brain-process occurs, murmur the appropriate term in their ears. Now "appropriate brain-process" will start out by meaning "brain-process constantly correlated with sincere utterances of 'I'm in pain' by people taught the use of 'pain' in the old rough-and-ready way." But soon it will come to mean, "the brain-process which we have always programed the machine to respond to with a murmur of 'pain.' " (A meter is [now, but was not always] what matches the Standard Meter; intelligence is [now, but was not always] what intelligence tests test; pains will be [but are not now] what the Standard "Pain"-Training Program calls "pain.") Given this situation, it would make sense to say things like "You say you are in pain, and I'm sure you are sincere, but you can see for yourself that your brain is not in the state to which you were trained to respond to with "Pain," so apparently the training did not work, and you do not yet understand what pain is." In such a situation, our "inability to be mistaken" about our pains would remain, but our "final epistemological authority" on the subject would be gone, for there would be a standard procedure for overriding our reports. Our inability to be mistaken is, after all, no more than our ability to have such hypothetical statements as "If you admit that I'm sincere and that I know the language, you have to accept what I say" accepted by our fellows. But this asset can only be converted into final epistemological authority if we can secure both admissions. Where a clear-cut public criterion *does* exist for "knowing the language," inability to be mistaken does not entail inability to be overridden.

Now Baier might say that if such criteria did exist, then we should no longer be talking about what we presently mean by "pains." I do not think that this needs to be conceded,[17] but suppose that it is. Would this mean that there was now a subject-matter which was not being discussed – *viz.,* the private subject-matter the existence of which Baier's argument was intended to demonstrate? That we once had contact with such a subject-matter, but lost it? These rhetorical questions are meant to suggest that Baier's explanation of the final epistemological authority of first-person reports of pains by the fact that this "logic" is "a function of this type of subject-matter" rather than, as Smart thinks, a convention – is an explanation of the obscure by the more obscure. More precisely, it will not be an explanation of the epistemological authority in question – but only an unenlightening redescription of it – unless Baier can give a meaning to the term "private subject-matter" other than "kind of thing which is reported in reports which cannot be overridden." These considerations show the need for stepping back from Baier's argument and considering the criteria which he is using to demarcate distinct subject-matters.

## VI   "Privacy" as a criterion of categoreal demarcation

The closest Baier comes to giving a definition of "private subject-matter" is to say that

> We must say that 'I have a pain' is about 'something private,' because in making this remark we report something which is (1) *necessarily owned* ... (2) *necessarily exclusive and unsharable* ... (3) *necessarily imperceptible by the senses* ... (4) *necessarily asymmetrical,* for whereas it makes no sense to say 'I could see (or hear) that I had a pain,' it makes quite good sense to say 'I could see (or hear) that *he* had a pain'; (5) something about the possession

---

[17] My reasons for thinking this concession unnecessary are the same as those presented in some recent articles by Hilary Putnam: cf. "Minds and Machines," in S. Hook, ed., *Dimensions of Mind* (New York, 1960), pp. 138–61, esp. pp. 153–60; "The Analytic and the Synthetic," *Minnesota Studies in the Philosophy of Science,* 3 (1962), pp. 358–97; "Brains and Behavior," in R. J. Butler (ed.), *Analytic Philosophy,* II (Oxford, 1965).

of which the person who claims to possess it could not possibly examine, consider, or weigh any evidence, although other people could ... and lastly (6) it is something about which the person whose private slate it is has final epistemological authority, for it does not make sense to say 'I have a pain unless I am mistaken.'[18]

Now this definition of "something private" entails that nothing could be private except a state of a person, and is constructed to delimit all and only those states of a person which we call his "mental" states. To say that mental states are private is to say simply that mental states are described in the way in which mental states are described. But it is not hard to take *any* Rylean category of terms (call it C), list all the types of sentence-frames which do and do not make sense when their gaps are filled with terms belonging to this category, and say that "something C" is distinguished by the fact that it is "necessarily X," "necessarily Y," etc., where "X" and "Y" are labels for the fact that certain sentence-frames will or will not receive these terms as gap-fillers. For example, consider the thesis that:

> We must say that 'The devil is in that corner' is about 'something super-natural' because in making this report we report something which is *necessarily intangible*, since it makes no sense to ask about the texture of his skin, not *necessarily simply-located*, since it does not follow from the fact that a supernatural being is in the corner that the same supernatural being is not simultaneously at the other side of the globe, *necessarily immortal*, since it does not make sense to say that a supernatural being has died, *necessarily perceptible to exorcists*, since it would not make sense to say that a man was an exorcist and did not perceive the devil when he was present.

Are devils hallucinations? No, because when one reports an hallucination one reports something which, though intangible, is simply located, is neither mortal nor immortal, and is not always perceptible to exorcists. Are reports of devils reports of hallucinations? No, because reports of devils are reports of something supernatural and reports of hallucinations are reports of something private. Is it simply because we lack further information about devils that we take exorcists' sincere reports as the best possible source for information about them? No, for this suggestion confuses the supernatural character of the subject-matter with the availability of external evidence. Those without the supernatural powers with which the exorcist is gifted may find ways of gathering *evidence* for the presence of supernatural beings, but they can never formulate an overriding and independent *criterion* for saying that such a being is present. Their

---

[18] Baier, p. 60; the numbers in parentheses have been added.

theories might become so good that we might sometimes say that a given exorcist was *lying*, but we could never say that he was *mistaken*.

If this pastiche of Baier's argument seems beside the point, it is presumably either (1) because the language-game I have described is not in fact played, or else (2) because "necessarily intangible, not necessarily simply located, necessarily immortal, and necessarily perceptible to exorcists" it does not delimit a subject-matter in the way in which "necessarily owned, exclusive, imperceptible by the senses, asymmetrical, etc., etc." does. In (1) one has to ask "what if it *had* been played?" After all, if the technique of detecting distinct subject-matters which Baier uses is a generally applicable technique, and not just constructed *ad hoc* to suit our Cartesian intuitions, then it ought to work on imaginary as well as real language-games. But if it is, we ought to be able to formulate rules for applying it which would tell us *why* (2) is the case. For if we cannot, and if the language-game described once was played, then Baier's objection to the Identity Theory is an objection to the theory that reports of visible supernatural beings are reports of hallucinations.

Baier gives no more help in seeing what these rules would be. But I think that the root of Baier's conviction that "something private" is a suitable candidate for being a "distinct subject-matter" is the thesis that certain terms are *intrinsically* observation predicates, and signify, so to speak, "natural explananda." When in quest of such predicates we look to the "foundations" of empirical knowledge, we tend to rapidly identify "observation predicate" with "predicate occurring in report having final epistemological authority" with "predicate occurring in report about something private." This chain of identifications leaves us with the suspicion that if there were no longer a private subject-matter to be infallible about, the whole fabric of empirical inquiry about public matters would be left up in the air, unsupported by any absolute epistemological authority. The suggestion that the distinction between items reportable in infallible reports and items not so reportable is "ultimate," or "irreducible," or "categorical," owes its intuitive force to the difficulty of imagining a stage in the progress of inquiry in which there was not *some* situation in which absolute epistemological authority about *something* would be granted to *somebody*.

There probably could *not* be such a stage, for inquiry cannot proceed if everything is to be doubted at once, and if inquiry is even to get off the ground we need to get straight about what is to be questioned and what not. These practical dictates show the kernel of truth in the notion that inquiry cannot proceed without a foundation. Where we slide from truth into error is in assuming that certain items are *naturally* reportable in infallible reports, and thus assume that the items presently so reportable always were and always will be reportable (and conversely for items not presently so reportable). A pain looks like the paradigm of such an item, with the situation described by "seems to me as if I were seeing something red" almost as well-qualified. But in both cases, we can imagine situations in which we should feel justified in overriding sincere reports using these predicates. More important, we see that the device which we should use to justify ourselves in such situations – *viz.*, "The reporter may not know how to use the word … " – is one which can apply in *all* proposed cases. Because this escape-hatch is always available, and because the question of whether the reporter does know how to use the word or not is probably not itself a question which could ever be settled by recourse to any absolute epistemological authority, the situation envisaged by Baier – namely, the body of current scientific theory foundering upon the rock of a single overriding report – can probably never arise. Baier sees a difference in kind between the weight of evidence produced by such a theory and the single, authoritative, *criterion* provided by such a report. But since there can be no overriding report until the ability of the speaker to use the words used in the report is established, and since this is to be established only by the weight of the evidence and not by recourse to any single criterion, this difference in kind (even though it may indeed be "firmly embedded in the way we talk" for millennia) is always capable of being softened into a difference of degree by further empirical inquiry.

## VII　Reductionist philosophical theories and categoreal distinctions

In the preceding sections of this chapter I have constantly invoked the fact that language changes as empirical discoveries are made, in order to argue that the thesis that "What people now call 'sensations' might be discovered to be brain-processes" is sensible and unconfused. The "deviance" of a statement of this thesis should not, I have been urging, blind us to the facts that (a) entities referred to by expressions in one Rylean category may also be referred to by expressions in another, (b) expressions in the first category may drop out of the language once this identity of reference is realized, and (c) the thesis in question is a natural way of expressing the result of this realization in the case of "sensation" and "brain-process." Now a critic might object that this strategy is subject to a *reductio ad absurdum*. For the same fact about linguistic change would seem to justify the claim that *any* statement of the form (S) "What people call 'X's' may be discovered to be Y's" is *always* sensible and unconfused. Yet this seems paradoxical, for consider the result of substituting, say, "neutrino" for "X" and "mushroom" for "Y." If the resulting statement is not conceptually confused, what statement is?

In answer to this objection, I should argue that it is a mistake to attribute "conceptual confusions" to *statements*. No statement can be known to express a conceptual confusion simply by virtue of an acquaintance with the meanings of its component terms. Confusion is a property of people. Deviance is a property of utterances. Deviant utterances made by using sentences of the form (S) *may* betoken confusion on the part of the speaker about the meanings of words, but it may simply indicate a vivid (but unconfused) imagination, or perhaps (as in the neutrino–mushroom case) merely idle fancy. Although the making of such statements may be *prima facie* evidence of conceptual confusion – i.e., of the fact that the speaker is insufficiently familiar with the language to find a nondeviant way of making his point – this evidence is only *prima facie*, and questioning may bring out evidence pointing the other way. Such questioning may show that the speaker actually has some detailed suggestions about possible empirical results which would point to the discovery in question, or that he has no such suggestions, but is nevertheless not inclined to use the relevant words in any *other* deviant utterances, and to cheerfully admit the deviance of his original utterance. The possibility of such evidence, pointing to imagination or to fancy rather than to confusion, shows that from the fact that certain questions are typically asked, and certain statements typically made, by victims of conceptual confusion, it does not follow that all those who use the sentences used to ask these questions or to make these statements are thus victimized.

This confusion about confusion is due to the fact that philosophers who propound "reductionist" theories (such as "There is no insensate matter," "There are no minds," "There are no physical objects," etc.) often *have* been conceptually confused. Such theories are often advocated as solutions to pseudo-problems whose very formulation involves deviant uses of words – uses which in fact result from a confusion between the uses of two or more senses of the same term, or between two or more related terms (e.g., "name" and "word") or between the kind of questions appropriately asked of entities referred to by one set of terms and the kind appropriately asked of entities referred to by another. (That these deviant uses *are* the result of such confusion, it should be noticed, is only capable of being determined by questioning of those who use them – and we only feel *completely* safe in making this diagnosis when the original user has, in the light of the linguistic facts drawn to his attention, admitted that his putative "problem" has been dissolved.) Because reductionist theories may often be choked off at the source by an examination of uses of language, antireductionist philosophers have lately become prone to use "conceptual confusion" or "category-mistake" as an all-purpose diagnosis for any deviant utterance in the mouth of a philosopher. But this is a mistake. Predictions of the sort illustrated by (S) may be turned to confused purposes, and they may be made by confused people. But we could only infer with certainty from the deviance of the utterance of a sentence of the form (S) to the conceptual confusion of the speaker if we had a map of the categories which are exhibited in all possible languages, and were thus in a position to say that the cross-category identification envisaged by the statement was eternally impossible. In other words, we should only be in a position to make this inference with certainty if we knew that empirical inquiry could *never* bring about the sort of linguistic change which permits the nondeviant use of "There are no X's" in the case of the "X's" to which the statement in question refers. But philosophers are in no position to say that such change is impossible. The hunt for categoreal confusions at the source of reductionist philosophical theories is an extremely valuable enterprise. But their successes in this enterprise should not lead linguistic philosophers to think that they can do better what metaphysicians did badly – namely, prove the irreducibility of entities. Traditional materialism embodied many confusions, but at its heart was the unconfused prediction about future empirical inquiry which is the Identity Theory. The confusions may be eradicated without affecting the plausibility or interest of the prediction.[19]

---

[19] I have been greatly helped in preparing this chapter by the comments of Richard Bernstein, Keith Gunderson, Amélie Rorty, and Richard Schmitt.

CHAPTER 7

# Do analysts and metaphysicians disagree?

My title suggests that there are two well-defined schools of philosophers – the "analytic" and the "metaphysical." I am aware of the sort of over-simplification which such labeling produces, but I think that it is sometimes justified. Despite the obvious differences between, say, Goodman, Wisdom, and Austin, and the equally obvious differences between Whitehead, Heidegger, and Maritain, some important metaphilosophical disagreements clearly exist between a position which is the least common denominator of the views of philosophers who have taken "the linguistic turn," and a position which is the least common denominator of the views of those who have not. The labels "analyst" and "metaphysician" are at least brief, and using them is no more unfair to one side than to the other.

As my title also suggests, I find it very difficult to formulate these metaphilosophical disagreements. They are usually conceived as centering around a disagreement about what *method* to pursue. My principal thesis in this chapter will be that none of the familiar ways of characterizing such alternative methods are successful.

I shall also argue that it would be a mistake to say that analysts and metaphysicians have different subject-matters. It is, to my mind, wildly misleading to say that analytic philosophers take language as their subject-matter, whereas metaphysicians take nature or experience as theirs. I should hold that the common subject-matter of both schools is, simply, the history of philosophy. In other words, I think that the only way of describing the subject-matter of either school which does not beg important metaphilosophical questions is to say that both take as their subject the various perplexities and paradoxes found in the philosophical tradition. The aim of both schools is to find a set of truths which will resolve these perplexities and problems – truths which will have a maximum of intuitive plausibility and, taken together as a system, a maximum of theoretical elegance. In my view, the dialectical moves which are made in formulating and defending such truths are much the same on both sides of the fence. Among both analysts and metaphysicians, the ultimate criteria are set by a common aim – that of striking a proper balance between effectiveness (at resolving problems), plausibility, and elegance. The apparent differences of subject-matter and method are illusions created by the use of different jargons in which to formulate these dialectical moves.

From here on, what I have to say falls into three parts. First, I shall offer a three-fold division between "critical," "speculative," and "empirical" philosophers and comment on how this division illuminates the quarrel between the metaphysicians and the analysts. Second, I shall take up, and criticize, the claim that analysts ask "second-order questions" and metaphysicians "first-order questions" (a distinction I am borrowing from Mortimer Adler's *The Conditions of Philosophy* – a book to which I shall recur from time to time throughout the chapter).[1] Third, I shall take up the distinction between "solving" and "dissolving" problems, and argue that this too is of little help in understanding the quarrel with which we are concerned.

By a "critical" philosopher I mean one who holds that philosophy is, in so far as it is a discipline in which argument and cooperative inquiry are possible, the attempt to dissolve all the traditional philosophical problems and thus to make the discipline of philosophy obsolete. As Adler notes, a currently popular view is that "philosophy is now barren because it has at last fully discharged its procreative function – its mothering of all the special sciences, both natural and social, which, one by one, have split off from the parent stem."[2]

By a "speculative" philosopher I mean one who holds the negative thesis that philosophical inquiry should not be thought of as a pursuit of truths of the sort about which agreement can be reached by argument. On this view, philosophy is much more like poetry than like the sciences. We need not quibble about whether poetry aims at a special sort of truth, as long as we agree that the sort of truth at which it aims is not one about which argument is possible (except in a very diluted and Pickwickian sense of "argument"). On this view, philosophy does not aim at finding solutions to problems. Rather, it aims at finding new ways of seeing things through finding new ways of saying things.

[1] Mortimer J. Adler, *Conditions of Philosophy* (New York, 1965).    [2] *Ibid.*, p. 5.

It is harder to specify what I intend by the term "empirical philosopher" but the following conditions will have to do: I shall call a philosopher an empirical philosopher if:

(1)   He believes that there are procedures by which rational agreement can be reached on solutions to at least some of the traditional philosophical problems.

(2)   He defends this first belief by saying that (i) philosophy's method is either simply a description of what experience is like, or else a form of the hypothetico-deductive method exemplified by the empirical sciences: (ii) that philosophy is distinguished from these sciences either by (a) being concerned with a different sort of experience than that which supplies the premises for arguments in any other empirical discipline, or (b) having as its task the proposal of hypotheses of a greater generality than those produced by the empirical sciences.

These three conceptions of philosophy are designed to include all traditional metaphilosophical views, with two exceptions. The first exception is real – the rationalistic view that philosophy consists in the deduction of conclusions from self-evident premises, with no appeal to experience to test these premises. I want to disregard this notion simply because it plays no part in the contemporary scene. The second exception I regard as merely apparent. It is the view that philosophy should pursue a transcendental method – not erecting hypotheses on the basis of experience but discovering conditions of the possibility of experience. I want to disregard this notion because I do not see, in any transcendental philosopher (as, for example, Kant or Hegel or Husserl or Strawson), any interesting way of distinguishing this enterprise from what I have called empirical philosophy. I have intentionally defined empirical philosophy so broadly that the notion covers whatever Kant is doing in the *Transcendental Analytic* and whatever Strawson is doing in *Individuals*. I do not see any except a rhetorical difference between philosophers who say that they are appealing to experience (or language) for the justification of general principles about the world and those who say that an examination of experience (or language) permits us to infer general principles about the possibility of experience (or language).

So much for my three-fold categorization. I do not recommend these categories as pigeonholes, into one of which every philosopher will fit. One rarely finds a pure case. But I think this trichotomy is a useful heuristic device for spotting difficulties in a philosopher's metaphilosophical views, and disharmonies between these views and his actual practice. Thus, the later Wittgenstein is professedly a critical philosopher, but his practice often makes him seem an empirical philosopher. Austin and Adler are professedly empirical philosophers, but their practice often makes them seem like critical philosophers. Santayana is a professedly speculative philosopher, but his practice often makes him seem an empirical philosopher. Heidegger sometimes talks as if he were an empirical philosopher and sometimes as if he were a speculative philosopher, but his practice is almost impossible to classify. Turning now to an application of these categories to the quarrel between the analysts and the metaphysicians, I think one has to say something like this: Analysts are, by and large, divided into professedly critical philosophers (like Wisdom, the early Carnap and the early Bergmann) and professedly empirical philosophers (like Austin, Putnam and Strawson). Nevertheless, one finds in the practice of all these philosophers a bent toward critical philosophy – in the sense that the test of success of the application of their empirical methods turns out to be the dissolution of certain traditional problems. Metaphysicians are, by and large, divided into professedly empirical and professedly speculative philosophers – into philosophers who have an explicit metaphilosophical view according to which some quasi-scientific procedure directed upon experience will produce philosophical truth, and philosophers who say "don't worry so much about decision-procedures and criteria, just try to find some way of expressing the nature of things, or some way of gaining wisdom." Nevertheless, one finds that a large proportion of the work of both sorts of metaphysicians consists in dissolving problems, in exposing the false presuppositions which have generated traditional problems – in short, in doing precisely the work the critical philosopher wants done. If these remarks accurately describe the contemporary situation, then the difficulty of my title question is clear. For if the analysts and the metaphysicians are, in practice, critical philosophers, and if neither school would whole-heartedly accept this description, then we need to find out why they would not, and, perhaps, wonder if something is wrong with our original trichotomy.

I turn now to the second part of my discussion – the distinction between first-order and second-order questions. By beginning here, I can say something about the suggestion that my trichotomy is incomplete and unwieldy. Such a suggestion might be backed up by saying that even if such postpositivistic analytic philosophers as Austin, Putnam, and Strawson are (in their explicit professions) neither critical nor speculative philosophers, they cannot be called empirical philosophers, since they deal with language rather than with experience, and pursue linguistic rather than empirical methods. I wish to bring these postpositivistic linguistic philosophers under the rubric of empirical philosophy. To do so, I need to attack the distinction between "questions of language" and "questions of fact." In my opinion, many linguistic philosophers and many critics of linguistic philosophy are still saddling themselves with an awkward and confusing pre-Quinian view of this distinction when they come to discuss metaphilosophical issues, even though they may have abandoned the distinction in discussing other matters.

The first point to be made about the distinction between premises drawn from language and premises drawn from experience is simply that language is part of what we experience. It is not self-evident why consulting language should be *opposed* to turning to experience, rather than thought of simply as a specification of the sorts of experience that are relevant to a given inquiry. The primary reason why the opposition exists is that analytic philosophers have often phrased their program in terms of the analytic–synthetic distinction, and have identified analytic propositions with "propositions about language." But it seems clear (if I may beg certain disputed questions about both analyticity and reiterated modalities) that it is a synthetic truth that certain sentences express analytic propositions. In other words, it is an empirical truth that the various expressions of our language exhibit the "logical" relations to one another that they do. So even if we say that analytic propositions are "about language," we can still say that the sort of linguistic philosophy which, in Strawson's phrase, aims at "describing the logical behavior of the linguistic expressions of natural languages" is an empirical discipline.

The second point to be made is that linguistic philosophers are no longer as confident as they once were about the claim that the "logical behavior" of linguistic expressions in natural languages can be clearly marked out from other facts about these expressions. One effect of this uncertainty is to make it evident that a claim to have detected such a piece of logical behavior cannot be backed up simply by inviting inspection of the language. Rather, what is required is a fairly complex theory about the expressions in question. Such a theory would contain, at a minimum, hypotheses about the meaning of these expressions; hypotheses which can compete successfully with alternative hypotheses. Such hypotheses are pieces of empirical theories, and the methods of constructing and testing such theories do not differ in any interesting way from those used in other empirical disciplines.

Given these two points, it seems reasonable to say that post-positivistic linguistic philosophy is using an hypothetico-deductive method, drawing upon a restricted range of experiences to confirm and disconfirm theories. If the matter could be left here, it would seem reasonable to say that this sort of philosophy was empirical, rather than speculative or critical. But we cannot leave it here, for it is not clear what relation such linguistic philosophers take to exist between hypotheses about the meaning (or, more generally, the logical behavior) of expressions on the one hand and solutions to traditional philosophical problems on the other. *Prima facie* there is a great gulf fixed between a straightforwardly and explicitly empirical philosopher like Adler and a linguistic philosopher like Austin, and the gulf obviously has something to do with differing conceptions of the relevance of linguistics to philosophy.

The difficulty in putting one's finger on these differing conceptions is that it is not clear what difference it makes whether we ask "What is the nature of x?" or "How do we use the word x?" There would be a difference if we were sometimes in a position to claim that we use the word "x" in such a way as to distort our conception of the nature of x, or to claim that more can be known about the nature of x than either language or science reveals. It is natural to suppose that metaphysicians are in such a position – for if they were not, why should they object to their analytic colleagues using the formal mode of speech? But, of course, it is not clear how a metaphysician could make good either claim. I shall come back in a moment to this question, but first let me note that the question cuts both ways. For one might equally well ask the analyst why he bothers with the formal mode of speech, and why he does not stick to the traditional "first-order" questions.

The older, positivistic, answer to the question of the utility of the formal mode of speech was that it served notice that answers to philosophical questions "told us nothing about the world." This answer presupposed a distinction between "truths of language" and "truths of fact" which ran parallel with the distinction between formal and empirical disciplines. Adler apparently accepts this older answer, since he wishes to classify analytic philosophy with pure mathematics – saying that it "deals with universals" and that its results are "not falsifiable by appeal to any experience." As I have remarked earlier, it would now be hard to find an analytic philosopher who would accept this view of the matter. The writings of Quine, Putnam, and Ziff have effectively sabotaged Carnap's original notion of philosophy as a formal discipline. The newer answer which would be given would, I think, run as follows: the only reason for using the formal mode of speech is to remind ourselves that there are no methods except attending to actual or possible linguistic behavior to decide questions about the nature of x, unless these questions can be settled by further data about the behavior of x's.

In other words, recent analytic philosophers would say that the only point to asking "How do we use 'x'?" is just to remind the metaphysicians that they have nowhere to turn to except to language. These philosophers would be quite happy, sometimes even eager, to say that discovering, for example, a set of necessary and sufficient conditions for the truth of sentences of the form "S knows that p" *does* tell us something about the world. It tells us what knowledge is – in any sense in which we can know "what knowledge is" without further psychological experimentation.

It would seem, then, that the only real issue between the analyst and the metaphysician is the one I referred to earlier – the question of whether the metaphysician has an alternative method of inquiry at hand. I may point out first that Adler's suggestion that philosophy is a "non-investigative" empirical discipline dealing with "common experience" is of no help here. In the first place, it is not clear that an analyst would disagree – since he would not want to say that in answering a question of the form "What expression would I use in the following circumstances?" a native speaker of a language consults any "special" experiences he may have had, nor that he performs an "investigation." In the second place, what we need is an answer to the question: can I find out anything about x by consulting "common experience" that I cannot find out by consulting the linguistic behavior of those who use the expression "x"?

If we try to answer this question by turning from Adler's general characterization of philosophy to the "tests of truth" he proposes, we find that these tests – empirical truth, logical consistency, harmony between principles pertaining to theory and those pertaining to practice, and ability of philosophical principles to resolve questions arising out of scientific inquiry – are ones with which no analytic philosopher would quarrel. Given this sort of agreement, and the fact that no metaphysician I know of has explained what procedure we might use to discover either the inaccuracy or the incompleteness of an account of the nature of x drawn from a description of the uses of "x," we are forced to speculate. The following suggestion perhaps expresses the metaphysician's discomfiture with the analyst's procedure: there could be no quarrel, he might say, with the claim that we found the nature of x by finding out how "x" was used if it were the case that accounts of the use of various expressions were always consistent with each other. But philosophical problems owe their origin precisely to the fact that our usage generates paradoxes, antinomies, and absurdities. So even if "linguistic phenomenology" is a necessary first step, it can hardly be the whole story.

If the metaphysician takes this line, analysts will tend to reply in one of two ways. Some would say that these paradoxes, antinomies and absurdities are not really there – that incomplete and prejudiced accounts of usage have made it appear that they are there, but better accounts remove this appearance. Others will say that although these perplexities are real, they are not to be resolved by finding out more about the nature of x, but by altering our usage so as to eliminate them – by reforming language. Most analysts would, I think, combine both replies – and say that we do not yet know whether perplexity can be removed by better accounts of usage, but that if not, linguistic proposals are the only alternative. If these proposals amount to urging the adoption of a full-scale "Ideal Language" – or, in older language, a metaphysical system – then so be it.

Here again we seem to be at an impasse. The metaphysician regards the analyst's appropriation of the term "metaphysics" as merely perverse. The analyst asks why regarding metaphysical systems as so many proposals for the reform of language should be so disturbing. If, the analyst may say, you want to consider these proposals for different ways of speaking as discoveries about the world, go ahead. Just do not pretend that you have any criterion for such discoveries save the absence of paradoxes, antinomies, and absurdities from the language you suggest we use.

Before acknowledging that this impasse is hopeless, however, we may try another tack. Coming back once again to Adler, we find him saying that "Therapeutic positivism and analysis try to cure philosophy of puzzles and paradoxes, all of which spring from 'the way of ideas' and the consequent 'doctrine of sense data,' while at the same time giving full sway to the psychologizing tendency that is the sole source of these puzzles and para-paradoxes."[3]

If we set aside the historically dubious claim that all the puzzles and paradoxes which analysts try to dissolve spring from the "way of ideas" (did Aristotle's perplexities about knowledge of particulars so spring?) we can note that Adler is here acknowledging that in their substantive anti-Cartesian and anti-Lockean conclusions post-positivistic analysts and empirical metaphysicians often do agree. Presumably, the "psychologizing tendency" which Adler speaks of now emerges only in these analysts' metaphilosophy, and no longer in their epistemology or their metaphysics. Adler seems to be suggesting that it is high time the analysts brought their

---

[3] *Ibid.*, pp. 277–8.

metaphilosophy in line with their newly found realistic epistemology and dropped their "second-order" inquiries. This suggestion is valid if it is indeed the case that

> to the extent that they (the analytic and linguistic philosophers) still accept the positivists' relegation of philosophy to the plane of second-order questions, they do so because they retain in some measure the view of man's cognitive powers that lies at the root of positivism – that is, a view opposed to [the position that affirms] man's mind or intellect as a cognitive power, distinct from and irreducible to all of his sensitive faculties.[4]

I do not think, however, that this diagnosis of the analysts' attitude is accurate. I have offered above an alternative account of analysts' preference for the formal mode of speech, and I have been arguing throughout that Adler's own notion of "relegation to the plane of second-order questions" is unenlightening unless we have a clearer understanding of why the mode of speech we employ should matter so much. Still, we can make one further attempt at a *rapprochement* with Adler. Setting aside the particular diagnosis which we offer of the analysts' predilections, we might nonetheless wish to say with Adler that "the answers philosophers give to second-order questions are determined or affected by their answers to first-order questions ... This means that first-order questions ... have primacy in philosophical inquiry."[5] To avoid some problems already discussed, I shall now construe "first-order questions" to mean simply "the traditional questions of metaphysics and epistemology" and construe "second-order questions" to mean questions about what linguistic expressions mean. I thus construe Adler as saying that it is only because we already have some metaphysical and/or epistemological views that we can choose between competing accounts of the meaning of expressions – at least in the case of expressions which are relevant to philosophical problems. This point is plausible enough. Doubtless such antecedent prejudices have played a role – for example, in the positivists' claim to have discovered the meaninglessness of metaphysics by an analysis of the term "meaningful." But the point can be turned around – and often is. Analytic philosophers are fond of remarking that certain metaphysicians have held certain metaphysical or epistemological views only because they misunderstood the meaning of certain expressions – or because they held confused notions about semantics, such as the doctrine that "all words are names." Such claims, it seems to me are no more and no less plausible than Adler's.

[4] *Ibid.*, pp. 77–8.   [5] *Ibid.*, p. 45.

It is hard to believe that all analytic philosophers are in self-deception when they resort to questions about language, and equally hard to believe that metaphysics would not have existed were it not for the prevalence of misunderstandings of language or of absurd (though implicit) philosophies of language. The story is obviously not as simple as all that. It is possible that in some particular cases one or the other of these diagnoses is correct, but there seems to me no clear way to verify this claim in any particular case.

My conclusion from this discussion of Adler's distinction between first-order and second-order questions is, then, that no interesting difference emerges between the analyst and the metaphysician when this distinction is used to contrast their procedures. All that we find is the superficial difference of jargon between the formal and the material modes of speech. Beneath the surface, we find the same activity being conducted – namely, uncovering the antinomies and paradoxes which common sense, or science, or both together, seem to present, and proposals for their resolution. The difference in jargon may perhaps be reflected in the metaphilosophical view taken of such resolutions: the analyst may describe them as proposals for an ideal language, the metaphysician as discoveries about the nature of things. But this difference strikes me as just as verbal and boring as the quarrel about whether electrons are "convenient fictions" or whether they are "real." It is hard to imagine a physicist caring greatly about which they are, and I find it equally hard to imagine that the vital difference between analysts and metaphysicians is simply that between realistic and instrumentalistic ways of describing their results.

It might be objected, however, that I have not come to grips with Adler's point. Specifically, it might be that the difference between realistic and instrumentalistic ways of stating conclusions is a reflection of deeply-lying epistemological disagreement – and that it is this epistemological disagreement which is the really interesting issue in the debate between analysts and metaphysicians. This is a familiar and tempting view, but I think that it is false. My first reason is simply that one can find both realists and instrumentalists in either camp. Carnap and Whitehead are roughly speaking, instrumentalists in their philosophies of science; Sellars and Adler are, roughly speaking, realists. But this agreement seems to bring them no closer in the area of metaphilosophy. My second reason is more general: it is that no epistemology that I know of has, in itself, direct metaphilosophical consequences of a sort that could dictate a choice between analytic philosophy and metaphysics. For example, nothing follows directly about philosophy and its methods from an epistemology that tells us that we can or cannot have *a priori* knowledge of synthetic truths, nor from one which tells us that we do or do not have an intuition of being, nor from one which tells us that there is or is not something unmediated and simply "given" in sensory experience. If one wants to get metaphilosophical consequences out of such epistemological views, one has to add a premise which presents tests of philosophical truth. Such premises would, for example, tell us how to determine that we had actually gotten a synthetic *a priori* truth, or were properly in touch with being, or had demarcated, the "given." Such premises, as I have suggested already, are woefully lacking in most metaphilosophical arguments. The sterility of most debate between analysts and metaphysicians is largely due to the fact that both of them commit this fallacy of leaping from an epistemological to a metaphilosophical claim without stopping to ask about criteria of philosophical truth.

Coming back now to realism versus instrumentalism, I would say that unless we find the difference between these two views reflected in the actual *methods* of philosophers who hold opposing views on this issue, we gain no insight from dwelling upon the contrast. If we found that analytic philosophers who viewed their resolutions of problems as linguistic proposals differed from their metaphysical colleagues by resorting to different patterns of argument, invoking different sorts of premises (where the difference was more than the difference between the formal and the material modes), or employed different criteria for resolution, then we would be getting somewhere. But I do not find any such differences in the literature. The closest approximation to such a difference is that between the analysts' claim to "dissolve" problems and the metaphysician's claim to "solve" them. I do not think that this difference is, in the end, more than a rhetorical one. But it is sufficiently interesting in itself to deserve discussion. So I will conclude my chapter by trying to show that no satisfactory answer to my title question can be found by dwelling on the difference between solving or dissolving philosophical problems.

The simplest and most straightforward way of stating the distinction between solving and dissolving problems is that offered in a recent book by James W. Cornman: "To solve a problem is to answer correctly the question or questions in which the problem is formulated ... To dissolve a problem is to show that at least one necessary condition of the truth of any possible answer to the questions is false."[6] Using this definition of "dissolve" it becomes obvious that dissolving philosophical problems is not a new-fangled notion of the linguistic analysts, but that it has been

---

[6] James W. Cornman, *Metaphysics, Reference, and Language* (New Haven, 1966), p. 228.

standard procedure for every metaphysician since Aristotle. As McKeon, for example, has argued in detail, every important metaphysician has either taken for granted, or argued, that all answers to certain crucial questions posed by his opponents have false presuppositions, and that these are misguided or pointless questions.

So if we want to use the distinction between dissolving and solving problems to describe the difference between analysts and metaphysicians, we shall have to try a different tack. We might say that the difference concerns the *scope* of proposed dissolutions – that although all metaphysicians dissolve *some* philosophical problems, all leave some intact. Analysts, on the other hand, want to dissolve *all* such problems. This is promising, but what would it mean to dissolve *all* philosophical problems? To do so, we should have to show that every possible answer to any question traditionally called "philosophical" would necessarily involve a false presupposition. But this is hard to imagine, for some common-sense beliefs count as answers to philosophical problems. For example, "we see trees, houses, and people" is an answer to a philosophical question about perception. Yet philosophers who embark on a wholesale program of dissolution tend to take common-sense beliefs as, by and large, true. So it seems that we must either say that no such program makes sense, or that some more sophisticated means of stating it needs to be found. The basic difficulty is that philosophers who want to say that common sense, or the conjunction of common sense and science, presents no philosophical problems, and that such problems are artificial and somehow phony, nevertheless seem to be committed to philosophical views. Yet it seems unfair and perverse to say that a man who sees no need to depart from common sense and science, and no need for such a discipline as philosophy, is holding a set of epistemological and metaphysical views. It is like saying to an atheist that "atheism is your religion."

The following way out of this perplexity might be suggested. We might say that an assertion like "we see trees, houses, and people" is not necessarily an epistemological view, and not necessarily an answer to a philosophical question. If we took this line, we might say that an assertion expresses a philosophical view only if it is defended by a certain sort of argument – an argument which contains at least one premise which is believed only by some philosophers and never by scientists or the man in the street. But then we would encounter a difficulty about knowing whether these presuppositions were false. For suppose they were distinctively philosophical propositions, and as such answers to distinctively philosophical problems. A program for the dissolution of all philosophical problems requires some appeal to propositions whose truth-value is agreed on by both sides; such a program will only work if the presuppositions in question are neither common-sensical nor defended by argument. But in concrete cases it will usually turn out that they *are* defended by argument. So the man who says he is dissolving all philosophical problems will turn out to be just one more philosopher, arguing for his chosen solution to a certain set of philosophical problems.

Alternatively, we might try a second way out. We might say that to dissolve a problem is not, as Cornman says, to show that all answers to a given question have false presuppositions, but to show that the question itself would never be asked by someone who did not have a false belief. Such a formula is, I think, somewhat closer to the intent of the explicitly critical philosophers among the analysts. But it is again hard to imagine how it could be carried out. What are the presuppositions of a question like "How many species are there?" or "Is the notion of insensate matter a case of misplaced concreteness?" I doubt that there is any way to detect anything that might reasonably be called a presupposition of one of these questions, except by seeing if there is some relevant proposition which is believed by all those who are inclined to ask the philosophical question and not believed by all those who find the question silly or pointless.

Such a method might in fact isolate certain interesting propositions which could reasonably be called the respective presuppositions of the various questions. But, once again, these propositions might often turn out to be distinctively philosophical. As such, it would not be clear how we were to know whether or not they were false.

We may conclude that a program for dissolving all philosophical problems would only work if the presuppositions detected according to the method just sketched were in fact (a) blatantly false, and (b) such that no one would wish to develop philosophical arguments in their favor. There actually are such presuppositions. To take a standard example, it does seem to be the case that some metaphysicians were bothered by questions which would not have bothered them if they had not been going on the assumption that all words were names – that is, that no word could have a use unless it had a referent. Since this diagnosis of certain philosophical perplexities became popular, no one has proceeded to argue that, oddly enough, all words *are* names. This is cheering, for this case is enough to refute the despairing view that since all philosophical argument is (or can be made) circular, and since any philosopher can construct a watertight system around any cherished belief, genuine controversy between metaphysicians and analysts is never going to take place. Further, it seems to me to refute the view that all the criticisms which analysts make of metaphysicians rest upon unargued-for metaphysical, or other specifically philosophical, assumptions. It is not the case that "not all words are names" expresses a philosophical view, unless we are to say (pointlessly) that all propositions relevant to one's judgments of philosophical views are themselves philosophical views.

Having said all this, have we now arrived at a clear picture at the difference between analysts and metaphysicians? I think not, simply because the activity I have described could just as well be a description of the sort of metaphysics which, for example, Adler recommends. For what is the difference, after all, between showing that everyone who disagrees with you does so because he raises questions which have false presuppositions, and showing that everybody who disagrees with you does so because he has not attended to those aspects of "common experience" to which you have attended? If philosophical method boils down to directing attention to certain evident truths, it seems to matter little whether we say that we are showing that our opponents raise bad questions because they have ignored these truths, or whether we just say the answers they give to these questions are bad because they have ignored these truths. There is at most a pedogogic difference.

I conclude, therefore, that the difference between solving and dissolving problems is no better than the difference between "first-order" and "second-order" questions as an analysis of the difference between analysts and metaphysicians. I shall conclude with an analysis which, though vague, seems to me at least less misleading than those I have been discussing. The difference has to do with wisdom. I think that analytic philosophers have in common the view that the pursuit of wisdom cannot be served by continuing the inquiries traditionally grouped together as "philosophy." Their examination of the history of philosophy leads them to think that philosophy is indeed a tree from which all, or nearly all, the branches have fallen. They think that the answers to the questions they pose in the formal mode of speech, and the truths which are brought forward to show the falsity of the presuppositions of some or all philosophical problems, are not truths which will give us wisdom. At best, they will give us the sort of wisdom which Socrates had – the wisdom which consists in not being fooled any more. For the sort of wisdom which Plato sought, we must turn to the sciences, the arts, and, perhaps, to speculative philosophy – to philosophy as the articulation of a vision rather than the solution or the dissolution of problems. They tend to conceive of empirical philosophy as a propædeutic to critical philosophy, and of critical philosophy as a propædeutic either to speculative philosophy or to a postphilosophical culture.

Metaphysicians, on the other hand, believe that some species of empirical philosophy will bring us to truths which will offer us wisdom in Plato's sense. They believe that the visions of the speculative philosophers can be backed by argument, and that criteria exist for choosing between such visions. Metaphysicians keep the Platonic faith that argument can bring us to truth – truth about the ultimately important things. Analysts have lost this faith. They have not lost it (*pace* Adler, Gilson, Heidegger, Blanshard, and many others) because they have adopted a false epistemology or a false metaphysics. They have lost it because they have looked at the history of philosophy and at our culture and arrived at a judgment about how human life may best be enriched. I believe that their judgment is sound. But I do not know how to prove that it is.

# CHAPTER 8

# Incorrigibility as the mark of the mental

In this chapter I argue, first, that various "topic-neutral" translations of mentalistic statements propounded by materialists are unsatisfactory in that they do not catch the specifically "mentalistic" element in these statements. I then go on to argue that to isolate this element one needs to insist on the incorrigibility of first-person reports of mental states. Finally, I consider whether this insistence is an obstacle to materialism.

We may begin by recalling that the origin of the attempt at "topic-neutral" translations of mentalistic statements was an attempt to avoid what we may call the "irreducible-properties objection" to the thesis that mental states are identical with brain states. This objection says that, even if the identity thesis frees us from nomologically dangling entities, it cannot free us from nomologically dangling properties – *viz.*, those properties by which we originally identified the mental entities as such. Thus, for example, a sensation of yellow has the property "of yellow," and the thought that *p* has the property "that *p*"; but it seems to make no sense for any brain-process to have either sort of property. So these properties seem irreducible. J. J. C. Smart originally tried to get around this objection for the case of sensations by saying that "I am having a sensation of yellow" was equivalent to (or could roughly be paraphrased as) "Something is going on in me like what is going on when I see something yellow."[1] More recently, D. M. Armstrong has employed the same technique in a program of translating (or paraphrasing) all statements ascribing mental states as statements containing the subject term "a state apt for the production of the following sorts of behaviour."[2]

---

[1] "Sensations and Brain Processes," *Philosophical Review*, 68, 2 (1959), pp. 141–56; reprinted in V. C. Chappell, ed., *The Philosophy of Mind* (Englewood Cliffs, 1962), pp. 166–7.
[2] *A Materialist Theory of the Mind* (London, 1968), ch. 6. See pp. 116–17 for the use of this analysis in replying to the "irreducible-properties objection."

It has been pointed out by many commentators that such "translations" do not succeed if construed as translations or meaning analyses in the strict senses of these terms. Armstrong has admitted the point,[3] saying that all that is offered is an "account," just as Smart suggested that he was merely giving the "general purport" of mentalistic statements. But it is important to see that nothing less than a translation will do, if we hold the view that two properties can be identified one with another only if we show synonymy of the expressions signifying those properties. If, in other words, we want to show that all properties of mental states are properties of brain-processes and if we believe that only showing that two terms mean the same thing can show that they signify the same property, our topic-neutral translations will have to be translations in the fullest sense of the term. To see the importance of this point, note that Smart himself has said that, in the light of criticism of his "translations," he feels compelled to say not that sensations and brain-processes have the same properties, but that the sensations of common sense simply do not exist and that the explanatory function fulfilled by reference to these pseudo-entities is better fulfilled by reference to brain-processes.[4]

By way of mapping the strategies available to materialists, we can say that if the irreducible-properties objection is to be overcome, materialists must either (a) improve topic-neutral translations so that genuine synonymy results, (b) drop the principle that properties are identical only if the terms referring to them have the same meaning (i.e., assert that there are contingent identifications of properties as well as necessary ones), or (c) adopt the principle that two things can be identical in a philosophically interesting sense even if they do not share all and only the same properties. The second alternative is adopted by Max Deutscher[5] and by Wilfrid Sellars.[6] The third alternative is the "Feyerabend" alternative – the

---

[3]  *Ibid.*, pp. 84–5.
[4]  See Smart, "Comments on the Papers," in C. F. Presley, ed., *The Identity Theory of Mind* (St. Lucia, Brisbane, 1967), pp. 91f: "I am even doubtful now whether it is necessary to give a physicalist analysis of sensation reports. Paul Feyerabend may be right in his contention that common sense is invincibly dualistic, and that common sense introspective reports are couched in the framework of a dualistic conceptual scheme . . . In view of Bradley's criticism of my translation form of the identity thesis, I suspect that I shall have to go over to a more Feyerabendian position."
[5]  "Mental and Physical Properties," in Presley, *op. cit.*, p. 75: "a distinction in meaning is not in itself sufficient reason to claim distinctness of properties."
[6]  "The Identity Approach to the Mind-Body Problem," in *Philosophical Perspectives* (Springfield, IL, 1967). Sellars here says that "the fundamental strategy of the identity theorist" must be "an appeal to a supposed analogy between the speculatively entertained identity of raw-feel universals with brain-state universals, and the once speculative but now established identity of chemical universals with certain micro-physical universals" (pp. 382–3).

adoption of (in Cornman's[7] phrase) "eliminative" rather than "reductive" materialism, according to which the sense of identity in question is the sense in which phlogiston is identical with (is replaced by, is eliminated in favor of) the kinetic motion of molecules.

Toward the end of this chapter, I shall make some remarks about the choice between the second and third of these strategies, arguing for the third. For the present, however, I want to argue simply that the first should be abandoned, not simply because of the detailed criticisms of the particular topic-neutral translations that have been offered (by, e.g., Cornman[8] and Bradley[9]) but for a more general reason. Briefly, the reason is that if Armstrong were right in saying that "The concept of a mental state is the concept of that, whatever it may turn out to be, which is brought about in a man by certain stimuli, and the cause within a man of certain responses"[10] then we should never have been able to make sense of the contrast between (a) dualism and materialism, or (b) between the mental and the physical, or (c) between materialism and behaviorism.

One form of this point – that involved in (a) – has already been made by Bradley, as follows:

> Descartes does indeed speak of non-material Substances of which the items constituent of experience are attributes; but it is hard to believe that he would ever have done so had he not thought that introspectible and physical qualities were utterly disparate. If, so to speak, he had been persuaded by Smart's attempt at a topic-neutral quasi-reduction of sensation statements, it seems natural to suppose that he would have then seen no point in postulating *two* sorts of Substance . . . Secondly, if Smart's offer of a choice between materialism and dualism, once "topic-neutral" translations have been adopted, is the merest gesture towards the possibility of a dualism, it is also a barely intelligible gesture, or perhaps not even that. For the "non-physical ghost stuff" will presumably not have introspectible (phenomenal) qualities, for if it did, they would, in consistency, have to be dealt with in a topic-neutral way. Its qualities must therefore be non-physicalism and non-phenomenal. What *they* might be baffles this reader at least.[11]

---

[7] James W. Cornman, "On the Elimination of 'Sensations' and Sensations," *Review of Metaphysics*, 22, 1 (1968), pp. 15–35, at p. 16.

[8] "The Identity of Mind and Body," *Journal of Philosophy*, 59, 18 (1962), pp. 486–92.

[9] M. C. Bradley, "Sensations, Brain-Processes, and Colors," *Australasian Journal of Philosophy*, 42 (1963), pp. 385–93.

[10] Armstrong, *op. cit.*, pp. 84–5.

[11] "Critical Notice" of Smart's *Philosophy and Scientific Realism, Australasian Journal of Philosophy*, 62, 2 (1964), pp. 262–83, at p. 278.

This point can be underlined and reinforced by noting that Smart and Armstrong think that topic-neutral versions of mentalistic statements can be reconciled with either immaterialism or materialism. They think, in other words, that we are being fair to Descartes as long as we give an analysis of the mental that leaves it open that mental events are taking place in an immaterial stuff. But this neglects the point that "immaterial" gets its sense from its connection with "mental." If the mental is merely the unknown cause of certain behavior or the unknown effect of certain stimuli, then no sense is given to "immaterial" because no example of the "nonextended" is available to us. The notions of "ghostly stuff" and of "immaterial substance" would never have become current if Descartes had not been able to use *cogitationes* as an illustration of what he intended. Even Aristotle, in looking for examples of form without matter, had to fall back on thought (the agent intellect of the *De Anima* and the "thought thinking itself" which is the "pure actuality" of *Metaphysics Lambda*) in order to find examples. "Immaterial" is not a notion we can hang on to once we have enfeebled our notion of mental in the way described by Armstrong.

Proceeding now to (b), the basic reason why dualism, and *a fortiori* the contrast between dualism and materialism, becomes unintelligible on Armstrong's view is that, if we have a contrast between two categories $X$ and $Y$, which are supposed to form an exhaustive and mutually exclusive division of the universe, we cannot mean by "$X$" something that might turn out to be either $X$ or $Y$. We cannot define "mental" as something that might turn out to be either mental or physical, because we cannot define any term as something that might turn out to refer to what is denoted by a contrary term. It is part of the sense of "mental" that being mental is incompatible with being physical, and no explication of this sense which denies this incompatibility can be satisfactory.

This point – that topic-neutral construals of what it is to be mental lose the mental–physical contrast – may also be brought out by noting that Armstrong's definition of a mental state covers many things that would normally be classified as physical states. Armstrong recognizes this difficulty and replies as follows:

> A certain state of the liver, for instance, may be apt for the production of ill-tempered behaviour. Yet it is not a mental state. This objection forces us to say that not all states of the person apt for the production of certain sorts of behaviour are mental states. What marks off the mental states from others? If we consider the secretions of the liver it is clear that, considered as causes, they lack the complexity to bring about such complexities of behaviour as

are involved even in ill-tempered behaviour. It is not until the chain of causes reaches the brain that processes of a sufficient complexity occur ... I think it can be replied that our concept of a *mental* state is the concept of a cause whose complexity mirrors the complexity of the behaviour it is apt for bringing about.[12]

This reply is inadequate. It confuses the question "What is the measure of complexity of a mental state?" with the question "What is the measure of complexity of a physiological state?" We know some rough answers to the latter question; but do we have any idea what it would be for a mere "state apt for the production ... " to be simple or complex? Armstrong is here assuming that it is already part of our concept of a mental state that it is to be identified with some physiological process or other. But the task he has posed himself is to give a concept of a mental state that makes no reference to such identification. Without such identification, the opposition between simple and complex makes no sense; for to say that a person is in a state apt for the production of certain sorts of behavior is merely to say that such behavior will, *ceteris paribus*, appear (where the *ceteris* may or may not be specified). This dispositional state cannot intelligibly be described as either simple or complex, except in so far as the *ceteris paribus* clause is filled in by spelling out the circumstances in which the behavior will be expected – in which case the length and complexity of the resulting subjunctive conditionals might be said to measure the complexity of the state. But then what we are measuring is the complexity of the behavior expected itself, not "the complexity of its cause." It is only the (physiological or "immaterial") state, which lies behind and explains the mental state (and with which the mental state may, on empirical grounds, be identified), that is a *cause*, and only it may be simple or complex. Before the discovery of such states-to-be-identified-with-mental-states we cannot use this contrast to characterize the mental states themselves.

To develop the point that, on Armstrong's analysis, mental states are mere shorthand for subjective conditionals, it will be useful to go on to (c) and to take up Armstrong's claim to have set out a genuine alternative to behaviorism. By refuting this claim, I wish to show that the materialism–behaviorism contrast itself makes no sense when "mental" is interpreted in Armstrong's way. Armstrong admits that his "talk about tendencies to initiate, and capacities for, behaviour" is "perilously close to the Behaviourist's dispositions," but insists that "Behaviourism and the Central-state theory still remain deeply at odds about the way dispositions *are to be*

---

[12]  Armstrong, *op. cit.*, pp. 118–19.

*conceived.*"[13] The difference, he says, is that the behaviorist holds a "Phenomenalist or Operationalist account of dispositions" according to which "to possess a dispositional property is not to be in a particular state," whereas the Central-state materialist holds a "Realist" view, described as follows:

> According to the Realist view, to speak of an object's having a dispositional property entails that the object is in some non-dispositional state or that it has some property (there exists a "categorical basis") which is responsible for the object manifesting certain behaviour in certain circumstances, manifestations whose nature makes the dispositional property the dispositional property it is. It is true that we may not know anything of the nature of the dispositional state.[14]

To take a Realist view of dispositions, according to this account, is simply to be willing to say that there is some explanation for the existence of a given disposition, even if this explanation is entirely unknown, and that this explanation is not itself to be given in terms of dispositional properties. But what is the force of this last restriction? To attribute a dispositional property, after all, is merely to say that a given subjunctive conditional is true. But subjunctive conditionals are derivative from nomological generalizations. How do we tell which new nomological statements attribute mere dispositions to the entity in question and which attribute new "categorical" features? I think the only answer to this last question is that Armstrong has in mind *micro-structural* explanations as the paradigm of the case in which new categorical features of the entity are found. (This is suggested by the examples he uses, e.g., the brittleness of the glass being explained by a molecular pattern.) When we merely find a new law regulating the behavior of an entity, without finding or postulating any new entities, we have merely explained one disposition with another. But when we find or postulate new entities, we are explaining a disposition by reference to a categorical state.

If this analysis of the Realist view of dispositions is correct, an odd consequence follows: physicalism *must* be true. Once we accept Armstrong's account of the mental together with the Realist view, it is no longer a scientific, but an *a priori*, truth, that there are unknown physical entities that explain our being in mental states and are the "categorical bases" of those states. For mental states cannot have their categorical bases in other mental states – the mental cannot be a

---

[13]  *Ibid.*, p. 85.     [14]  *Ibid.*, p. 86.

self-sustaining realm – since mental states are dispositions to behave and cannot be explained (for a Realist) merely by other dispositions to behave. Further, unless we fall back on the dodge that these nonmental categorical bases might be states of a nonphysical substance, only physical states will do. But this dodge will not do, for the reason given above: the notion of a "nonphysical and nonmental immaterial substance" is a notion without content. "Material" and "physical" would be vacuous notions without the contrast with "mental." "Immaterial" and "non-physical" are notions that have sense only if the mental is given as an instance of them. So to adopt Armstrong's position is to be committed, on *a priori* grounds, to postulating physical entities "whose nature makes the dispositional properties the particular dispositional properties they are."

This result, though unwelcome to Armstrong, is to be expected, given his *prima facie* resemblance to the behaviorist. Both behaviorism and the "topic-neutral" analysis assign mental entities a character that one might call "explanation-hungry"; both dispositions and "states apt for … " cry out for something behind them that accounts for them. (Note, incidentally, that there is no reason why Ryle himself should not be a Realist about dispositions.) By making the realm of the mental a realm that contains only relations among physical entities and by accepting the common paradigm of explanation of modern physical science according to which the best explanations of relations among particulars are those which discover new ("micro-") particulars, one naturally smooths the way for materialism. Unfortunately, however, the way is too smooth. By making materialism an *a priori* truth, we deprive the Identity Theory of any interest. The interest of the Identity Theory consists in saying that what used to be thought to be entities that had a nature incompatible with being physical, now turn out to be physical. But Armstrong's topic-neutral explication of mentality, by making mental entities mere stand-ins for physical entities, leaves nothing to *turn out* to be identical with physical particulars. The materialist who wishes to hold that it is an empirical question whether or not the realm of the mental is self-sustaining – i.e., whether the ideal scientific account of the world might include mental entities as well as physical ones – must insist, against *both* Ryle and Armstrong, on preserving mental entities that have characters incompatible with being physical.[15]

---

[15] I pass over without detailed comment two further points that Armstrong makes in connection with his distinction between Realist and Phenomenalist views of dispositions. In what he calls an *a priori*

The upshot of my discussion of Armstrong's reply to the behaviorist is that the difference between Armstrong and Ryle is, at most, the difference between a behaviorist analysis with, and one without, a faith in the possibility of micro-structural explanations of the occurrence of those dispositions to behave which we call mental states. (I say "at most" because, as I have suggested, nothing in *The Concept of Mind* prohibits such faith.) Both types of analysis would, if accepted, reduce the notion of the mental to a notion of relations among (known and unknown) physical entities, and would thereby deprive the notion of "the physical" of sense by stripping it of its contrast with another realm of entities having properties incompatible with physicality. Whether or not Ryle is right in thinking that such an analysis gives us our common-sense notion of the mental as contrasted with the notion held by Cartesian philosophers,[16] it seems clear that it is the notion held by Cartesian philosophers that we must explicate if we are to make sense of materialism. This latter notion must contain properties incompatible with properties of physical entities. I now proceed to canvass alternative candidates for the position of being these key incompatible properties, and to argue that incorrigibility is the best candidate.

In settling upon a mark of the mental, it is important to begin by distinguishing between two different notions of what counts as mental. The distinction I have in mind is that between the sort of mental entity that is an *event* and the sort that is not. In the first class fall,

---

argument for the former view (*op. cit.*, pp. 86–7) he argues that the Phenomenalist cannot explain why counterfactual conditionals are true whereas the Realist can. As far as I can see, this argument presupposes that inductive arguments to the presence of dispositional properties are *ipso facto* weaker than inductive arguments to the presence of categorical properties. *Pace* Armstrong, the Phenomenalist, can reply to the question "Why should a thing not change its dispositional properties?" *not* by an appeal to underlying categorical properties, but simply by an appeal to the constancy of the dispositional property in the past.

The second further point Armstrong makes is that on the Phenomenalist view "dispositions cannot be causes," whereas, since the Realist identifies dispositions with *states*, his view permits them to be causes. Once again, it is not clear that the distinction between dispositions-as-states and dispositions-as-non-states comes to more than the distinction between behavioral law backed up by reference to new particulars, and those not so backed up. But it is not clear why explanation by reference to unbacked-up behavior laws should not count as causal explanation.

[16] I do not mean to suggest that I think Ryle *is* right about this. On the contrary, I should hold that common sense is irredeemably Cartesian on the point. I should argue that Ryle's purported distinction between the concept built into our language and the Cartesian concept is actually a distinction between the concept most congenial to a verificationist and operationalist philosopher and the concept actually built into our language. On the operationalist presuppositions of *The Concept of Mind*, see Albert Hofstadter, "Professor Ryle's Category-Mistake," *Journal of Philosophy*, 48, 9 (1951), pp. 257–70. On its verificationist presuppositions, see Stuart Hampshire's review in *Mind*, 59, 234 (1950), pp. 237–55.

paradigmatically and perhaps solely, thoughts and sensations. By "thoughts" here I mean not beliefs, but occurrent, datable, thoughts – e.g., the entity referred to when one says "The thought that *p* suddenly struck me." By "sensations" here I mean not perceivings – not acquisitions of beliefs – but simply the entities that are reported in such ways as "Then I had a sensation of red" or "Then I had a painful sensation in my leg." These two sorts of entities make up the content of the stream of consciousness – what one finds when one asks "What's going on in me now?" In the second class fall all those mental entities which are not events and which are only dubiously "entities" at all – beliefs, moods, emotions, desires, purposes, intentions, motives, etc., etc. These might better be called "mental features" than "mental entities." Not only are they not events, but it strikes one as an odd, peculiarly philosophical, hypostatization to think of them as *particulars* of *any* sort.

Another way of contrasting these two classes is to note that they are recalcitrant to behaviorist "reduction" in different ways. To say that thoughts and sensations are dispositions to behave sounds counterintuitive – as counterintuitive as saying that molecules are dispositions of macroscopic objects to behave. A Rylean approach to thoughts and sensations runs into the obstacle that here ordinary language seems to steadfastly support the Cartesian notion of a double series of events – one mental and the other physical – which when put together make up the human being. Here, if anywhere, we genuinely have a ghost in the machine – a set of nonphysical occurrences. When we come to beliefs, emotions, desires, purposes, and the like, however, we are no longer tempted to count them as episodes rather than dispositions. Here, Ryle's general approach – that talking about these things is a way of talking about what behavior may be expected – has great intuitive plausibility. The recalcitrance in these cases is rather that when we try to give equivalents in terms of bodily movements for such expressions as "He wants *X*" and "He intends to *A*" we seem to fail. We cannot break out of the circle of terms whose most prominent members are "belief" and "desire," because, roughly, the putatively equivalent hypothetical sentences about physical movements always seem to require in their protases such qualifying phrases as "Provided he believes that … " and "Provided he wants that … ". Whereas thoughts and sensations were recalcitrant to reduction because they did not seem like dispositions at all, beliefs and desires (and the rest) are recalcitrant to reduction because, though they may be dispositions, they cannot be isolated without reference to other such dispositions.

I wish now to argue that only the former class of mental entities generate the opposition between the mental and the physical, where this opposition is considered as an opposition between two incompatible types of entity, rather than an opposition between two ways of talking about human beings. The former class of entities – the thoughts and the sensations – are the paradigm illustrations of what is meant by the Cartesian notion of the mental as a separate realm. The latter class of entities are entities which, *if we had never heard of thoughts and sensations*, would never have generated the notion of a separate "realm" at all. If we had no notion of a mental *event*, but merely the notion of men having beliefs and desires and, therefore, acting in such-and-such ways, we would not have had a mind-body problem at all, and Ryle would have had no motive for writing. Believing and desiring would have appeared simply as distinctively *human* activities, and our only dualism would have been one between human beings *qua* agents (i.e., *qua* moving in ways to be explained by reference to beliefs and desires) and as mere bodies (i.e., *qua* moving in ways that can be explained without reference to beliefs and desires). This dualism would have been a dualism not between mind and body, nor between the mental and the physical as distinct realms, but simply between ways of explaining the doings of human beings – psychological explanations and nonpsychological explanations.[17]

I have presented this distinction between mental events – the content of the stream of consciousness – and mental features in order to explain why I shall be concentrating on the former in looking for a mark of the mental. In what follows, I shall be asking the question: what features or feature do thoughts and sensations have in common with each other, and with nothing physical? It will turn out that their single common feature – incorrigibility – is only in a weak and diminished sense a mark of such things as beliefs, desires, purposes, emotions, etc. I shall be forced to conclude, therefore, that there is no single mark of all the entities customarily called mental. But I believe that isolating the features of the paradigmatically nonphysical, the mental *events*, serves two useful purposes. In the

---

[17] My distinction between the mental entities that are events and those which are not might thus be expressed as a distinction between the *mental* and the *psychological*. This way of putting the matter would have the merit of calling attention to the difference between Descartes's distinction between the mind and the body and Aristotle's distinction between the soul and the body. However, I do not wish to press this terminology, for I cannot, in the space of the present chapter, offer a full-blown account of the "Aristotelian" as opposed to the "Cartesian" notions of where the interesting lines fall. Cf. Wallace Matson, "Why Isn't the Mind-Body Problem Ancient?," in Paul Feyerabend and Grover Maxwell, eds., *Mind, Matter, and Method* (Minneapolis, 1966), pp. 92–102.

first place, it lets us see how the notion of mutually exclusive realms of being came to exist. In the second place, it lets us see that there are family resemblances between mental events and mental entities that are not events – resemblances which account for the tendency to use the term "mental" of both, despite the differences I have mentioned and despite the fact that one can construct no set of necessary and sufficient conditions for mentality.

Proceeding now to candidates for marks of mental events, we may begin by noting that two familiar marks of the mental – intentionality and "purposiveness" – are excluded from consideration by our inclusion of *sensations* as mental. None of the marks of the intentional – e.g., those proposed by Chisholm – would make "I am having a sensation of red now" or "I am having a painful sensation now" an intentional sentence. To have a sensation, unlike having a thought, is not to be in a state which has "aboutness" or which can somehow refer to the inexistent. Nor does there seem to be anything distinctively "purposive" about sensations. We can explain what a sensation is without any reference to beliefs or desires. The notion of sensation is not a part of the circle of terms used to explain action as opposed to movement (although of course reference to sensations may enter into such explanations, just as reference to physical objects may enter). If we are to find something that sensations and thoughts have in common with each other and not with anything physical we must look away from intentionality and purposiveness to the following group of marks: *introspectibility, nonspatiality,* and *privacy.* These are the sorts of characteristics that distinguish the contents of the stream of consciousness from "the external world" and generate the notion of the physical and the mental as distinct realms.

To begin with introspectibility, although everything mental is introspectible and conversely, nevertheless it is unhelpful to cite this as a mark of the mental. The unhelpfulness comes out when we try to distinguish introspection from such borderline cases as sensing that one's stomach is fluttering or that a vein in one's leg is throbbing. These latter cases do not count as cases of introspection simply because the object reported on is physical. In short, we cannot explain what introspection is except by reference to an antecedently understood notion of what is mental. To say that all and only mental events are introspectible is no more informative than saying that all and only these are knowable in that unique way in which we know our own mental events.

Nor is non-spatiality a satisfactory mark of the mental. The difficulty here is that it makes excellent sense to give thoughts and sensations a location, though a vague one – namely, to say that they are located where the person doing the thinking or the sensing is located. From the point of view of the Identity Theory, this position has the advantage that, given reasons for identifying thoughts and sensations with brain-processes, it will make sense to make the location of the former more precise than it was previously. From the point of view of our search for marks of the mental, it should be noted that we cannot make "vague spatiality" as opposed to "precisely locatable spatial position" a mark of the mental, because the same vagueness applies to the location of my weight, my build, my health, and my behavior – all of which are located where I am, but are not more precisely locatable, and none of which are "mental." Nor can we back up the notion that the mental is unextended and the physical extended by claiming that the *shape* or *size* of thoughts and sensations is a contentless notion, whereas all physical things have shape and size. The mass or the weight of physical objects does not have shape or size, and indeed no *state* of an object, as opposed to the object itself, does. To insist that mental events are shapeless and sizeless is merely to remind us that they are states of persons.

The temptation to explicate "mental" as "unextended" comes, I think, from taking a special case – images of physical objects had in dreams or hallucinations – as paradigmatic of the mental. It is easy to say that Macbeth's "dagger of the mind" does not occupy space, or at least not "physical" space, and then extrapolate from there. But it is a bad example to extrapolate from, since it is an example of something that does not exist. What do exist are certain sensations (sense impressions of something daggerlike) and thoughts (that there is a dagger there) in Macbeth. And these are not on the table where the dagger seems to be, but where Macbeth is. The temptation here is to think that mental things are objects rather than states, that all objects must have features homogeneous with those of real physical objects (e.g., color, shape, and size), that "mental objects" have such features only in some Pickwickian sense (e.g., "phenomenal" color or size or location), and then to conclude that it is this Pickwickian possession of familiar features that characterizes the mental. But this is to confuse the mental with the inexistent or the imaginary, to confuse thoughts with their intentional (and possibly inexistent) objects (as if to think about unicorns was to have a nonexistent unicorn in our minds), and sensations with the objects that the presence of certain sensations may lead us (mistakenly) to believe exist. Descartes's preoccupation with dreaming, and the habit of treating objects dreamt of as "mental objects," led to this confusion and thus to much of the obscurity surrounding the notion of the mental.

To supplement these last remarks, and also as a way of introducing the topic of incorrigibility, it will be useful to digress for a moment to a view about marks of the mental which is suggested by Sellars. Sellars emphasizes the point we have just made – that sensations and thoughts are states of persons rather than quasi-substances – and adds the further point that their intrinsic features are features that are not shared by physical objects, real or imagined. On his "mythical" account, thoughts were originally theoretical entities, postulated as "inner" states that explained certain sorts of behavior. But they were not merely Rylean dispositions nor Armstrongian "states apt . . . "; for they had certain intrinsic features. For example, they were true or false, and were *about* things, in the way in which sentences are. They shared, in other words, the "semantical" features of sentences – the features sentences possessed not *qua* physical objects (inscriptions) but *qua* types (as opposed to tokens) – but had no other features. Sensations, in turn, were also originally theoretical entities – "inner" states postulated to explain the occurrence of certain thoughts (e.g., the thought that there is a red triangle before me, when there isn't). They too had certain intrinsic features, but, again, features not shared by any physical objects *qua* physical objects. Their intrinsic features were, e.g., being "of red" and "of a triangle." ["Of" here is not a relational expression, but is a device for introducing such new theoretical predicates as (using hyphens to mark unanalyzability) "of-red" – a predicate which applies *only* to sensations and gains application through such "correlation rules" as that which says that red triangles perceived in standard conditions give rise to sensations that are "of-red" and "of-a-triangle."] When originally proposed as theoretical entities (by Jones, the man who, in Sellars's myth, invented the concept of mind) sensations and thoughts were not conceived of as immediate experiences – they were not the objects of noninferential introspective reports, much less of incorrigible reports. Instead, they were inferred entities – known to exist in the way in which positrons are known to exist, by inference from the behavior they cause. It is only after Jones has instructed others in his theory and subjected them to a prolonged training process that it turns out they can make noninferential reports of their own inner states.[18]

---

[18] This paragraph summarizes pp. 186–96 of "Empiricism and the Philosophy of Mind," in Sellars's *Science, Perception and Reality* (New York, 1963).

What, we may now ask, is the mark of the mental on Sellars's account? What intrinsic features do sensations and thoughts have in common? Oddly enough, the answer is that they have *no* features in common save the Armstrongian one of being "inner" states apt for the production of certain behavior. Though they both have intrinsic features, and not merely relational features, they have no *common* intrinsic features save "innerness." But what does being "inner" come to? I suggest that all the term can mean (before the day when Jones trains his fellows to make not merely noninferential, but incorrigible reports, of their thoughts and sensations) is "beneath the skin." To postulate such states, like postulating Rylean dispositions or Armstrongian states, is not to give a basis for the notion of the "nonphysical" – or, to put it more accurately, does not provide a means for giving the notion of "physical" a sense by contrasting it with something else. Rather, the natural thing for Jones's pupils to think is that he is telling them that something happens somewhere in their bodies which accounts for their behavior, something on all fours with internal secretions or muscle movements.

To see this point, it helps to notice that Jones might just as well have introduced the notion of "brain-process-about-$p$" or "brain-process-of-a-red-triangle" as have invented the neologisms "thought about $p$" and "sensation of a red triangle." What counts is not whether a new word or an old is used, but merely the theoretically postulated intrinsic features of the entities in question and the relevant "correlation rules." It would have been just as good an explanation of intelligent behavior to say that some brain-processes had, like sentences, the special feature of being "about" things, as to say that an invented state called a "thought" did. These new properties of brains would have been, if Jones had phrased his theory in this way, "unobservable" properties, but they would not have been non-physical properties, any more than the spin of an electron is a nonphysical property.

Coming now to the point, I want to say that Jones did not invent the concept of *mind* by inventing the notions of unobservable inner states with certain intrinsic features. Given Sellars's description of his theory, all that Jones did was to propose a micro-structural account of the causes of human behavior, but not an account in terms of specifically mental events. We cannot make Armstrongian "states apt . . . " into *mental* states just by adding an assortment of intrinsic features to them unless there is among those features one which separates off all such states from any other states we know of and, thereby, establishes a new category of existence.

This seems a strong requirement, but it is exactly what is supplied by the *privacy* of mental events. We must be careful, however, to isolate the right sense of "private." As A. J. Ayer has pointed out,[19] mental events have been said to be private in at least the following four senses: incommunicability, special access, unsharability, and incorrigibility. In the first sense, things are private to a person if only he can know of their existence or some of their features. Mental events are clearly not private in this sense, unless one believes that thoughts or sensations have special felt qualities that are not signified by any term in a public language. But the latter view is hardly part of common sense or of our normal conception of the mental. In the second sense, things are private to a given person if he can know about them in ways different from those in which anyone else can know about them. But in this sense my stomach is private to me, for I can know that it is fluttering by feeling that it is, and no one else can do that. So this sense will not give us what we want. In the third sense – "unsharable" – things are private to a given person if it is impossible for anyone else to have them. But this again extends too far, for no one else can have my state of health or my behavior. Nor is it clear, because of the possibility of telepathy and of interlocked brains, that thoughts and sensations *are* unsharable. If we want to say they are, we have to rule that in telepathic communication we only have the same *kind* of thought and not the same thought, but this ruling seems arbitrary and *ad hoc*. The fourth sense of privacy, however – incorrigibility – does give us what we want. Mental events are unlike any other events in that certain knowledge claims about them cannot be overridden. We have no criteria for setting aside as mistaken first-person contemporaneous reports of thoughts and sensations, whereas we do have criteria for setting aside all reports about everything else.

We may accept Sellars's "myth" as a reasonable account of how terms that were eventually to refer to the mental entered the language, but we must guard against thinking that the notions of inner states "about *p*" or "of red" give us the notion of something mental, something categorically distinct from everything else. Only after the emergence of the convention, the linguistic practice, which dictates that first-person contemporaneous reports of such states are the last word on their existence and features, do we have a notion of the mental as incompatible with the physical (and thus a way of making sense of such positions as parallelism and epiphenomenalism). For only this practice gives us a rationale for saying that thoughts and sensations must be *sui generis* – the rationale being

[19] Cf. *The Concept of a Person* (New York, 1963), p. 79.

that any proposed entity with which they could be identified would be such that reports about its features were capable of being overruled by further inquiry. Before this practice arose, it would have made no sense to ask whether Jones was giving us a theory about mental or about physical entities.

The force of this point may be brought out by noting that if, as we suggested above, Jones had produced a theory of "brain processes about *p*" and "brain processes of red" he would still, *if the same linguistic practice had arisen*, have invented something that turned out to be mental. Instead of states of a person that were incorrigibly reportable, there would have been states of brain processes that were incorrigibly reportable. There would, so to speak, have been no mental *entities*, but brain processes would have had mental *properties*. What makes an entity mental is not whether or not it is something that explains behavior, and what makes a property mental is not whether or not it is a property of a physical entity. The only thing that can make either an entity or a property mental is that certain reports of its existence or occurrence have the special status that is accorded to, e.g., reports of thoughts and sensations – the status of incorrigibility.

In what precedes, I have given reasons for denying to the following the title of the mark of mental events: intentionality, purposiveness, nonspatiality, introspectibility, privacy as incommunicability, privacy as special access, and privacy as unsharability. I have also urged that Sellars's account of thoughts and sensations in terms of certain special features (being "about *X*" or "of red") will not do the job. I have emerged with the conclusion that only incorrigibility marks off a common feature of our paradigms of mental events – thoughts and sensations – which distinguishes mental events from anything physical. I now turn to making this notion of "incorrigibility" more precise and to defending against objections the claim that we have incorrigible knowledge.

It is customary to define incorrigibility in terms of the notions of entailment or logical possibility. Thus, Armstrong[20] offers the following definition of "*p* is logically indubitable for *A*":

(i)    *A* believes *p*
(ii)   *(A's belief that p)* logically implies *(p)*

and George Nakhnikian[21] gives the following definition of "it is incorrigible for *S* at *t* that *p*":

---

[20] Armstrong, *op. cit.*, p. 101.
[21] "Incorrigibility," *Philosophical Quarterly*, 18, 72 (1968), p. 207.

(i)   It is logically possible that at $t$ $S$ believes attentively that $p$, and

(ii)   "At $t$ $S$ believes attentively that $p$" entails "At $t$ knows that $p$"

I wish, however, to eschew reference to logical modalities, both because of general Quinean doubts about the existence of necessities other than "natural" ones and because of a particular difficulty that arises when we try to spell out "logically possible" in this context. Suppose that, in the familiar manner, we try to spell out the force of this term in such sentences as "It is logically impossible that I believe that I am thinking that $p$, and not be" by the notion "impossible by virtue of the meaning of terms." We shall then arrive at the conclusion that the meaning of the terms "thinking" and "thought" is such that it is impossible to have incorrect contemporaneous beliefs about what one is thinking. But now let us recur to Jones, who uses the word "thought" before people have learned to make introspective reports of their thoughts, much less come to view such reports as incorrigible. Must we say that when Jones first invented the notion of "thought," meaning by it "inner state that can be about $X$, be true or false . . ., etc.," he did not mean by the word what we do? Did the meaning of "thought" change when people came to make noninferential reports of their own thoughts? Did it change when these reports came to be regarded as the last word? Would it change if cerebroscopes came to be regarded as offering better evidence for what someone was thinking than his own introspective reports?

I regard these questions as unanswerable, and affirmative answers to them as dogmatic pieces of what Hilary Putnam calls "unreasonable linguistics."[22] We have here a case where Quine's thesis of the indeterminacy of translation – the point that we may regard either *meanings* or *beliefs* as having changed, with no clear reason for choosing one alternative over the other save elegance or simplicity – is directly relevant to philosophical issues. My own preference would be to say that in none of the imagined cases does the meaning of "thought" change and to defend this claim by invoking Putnam's notion of a "cluster-concept."[23] I do not wish to defend this piece of impromptu linguistics, however, but merely to urge that we should not let a definition of incorrigibility in terms of logical modalities drive us to such conclusions as that Jones did not mean by "thought" what we do. Whether the myth of Jones be true or not, we should at least have

---

[22] "Brains and Behaviour," in R. J. Butler, ed., *Analytical Philosophy*, II (Oxford, 1965), p. 19, where Putnam is arguing against the view that the ascription of pain to beings who never wince nor admit to being in pain *purely* on the basis of brain waves involved a change in the meaning of "pain."

[23] *Ibid.*, p. 5.

the ability to tell a coherent story along the lines of the Jonesian myth. We can do this if we define incorrigibility "naturalistically," so to speak, in terms of the linguistic practices adopted by Jones's successors.

What, then, did these successors do when they "made" reports of sensations and thoughts incorrigible (and thus, on my view, made sensations and thoughts mental)? Well, something like this. They found that, when the behavioral evidence for what Smith was thinking about conflicted with Smith's own report of what he was thinking about, a more adequate account of the sum of Smith's behavior could be obtained by relying on Smith's report than by relying on the behavioral evidence. Thus, for example, if Smith's cave-reentering and ax-grasping behavior seemed to point to his just having had the thought that he had left his ax in the cave, his subsequent use of the ax nevertheless confirmed the truth of his report that what he had actually thought at the moment in question was that he might have broken the ax-handle yesterday. The growing conviction that the best explanation in terms of thoughts for Smith's behavior would always be found by taking Smith's word for what he was thinking found expression in the convention that what Smith said went. The same discovery occurred, *mutatis mutandis*, for sensations. It became a regulative principle of behavioral science that first-person contemporaneous reports of these postulated inner states were never to be thrown out on the ground that the behavior or the environment of the person doing the reporting would lead one to suspect that they were having a different thought or sensation from the one reported. In other words, it became a constraint on explanations of behavior that they should fit all reported thoughts or sensations into the overall account being offered. This constraint came to be reflected in linguistic practice, so that the expression "You must be mistaken about what you're thinking," which had had an established use in the past (*viz.*, to reflect apparent conflicts between behavior or environment and reports), fell into desuetude.

If this is a plausible myth, it can be described either as the history of how the meanings of "thought" and "sensation" changed or as the history of how people came to acquire new beliefs about thoughts and sensations (viz., that certain reports about them could not be mistaken). For the reason given above, I prefer to describe it in the second way. This choice means that I must define incorrigibility in terms not of logical possibility, but of the procedures for resolving doubts accepted at a given era. Thus, I submit the following:[24]

---

[24] Cf. my article "Intuition" in Paul Edwards, ed., *The Encyclopedia of Philosophy* (New York, 1967), IV, pp. 204–12, where I present a variant of this definition in the context of an account of intuitive knowledge.

*S* believes incorrigibly that *p* at *t* if and only if

(i)   *S* believes that *p* at *t*.
(ii)  There are no accepted procedures by applying which it would be rational to come to believe that not-*p*, given *S*'s belief that *p* at *t*.

As an initial comment on this definition of incorrigible belief, let me note that it is immune from certain familiar objections which Armstrong and others have brought against incorrigible belief as belief that implies its own truth.[25] Armstrong points out that there is a *prima facie* incompatibility between the materialist claim that knowledge of one's own mental states is a result of self-scanning by the brain and the claim that we possess logically incorrigible knowledge of such states. For how could it be logically impossible for the scanning process to go wrong? On our definition, this is not a problem. All we are asserting, when we say that contemporaneous beliefs about our own mental states are incorrigible, is that there is no assured way to go about correcting them if they should be in error. Viewing the matter in this way reduces incorrigibility to what Armstrong refers to as "empirically privileged access"[26] – an epistemological status relative to the state of empirical inquiry, and one capable of being lost if, for example, cerebroscopes should come to overrule first-spoken reports. Against such privilege, Armstrong has nothing to say. In particular, his argument that there can be no logical connection between distinct existences – e.g., between our mental state and our awareness of our mental state – is irrelevant to a sense of "incorrigible" that eschews reference to logical connection.

If our definition has the advantage of circumventing familiar objections to incorrigible knowledge, it has the disadvantage of including more than just knowledge of the mental. For there are three varieties of statements that may be believed incorrigibly in the sense just defined: (a) statements knowable *a priori*; (b) statements reporting mental events; and (c) statements about how something appears, looks, or seems to someone. In the

---

[25]  Cf. "Is Introspective Knowledge Incorrigible?," *Philosophical Review*, 72, 4 (1963), pp. 417–32, and *A Materialist Theory of the Mind*, pp. 100–13. See also Smart, *Philosophy and Scientific Realism* (London, 1963), p. 100, and the references given there.
       I shall not take up here the argument against incorrigible knowledge that Malcolm, in his review of *Philosophical Investigations*, imputes to Wittgenstein – *viz.*, that where we cannot make a mistake we cannot make a knowledge claim, so that it is nonsense to say "I know that I am in pain." I have tried to rebut this argument in another article – "Wittgenstein, Privileged Access, and Incommunicability," *American Philosophical Quarterly*, forthcoming [*American Philosophical Quarterly*, 70, 3 (1970), pp. 192–205; Chapter 9 in this volume].
[26]  Cf. *A Materialist Theory of the Mind*, p. 108.

case of *a priori* knowable propositions, the phrase "given $S$'s belief that $p$" in the above definition can be ignored, since our belief in such statements as "$2 + 2 = 4$" and "Every event has a cause" is guaranteed simply by the absence (at the moment) of accepted procedures for overthrowing them. In the case of (b) and (c), however, the phrase is essential. It serves, roughly, to summarize the fact that present procedures for adjudicating belief claims are such that the fact of $S$'s belief at $t$ that $p$ is at least as strong evidence for $p$ as any imaginable state of affairs could be for not-$p$. This is the situation that obtains for statements like "It looks brown to me now" and like "I'm in pain now." In both cases we may doubt the fact expressed, wondering whether it really looked brown or really *was* pain, and others may follow us in these doubts, but we have no procedures available for resolving such doubts. Granted that, as Austin says, we may come to suspect that it just wasn't *brown* that it looked to be, there is no way we can rationally decide that it *didn't* look brown in the face of the contemporaneous belief. We are condemned to hesitation. (This is why I prefer to speak of *incorrigible* rather than *indubitable* belief; any belief can be doubted, but not all such doubts are rationally resolvable.)

Given this definition of "incorrigible belief," how now may we put it to use to mark off the mental? I propose the following strategy. The thesis presented is that all and only mental events are the sorts of entities certain reports about which are incorrigible. We may get rid of *a priori* statements by noting that they are not *reports* – they are not descriptions of particular states of affairs.[27] What about "appears" statements? These do seem to be reports of particular states of affairs. Are they, and are they then, reports of mental states? This is a subtle question. One move would be to say "yes" to both questions – to say that they are reports of thoughts, "It looks brown to me now" being equivalent to "I am thinking that it may be brown." I do not wish to make this move, however, because "appears" statements seem to me, in their primary meaning, statements one could use without ever having heard of thoughts or sensations – statements which, so to speak, have a pre-Jonesian use. In this use, they simply mark refusals to commit oneself to making a report of a certain sort. To say that "$X$ looks brown" is, at the least, to express hesitation about saying that $X$ is brown. Is it also to make a report – a report that one is in a state of hesitation about saying

---

[27] It might be urged here that "This bachelor is unmarried" *is* a description of a particular state of affairs, though knowable *a priori*. To exclude such cases, we can include an additional restriction on the notion of "report" – *viz.*, that reports are not known to be true by virtue of knowing that universally quantified statements are true.

that *X* is brown, that one is tempted to do so but not quite willing to do so? I would claim that (post-Jones) it may be and that, when it is, it is a report of a mental slate, a thought of a given sort. But I would urge that it may not be, and may be simply an *expression* of hesitation, rather than a *report* of a hesitation. So I wish to use the notion of "report" to mark off among incorrigibly believable statements those which are about mental states. Only the reports are about mental states; the others are not. By "reports," once again, I mean descriptions of particular states of affairs. An "appears" statement may be a description of a particular state of affairs, and in that case it is a description of the mental. But it may be simply a refusal to make a description of a particular state of affairs, and this is its primary, pre-Jonesian use.

We can sum up the results of this strategy by noting that we now have a set of necessary and sufficient conditions for something being a mental *event*, namely

> If there is some person who can have an incorrigible belief in some statement *P* which is a report on *X*, then *X* is a mental event.

We now, however, have to face up to the question of whether we have necessary and sufficient conditions for something being a mental *entity* – whether, in other words, our criterion can be made to apply to beliefs, desires, moods, emotions, intentions, etc., as well as to thoughts and sensations. Here the answer, unfortunately, is "no." Those mental entities which I have contrasted with mental events as mental *features* are such that our subsequent behavior may provide sufficient evidence for overriding contemporaneous reports of them. If I say that I believe that *p*, or desire *X*, or am afraid, or am intending to do *A*, what I go on to do may lead others to say that I couldn't *really* have believed *p*, or desired *X*, or been afraid, or intended to do *A*. This fact is what we should expect, given the non-episodic, dispositional, character of these entities. Statements about beliefs, desires, emotions, and intentions are implicit predictions of future behavior, predictions which may be falsified. Such falsification provides an accepted procedure for overriding reports. In this, they are distinct from reports of thoughts and sensations, which are compatible with any range of future behavior.

But the fact that we are not incorrigible in our reports of mental features as we are about mental events should not blind us to the fact that we are *almost* incorrigible. The possibility of overriding reports about such features is real, but it is actualized only rarely and with trepidation. We are far less likely to have a report about a mental state, even one that is not an event, overridden than to have a report about something physical overridden. Further, as such mental features as beliefs and desires become more particular and limited and, thus, approach the status of episodes rather than dispositions, they become *more* incorrigible. It is not clear that there *are* accepted procedures for overriding someone's sincere report that he believes there is a table before him or that he desires a peach now. This may be explained by noting that there is no clear distinction between saying I believe that there is a table before me and saying that the thought has struck me that there is a table before me, nor is there a clear distinction between saying I want a peach now and saying that the thought "Would that I had a peach!" has just struck me. Again, there is no clear distinction between saying I am afraid of the tiger I just encountered and saying I had a sensation of fright when I encountered him. Beliefs and desires about momentary matters tend to collapse into thoughts, and momentary emotions tend to collapse into sensations. Short-run beliefs, desires, emotions, and intentions are less like predictions of future behavior than like avowals of contemporaneous thoughts or sensations. That is why they are more like episodes than like dispositions.

The two factors we have just mentioned – the near-incorrigibility of reports of mental features, and their tendency to become strictly incorrigible as they become more particular and limited – account, I believe, for the term "mental" having been stretched from the paradigm cases of the nonphysical – thoughts and sensations – to such things as beliefs, desires, emotions, and intentions. If I am right in saying that strict incorrigibility is the mark of mental events and if I was right in saying above that it was mental events, as opposed to mental features, which engendered the Cartesian notion of the mental and the physical as separate realms, then it is appropriate that near-incorrigibility should be the basis for widening the realm of the mental. The likeness of near-incorrigibility to strict incorrigibility is the family resemblance that ties the various things called "mental" together and makes it possible to contrast them all with the physical. But the distinctness of near- from strict incorrigibility is what makes it impossible to find any interesting set of necessary and sufficient conditions for mentality.

I have now completed my search for marks of the mental. I shall end by turning to the relevance of my results to materialism. I began by arguing that the attempt to avoid the "irreducible-properties objection" to mind-brain identity foundered on the incompatibility between the mental and the physical. I have now isolated that incompatibility as the incompatibility between what we are strictly or nearly incorrigible about and what we are straightforwardly corrigible about. What can the materialist do in the face of this incompatibility?

I suggest that he can say, simply, that it might turn out that there are no entities about which we are incorrigible, nearly or strictly. This discovery would be made if the use of cerebroscopes (or some similar mechanism) led to a practice of overriding reports about mental entities on the basis of knowledge of brain states. If we should, as a result of correlations between neurological and mental states, begin taking a discovery of a neurological state as better evidence about a subject's mental state than his own report, mental states would lose their incorrigible status and, thus, their status as *mental*. This possibility is a result of the way in which we defined "incorrigible belief." By phrasing our definition in terms of accepted procedures, rather than in terms of the logical impossibility of error, we leave room for the sort of change that would confirm "eliminative" materialism.

There is, however, another way in which materialism could be vindicated, but this too involves a shift in linguistic practices on the part of our descendants. If it came to pass that people found that they could explain behavior at least as well by reference to brain states as by reference to beliefs, desires, thoughts, and sensations, then reference to the latter might simply disappear from the language. Reports of thoughts and sensations, e.g., might be replaced by reports of brain-processes. To invoke a possibility I have explored in another article,[28] reference to mental states might become as outdated as reference to demons, and it would become natural to say that, although people had once believed that there were mental states, we had now discovered that there were no such things. Instead of our continuing, as in the first alternative suggested above, to speak about thoughts, desires, and the like but ceasing to let ourselves be incorrigible about them, we might simply cease to talk about them at all (except for antiquarian purposes). Either of these changes would give the "eliminative" materialist the right to say that it had been discovered that there were no mental entities.

This conclusion amounts to saying that only the third of the three strategies I described at the outset as available to the materialist is viable. The first strategy, involving "topic-neutral" translations, has already been discussed. The second involves circumventing the "irreducible-properties objection" by making contingent identifications of mentalistic properties with neurological properties. But the second strategy, like the first,

---

[28] Cf. "Mind-Body Identity, Privacy, and Categories," *Review of Metaphysics*, 19, 1 (1965), pp. 24–54 [Chapter 6 in the present volume].

founders on the incompatibility of the mental and the physical. Even if we could identify "being about *p*" or "being of red" with neurological universals, we are never going to identify the property of being the subject of an incorrigible or near-incorrigible report with any neurological property. For this is not a feature which mental states have, so to speak, by themselves and which might be found mirrored in neurology – it is a feature attached to them by the linguistic practices of a community. This property may cease to hold of thoughts, beliefs, sensations, desires, etc. – in which case these things would cease to be *mental* entities. Or these entities might be rejected altogether. But nothing would count as finding a neurological property that *was* the property of being the subject of incorrigible reports.

Only the third strategy, therefore – the one which admits that there is an incompatibility between being mental and being physical, but suggests that there may be no mental entities – will do as an explication of the materialist thesis. But to say that it might turn that there are no mental entities is to say something not merely about the relative explanatory powers of psychological and physiological accounts of behavior, but about possible changes in people's ways of speaking. For as long as people continue to report, incorrigibly, on such things as thoughts and sensations, it will seem silly to say that mental entities do not exist – no matter what science may do. The eliminative materialist cannot rest his case solely on the practices of scientists, but must say something about the ontology of the man in the street.

Yet it may seem outrageously paradoxical to say that the truth of an ontological thesis depends in part upon what linguistic practices are adopted by the community. One's feeling is that it should be the other way around – that such practices should shift as a result of the discovery of ontological truths. Perhaps the paradoxical flavor may be diminished, however, by noting the near-invisibility of the difference between the identity thesis and a certain form of parallelism. On this form of parallelism, there are neural-mental correlations of such a sort that every "natural kind" of mental state is constantly correlated with a "natural kind" of neural state.[29] If such correlations occurred, every explanation of behavior

---

[29] The possibility I am suggesting here is one envisaged by Charles Taylor in "Mind-Body Identity: A Side Issue?," *Philosophical Review*, 76, 2 (1967), pp. 201–13 – that not only will every mental state be correlated with a brain state, but that regularities among brain states adequate to the explanation of behavior will appear not only when, in Taylor's phrase, we "characterize these events as *embodiments* of the corresponding thoughts and feelings" but also when we consider them purely in their own, neurological, terms. Taylor thinks that this "(ultimately empirical) question of the most fruitful forms of explanation of behavior" is "the major question in dispute between

in terms of mental states would be isomorphic to an explanation of behavior in terms of neural states, neither mode of explanation being simpler or more elegant or more fruitful than the other. The discovery of this form of parallelism would, it seems clear, be a necessary condition for either of the changes in linguistic practices I have described. (No one should be inclined to let cerebroscopes correct introspection, nor to stop talking about mental states altogether, unless this degree of "interchange-ability" of the mental and the neural ways of speaking had been discovered.) But it seems equally clear that it is not a sufficient condition. The further condition necessary would be, roughly, a preference for Occam's Razor over old ways of speaking.

Whether this preference is felt by the community as a whole in the way the materialist would like it to be felt is something very close to being a matter of taste, not to be decided by either empirical discoveries or philosophical argumentation. But even if the general will goes against him, the proponent of the identity thesis should not be abashed. He can still say that it would be *rational* to go beyond parallelism to identity. But would he bother? Would not the purported advantage of saying "identical" rather than "correlated" have begun to seem a mere shibboleth? Would the identity thesis still be an interesting point of controversy, once parallelism of the sort we have described is found to hold? I suspect not, and therefore I take what I have said about the need for changes in linguistic practices in order for the identity thesis to be affirmed, although formally correct, to be somewhat misleading. When ontological issues boil down to matters of taste, they cease to be ontological issues. If parallelism of the sort described were discovered, there would, I think, cease to be an issue about material-ism. For the materialist would have succeeded in showing that all phe-nomena can be explained completely in physicalistic terms, and this would be enough to satisfy his ontological intuitions. Insistence on the "identity" of the mental and the physical would seem an unnecessary rhetorical flourish.

materialists and their opponents" and that the materialists win if such purely neurologically characterizable regularities appear. I am arguing that, for the materialist to win, a further step would be necessary – a change in linguistic practices.

# CHAPTER 9

# Wittgenstein, privileged access, and incommunicability

## I Introduction

In this chapter, I wish to argue for the following theses:

(A)  None of the arguments about the possibility of a private language or about the privacy of sensations and thoughts which Wittgenstein advances in the *Philosophical Investigations* provide good reason for doubting

  (a)  that words like "toothache" and "pain" are the names (in a nontrivial sense) of sensations which people sometimes experience, or

  (b)  that when I assert truly "I have a toothache" or "I am in pain," I am describing the state of my consciousness, or

  (c)  that when I assert of another person "He has a toothache" or "He is in pain" I claim that he is experiencing the same sort of sensation that I do when I have a toothache or am in pain.

(B)  None of these arguments give good reasons for rejecting as senseless the claim that "sensations are private."

(C)  None of these arguments give good reasons for rejecting as senseless the claim that "I know that I am in pain because I feel it."

I have drafted these theses with an eye to recent discussions of Wittgenstein's views about the privacy of sensations, and in the belief that certain confusions committed by Wittgenstein or his interpreters – notably between "privacy" in the sense of "susceptibility to privileged access" and in the sense of "incommunicability" – have led sympathetic commentators to attribute unnecessarily paradoxical views to him, and hostile critics to attack him by attacking these paradoxes.

Wittgenstein's central insights have thus, I believe, been obscured. Accordingly, this chapter will consist of commentary on commentaries on Wittgenstein. By reviewing the literature on the topic, I hope to make possible a fresh look at some of Wittgenstein's central themes.

The wording of clauses (a), (b), and (c) in (A) above are taken from George Pitcher,[1] who argues that these three clauses express the view which Wittgenstein believed his arguments to have overthrown. (Pitcher does not believe that these arguments *do* overthrow this view, but many of Wittgenstein's readers have thought they did.) John Cook,[2] in contesting Pitcher's account of what Wittgenstein thought he had shown, argues that Wittgenstein's aim was rather to show the senselessness of the assertions quoted in (B) and (C). In section II, I argue for (A) by rebutting arguments which Pitcher attributes to Wittgenstein. In section III, I argue for (B) and (C) by rebutting those attributed to him by Cook. (I shall not attempt to settle the question of whether Wittgenstein actually advanced either set of arguments.)

## II   Pitcher's interpretation

Pitcher calls the view expressed by the three clauses cited under (A) above "View V" and claims that they – and, in particular, (b) – entail that "I can never know for certain whether . . . another person is in pain or not – for I cannot feel another person's pain."[3] He regards this as a *reductio*, but does not argue for the entailment. Bating the question of whether the conclusion is absurd, it would seem that the entailment would only hold if

I know for certain that Jones is in pain entailed
I feel Jones's pain.

But one would accept this latter entailment only if one held

(1)   If Jones is certain that he is in pain, and if I am certain that he is in pain, we must both have the same grounds for certainty

and there seems no plausibility to this view.

Again, Pitcher claims that V entails that "I cannot conceive that another person feels the same sensation that I do when I feel a pain."[4] He supports this by saying that

---

[1] *The Philosophy of Wittgenstein* (Englewood Cliffs, 1964), p. 285.
[2] "Wittgenstein on Privacy," *Philosophical Review*, 74 (1965), pp. 281–314. Reprinted in George Pitcher, ed, *Wittgenstein: The Philosophical Investigations: A Collection of Critical Essays* (New York, 1966), pp. 286–323.
[3] Pitcher, p. 285.     [4] *Ibid.*, p. 288.

There are in fact no specifiable conditions under which I could determine that another person feels the same sensation I do: to do that I would have to be able to feel his pain (see *PI*, sect. 253); and that is impossible. He can, of course, describe his pain to me as "sharp," "dull," "severe," and so on, but this is no help whatever; for I have no way of telling what corresponds to these adjectives in this case. The adjectives are here being used analogically ... Since there is no way of specifying how the truth of the assertion "He feels the same sensation I do" could possibly be determined, the assertion is unintelligible.[5]

In this passage, and elsewhere, Pitcher is assuming that View V entails

(2)    "Pain" is the name of a kind of private sensation
      and that this in turn entails
(3)    I only learn what pain is from my own case
      which in turn entails
(4)    I can only apply the word "pain" to my own sensations.

But it is not clear why (2) entails (3). Here, we encounter the problem of the meaning of "privacy," and it will therefore be helpful to recall some distinctions, drawn most explicitly by Ayer, between possible meanings of this term.[6] Ayer notes that we might say

(P1)    Things are private to a given person if their existence, or one or more of their qualities, could be known by him but not conceivably by anybody else.

or

(P2)    Things are private to a given person if there is at least one way in which he can detect either their existence, or one or more of their qualities, but others cannot.

or

(P3)    Things are private to a given person if his authority about either propositions like "There is an ..." or "There is an ... which has a certain quality" cannot be overridden.

or

[5] *Ibid.*, p. 288.
[6] Cf. *The Concept of a Person* (New York, 1963), p. 79. In stating these possible meanings, I have touched up Ayer's statement of them by speaking of "the existence of, or some quality of" an object, rather than simply of "the existence of" the object.

(P4)   Things are private to a given person if he has something which he can either not share with another person, or which he can share only partially (in the sense that he can have the same *kind* of thing as another person, but not the numerically identical thing).

Now View V does not commit us to (2) even if (2) is interpreted in the weak sense of (P4). (When so interpreted, we should notice, (3) does not follow.) As it stands, View V says nothing about epistemological questions, and thus does not commit us to the privacy of sensations in any other sense. However, Pitcher is, reasonably enough, assuming that one who holds V will also hold

I know about my pains by feeling them

and

Nobody else can feel my pains, nor can I feel anybody else's.

These propositions would commit the holder of V to interpreting (2) in the sense of P2 as well as that of P4. But even this would not allow the inference to (3). For we might well say that I can learn what pain is (and/or what "pain" means) in all sorts of complicated ways, and could learn this even if I never happened to have had a pain. Even if we granted that we could not learn what pain was unless we had received appropriate linguistic training concurrently with being in pain – thus granting (3) though not the entailment of (3) by (2) – one would still not be in a position to go from (3) to (4) without the help of some such premise as

(5)   If I learn the meaning of a word by ostention (i.e., if ostensive definition is a necessary part of the process of learning the meaning of the word), then I can meaningfully apply that word only to objects ostensible to me in the same way in which the original cases (the ones used in training me) were ostensible.

But nothing in View V seems to support such a *prima facie* implausible premise. Why should one who holds V not answer Wittgenstein by saying that the criteria for the truth of "He feels the same sensation I do" are the standard behavioral and environmental ones? Pitcher implicitly grants the possibility of this reply when he says that "The foregoing considerations [various arguments, including the one now under discussion] do not show that 'pain' is not the name of a private sensation. They show only that some outward manifestations of pain are required for the teaching and learning of the use of the word 'pain'."[7] Pitcher says the admission of this

---

[7] Pitcher, p. 292.

latter point constitutes a "modification" of V, but it is not clear that it is. He so describes it, I believe, because he implicitly assumes that one who upholds V is also committed to "If 'N' is the (common) name of things of a certain kind, then (for at least some kinds) nothing save awareness of such things, plus correlated utterances of 'N' by those who know the language which contains 'N', are required to learn what 'N' means." This assumption is one which I think Wittgenstein *does* have a good argument against. Here, however, I want simply to note that it is logically independent of V. First, however, for the sake of completeness, let us look at a final argument which, according to Pitcher, Wittgenstein advances against the "unmodified" form of V.

This argument rests on the premise that "The expression of doubt has no place in the language-game" (which we play with utterances like "I am in pain now").[8] Pitcher presents Wittgenstein as saying that if V were correct then "when a sensation appears before a person's mind, he must identify that item (as, say, a pain rather than itch or an ache or a twinge). In that case, the possibility arises at once that he might make a mistake in his identification. He might always misidentify it, and hence it must always be possible for him to wonder whether he has done so or not."[9] But the quoted premise shows that he cannot so wonder. Pitcher is here suggesting that Wittgenstein infers from

(I)    I can identify a certain particular

to

(II)   It is in principle possible for me (given present practices, and barring misuse of language, or failure to master the language) to make a mistake in identifying that particular (a mistake which is not a result of ignorance of the language – of, e.g., the meanings of terms like "pain," "sensation," "stabbing," etc.).

to

(III)   I have criteria for identifying that particular.

But, defenders of V may reply, why does not the case of mental particulars simply show that the inference from (I) to (II) is fallacious? Why should all cases of identification be cases of corrigibility?

When we have to choose between an analysis of a concept like "identification of a particular" (e.g., one which would license the inference from

[8] *Philosophical investigations*, Pt I, sect. 288.     [9] Pitcher, p. 290.

(I) to (II)) and a piece of conventional wisdom such as View V, what is our criterion? It is not too much to say that certain interpreters of Wittgenstein have argued as follows: "We can make mistakes when we identify, but not when we express feelings. There are no mistaken pain-reports. Therefore pain-reports are expressions of feeling, rather than identifications of particulars." So put, the argument is to say the least of it, an obvious *petitio*. To get a good argument we need to argue that no analysis of "identifying a particular" which does not permit the inference from (I) to (II) will be adequate. But I do not think that any interpreter of Wittgenstein has offered such an argument. Rather, they have assumed that any adequate analysis of "identifying a particular" will include the notions of "observing the particular (or its effects)," "noting whether the particular satisfies certain criteria," etc. Since they note, rightly, that the Cartesian tradition in philosophy has built up a host of philosophical perplexities out of the assumption that we possess an inner eye which inspects (and, so to speak an "inner mind" which forms judgments about) mental particulars, they assume that the fastest way to overthrow this tradition is to abandon the notion that when we report, e.g., pains or thoughts we are identifying particulars. It is indeed a fast way, but it is certainly not the only way.

More will be heard of the fact that we cannot have doubts about whether we are in pain when we come to Cook's interpretation of Wittgenstein. We may turn now, however, to Pitcher's account of Wittgenstein's arguments against the "modified" version of V. On this account, "the ways in which the names of public objects and qualities denote their objects cannot be even remotely like the ways in which 'pain' denotes a sensation," and this is seen by noting that

> I can do practically none of the things [with pains] I can do with physical objects or colors or shapes, i.e., with publicly observable things, and so the modes of behavior in which alone the connection between the name of something public and the thing it names is made are not available in the case of "pain."[10]

The defender of V is then envisaged by Pitcher as replying that the process of learning by ostensive definition which we undergo while coming to use "tree" or "red" correctly may, in fact, be paralleled by a similar process – namely, the one which the celebrated "private diarist" conducts when he decides to call a given sensation '*E*'. Having taken this line, he is now a

---

[10]  *Ibid.*, pp. 293–4.

patsy for the familiar objection that "the concept of correctness and incorrectness does not apply" to '$E$'.[11]

Here we need merely ask: is this appeal to a private diary the only rejoinder which one who holds V can make to the argument which Pitcher attributes to Wittgenstein? The difficulty in answering this question is a result of the vagueness of the phrase "the way in which names denote . . . ." How much like the way in which "tree" denotes trees does the relation between "pain" and pains have to be? What parameters of similarity and difference are appropriate here? Does the fact that we can do "practically none of the things" with trees and "tree" that we do with pains and "pain" count as showing that what Wittgenstein calls "the model of 'object and name'" is out of place here? May it not be that the model can be kept, as long as we are on our guard not to assume that, because the same model is used for "tree" and for "pain," everything that holds for the former holds for the latter? By putting the claim that "we can keep a private diary" in the mouth of the holder of V, one seems to assume that

(6)    We cannot come to know what the referent is of an observation-term (i.e., a referring expression which very frequently occurs in noninferential reports – reports which people make without having gone through a conscious process of inference) except by ostention.

Since "pain," under this definition, obviously *is* an observation-term, the truth of (6) would commit those who hold that " 'pain' is the name of private sensation" to something like the "private diary" picture of how we learn the names of mental particulars. But, given Wittgenstein's critique of the whole notion of "ostensive definition," and the doubt this critique casts on (6), cannot we simultaneously repudiate (6) and maintain V? Once again we need to ask whether we cannot simply appropriate Wittgenstein's theories about language and the learning of language without thereby giving up V. As in the case of choosing an analysis of "identifying a particular," there may be a perfectly good analysis of "denoting" which covers both "tree" and "pain." At least we may say that unless it is shown that such an analysis cannot be given, and that any adequate analysis will entail (6), the "private diary" argument does not show that "pain" may not be the name of a private sensation, where "private" has the senses of (P2), (P3), or (P4).

[11]   *Ibid.*, p. 297.

In my examination of the arguments so far, it may seem that I have perversely evaded the point. It seems clear that, despite the gaps in the arguments which I have tried to point out, there is *something* to these arguments, and that our treatment so far has not got at it. I think this is so, and I think that many threads can be knotted together by focusing on the central premise of the next (and last) argument which Pitcher presents – his interpretation of Wittgenstein's "beetle-in-the-box" argument. This premise is: "Everyone acknowledges that sensations are private, that no one can experience another person's sensations, so that the special felt quality of each person's sensations is known to him alone and to no other."[12] What Pitcher does in this sentence is to move from privacy in the sense of (P4) to privacy in the sense of (P1) – from

(7)  Sensations cannot be shared

to

(8)  We cannot communicate certain qualities (the "special felt qualities") of our sensations to others.

Given (8), Pitcher can continue "Thus, when you are in pain, I do not know, cannot know, the character of your sensation – whether, for example, it is exactly like what I might feel if my hand were wounded as yours is now, or whether it is something altogether different." But, restricting ourselves to V and its consequences, this line of argument is no more convincing than the skeptical suggestion that you and I, when we inspect a patch of red or a beetle, are having wildly different experiences or seeing wildly different things, even though we say all the same things. If we both say the same things about our sensations, the patch, or the beetle, then it is not clear what it means to say that there are certain qualities of sensations, patches, or beetles which are "incommunicable." We may wish to squash skepticism about our knowledge of beetles by noting that a difference which is not reflected in a possible difference in what we say is in some sense, not a real difference. But one may happily grant this point and yet insist that the fact that pains cannot be shared does nothing to show that the relation between "pain" and pains differs from the relation between "red" and red patches or "beetle" and beetles. If one refuses to take skepticism about patches or beetles seriously – on the ground that the skeptic's suggestion that it might be, so to speak, sheer chance that we all agree in what we say about them does not make sense – then one should

---

[12]  *Ibid.*, p. 297.

not take skepticism about pains seriously either, and thus one should not grant (8). Nor does it help to say that it is only the false view of pains as private sensations which licenses the skepticism of (8). For one who holds view V may be committed only to sensations as private in the sense of (P4) (and possibly (P3) and (P2) as well), not to their privacy in the sense of (P1), and thus not to (8).

Given this point, we can account for our sense that there is *something* to the various arguments which Pitcher attributes to Wittgenstein by noting that *if* (8) *is* accepted – or, more generally, if privacy in the sense of (P2), (P3), or (P4) is taken to entail privacy in the sense of (P1) – then a number of dubitable premises which we have isolated above – e.g., (1), (3), (5), and (6) – look a good deal more plausible than they do in isolation. They look still more plausible if we adopt two more principles, *viz.*,

(9)    I know what a given sort of sensation is only because I know about certain incommunicable "special felt qualities" which are characteristic of certain sensations I myself have.

and

(10)    I do not know whether it would be appropriate to apply the name of a given sort of sensation – e.g., "pain" – unless I know whether I am talking about something which has certain incommunicable "special felt properties."

I think that the plausibility of Wittgenstein's arguments, as they have been presented by Pitcher, arise from his tacitly treating (8), (9), and (10) as an intrinsic part of view V. This treatment is by no means disingenuous, for it is the case that *philosophers* who held V had frequently held (8), (9), and (10) as well. But it is nevertheless important both to distinguish between what philosophers have tacitly accepted and what common sense would say, and to recognize that these various theses are at least a few steps farther away from common sense than the three assertions which express Pitcher's "official" version of V.

I want now to finish the job of showing that, in Pitcher's account of Wittgenstein's arguments, *everything* turns on the truth of the additional premises (8), (9), and (10). So I now come back to the argument which Pitcher constructs on the basis of his premise about "special felt qualities." Pitcher quotes the celebrated "beetle-in-the-box" passage and says

> The analogy with pain is perfectly clear. If "pain" is supposed to denote a somewhat (including a nothing) which each person can observe only in his

own case, then the somewhat "cancels out"; and if the sole function of the word "pain" is to denote it, the word is at once deprived of any use.[13]

There are various objections which might be made here – notably about the parenthetical clause "including a nothing" and about the attribution to holders of V of the claim that this is the "sole function" of "pain." But let us bate these issues and consider simply what is being said when we say that "the somewhat 'cancels out'." The original passage in Wittgenstein, after describing people's privileged access to the contents of their boxes, says

> But suppose the word "beetle" had a use in these people's language? – If so, it would not be used as the name of a thing. The thing in the box has no place in the language-game at all; not even as a *something*: for the box might even be empty. – No, one can "divide through" by the thing in the box; it cancels out, whatever it is.
>
> That is to say, if we construe the grammar of the expression of sensation on the model of "object and designation" the object drops out of consideration as irrelevant.[14]

Pitcher says that Wittgenstein is here

> only denying a particular thesis about language, namely that the word "pain" names or designates this something that the person feels, in a way which is even remotely like the way that words for publicly observable things name or designate them. In the language-games we play with words like "tree" and "red," trees and redness (red things) play some part, and it is in these games that the connection between the name and the thing named is established. But in the numerous language-games we play with the word "pain," private sensations play no part, and so "pain" cannot denote them in anything like the way that "tree," for example, denotes that kind of object. What does play a part in pain language-games is pain-behavior . . . and pain-comforting behavior . . . – in short, the external circumstances in which the word "pain" is used.[15]

Pitcher thus identifies "is canceled out" with "plays no part in the language-game." Two points may be made about this passage. First, in saying that "private sensations play no part" Wittgenstein is either committing a *petitio* or else using "private sensations" as an abbreviation for "those special felt qualities of private sensations which are not communicable in language." In the latter case, he is perfectly justified in his claim, but then we must realize that it is not self-evident that there are such qualities, and that even if there

---

[13] *Ibid.*, p. 298.     [14] *Philosophical Investigations*, Pt I, sect. 293.     [15] Pitcher, pp. 298–9.

were it might be that private sensations had plenty of *other* qualities which *were* communicable. Secondly, consider the following parodies:

> But in the numerous language-games which we play with "tree," the tree-in-itself plays no part, and so "tree" cannot denote in anything like the way that words which refer to directly experienced entities (e.g., green sense-data) denote. What does play a part in tree language-games is sense-data, and certain other mental entities (intentions, judgments, volitions, desires, etc.) – in short, the directly apprehended objects of awareness which are before our consciousness in situations in which we learn how to use "tree."
>
> But in the numerous language-games which we play with "neutron," the neutrons themselves play no part, and so "neutron" cannot denote in anything like the way that words which refer to directly experienced entities (e.g., cloud-chamber tracks) denote. What does play a part in neutron language-games are pointer-readings, unexpected results in mathematical calculations.. . .

I take these parodies to show if we use the notion of playing no part in the language-game to explicate "cancels out," it will be much too easy to cancel things out.[16] The trouble is that it is never very hard to describe the process of learning and using a given term – one which, *prima facie*, seems to be used to denote particulars – in a language which makes no reference to these particulars. All that one has to do is to use only terms which occur in criteria for applying the term in question. One will thus be able to argue that the particulars putatively denoted "play no part" in the language-game played with the putatively denoting term, and thus "cancel out."

I have developed the second point to emphasize the importance of the first, and to show that, on Pitcher's interpretation, the "beetle-in-the-box" argument reduces to the argument that what is *incommunicable* can play no part in a language-game. This argument may be expressed as follows:

(a)   Suppose that $Q$ is an incommunicable quality of a particular – a quality which cannot be characterized in language.

(b)   Let $G^*$ be the (indefinitely large) set of rules which govern the correct application of a (putatively) referring expression '$P$'.

---

[16] The fact that such parodies can be constructed has suggested to such writers as Strawson, and Chihara and Fodor, that Wittgenstein is taking for granted the sort of operationalism which inspired Berkeley, the Absolute Idealists, and positivistic phenomenalists. I think that he did indeed do this, confusing the kernel of truth in the verificationist theory of *meaningfulness* with a stronger, false, theory about *meaning*.

(c) Suppose that we cannot tell whether '*P*' has been correctly applied unless we know whether it is being applied to something that is *Q*.

(d) Then, by (c) *G*\* must contain some rule of the form (*R*) "Call it a *P* only if you have good reason to think that it is *Q*."

(e) But then *G*\* is inexpressible in language, for, by (a), no expression in any language characterizes *Q*, and (*R*) is therefore inexpressible.

(f) But the notion of there being rules for using a language which cannot themselves be expressed in any language is incoherent.

(g) Therefore (a) and (c) are mutually incompatible hypotheses.

If one grants (f), then I think that this argument is sound.[17] But we now see that, the argument – in (c) – presupposes (10) – *viz.*, that the incommunicable "special felt" qualities of my private sensations are of the *essence* of those sensations. The reason why Wittgenstein (according to Pitcher) thinks that private sensations cancel out but that trees and neutrons do not is that the former, but not the latter, are "beyond the reach of language." If I am right in suggesting that the denials of (8)–(10) are absolutely central to Wittgenstein's thought, then it is easy to see why Wittgenstein should have attached so much importance to denying that the relation between pains and "pain" can be construed "on the model of 'object and designation'." If (8)–(10) *were* true, then we would have to grant the existence of knowledge unmediated by language – the central Cartesian fallacy. For we would have to grant that words in a public language could be learned and used only by calling upon knowledge of (as yet) incommunicable qualities – the usual Cartesian–Lockean picture of language-learning.

This exegesis of the final argument which Pitcher attributes to Wittgenstein may be confirmed by noting one more remark which he makes:

> If, after you say to someone "I am in pain," he sympathizes with you, comforts you, does what he can to help you, then the word "pain" has done its work – and it was not used to tell him the nature of what you had before your consciousness, because that cannot be told.[18]

The first clause here is unexceptionable, but the second clause ("and it was not used . . .") rests on nothing except the claim that "that cannot be told" and the vague suggestion that if an utterance does one job, it cannot do two. If we discount the latter suggestion (as I think we should) then we are

---

[17] I think that (f) is true, and that Wittgenstein thought so too. But I do not think he had any convincing arguments in its favor, nor do I.

[18] Pitcher, p. 299.

left with the claim that what is before my consciousness "cannot be told." This claim rests *entirely* on (8) and (10).


### III   Cook's interpretation

In the article referred to earlier, Cook criticizes Pitcher for attributing to Wittgenstein the view that "I cannot 'determine that another person feels the same sensation I do'."[19] Cook argues that Wittgenstein did not commit himself to (8) – on a construal of (8) according to which the "special felt qualities" are objects of knowledge – nor to (9) and (10). But his argument depends on attributing certain other dubious theses to Wittgenstein, notably the following:

> There is no criterion of numerical (as opposed to generic) identity of sensations.
> The notion that "sensations are private objects" is senseless.
> It is senseless to say that "I know that I am in pain because I feel it."

Since we have presupposed the contradictories of all three of these theses in our discussion of Pitcher's interpretation, we need now to inquire whether Wittgenstein provides good arguments in favor of any of them.

Although Cook's criticism of Pitcher comes at the very end of his discussion, it will be convenient to begin with an analysis of this criticism to connect the remarks I have already made about Pitcher's version of Wittgenstein with the criticisms I wish to make of Cook's. Cook says that Pitcher thinks that Wittgenstein is criticizing a common-sensical view (V), whereas he is in fact only criticizing a "philosopher's picture," Cook notes that Pitcher does not quote the last sentence of Wittgenstein's "beetle-in-the-box" passage, *viz.*, "That is to say: if we construe the grammar of the expression of sensation on the model of 'object and name' the object drops out of consideration as irrelevant." He continues

> The word "if" here is crucial, for it is not Wittgenstein's view but the one he opposes that construes the grammar of the expression of sensation on the model of "object and name," and therefore it is not Wittgenstein, as Pitcher thinks, who is committed to the paradoxical consequence that in the use of the word "pain," for example, the sensation drops out as irrelevant. The point of the passage, then, is quite the opposite of what Pitcher supposes. Rather than showing that sensations cannot have names, it shows that since

---

[19] Cook, p. 313 (p. 322). The number given in parentheses in references to Cook's article is the page number in Pitcher's anthology (see n. 2 above).

the view that sensations are private allows sensations to have "no place in the language game" and thereby makes it impossible to give any account of the actual (that is, the "public") use of sensation words, we must, if we are to give an account of that language game, reject the view that sensations are private.[20]

Roughly speaking, Pitcher takes Wittgenstein to say that since sensations are private, they can't have names, whereas Cook takes him to say that since sensations have names, they can't be private. Both, then, seem to agree that Wittgenstein needs as a premise

Private objects can't have names.

I wish to argue that Wittgenstein has given no good reasons for holding this view. In examining it, we are once again led to ask for an explanation of "private," but Cook is no help here. He thinks that it is pointless to criticize Wittgenstein for not having explained more clearly what he meant by "private language" because "the idea under investigation turns out to be irremediably confused and hence can be only suggested, not clearly explained. Moreover, the philosophical idea of a private language is confused not merely in that it supposes a mistaken notion of language (or meaning) but in its very notion of the privacy of sensations."[21] Cook here seems to be saying that the very notion of a "private object" is too confused to be explained. In the light of Ayer's vigorous efforts to formulate explanations of various senses of this notion, this is a strong claim. Cook backs it up by claiming that only a false presupposition that sensations can be numerically identical permits Ayer to formulate his explanations. Thus, according to Cook, when Ayer says that in the sense in which two people can have the same pain or the same thought we do *not* have "numerical identity" in mind, he is presupposing the view that sometimes we *do* have numerical identity in mind, and this is false. Cook thinks that we must answer "no" to the question "is there, then a familiar use of sensation words with a criterion of identity that is reflected in 'But surely another person can't have this pain'?" His argument for this negative answer comes out best in the following passage:

Thus, if a mother has described one of her children's tantrums, someone else might remark that her child had had a tantrum "exactly like that" … "Exactly like" is used here in contrast, not with "same," but with "rather like," "rather different," and so forth. That is, it would not be asked: "Do you suppose they may have had the same one and not just two exactly

---

[20] *Ibid.*, p. 312 (pp. 322–3).    [21] *Ibid.*, p. 281 (pp. 286–7).

alike?" This kind of identification question has no place in the grammar of "tantrum," and so neither do its two answers: "Yes, they did have the same one" and "No, they did not have the same one, only two exactly alike." Now this same point holds for the grammar of "toothache"... That is, it would not make sense to say, as if in answer to that question, *either* "They had the same toothache" or "They did not have the same toothache."[22]

We can agree that such questions "should not be asked," but we can also hold that the reason they are not asked is not that we lack a criterion for numerical identity of toothaches, but simply that it is obvious that the criterion for numerical difference is satisfied. Consider the following definition:

(D)    Two sensations are generically the same if and only if the persons who have them describe them in exactly the same terms, answer questions about them in exactly the same way, etc., and two generically identical sensations are numerically different if and only if they are had by different persons or by the same person at different times.

What is wrong with (D) – simple-minded as it is – if one wants a criterion for the numerical identity of toothaches? Cook is right in suggesting that Ayer would not accept it, since Ayer wishes to leave open the possibility of "co-consciousness," and thus does not want its impossibility built into the language-game. But suppose that, for the moment, we just decide to describe all cases of possible "co-consciousness" (e.g., cases of split personality, cases of interchanged or intercommunicating organs, etc.) in a way compatible with (D). Do we not then have all we need to give sense to the notion of "generically the same, but numerically different, sensations"?

Cook would presumably say that we do not and would insist that

(I)    If a yes-or-no question does not normally occur in extra-philosophical discourse (although all the words used in it do), then the question, and all direct answers to it, are senseless.

Cook regards this principle as superior to the one usually adopted by philosophers who claim that "It is a necessary truth that no two people can have the same toothache" – *viz.*, a principle such as

(II)    If a yes-or-no question does not occur in extraphilosophical discourse because it is never the case that the answer to it is "yes"

---

[22] *Ibid.*, p. 308 (p. 312).

(or because it is never the case that the answer to it is "no"), then a suitably generalized form of the answer which *would* invariably be given (if the question *were* asked) expresses a necessary truth.

One may sympathize with Cook's doubts about (II), since the notion of "necessary truth" (or "conceptual truth" or "grammatical truth") is indeed very murky. But I think the attempt (which is a major theme of Cook's article) to substitute notions of "confusion arising from mixing up distinct language-games" and of "senselessness" for such notions is a cure which is worse than the disease. One can applaud Cook's remark that "This talk of grammar 'forbidding us' to say something is nothing but the most recent jargon for calling a halt to an analogy whose oddness has begun to dawn on one,"[23] while regretting that Cook himself does not stick to blocking bad analogies, rather than resorting to charges of "senselessness" and invoking (I). To see what is wrong with (I), consider the following argument against the claim that there is a criterion of numerical identity for mountains:

> It might be discovered that two mountains – one in Alaska and one in Antarctica – were exactly like each other. They had precisely the same configuration, the rock of which they were made seemed qualitatively identical – and so on for all features within a radius of, say, two air miles from their respective peaks. "Exactly like" is used here in contrast, not with "same," but with "rather like," "rather different," and so forth. That is, it would not be asked "Do you suppose they may be the same mountain?" This kind of identification question has no place in the grammar of "mountain," and so neither do its two answers: "Yes, they are the same" and "No, they are not."

This argument does not show anything except that if we know that two mountains have different locations, we don't ask whether they are the same mountain. It certainly does not show that "The same mountain cannot be in two different places at the same time" is senseless. So *sometimes* (I) is false.

On the other hand, Cook has an example which makes (I) look fairly plausible. This is the noun "build," as in "His build is exactly like his father's." Here indeed the question "Do they have the same build?" cannot be construed in different ways – once in regard to qualitative identity and again in regard to numerical identity. Further, the answer "No, the builds are different, but they're exactly alike" *is* "senseless," if any grammatical English sentence is. But this example just forces us to ask: (a) "Are pains

---

[23] *Ibid.*, p. 303 (p. 311).

more like mountains or like builds?"; (b) since (D) would, *mutatis mutan-dis*, seem to work for builds as well as for sensations, is not our so-called criterion for numerical identity of sensations susceptible to a *reductio ad absurdum*?

The answer to (a), I think, is that pains are more like mountains simply in the respect that we *do* sometimes say things like "But nobody can have *this* pain" and "But the one in Antarctica can't be *this* mountain" and *don't* say things like "But nobody can have *this* build." (If it were said that nobody but a philosopher would use the first of the quoted sentences, I would not wish to argue a point which seems to me irrelevant. It would be relevant only if philosophers played on the limited – and, to my mind, quite innocent – analogy between pains and mountains created by their odd linguistic habits in order to infer to some *further* analogy.) There is no particular reason, as far as I can see, why we treat pains but not builds as particulars, but then why shouldn't we? The answer to (b) is that we *could* treat builds as particulars, in which case we doubtless *would* use a modification of (D) as a criterion of numerical identity for builds. It just happens that we don't.

In making these points, I have no wish to deny Cook's point that builds and pains are analogous in a way that neither are analogous with coats. Cook says that the "my" in "my coat" is a "possessive of ownership" because the question of whether it's my coat (whether I own it) is not settled by the fact that I've got it. In this (stipulated) sense, the "my's" in "my build" and "my toothache" are, to be sure, not possessives of ownership. But Cook goes from

> In cases where "my" is not a possessive of ownership, "is my *X* the same as his *X*?" is not a "genuine identification question"[24]

to

> "Is my *X* the same as his *X*?" is senseless, and so are all direct answers to it,

and I do want to criticize this inference. If a "genuine identification question" means "one that would not be asked by anybody who knows the language" then we still have to ask "Do we not ask it because the answer is so obvious, or because we can't make sense of it?" In the case of builds, I am inclined to say "because we can't make sense of it," although I can imagine someone making sense of it by creating a new language-game in which "my build" is treated as the name of a particular, rather

---

[24] Cf. *Ibid.*, p. 296 (p. 303).

than as the name of a collection of qualities. In the case of pains, I am inclined to say "because the answer is so obvious." All that Cook has done is to note that there would be no great difficulty in treating "my toothache" as the name of a sharable collection of qualities. He has not shown that we *do* so treat it or that we *should* so treat it. To show the former he would have to establish some sort of invidious distinction between language-games played (mainly) by philosophers and language-games played by non-philosophers – one which enables us to discount the former as *ipso facto* "mistaken" or "confused." To show the latter, he would have to show that the philosophers' habit of treating "my toothache" as the name of a particular has had disastrous philosophical consequences, and that the only (or the best) way of avoiding these consequences was to break the habit.

I think that the latter project is closest to Cook's actual intention, for he says that when " 'no two people can feel the same toothache' comes to be called a necessary truth," then "one easily concludes that we cannot know anything about another person's toothaches."[25] But this is not an easy conclusion. It does not follow at all unless one grants some further premises – e.g., (1), or (5), or (8) – all of which, I have argued above, are dubious. A philosopher who refuses to grant any of these further premises, while holding out for the view that "sensations are private" and explicating "private" in the sense of (P2), (P3), or (P4), is not thereby going to get involved in any of the standard puzzles about other minds, knowledge of the external world, and the like. If he interprets "private" in the sense of (P1), and thus assents to (8), he will indeed be in trouble. But, once again, we need to notice the distinction between "privileged access" ("privacy" in the combined senses of (P2) and (P3)), "unsharability" ("privacy" in the sense of (P4)), and "incommunicability" (privacy in the sense of (P1)) and to ask whether, if these distinctions are borne in mind, we cannot get the benefits of Wittgenstein's treatment of private particulars without accepting Cook's paradoxes.

I have now done all I can to show why Cook is wrong in saying that "sensations are private" is senseless, and thus all I can to argue for the claim labeled (B) in the first paragraph of this article. I turn now to the one labeled (C), and ask whether Cook has produced good arguments for rejecting "I know that I am in pain because I feel it" as senseless. If he can do this, he will have shown that to interpret "privacy" in the sense of (P2) is wrong-headed.

---

[25] *Ibid.*, p. 309 (p. 318).

Cook sets about making this latter claim in an odd way. He says that Wittgenstein wants to get around "Argument A" which goes as follows:

(i)   No one can feel (experience, be acquainted with) another person's sensations.

(ii)  The proper and necessary means of coming to know what sensation another person is having is to feel that person's sensation.

(iii) Anyone who has a sensation knows that he has it because he feels it, and whatever can be known to exist by being felt cannot be known (in the same sense of "known") to exist in any other way.

Conclusion: No one can know what sensations another person is having.[26]

One would think that (ii), and the second half of (iii), were so implausible that an attack on them would suffice to get around Argument A. But Cook employs an indirect method, arguing that (ii) and (iii) presuppose that

(iv)  There is a genuine use of the verb "to know" as an expression of certainty with first-person present-tense sensation statements.[27]

and that this presupposition is false.

The odd thing about this argument is that neither "certainty" nor "certain" appears in (ii) or in (iii), and thus it is hard to see how either could presuppose (iv). Suppose we forget about "certainty" for a moment and ask simply: can we find an account of the meaning of "I know that ..." according to which "I know that I am in pain" would be sensible? Let us try a conventional analysis, according to which "I know that $p$" is true *if $p$*, I believe that $p$, and I have adequate evidence for my belief that $p$. Do I have good reasons for believing that I am in pain, when I believe that I am? Two answers suggest themselves:

(A)   My reason is that I feel it

and

(B)   My reason is that I know the language, and consequently know which states are called "pains," which "anxieties," which "thrills," etc., etc.

Since Cook has a rather detailed discussion of (A), to which we shall shortly turn, let us concentrate first on (B). At first sight, (B) seems merely

---

[26] Cf. *Ibid.*, pp. 283–4 (pp. 289–90).     [27] *Ibid.*, p. 285 (p. 240).

to say "I know that I am in pain because I know what pain is," and this does not seem satisfactory. But now let us read (B) as an abbreviation for

(B′)  My reason is that I am inclined to say "I am in pain," and I know that this inclination, had by one who knows the language, is itself evidence, and indeed conclusive evidence, for the truth of what is said.

Here the person who is asked to justify his belief that he is in pain is calling attention to a convention of the language – the convention that the utterance of, or the disposition to utter, certain first-person present-tense reports are taken as the best possible evidence (and, indeed, evidence which cannot be overridden) for their own truth. In other words, he is distinguishing between the fact that he is in pain and his own belief that he is in pain, and saying that the latter is evidence of the former. One could rule this answer out if one held that

Beliefs can never be evidence for the truth of the proposition believed

but this is false, since other people certainly take my beliefs about my mental states as evidence for their own beliefs about my mental states. So why shouldn't I? Can we justify holding

I can never take the fact that I believe *p* as adequate evidence for the truth of *p*?

Perhaps we can, but I do not see how. It seems to me that we have a choice between letting "privileged" reports count as expressions of knowledge by letting this sort of evidence count, or else ruling them out by ruling out this sort of evidence. I do not know how to make this choice except by looking to the degree of paradoxicalness of the views which will result from each alternative. If we choose the former, we have to say "Sometimes the fact that beliefs are held can be adequate evidence for the truth of those beliefs," which sounds a little funny. If we choose the latter, we have to say with Wittgenstein "It is wrong to say 'I know what I am thinking'," which also sounds a little funny. Unless we are simply to fall back on our intuitions about which sounds *more* funny (a result which would, as the recent literature shows, lead to an irresolvable impasse), we have to look further and ask which of the two views leads to the greater *quantity* of funny-sounding views. In other words, we have to look to the further philosophical consequences of taking one alternative rather than the other. Wittgensteinians, by and large, think that a willingness to say "It is wrong to say 'I know what I am thinking'" is the price we have to pay for not having to say the bulk of the funny things which epistemologists in the Cartesian tradition have been wont to say. But, as I remarked above, the familiar Cartesian puzzles would only follow if one accepted, not merely the presupposition of (ii) and (iii) that it makes sense to talk about knowing that one has a certain sensation, but (ii) and (iii) themselves. Once again, we are led to ask why Cook does not attack the premises rather than their presupposition.

A partial answer to this question will emerge if we go back to the phrase "as an expression of certainty" which Cook drags in, seemingly *ab extra*, in formulating (iv). The reason why he does so is suggested by his saying "Whereas it makes sense to speak of ignorance and knowledge, doubt and certainty, in the case of the stone in the shoe, it does not make sense to speak this way in the case of the man in pain."[28] The crucial move here is the implicit suggestion that

(v)   Where it does not make sense to say "I doubt that *p*" it does not make sense to say "I am certain that *p*," and conversely.

and that

(vi)   Where it does not make sense to say "I am certain that *p*" it does not make sense to say "I know that *p*" (in the sense of "know" intended in (ii) and (iii),) and conversely.

Since one is much more ready to say "I cannot have doubts about whether I am in pain" than to say "It is wrong to say 'I know that I am in pain' " to accept (v) and (vi) is to have persuasive reasons for saying the latter. If Cook and Wittgenstein did not have this move to help them, it is doubtful that they would have been quite so certain that those who believe (iv) are "confused." But this move is at bottom the same as the move which Pitcher attributes to Wittgenstein from

I can identify a certain particular

to

It is in principle possible for me to make a mistake in identifying that particular (a mistake which is not a result of ignorance of the language),

a move which I criticized earlier. Cook is asking us to accept an analysis of "knowledge" according to which so-called "incorrigible knowledge" is not to count as knowledge. In both cases, the argument is clearly "reversible"

[28] *Ibid.*, p. 288 (p. 294).

(in Waismann's phrase). That is, it is not clear whether we should accept the analysis and get rid of the (potentially) embarrassing fact that we possess incorrigible knowledge, or whether we should reject the analysis because it does not cover a certain sort of knowledge (while trying to overcome our embarrassment by other tactics). *Prima facie*, my certainty that I am in pain is an obvious counterexample to (v). If I am told that I cannot render a satisfactory account of the meaning of "certain" that will not entail (v), and of "know" that will not entail (vi), then we are driven back to the question about whether the fact of believing *p* may not sometimes be adequate evidence for *p*. For if it may be, then I am entitled to reject the conjunction of (v) and (vi) as false.

The importance of (v) and (vi) for Cook's view will be evident from the following passage. In discussing the reasons one might adduce in support of "I know it's raining" – e.g., "I'm looking out the window" – Cook says:

> What makes it possible to use "I know" here as an expression of certainty is that it would be intelligible for someone to suppose that the speaker is not, in the particular instance, in as good a position as one could want for correctly answering a certain question or making a certain statement. More generally, for "I know that . . . " to be an expression of certainty, it is at least necessary that the sense of the sentence filling the blank allow the speaker to be ignorant in some circumstances of the truth-value of statements made by means of the sentence (or equivalents thereof).[29]

The first sentence of this passage makes clear that Cook tacitly adopts (v). His taking for granted the relevance of "as an expression of certainty" to (ii) and (iii) demonstrates his adoption of (vi). His refusal to consider the possibility that "knowledge of the language" can count as a good reason for knowing that I am in pain can be seen by the fact that his necessary condition for "I know that . . . " being an expression of certainty, as it stands, excludes nothing whatever. For if I do not know what some words in the sentence in question mean, then *that* is a circumstance in which I can be ignorant of the truth-value of statements made by means of the sentence. Since there is no reason to think that everybody knows what "pain" means, this necessary condition, as it stands, is worthless for Cook's purposes. What he obviously intends is that we should take "the speaker" (in both the sentences quoted above) as short for "someone who knows the language." If we make this emendation, then we see that Cook has simply ruled out "knowing the language" as a factor to be taken into account in

---

[29] *Ibid.*, pp. 285–6 (pp. 291–2).

determining whether someone is in "as good a position as one could want for correctly answering a certain question or making a certain statement." If he did not rule it out, then we could simply reply to him and Wittgenstein: "Certainly I need not suppose that Jones is in as good a position as one could want for determining whether he is in pain; after all, the poor boy is only three, and he still uses 'pain,' 'hurts,' etc., in some very peculiar ways."

Once again, we find ourselves brought back to the alternatives presented earlier: either admit that "knowing the language" counts as part of "being in a good position" (i.e., as a sufficient belief-justifying reason) and accept first-person present-tense pain-reports as cases of knowledge, or rule "knowing the language" out and refuse to allow these cases to count as knowledge. The primary reason why Cook prefers the latter alternative is that he thinks that making sensations "objects of knowledge" engenders philosophical perplexities. Specifically, it suggests the question: what is so special about mental states as to make our knowledge of them incorrigible? Now if we answer this by saying "They are directly present to consciousness, and nothing else is," and add on a few other plausible premises, the resulting epistemological dualism will beget metaphysical dualism (which will beget Idealism, which will beget Neutral Monism, which will beget Logical Positivism) as surely as Sin gave birth to Death. But suppose we answer the question by saying: "There is nothing special about them, apart from a convention that first-person present-tense reports of them are taken as the best possible evidence about them." If we add, with Wittgenstein,[30] that when we reach conventions we reach rock-bottom, we will not be tempted to go on to ask "And why do we apply this convention to some things and not others?" We will not fall under the spell of what Pitcher calls the "Platonist principle" that differences in degrees of certitude, or of corrigibility, correspond to metaphysical differences in the objects known.

This last suggestion is merely a sketch of a "conventionalist" view of non-inferential knowledge, one which I cannot argue here.[31] It is inserted here merely to show that there may not be as much reason as Wittgenstein thought to be frightened of the view of sensations as private objects of knowledge. Returning to the business at hand, I shall conclude my discussion of Cook by making one further criticism of detail and then spelling out a more general criticism, which I have sketchily adumbrated

---

[30] Cf. *The Blue and Brown Books* (Oxford, 1958), p. 24.

[31] It is a view which has been elaborated at length by Sellars, and which I try to summarize in "Intuition," *The Encyclopedia of Philosophy* (New York, 1967), IV, pp. 204–12.

above. The criticism of detail concerns his discussion of "the perceptual sense of 'to feel'." Here, the defects of Cook's general method of argument seem to me particularly obvious. He wants to argue, in the face of cases like "I feel a pain in my knee," that "Sensation words cannot be the objects of verbs of perception in first-person sentences."[32] Clearly, he needs to say that "feel" in the sentence cited, is not "a verb of perception." So he defines "the perceptual sense of 'to feel' " as the sense in which "feel" is used in the sentence "I know it because I feel it." He then says that in such sentences as "I feel a slight pain in my knee when I bend it" the words "I feel" may be replaced by "I have" or "there is" without altering the sense of the sentence. So far so good, and all we need now is an argument to show that when "feel" is used in the perceptual sense such substitution is impossible. But we do not get this. All we get is the fact that in *some* cases of the use of perceptual sense of "feel" – e.g., "I feel a stone in my shoe" – such substitution is impossible. This does nothing whatever to show that satisfaction of the initial definition entails satisfaction of the criterion of the nonsubstitutability of "There is" for "I feel." One disanalogy does not make a difference of sense, and even if it did, it would not necessarily make the very special difference of sense which Cook needs for his argument. The fact that when we feel stones in our shoes we have methods for checking whether there is one, but that when we feel pains in our knees we do not, hardly shows that it is a "confusion" to answer the question "How do you know that there is a pain in your knee?" by "Because I feel it." Here, as in his comparing "pain" with "build" rather than with, say, "mountain," Cook uses one analogy or disanalogy between uses of a term to convict his opponents of confusion. If he had confined himself to pointing out that pains, and the way we know about them, differ from stones and the way we know about them, and that something in Argument A, or some other argument with a philosophically undesirable conclusion, depended upon the assumption that we knew about them in just the same way, then all would be well. In certain passages – passages which, to my mind, are the best parts of his article – he does just this. Thus, for example, he notes that "the plausibility of A depends on its seeming to be analogous to something like this: to ascertain whether my neighbor's crocuses are in bloom, as opposed to merely taking his word for it, I must see his crocuses."[33] Later he points up the relevant disanalogy as follows:

---

[32] Cook, p. 289 (pp. 295–6).     [33] *Ibid.*, p. 290 (p. 296).

> It [Argument A] makes out the difference between first-and third-person statements to rest on a matter of circumstance (like being unable to see my neighbor's crocuses) whereas Wittgenstein has made us realize that the difference resides in the language-game itself. The difference does not rest on some circumstance, and therefore Argument A, which purports to name such a circumstance with the words "being unable to feel another's sensations" is inherently confused.[34]

I think that in the first sentence of this passage Cook accurately characterizes an important part of Wittgenstein's contribution to our understanding of the notion of "privacy." In the second sentence, however, he confuses the fact that we may be inclined to accept the false propositions (ii) and (iii) on the basis of a false analogy between knowing-about-pains and knowing-about-crocuses, with the claim that (ii) and (iii) are not simply false, but are inherently "senseless" or "confused." There is a difference between people being willing to accept a false proposition (or senseless quasi-proposition) $p$, because they accept another proposition (or senseless quasi-proposition) $q$, and $p$ entailing or presupposing $q$. Sometimes the phenomena are co-extensive, but it has been the burden of my argument that, in the case at hand, they are not. The claim that the difference between first- and third-person statements about sensations is built into the language-game *can* be accepted by someone who accepts all the premises of Argument A, without his thereby involving himself in logical contradiction, or in making senseless utterances. For, if the foregoing criticisms are sound, Cook cannot get from this difference to the "senselessness" of any relevant statements. Nor need he try, since the implausibility of (ii) and (iii) is such as to let us dismiss the argument at once. Granted that it took Wittgenstein to break the spell which these premises exerted, we need not continue to recite the powerful incantations (such as "It is incorrect to say 'I know what I am thinking'") which Wittgenstein used for this purpose. (It took Hume's paradoxical views to wake eighteenth-century philosophy from its dogmatic slumbers, but we are fortunate that no misguided sense of gratitude led Kant to reiterate Hume's slogans).

## IV   Conclusions

My discussion of Pitcher and Cook has suggested the following view of Wittgenstein. Wittgenstein wanted to cut Cartesian skepticism off at the

---

[34] *Ibid.*, p. 291 (p. 297).

roots, and hoped to do so by arguing that the Cartesian picture both of non-inferential and of incorrigible knowledge was incoherent. In particular, he noted that the Cartesian tradition assimilated the language-game played with sensations terms like "pain" to that played with physical-object terms like "tree," and thus produced various false analogies. These analogies inclined philosophers to make various false statements (or to invent a new, specifically philosophical language-game, and then, by combining premises drawn from this artificial language-games with premises drawn from more "natural" language-games, to produce arguments which committed fallacies of ambiguity). Pitcher emphasizes the differences between the way in which we *name* trees and pains, and Cook the differences between the way in which we *know about* trees and pains, but both agree that

> If sensations are private objects, they can't have names (in the same sense of "name" in which trees have names)

and

> If sensations are private objects, we can't know about them (in the same sense of "know" in which we know about trees).

Both, in other words, focus on what Strawson calls Wittgenstein's "hostility to privacy," rather than on what Strawson calls his "hostility to immediacy."[35]

In the discussion so far, I have admitted that it is possible to construct analyses of "know," and of "name" (or "denote," "refer," or "identify"), which will entail the two theses just mentioned, or alternatively to construct distinctions between different "senses" of these terms which will produce the desired result. But I have argued that Cook and Pitcher present no good reasons for saying that we should adopt such analyses or make such distinctions. I have argued further that both men pick up the problem by the wrong end, that what needs analysis, or distinctions between senses, is "privacy," and that Ayer's distinctions suffice to do this job. I have suggested that it was Wittgenstein's failure to make the distinctions which Ayer makes, and to recognize that an object can be "private" in one of these senses without being "private" in all the others, which accounts for his "hostility to privacy."

In another article, forthcoming ["Verificationism and Transcendental Arguments," *Noûs*, 5 (1971), pp. 3–14; Chapter 13 in this volume], I hope to

---

[35] Cf. P. F. Strawson, review of *Philosophical Investigations*, *Mind*, 63 (1954), esp. pp. 90ff.

show that the proper thrust of those portions of the *Investigations* which Malcolm has grouped together as "arguments against the possibility of a private language" is against the notion that we can have knowledge of something distinct from the knowledge that certain propositions are true of it, and against the notion that we can have knowledge of the truth of propositions which are not formulated in language. In other words, I want to argue that what is novel and exciting in these portions of the *Investigations* is the attack on the Cartesian notion of prelinguistic awareness – the notion that there is a species of awareness which antedates and underlies our coming to be able to justify the utterance of sentences. But this is a separate topic, which I have only had space to hint at in the present article.

# CHAPTER 10

# In defense of eliminative materialism

In this brief note, I should like to comment on two replies to my "Mind-Body Identity, Privacy, and Categories"[1] – one by James Cornman[2] and the other by Richard Bernstein.[3] I shall concentrate upon a single point which is made by both critics.

In my article, I attempted to work out an analogy between talking about demons and talking about sensations, urging that sensation-discourse might go the way of demon-discourse, given the proper neurological discoveries and resulting neurological ways of explaining behavior. More specifically, I argued that "sensation" might lose its reporting role as well as its explanatory role, just as "demon" had lost both its roles, and that both of these roles might be taken over by reference to brain-processes.

In response to this strategy, Cornman argues that

> Even if we grant that a pain is identical with a stimulation of C-fibers, it would seem that we still need sensation-terms to make the true descriptions of certain pains, or stimulation of C-fibers, as, for example, intense, sharp, and throbbing. No neurophysiological sentence is synonymous with "This pain (stimulation of C-fibers) is intense, sharp, and throbbing," and thus no neurophysiological sentence can be used to make the same true description. Thus to eliminate the sensation-terms we apply to what we experience would seem to diminish our ability to describe considerably.[4]

My general line of reply to this point is to say that three neurological properties of the stimulation of C-fibers would correspond to "intense," "sharp," and "throbbing," and that terms signifying these properties would take over the roles of these latter terms just as "stimulation of C-fibers"

---

[1] *Review of Metaphysics*, 19 (1965), pp. 24–5 [Chapter 6 in the present volume].
[2] "On the Elimination of 'Sensations' and Sensations," *Review of Metaphysics*, 22 (1968), pp. 15–35.
[3] "The Challenge of Scientific Materialism," *International Philosophical Quarterly*, 8 (1968), pp. 252–75.
[4] Cornman, *op. cit.*, p. 30.

took over the role of "pain." Cornman, however, anticipates this reply and attempts to rebut it as follows:

> Let us assume that "Jones' C-fibers are very stimulated" has acquired the descriptive role of "Jones' pain is intense," and that it also retains its theoretical role. Let us also grant that if this role change occurs, then "Jones' pain is intense" is no longer needed to make a true description of Jones because "Jones' C-fibers are very stimulated" gives us this description of Jones and more ... The objection is ... that the reason we would no longer need "Jones' pain is intense" is that *what it states would be entailed by "Jones' C-fibers are very stimulated."* Consequently, we could no longer even make certain physiological claims about the brain without implying that there are sensations ... It is not important, then, which words we use now or ever. What matters is which descriptive roles they play ... Thus because "stimulation of C-fibers" taking on the descriptive role of "pain" accomplishes only the elimination of "pain" and not its role in true descriptions, such an elimination of sensation-terms fails to help the eliminative materialist. Indeed, if this is the only way sensation-terms can be eliminated, we should reject eliminative materialism, because we must either keep sensation-terms to make true descriptions or change physicalistic terms in such a way that using them descriptively implies that there are sensations [italics added].[5]

The same point is made by Bernstein:

> We might concede that neurophysiological discourse is a better way of scientifically explaining and describing the relevant phenomena and I may agree that "sensations" turn out to be brain processes. But if I am to describe these brain processes as *I experience* them then I must use phenomenal predicates to describe them or if I adopt a new language, the new expressions must at least *express what I now express* when I report and describe my "sensations" [italics added].[6]

Both Bernstein and Cornman are claiming that if two terms play the same descriptive role, then sentences using the one must "entail" what is stated by the other (Cornman) or "express" what the latter sentences express (Bernstein). Both agree that our ability to describe would be diminished if we were no longer able to express what we expressed by words like "intense" and "throbbing," and both insist that the new language which I am suggesting we might use would either continue to express this or be deficient.

As a first attempt at getting around this objection, I can remark that the sentence "I am having an hallucination of a fat red man-like shape" which

---

[5] *Ibid.*, pp. 30-2.    [6] Bernstein, *op. cit.*, p. 271.

takes over the descriptive role of "There is a fat red demon" does not seem to entail the latter nor to express what the latter expresses. But this may seem a limp reply, since, as Bernstein points out, "there is no question here of changing or dropping the predicates and the types of descriptions used to describe these hallucinatory experiences. Imaginary demons can be short, red and fat just as real demons can."[7] Bernstein is quite right in noting that there is a disanalogy between the demons and the sensations, in that some of the predicates appropriate to demons are also appropriate for describing hallucinations, whereas I want to say that none of the predicates appropriate to sensations are appropriate to brain-processes. Nevertheless, this disanalogy does not damage the point that a sentence about hallucinations does not seem to entail a sentence about demons. So why should "My C-fibers are very stimulated" entail "My pain is intense" (or perhaps "The stimulation of my C-fibers is very intense")? Granted that in the demon case the old-fashioned adjectives don't follow the old-fashioned referring expression into desuetude, why shouldn't they in the case of sensations? If referring expressions can go out of date, why not adjectives as well?

Since I assume that neither Cornman nor Bernstein really sees any great difference between nouns and adjectives here, are they saying that even when we admit that demons are only hallucinations or that sensations turn out to be brain-processes we must still grant that "Here is an hallucination of a certain sort" entails (or "expresses what is expressed by") "Here is a demon" and "My C-fibers are stimulated" entails (or "expresses what is expressed by") "I am in pain"? But this seems paradoxical, for what does it mean to say "There are no demons" if not that the entailment does *not* hold? And if it doesn't hold in the demon case, why should it hold in the pain case? Why need we say that the employment of "My C-fibers are stimulated" to report immediate experience *changes the meaning of this expression* in such a way that it now entails "I am in pain"?

At this point in the argument, it seems to me, Cornman and Bernstein must either (a) find a way of squaring the claim that "I am having a certain sort of hallucination" entails (or "expresses what is expressed by") "There is a demon" with the fact that there are no demons, or (b) say that there is a further disanalogy between the demon case and the sensation case such that the entailment doesn't hold in the former but does in the latter. Since I see no way in which (a) can be followed up, and since there is evidence for (b), I shall focus on that alternative.

---

[7] *Ibid.*, p. 271.

The evidence that Cornman and Bernstein see a further disanalogy between the two cases is that both devote attention to the difference between, as Bernstein says, "the context of the scientific evaluation of competing or alternative *theories*" and the case of replacing sensation-discourse. Bernstein thinks that it "begs the issue" to assume that "sensation-discourse, especially in its reporting role, is a quasi-scientific theory."[8] Cornman says that "sensation-terms are used to report phenomena we experience whether or not they have any explanatory function, and therefore we cannot justify their eliminability merely by eliminating their explanatory function."[9] Both remarks suggest that the principle being invoked to distinguish the sensation case from the demon case is something like the following:

> (T) If a theory-laden term takes on the reporting role of a non-theory-laden term, then statements using the latter term are entailed by ("express what is expressed by") statements using the former, whereas if a theory-laden term takes on the reporting role of another theory-laden term, this is not the case.

The rationale for (T) might go something like this: the descriptive roles played by non-theory laden terms (like "sensation" or "intense") are roles which must be played in any language which is adequate to describe what is experienced, whereas the descriptive roles played by theory-laden terms (like "demon" or "hallucination") may or may not be played, depending upon whether the explanatory theory which contains them is accepted. Both Cornman and Bernstein say things which suggest that they would accept a distinction between terms which are necessary to describe the objects-as-they-are-experienced and eliminable "theory-laden" terms – Bernstein in the passage quoted above about the need to describe brain-processes "as I experience them" and Cornman in the following passage: "It is most implausible to claim that a man's sensory phenomena have nothing like the features he experiences them to have, with the consequence that he has no special epistemological status even regarding those features he believes his sensory phenomena have."[10]

Furthermore, Cornman has devoted a separate article[11] to arguing that Quine's version of eliminative materialism will not work because "sensation,"

[8] *Ibid.*, p. 270.     [9] Cornman, *op. cit.*, p. 23.     [10] *Ibid.*, p. 35.
[11] J. Cornman, "Mental Terms, Theoretical Terms, and Materialism," *Philosophy of Science*, 35 (1968), pp. 45–63.

though a theoretical term, is a theoretico-reporting term. That is to say, it is used to refer to something that we are aware of, and therefore not to something postulated.[12] Cornman's assumption in this article is that "What we are aware of is not postulated, and only the postulated is eliminable";[13] and this assumption seems to occur also in his reply to me in the form "What we are aware of must be expressed in any adequate language," whereas what we are not aware of need not be – or, in other words, "What we are aware of is not eliminable by changes in our ways of explaining things." More specifically, it seems likely that Cornman would distinguish "demon" as a "theory-laden" theoretico-reporting term – because, although we are aware of demons, talking of demons entails talk about unobservable properties (e.g., those having to do with demonic intercourse with unobservable supernatural beings) – from "sensation" as a theoretico-reporting term which carries no commitment to unobservable properties.[14]

Now my answer to (T) is that what appears to us, or what we experience, or what we are aware of, is a function of the language "We customarily use 'F' in making non-inferential reports about X's." In other words, I would claim that if we got in the habit of using neurological terms in place of "intense," "sharp," and "throbbing," then our experience would be of things having those neurological properties, and not of anything, e.g., intense. It seems to me that Cornman and Bernstein are taking for granted that there is a sort of prelinguistic givenness about, e.g., pains which any language which is to be adequate must provide a means of expressing. This is why they claim that sentences using the neurological term in its reporting use would entail, or express what is expressed by, sentences using the "phenomenal" term. If it were the case that we experienced the same thing when we used the new vocabulary as when we used the old, then their point would be sound. But there is nothing to be this "same thing."

---

[12] *Ibid.*, p. 61.

[13] *Ibid.*, p. 61. Although this article is a reply to Quine, and in "On the Elimination" Cornman regards me as taking a "new line" which goes beyond Quine's form of elimination and requires separate refutation, it seems to me that the basis of Cornman's objections to me and to Quine is the same. All my new line amounts to is the suggestion that the reporting role of sensation-discourse could be taken over by a neurological vocabulary. All that Cornman's reply to this new line comes to is that the new use of a neurological vocabulary will entail sentences phrased in the old vocabulary. But, if my comments so far have been sound, Cornman would not argue that such entailment holds if the entities referred to in the old vocabulary are *postulated* entities (like demons). So to both Quine and me, Cornman is saying: your eliminative tactics will work only on what we are not aware of.

[14] See Cornman, "Mental Terms," p. 51, for a definition of "theory-laden term," and p. 61 for the claim that "sensation" is not such a term.

To see this point, let us imagine two sets of people, one raised to speak conventional English and the other raised to use only neurological predicates in the place of those conventionally used in introspective reports. Are these two groups experiencing the same things when they are simultaneously manipulated in various ways? Intuition perhaps suggests that they are. But what is this same thing, the intensity of the pain or the X-character of the brain-process? Here, I think, intuition is baffled, and rightly so. Either answer would do equally well. On the Cornman–Bernstein view, however, we are forced to say either "both" or "something common to both." For if we want to claim that the neurologically speaking people are using sentences which "entail what is stated by" or "express what is stated by" or "express what is expressed by" sentences used by the conventional English speakers, then we have to allow the claim in reverse also. If both sets of sentences are playing the same reporting role, then either "entails what is stated" by the other or "expresses what is expressed" by the other. So it will turn out that conventional speakers cannot speak of the intensity of a pain without implying the existence of certain neurons and their features, just as the neurologically speaking people cannot use their language without implying the existence of something mental.

I suggest that rather than draw either of these consequences we should admit that there is nothing in common between the two experiences save that they are had under the some conditions – *viz.*, the manipulation of the body in certain specified ways. That the "same descriptive role" is played is not a matter of the same feature or features being reported in either case, but simply a matter of the two sentences being used to answer the same question – *viz.*, what do you experience under the following conditions? I suspect that Cornman and Bernstein think that changing from "intense" to "X-character" is a mere change of words without a change of descriptive role because they think of "descriptive role" as "role of referring to the same experiential feature." But they cannot, without begging the question, claim that "intense" refers to an experiential feature but "X-character" does not. They cannot make use of our intuition that the same feature is being experienced no matter which word is used in order to give the preference to "intense." For this intuition is neutral as between the two different languages.

To put the matter more generally, I think that the putative intuition that we will continue to have the same experiences no matter which words we use is in fact a remnant of what Sellars has called the Myth of the Given – the view that awareness comes first and language must follow along and be adequate to the initial awareness. The trouble with this view is that "adequate to" is an empty notion. There is no criterion for the adequacy of a bit of language to a bit of nonlinguistic awareness. Indeed, the notion of a nonlinguistic awareness is simply a version of the thing-in-itself – an unknowable whose only function is paradoxically enough, to be that which all knowledge is about. What *does* exist is the causal conditions of a noninferential report being made. But there is no unique vocabulary for describing these causal conditions. There are as many vocabularies as there are ways of explaining human behavior.

I shall conclude this note by taking up a different but related topic. Both Cornman and Bernstein suggest that I am adopting, or for consistency must adopt, the view that, in Bernstein's words, "'ultimately' *the* legitimate form(s) of description is scientific description."[15] Bernstein says that without this presupposition my arguments cut no ice against the view that "my present language for reporting and describing sensations is another, different, supplementary, legitimate mode of discourse for describing my experiences." Cornman claims that "there is one last move an eliminative materialist might try" – *viz.*, "an extreme version of scientific realism, one which holds that in all cases those pure theoretical terms of science that provide the best available explanations of behavior also provide the best available descriptions of the things whose behavior they explain."[16]

Against Bernstein, I can say that I am not in any sense claiming that the customary vocabulary of introspection is "illegitimate." Rather, I am merely claiming the same legitimacy for the neurological vocabulary – where "legitimacy" means the right to be considered a report of experience. My attitude is not that some vocabularies are "illegitimate," but rather we should let a thousand vocabularies bloom and then see which survive. The materialist predicts that the neurological vocabulary will triumph. He may be right, but if he is, it is not because of some special feature of this vocabulary which consists in its having originated in theoretical science. Given different cultural conditions, one can imagine the neurological vocabulary having been the ordinary familiar one and the mentalistic one the "scientific" alternative.

To make the same point in another context, I shall take up another of Bernstein's remarks:

> On the one hand when Rorty makes claims like "Elimination of the referring use of the expression in question ... from our language would leave our ability to describe and predict undiminished," he seems to be

---

[15] Bernstein, *op. cit.*, p. 273.    [16] Cornman, "On the Elimination," p. 34.

presupposing a metalanguage or metatheory in which we can evaluate different types of descriptive expressions and determine whether our ability to describe is or is not diminished. But on the other hand, Rorty sometimes writes as if the radical displacement of languages takes place without any inter-theoretical justification. Like Marx's concept of the state, one form of discourse withers away (in fact or in principle) when it no longer serves any function or purpose that isn't better performed by another mode of discourse. Thus an entire mode of discourse including its *entire descriptive vocabulary* can be displaced. But then it is no longer clear what it means to say that our ability to describe is undiminished.[17]

To say that our ability to describe is undiminished is merely to say that by using some portion of language common to the competing vocabularies (e.g., "What do you experience when I do *that* to your arm?") we can isolate the questions to which alternative answers might be given and note that both vocabularies offer something to say in reply. No general meta-language is needed, but merely some way of locating the place in the language-game which is to be filled by either of the alternative candidates. I quite agree with Bernstein's implicit suggestion that any general meta-language or metatheory would be question-begging, and in particular any which always awarded the prize to the "scientific" alternative would be. Therefore, I grasp the second ("withering away") horn of the dilemma he sketches. But I take no sides on the question of whether the materialist is right in his prediction that the ordinary ways of reporting on introspections will wither away. In my view, the truth of the prediction is of much less philosophical interest than the fact that the prediction is itself a coherent suggestion. (To back up the claim that it is coherent to suggest that "the entire descriptive vocabulary of a mode of discourse" might wither away while leaving our descriptive ability undiminished I can offer no better argument than the example of demons. I grant that in this case the adjectives used for describing demons persist. But, as I have said above, I do not think that the persistence of these adjectives counts against the force of the example.)

Turning now to Cornman's suggestion that I might fall back on an extreme form of scientific realism, I note that even this move will do me no good if (T) is true. For even if I claim that the "pure theoretical terms of science" provide the "best available descriptions," these best descriptions will still, according to (T), entail all the old-fashioned descriptions which scientific realism would wish to discard. So I construe Cornman as, in this

---

[17] Bernstein, *op. cit.*, pp. 272-3.

passage, suggesting that extreme scientific realism could be used as the basis for a denial of (T). But on my view (T) is false whether one is a scientific realist or not. What defeats (T) is what defeats the Myth of the Given – not scientific realism, but an appreciation of the internal difficulties engendered in traditional empiricisms and rationalisms by the notion of a prelinguistic item of awareness to which language must be adequate. To attack the Myth of the Given is to insist that predicates like "intense" are in principle replaceable. To adopt scientific realism is to say that they ought to be replaced, given the superior explanatory ability of neurological theory. I wish to take the first step – insisting on in-principle-replaceability – without taking the second.

# CHAPTER 11

# Cartesian epistemology and changes in ontology

Many philosophers nowadays ignore or ridicule traditional ontology, but few are happy with the breezy "refutations" of metaphysics which were fashionable a decade or two ago. On the one hand, quarrels between Absolute Idealists and Physical Realists, interactionists and epiphenomenalists, process philosophers and substance philosophers, seem as inconclusive as ever. Even streamlined versions of old ontological theses (for example Strawson's claim that material objects are basic particulars or Quine's that we can get along with physical objects and classes) do little more than excite a certain languid admiration of their authors' ingenuity. On the other hand, few of us can swallow the notion that Plato, Aquinas, Spinoza, Kant, Russell, and Whitehead were simply "confused about language." Even if one suspects that the systems they erected simply worked out the absurd consequences of a few blunders,[1] one wants a longer story about how some of the most intelligent men who ever lived made such blunders, and about why they devoted their lives to piling paradox upon paradox.

I do not think that a satisfactory story of this sort has yet been told. Most such stories either blithely dismiss pre-twentieth-century philosophy or else make what is, I suspect, a serious mistake. The mistake is the assumption that there is a single discipline called "ontology" or "metaphysics" which was practiced by Aristotle, Aquinas, Descartes, Hegel, Whitehead, and Russell, and which is still being practiced by Quine, Strawson, Sellars, and J. J. C. Smart. It is tempting to think that we shall always come back to the good old metaphysical problems despite changes in jargon, for this way of viewing the matter also suggests that no radical change has occurred. On this view, the rise of "analytic" philosophy is *just* a change of idiom, and the positivistic rejection of

[1] Cf. Austin's remark (in conversation) that "Plato thought that all general terms were proper names, and Leibniz that all proper names were general terms."

metaphysics was just juvenile rhetoric, on a par with Descartes's self-deceptive attacks on the scholastics.

Only time will tell whether a genuine world-historical change is now going on in philosophy. It may be that the present split between "metaphysicians" and "analysts" is a mere provincial squabble which will strike our descendants as comic, but I doubt it. Self-deceptive as Descartes may have been concerning his relation to his scholastic teachers, it was no small change that came over men's notions of what it was to do philosophy at the end of the seventeenth century. Self-deceptive as the positivists may have been, I believe that no smaller change is taking place now. To appreciate this change, I think we have to see that the ways of answering the ontological question "What is really real?" are very different at different epochs. Specifically, the criteria for a satisfactory answer to this question changed in the seventeenth century, and are changing now. A full-blown history of these changes would offer a comparative account of the criteria used by the Greeks and the medievals, those used by philosophers between Descartes and Russell, and those being invoked nowadays in, say, controversies between Strawson and Quine. I shall not attempt this, for two reasons. First, I do not think that I understand the Greeks well enough to get them right. Second, I do not think that the most recent discussions of "ontology" have lasted long enough for criteria to have emerged.[2] I shall, however, try to offer an account of the criteria used in what I shall call the "Cartesian" period of philosophy – the one which stretches from the end of the seventeenth to the middle of the twentieth centuries. If my account is right, then it will at least be clear that present-day motives for doing ontology and present-day criteria for having produced the true ontology are altogether different than in earlier periods. One can, of course, use the term "ontologist" to cover Aristotle, Hegel, and Quine, for they all are concerned with what there is; but this is about as helpful as using "atomic physicist" to cover Leucippus, Dalton, and Gell-Mann.

So much for prefatory remarks about my aims. The claims which I want to make are as follows:

---

[2] For an exploration of criteria which might be invoked by a reductionist program like Quine's, see Gilbert Harman, "Quine on Meaning and Existence, II," *Review of Metaphysics*, 21 (1967), pp. 362–7. As Harman notes, treating ontology as subject to the same sorts of requirements as a scientific theory raises problems about how we decide which of the purposes served by the "reduced" entities we want to continue to be served, as opposed to those we want to repudiate. I think that more would have to be said about criteria for such a decision before we could do much to adjudicate disputes about what there is between philosophers like Quine, Davidson, Strawson, Martin, and Sellars. More would also have to be said about the criteria for the validity of "transcendental" arguments and about the relation between such arguments and reductionist programs.

(1)  A necessary condition for participating in ontological discussion
     during what I shall call the "Cartesian period" was that an answer
     be given to the question: given that we have incorrigible knowledge
     only of the contents of our minds, how is it that we can know about
     anything else?

(2)  The paradigm of an answer to this question was the claim that the
     nature of the object of knowledge – reality as opposed to appearance –
     was different than either common sense or science conceived it.

(3)  The justification for the existence of ontology as a distinct discipline
     came to be the fact that neither science nor common sense could offer
     an adequate reply to the epistemological skeptic. Giving such a reply
     became the *paradigm* of what it was to do philosophy.[3]

(4)  The refusal of many contemporary philosophers to take seriously the
     suggestion that reality is different from either common sense's or
     science's picture of it is due to the fact that they no longer accept or
     find it necessary to answer the epistemological skeptic.

(5)  The reasons why this premise is no longer accepted can be traced
     back to the abandonment of certain more general principles.

(6)  These principles are such that, once they are accepted, it is not clear
     why there need be a discipline called "ontology" over and above
     empirical science. The justification of the existence of such a discip-
     line thus requires to be rethought.

I should like to argue for all of these, but as regards the historical claims,
(1) – (3), I can do no more than suggest how they *might* be argued for.
Specifically, I shall make some dogmatic remarks about the Cartesian
period in philosophy as a suggestion of how I would meet *prima facie*
objections to these historical claims. On the last three points, the reasons
why epistemological skepticism no longer seems a live issue to many
philosophers, and the implications of these reasons, I shall be able to
actually do some arguing, and thus be more susceptible to refutation.

     One might object to my first claim – that the answering of an epistemo-
logical question was, in the Cartesian period, a necessary condition for a
satisfactory ontology – by saying that the task of ontology is, after all, just

---

[3] The science of a given period tends to take *one* solution as a paradigm, whereas since Descartes
philosophers have argued about which of the "classical" solutions was correct. This helps account for
the "unscientific" character of philosophy as a discipline. For this reason, however, it is perhaps more
fruitful to say that scientific epochs are defined by the *solutions* they take as paradigmatic, whereas
philosophical epochs are defined by the *problems* they take as paradigmatic. (As may be obvious, I am
here drawing upon a terminology and an outlook put forward by T. S. Kuhn in his *The Structure of
Scientific Revolutions* [Chicago, 1962].)

to tell us what there is – or what things are really real. One would think this could be done, and has been done, even if by those who never heard of a problem about our knowledge of the external world. I think that one can meet this objection by asking how, in such a view, one would distinguish ontology from the empirical sciences. In the sense in which pre-Sophistic philosophers like Anaximander and Democritus were asking about what is really real, modern science is a satisfactory answer to the question. If by "what there is" or "what is really real" one means anything like "that by reference to which we can explain everything else, in a relatively simple and elegant way," then, in Sellars's words "Science is the judge of the things that are that they are and of the things that are not that they are not." If explanation and prediction are the only purposes to be served by the construction of an ontology, there is no excuse for an armchair substitute for science. One can only make sense of ontology as an armchair discipline if one sees the ontologists' definition of "really real" or "what there is" as something like "what there would have to be if certain principles which we do not wish to give up are to be maintained." The principles referred to will have to be generalizations at a level not evidently susceptible to empirical refutation – such principles as that "We can know what colors things have," "We can tell right from wrong," "We can communicate with each other," and "Tables are solid objects." To say that we need better answers to the question "What is there?" than either science or common sense gives us makes sense only if we see some such principle endangered by either science or common sense. If to be a philosopher who does ontology is to be something different from an armchair scientist, the difference will only appear by isolating the questions which impelled him to become an ontologist. What sets apart the ontologies of professional philosophers is that they are created in response to questions arising within other areas – specifically, epistemology, ethics, logic, and semantics. This is the reason for the notorious difficulty of drawing a line, within a given philosophical system, between ontology and these other areas, and the difficulty (or pointlessness) of answering questions like "Is Aristotle's doctrine of substance an answer to a logical or an ontological question?" Typically, the scientist's (and the man in the street's) view about what really exists is not influenced by questions about how we can know what we know, or name what we name, nor (except when the existence of God is under discussion) by questions about whether we should value what we value. By and large, the man in the street, the scientist, and pre-Sophistic philosophers are not bothered by such questions. Typically, post-Sophistic philosophers are. When we go through the history of thought and try to divide off the scientific from the specifically philosophical elements (in, for example, the works of Aristotle, Descartes, Newton, Freud, or Quine) we do so by putting the doctrines which can be evaluated without reference to such questions under the heading "science" and the rest under the heading "philosophy." I would argue that such an historically oriented approach is the *only* way in which we can catch the felt difference between science and philosophy, once we grant Quine's point that Carnap's internal–external distinction has to be reformulated and made a difference of degree. To use a loose analogy, we can only define the class of philosophical theories by enumerating a set of philosophical problems, just as Quine can only define the class of logical truths by enumerating the logical constants. To practise a discipline called ontology, as opposed to simply having a set of beliefs about what exists, one needs to be motivated by one or another of the ethical, epistemological, or semantic questions which provide part of the enumerative definition of the term "philosophical problem."

If there is any point at all in classifying philosophy into periods, this classification must be done by picking out the, as it were, pre-ontological questions which made it seem necessary to create a third view of what there is over against both common sense and science. I do not think that the questions raised by epistemological skepticism are the *only* questions which moved philosophers during the Cartesian period; one cannot neglect the Platonic notion of ontology as a way of justifying our claims to be moral which persists in Spinoza and Hegel. I think that inspection of the controversies between philosophers in this period would show that a philosopher who put forward a competitor to common sense and to science (as Spinoza, Leibniz, Berkeley, Kant, Hegel, and Russell did) always argued for this theory by claiming that if his ontology were not accepted we could not have the knowledge we appeared to have. Philosophers who put forward no such competition (e.g., Locke and Hume) were skeptics, the men who were prepared to admit that we knew less than we seemed.

I turn now to a more concrete form of the objection I have just discussed. Surely, it might be said, the great metaphysical issue of the period was the mind-body problem. Doubtless this problem is intimately linked to the problem of the possibility of knowledge of body by mind, but why suggest that one is more fundamental than the other? Here, I want to claim that a certain view of knowledge – the one which engenders epistemological skepticism – just *is* fundamental; there would have been no mind-body problem without it.

The mind-body problem is an offspring of the theory that knowledge consists in the having of certain representations of reality (including perceptual ones), by the subject. As Matson has recently pointed out,[4] the Greeks had a soul-body problem but not a mind-body problem – or, at least, not the mind-body problem which has bothered philosophers from Descartes to Feigl. Before *this* mind-body problem can be made to seem urgent (as Matson also notes) one has to have the notion of "immediate awareness," and to believe that the things we want to know about (tables, other men, stars, the moral law, and the gods) are not things which we are immediately aware of. Once one believes all this, one will have to grant the existence of a realm to contain the objects of immediate awareness. This will be the Mind, or the Subject *qua* Subject. Psychophysical dualism follows from epistemological dualism.[5] In the great systems of the Cartesian period, the primary task of ontology was to get the Subject and the Object back together. Solutions to the mind-body problem appear as simple corollaries to solutions of the Problem of Knowledge.

Thus, the ontologies of almost every important non-skeptical philosopher from Spinoza to Russell consisted in a redescription of the Object – that which we want to know about – according to which the Subject and the Object turned out to be much the same. The concomitance of the modes of the two known attributes of Spinoza's God, the pre-established harmony of Leibniz's monads, the variations on what Austin calls "the ontology of the sensible manifold" (Berkeley, Kant, Russell), the perfect union of appearance and reality in Hegel's or Royce's Absolute, and Whitehead's panpsychism are so many ways of showing that if you know enough about the sort of thing you are directly aware of (the contents of your mind) you will know everything there is to know about everything. In short, the mainstream of ontology has been a redescription (specifically, a "subjectivizing") of the Objects – a redescription which would not have been thought necessary had not the original claim about direct awareness been swallowed.

If it is admitted for the sake of argument that the problem of overcoming epistemological skepticism was the original motive which, during the Cartesian period, called ontology into being, one might still be tempted to say that as soon as ontology got going a host of further problems were

---

[4] Wallace Matson, "Why Isn't the Mind-Body Problem Ancient?," in Paul Feyerabend and Grover Maxwell, eds., *Mind, Matter, and Method* (Minneapolis, 1966), pp. 92–102.
[5] The genesis of the latter dualism from the former is well displayed in Arthur O. Lovejoy's *The Revolt against Dualism* (Princeton, 1971), ch. 1.

revealed. There are, after all, plenty of metaphysical issues other than the relation of the knower and the known, or of the mind to the body. So it might be objected that the initial justification for doing ontology is no longer needed once this whole range of urgent problems becomes visible. In replying to this, I should want to make two points.

First, the other metaphysical issues which have found their way into the textbooks could hardly have occurred to anyone who had not had the conception of the relation between the mental and the physical which created the mind-body problem – *viz.*, the mind as the home of representations of which the knower is immediately aware. Since the Realm of the Mental was not spatially locatable, and maybe not even temporal, it was easy to go on to postulate as many Realms of Being as might seem necessary to contain anything which we wanted to talk about, but which did not fall within the purview of either common sense or science. Propositions, values, numbers, the True, the Right, the Absolute, and unicornhood were all admitted as candidates on the ground that if ideas could be real, then anything "spiritual" – *viz.*, anything which was like an idea (in not being a physical object) – could be real, too. With the introduction of these candidates, the game of ontology became more complex, for new rules were added. Instead of simply getting the Subject and the Object back together again, you had to spell out what you proposed to reduce to what and what you were going to make irreducible. (Were numbers, for example, reducible to ideas about quantities of physical objects? Were they objects of which we had mediate awareness? If the latter, did God have to have immediate awareness of them? If so, did we have to be immediately aware of God? etc.) Again, the Realm of the Mental had to have some sort of unity, and thus it was discovered that there was a problem about the Nature of the Self. (Could it know itself directly? If so, then the subject of ideas would have to be an idea. So perhaps it was a kind of Idea of Ideas? etc.) Given this more complicated problematic, philosophers won points for elegance of reduction and lost points for paradoxicalness. Roughly speaking, the best ontology was the one which did enough reducing so that the universe looked reasonably neat, but not so much that one had to say such *outré* things as "Numbers are really inscriptions" or "Pains are really neural events" or (but this one was hard to avoid) "Physical objects are merely permanent possibilities of sensations."[6]

---

[6] I owe this way of looking at the matter to Milton Fisk.

The second point which I want to make in reply to the above-mentioned objection emerges if we ask why philosophers were so concerned about what could be reduced to what. One might reply that it is simply an aesthetic delight to find a system in which appearances are saved with just the right balance between number of entities countenanced and degree of paradoxicalness. But this aesthetic attitude towards ontology, though presently flourishing,[7] is a very recent development. To explain three hundred years of ontologizing, it will not suffice to dwell on the familiar pleasures of finding, or proving the impossibility of finding, necessary and sufficient conditions for this and that. I think that the way to explain it is to realize that for philosophers during the Cartesian period it seemed as if there were only four possible answers to the question "How do we justify claims about X's?," *viz.*

(1)   We are directly acquainted with (have immediate awareness of) X's.

(2)   To talk about X's is just a relatively misleading way of talking about Y's, which we *are* directly acquainted with. (E.g., Berkeley's phenomenalism, Kant's identification of "nature" with the ordering of intuitions by concepts.)

(3)   To talk about Y's, which we are directly acquainted with, is just a relatively misleading way of talking about X's. (E.g., Spinoza's identification of our ideas with modes of the One Substance, Hegel's identification of everything with an appearance, or facet, or stage, of the Absolute Spirit.)

(4)   Appearances to the contrary, we *can't* justify claims about X's. (Skepticism.)

As long as these seemed the only answers, reason tottered every time it looked as if something else (the moral law, God, numbers, meanings) was neither an object of immediate awareness nor somehow identical with such objects. To show that X's were really real was a matter of showing that they could be known, which in turn was a matter of showing that somehow we were directly aware of them. This coalescence of reality and knowability was the reason why no one – not even Kant himself, in some passages – could put up with the notion of "things-in-themselves." The identification of knowability with being an object of immediate awareness is less easy to see, but I think that an analysis of particular cases would show that "the quest for certainty" which was initiated by Descartes, combined with the

---

[7]  See Nelson Goodman, "The Significance of *Der Logische Aufbau der Welt*", in P. A. Schilpp, ed., *The Philosophy of Rudolf Carnap* (La Salle, 1963), especially pp. 551–3.

lingering influence of Plato's principle that only what is a matter of knowledge, rather than opinion, is fully real, produced just such a coalesence.[8]

I have now done all I can in the space at hand to support the first three points I listed – my historical remarks about the character of ontology during the Cartesian period. Nothing, of course, can substitute for detailed inductive argument when one is trying to establish an historical thesis, but I hope that I have given some plausibility to my claim that ontology during this period centered around problems raised by epistemological skepticism, and more specifically by a certain notion of "incorrigible knowledge." I know that "centered around" is horribly vague, and I should prefer to put my thesis as "had these notions not been held, there would have been no such thing as ontology during this period" – but this seems on a par with such a pointless counterfactual as "if there had been no quarrels between the popular and aristocratic parties in Rome, the Republic would not have been replaced by the Empire." (Pointless because the Republic would not have been the Republic, nor the period the period, if the antecedent had held.) So I have stuck to the more modest claim that an attempt to get the Subject and the Object together again constituted the paradigm of doing ontology.

I turn now to defending my last three points – points which can be summarized as the claim that contemporary philosophy no longer sees the point of the question "since we have incorrigible knowledge only of the contents of our minds, how can we have knowledge of anything else?" and that the principles which lead to denying sense to this question make it difficult to see why there need be a discipline called "ontology." The lynchpin of my argument here is the claim that the most important element in contemporary philosophy is the adoption of what I shall call the Principle of the Relativity of Incorrigibility – or, bowing to Sellars, the Principle that the Given is a Myth. I shall mean by this the following thesis:

*That a given sentence is used to express incorrigible knowledge is not a matter of a special relation which holds between knowers and some object referred to by this sentence, but a matter of the way in which the sentence fits into the language of a given culture, and the circumstances of its user, at a given time.*

[8] George Pitcher, in a forthcoming book on perception [*A Theory of Perception* (Princeton, 1971)], has analysed the role of this "Platonic principle" in the creation of sense-data theories; I owe a sense of its importance to his discussion, and I was greatly helped by his comments on an earlier version of this chapter.

If this principle seems too innocuous to have such importance, I would point out the phenomenon of epistemological skepticism itself. Why, after all, should the fact that we have incorrigible knowledge only of the mental cast doubt on the claim that we have corrigible knowledge – but still *knowledge* – of the non-mental? The first stage of answering this question is simply to cite Malcolm's point that the epistemological skeptic trades on an assimilation of "know" to "know for certain" – where "known for certain" is equated with "indubitable," and the latter is illustrated by reference to our knowledge of our own mental states, or our knowledge of how things appeared to us. But why was such an assimilation ever accepted? I don't have a really good answer to this, but I think that one can begin by noting that no one would have been tempted to make such an assimilation had they not believed that the fact that no doubt was possible about these matters was a clue to the *nature of knowing*. To put it another way, no one would have been tempted to this assimilation had they not believed that knowledge is the sort of thing that *has* a nature. One must further believe that this nature can be isolated, thereby segregating cases of true knowledge from cases of pseudo-knowledge, not simply in the common-sense way in which we tell the wise man from the fool, but in some deeper and more interesting way. An epistemological skeptic cannot think of knowledge-claims as cultural phenomena like marriage ceremonies; for viewed *that* way a universally accepted knowledge-claim is automatically a sound one – at least until further evidence comes in (not evidence of some new and deep sort – but evidence of a sort which would be accepted as such by those making the claim), just as something universally accepted as marriage *is* automatically marriage. Treating knowledge as having a nature which may turn out to be very different from what a given culture takes knowledge to be is the hallmark of epistemological skepticism. The importance of the principle of the Relativity of Incorrigibility is that it undercuts the attempt to discover this nature by casting doubt on the first move which the skeptic makes – namely, to have found some case of knowledge which is a clearer case than others, and is thus a clue to the essence of what it is to be knowledge. It casts this by saying that the cases in which "doubt plays no role" are cases in which *we* do not *let* doubt play a role, not cases in which we are in a different natural state.

To summarize the contrast between the Cartesian tradition and the Principle of the Relativity of Incorrigibility, the former thinks that the nature of knowledge is:

That about which no doubt is possible, or which can be inferred from propositions about which no doubt is possible (including both "truths of reason" and truths about mental events),

whereas the latter takes knowledge to be simply "justified true belief," where "justified" is defined not by any reference to certainty but simply by enumeration – by pointing to actual procedures of justification which are used. To put the contrast still another way, the Cartesian tradition jumped on the fact that knowledge must be belief in what is true, and thought that by learning more about knowledge we could learn more about what is true. Thus, we got *a priori* ontological conclusions deduced from sheer reflection on the nature of knowledge. The post-Cartesian tradition (exemplified by Wittgenstein, Austin, Sellars, Dewey, and Quine) rallies around the principle that empirical knowledge needs no foundation, emphasizes "justified" rather than "true," recognizes that "justified" does not mean "justified now and forever, beyond the possibility of revision," and consequently does not imagine that an exploration of how we know could lead us to conclusions which would clash with either common sense or science.

Yet another way of emphasizing the importance of this contrast is by noting different definitions of "incorrigible" knowledge which would be put forward by the two traditions. The definition used by those who accept the Principle of the Relativity of Incorrigibility is:

> To have incorrigible knowledge that *p* is to have a belief that *p* such that the question "How do you know" – given a knowledge of the language and of your circumstances – is inappropriate, and such that there are no accepted procedures for resolving doubts about *p*, given the belief.

If this definition is accepted, then the Principle follows once it is granted that such procedures can come into acceptance and go out of acceptance. The definition offered by the Cartesian tradition is as follows:

> To have incorrigible knowledge that *p* is to have a belief that *p* based on immediate awareness of the entities referred to by "*p*."

I cannot now try to give all the reasons I would like for holding that the notion of "immediate awareness" is a mere philosopher's invention. I would merely suggest that such a definition is circular, in that no criterion for "immediate awareness" can be offered save references to the incorrigible knowledge we have of the entities of which we are putatively immediately aware. We are immediately aware of what we can have no doubts about, and vice versa. So nothing is explained by such a definition. Its popularity, I believe, was due to picture-thinking – to thinking of the mind as an "inner eye" which was capable of seeing only inner entities. But if we grant that nothing is gained by such a definition, then we are in a fair way to granting the principle of the Relativity of Incorrigibility. For the Principle says that our ability to have incorrigible knowledge about so-and-sos is not a function of a special relation in which we stand to so-and-sos. But "immediate awareness" is just the name for that special relation. If it is seen that reference to this notion explains nothing, then the same arguments will work to show that no other name for this "special relation" will explain anything either.

I have now said all I have time for about the importance of the Principle of the Relativity of Incorrigibility, but I have not yet given arguments for its truth. However, I do not know how to do this save by rebutting objections. Instead of dreaming up some objections and then knocking them down, I want to introduce a new topic into the discussion – one which provides an illustration of the way in which this Principle can be put to work in practice. By offering such an illustration the strengths and the weaknesses (if any) of the Principle can be displayed. Further, this new topic – the present fate of materialism – will permit me to develop my claim that the tradition which accepts this Principle finds it hard to take seriously the traditional problems of ontology. I shall be arguing that an adoption of this Principle makes it uninteresting whether or not materialism is true.

Until recently, debates about materialism have gone something like this:

HYLAS: Since science seems to need to talk about nothing save atoms and the void in order to explain everything that happens, only atoms and the void are really real.

PHILONOUS: But what is science save a scheme for ordering our experiences? Or, if it is more than this, how can it possibly deny that it rests upon experiences, and that these experiences are something different from either the atoms or the void?

H: What you call "experience" is but another name for bounding atoms in the brain.

P: That is the sort of thing one would only say if one were defending a theory at all costs. What criterion of "same" could one possibly use to show that two such different things were the same?

H: Two things are the same thing if talking about the one serves all the same purposes as talking about the other.

P: There you are. Talking about atoms and the void is never going to serve the purpose of describing what's immediately present to my consciousness – what I'm immediately aware of. No matter how much explanatory power such talk has, there will always remain the explananda.

H: But those things we are directly aware of are mere appearances.

P: Worse and worse. "In the case of stabbing pains, it is not possible to hold that the micro-picture is the real picture, that perceptual appearances are only a coarse duplication, for in this case we are dealing with the perceptual appearances themselves, which cannot very well be a coarse duplicate of themselves."[9]

For a long time, this rejoinder has seemed decisive. In recent years, however, Hylas has found a new move to make. He now replies:

H: There are no such things as "natural explananda." What we are "directly aware of can be described in many different ways. One could train people to use the language of physiology to report on their inner states, simply by training them to use the name of the correlated physiological state whenever we now use "stabbing pain," "bitter taste," etc. I will, if you like, withdraw the term "mere appearance," but I insist that there is no way of showing that it is *more* appropriate to report my reactions to stimuli in phenomenalistic language than in physicalistic language.

Hylas here invokes the Principle of the Relativity of Incorrigibility – the insight that what counts as an object of incorrigible awareness is a matter which is subject to revision in the course of empirical inquiry. If we did indeed train the next generation to abstain from phenomenalist language, then there would be no incorrigible knowledge of any statement of the sort usually classified as "synthetic" (for introspective reports would now be corrigible by cerebroscopes). But no knowledge would have been lost, nor would any realm of being be lost to human sight, a given language-game would, for better or worse, no longer be played, but that is all that would have happened.[10]

Faced with this move, those who dislike materialism have moved a step backwards. They now focus on Hylas's claim that, roughly, two things are the same if the language used for describing the one serves all functions fulfilled by the language used for describing the other. This claim is hardly self-evident, as Brandt and Kim have noted in a recent article.[11] These

---

[9] The quotation is from Richard Brandt, "Doubts About the Identity Theory," in S. Hook, ed., *Dimensions of Mind* (New York, 1960), p. 70.

[10] I have argued for some of these points in the article on "Intuition" in P. Edwards (ed.), *The Encyclopedia of Philosophy* (New York, 1967), and in "Mind-Body Identity, Privacy, and Categories," *Review of Metaphysics*, 19, pp. 24–54.

[11] "The Logic of the Identity Theory," *Journal of Philosophy*, 64, pp. 515–37.

authors rightly point out that the materialist can hardly accept a weaker criterion for the identity of events than the following: two events are the same, if all and only the same universals are truly applicable to them. But this means that those who hold that, e.g., thoughts and brain-states are identical have to say that the universals signified by a phenomenalistic language are the same universals as those signified by some part of a physicalistic language. Since, however, there are no rules for determining identity of universals (except the question-begging one that two universals are the same if they hold of all and only the same events), there is no reason to accept the identity of physical and phenomenal events save what Brandt and Kim call "parsimony of a rather metaphysical sort."

I think that there is indeed no other reason, and I think Brandt and Kim are right in saying that it is hard to imagine what importance the Identity Theory could have. But this is surprising, and needs explaining. In the recent past, materialism roused philosophical passion. In these latter days, its opponents no longer argue that it *can't* be true, they merely argue that there is no particular reason to think it true. Both friends and enemies of materialism tend to agree that the Identity Theory has (*pace* Smart) no explanatory power not possessed by a simply nomological correlation of the physical and the psychical. Both sides agree that the difference between mind-body identity and mind-body parallelism is of no scientific interest – that what interest it has is purely philosophical. But instead of arguing in the good old ontological way, the controversy has shifted to quarrels about senses of the term "identical" – quarrels whose upshot seems to be that there are various analogies and disanalogies between, e.g., the identification of chemical with physical universals and the identification of psychological with physiological universals, but no disanalogy so sharp as to make the latter identification outrageous and no analogy so close as to make it inescapable.[12]

---

[12] This curt remark does not do justice to the careful and useful analyses of senses of "identity," "reduction," and related concepts found in, for example, May Brodbeck's "Mental and Physical: Identity vs. Sameness," in Paul Feyerabend and Grover Maxwell, eds., *Mind, Matter, and Method* (Minneapolis, 1966), pp. 40–58, and Richard Routley's and Valerie Macrae's excellent article "On the Identity of Sensations and Physiological Occurrences," *American Philosophical Quarterly*, 3 (1966), pp. 87–110. I do not mean to suggest that these analyses and distinctions are unimportant, but simply that they do not issue in a decisive difference between the two identifications mentioned. Nor can I do justice here to two attempts to show that there *is* such a decisive difference – that offered by Putnam and Fodor (cf. Hilary Putnam, "The Mental Life of Some Machines," in Hector-Neri Castañeda, ed., *Intentionality, Minds and Perception* (Detroit, 1967), and "Robots: Machines or Artificially Created Life?," *Journal of Philosophy*, 61 (1964), pp. 668–91; Jerry Fodor, "Explanations in Psychology," in Max Black, ed., *Philosophy in America* (Ithaca, 1965)), and that offered by Wilfrid Sellars, "The Identity Approach to the Mind-Body Problem," in *Philosophical Perspectives* (Springfield, IL, 1967).

Nobody now argues that dire philosophical consequences will ensue if we do or do not accept materialism. Here is just the sort of historical shift which our account of the history of ontology as a discipline should be expected to clarify.

To explain the fact that philosophers used to feel that a great deal hung on materialism, or its denial, and now don't, we must hark back to the genesis of the mind-body problem. It used to be that parsimony was *not* the only motive for, if possible, getting rid of the mental. There were two other motives: if materialism were true, then (i) there would be no problem about how causal interaction was possible between these different ontological realms, (ii) there would be no problem about whether and how sensations and ideas could be representations of reality, for the whole notion of "representation" would be replaceable by a straightforward, if complex, account of knowledge in terms of appropriate responses to stimuli; an epistemic vocabulary would be replaceable by a causal one.

The first motive has gradually disappeared since Hume revised our notions of causality. These revisions have made it difficult to give an interesting sense to the question "How can mind act on matter, and vice versa?," and the absence of empirical support for interactionism (as opposed to parallelism) has discouraged people from even trying. But, more important for our present interests, the first motive has been weakened by the fact that philosophers have increasing trouble making sense of the mental as a "different ontological realm." This latter notion depends upon the assumptions that mental entities (a) are "homogeneous" with physical entities in that some of the same "primitive" descriptive predicates apply to both, and (b) can be described independently of their relation to the person with whom they are associated. More specifically, it depends upon the distinction between, e.g., a real dagger and an imagined dagger being a distinction between two *particulars*, both describable (in their "essential" features) without reference to any other particular, rather than between one particular (a dagger) and *state* of another particular (a person). As long as we think in terms of two sorts of daggers – one simply located and conforming to one set of regularities, another not simply located and conforming to a different set of regularities (if to any) – the notion of "distinct realms" makes sense.[13] The metaphor of

[13] The way in which the "two sorts of daggers" way of thinking forms the foundation for traditional dualisms is beautifully illustrated by Lovejoy, *op. cit.*, pp. 12–32. In emphasizing the importance of the distinction between particulars and states, I am borrowing heavily from Sellars ("Empiricism and the Philosophy of Mind," in *Science, Perception and Reality* [London, 1963]). See also J. J. C. Smart,

"realms" is founded on the image of subjects living divers laws in divers regions. It is destroyed once the subjects that are supposed to be in different realms are no longer thought of as describable in the same terms. (This is why Ryle's remark that "imagined sights and sounds are not sights and sounds" has such poignancy.)[14] It is not philosophically exciting to ask "How can states of persons cause, and be caused by, daggers?" since this question naturally suggests a program of research in physiology rather than a metaphysical or "conceptual" perplexity.

Why did the philosophical tradition think of mental entities as particulars rather than states? The answer, I believe, is that they made the following assumptions:

(1)   All our knowledge is either expressible in incorrigible statements or validly inferable from such statements.

(2)   We do not have incorrigible knowledge about anything except mental entities.

(3)   No inference to propositions about the qualities of nonmental objects can be valid unless the incorrigible premises of these inferences themselves mention the *same* qualities of mental objects. (E.g., we can't know that tables are brown or that parallel lines never meet unless some mental entity is brown, or is parallel, or has some qualities which provide a *definiens* for "brown" or "parallel.")

(4)   Persons who do not have certain qualities (e.g., being brown, or parallel to something) can nevertheless know that other (non-mental) things have these qualities.

Accepting all this commits one to:

(5)   Persons have immediate knowledge of mental entities characterizable by qualities which the persons themselves do not have.

It will then seem paradoxical to insist that mental entities, such as sensations and ideas, are states of persons. For how can I be aware of

---

"Sensations and Brain Processes," *Philosophical Review*, 68, (1959), pp. 141–56, and Thomas Nagel, "Physicalism," *ibid.*, 74 (1965), pp. 339–56.

[14]   *Concept of Mind* (London, 1949), pp. 250–1. This mention of Ryle should not be taken to mean that an adoption of logical behaviorism is required to overcome traditional psychophysical dualism. All that is required to overcome the epistemological dualism which begets psychophysical dualism is something much milder – the claim that the vocabulary for making statements about mental events can be introduced into language without antecedent awareness of such events serving as ostensive definienda for the terms of this vocabulary. As Sellars has shown, this claim is compatible with common-sense notions of sensations and thoughts as causes of behavior rather than, so to speak, abbreviations for behavior.

something brown which is a state of myself, but not a state of my body? To avoid this paradox, we imagine ourselves as aware not of our own states, but of *particulars* (which we "have" in some ill-defined way) which *are* brown, parallel, *et al.* Knowledge of these particulars will then stand in the same relation to knowledge of nonmental entities as knowledge of pictures to knowledge about the things pictured. Mental entities will be both particulars and representations.

As long as (1), (2), and (3) went unquestioned, the notion of mental particulars homogeneous with (in the sense of sharing some "basic" qualities with) physical particulars, as well as epistemological skepticism and the mind-body problem, were inevitable. As long as the problem of getting the Subject and the Object (and, *a fortiori*) the mind and the body, back together, there were motives for being a materialist. Once the notion of two sorts of daggers – or, more generally, the notion of "homogeneous" mental and physical entities – loses its hold, *both* traditional motives for being a materialist vanish, and are replaced by a purely aesthetic motive – "parsimony of a rather metaphysical sort." It is because (1) – (3) are no longer accepted, much less taken for granted, that (in Taylor's phrase) mind-body identity has become a "side-issue."[15]

Summarizing, we may say that controversies about materialism have lost their interest because we no longer accept the traditional notion of mental particulars. But we can press the matter further. If the notion of mental particulars depended on accepting (1) – (3), which of these premises has now been dropped, and why? This question is too large for the present chapter, but two points can be made fairly briefly. First, even if we accept (1) and (2), we shall still not be in a position to argue for the existence of mental particulars unless we accept (3). But (3) loses any plausibility if we follow common sense in holding that statements about persons' beliefs are sufficient grounds *all by themselves* for statements about utterly heterogeneous things. (E.g., that the inference from "we all think there is something red there" to "Probably there is something red there" or the inference from "None of us can imagine that parallel lines could meet" to "Parallel

---

[15] Charles Taylor, "Mind-Body Identity: A Side-Issue?," *Philosophical Review*, 76 (1967), pp. 201–13. Taylor's own view is that everybody now grants that mind-body identity *might* be true and that the interesting question is whether it is, in fact, empirically true – which boils down to "whether the most fruitful explanations are in psychological rather than physiological terms" (p. 211). I agree with most of what Taylor says in this paper, but I think it a bit misleading to suggest that philosophers should turn their attention to the empirical question he raises. Philosophers here can only wait and see, meanwhile appreciating the impact upon their own discipline of the fact that the only questions left to argue about in this area are empirical ones.

lines never meet" do not require additional non-empirical premises expressing "transcendental" or "conceptual" truths.) In other words, (3) loses its
appeal if we cease to assume that in addition to the ordinary ways of
justifying beliefs there must be a way of justifying this justification itself
(specifically, a way of guaranteeing that the *received opinion* about colors,
or geometry, is not just a good guess, but bound to be right).[16] This recent
willingness to let common-sensical inferences stand on their own feet is
not easily separable from the dissolution of epistemological skepticism
which ensues upon the dissolution of mental particulars. But, as the
example of Moore shows, it can be adopted even when traditional notions
of mental particulars are retained. An adequate history of the twists and
turns of recent philosophy would unravel this strand.

The second point is that the assault on "givenness" common to so many
recent philosophers is not (or should not be) an attack on (1) and (2). If
one defines "incorrigible" beliefs as beliefs which are (a) normally accepted
simply by virtue of being held, and (b) are such that no generally accepted
means for resolving doubts about these beliefs exist, then I think we can
escape Austin's strictures[17] against incorrigibility. We can hold that certain
sentences, used to make sincere statements by one who knows English
(e.g., "It now seems to me that I am seeing something red"; "I cannot
imagine parallel lines meeting") do indeed always express incorrigible
beliefs. Nor need one deny (2) – for one could, given enough time and
trouble, provide a justification for every other piece of knowledge one has
in the form of an inference from such beliefs. (Though this is not to say
that such an inference is in fact "unconsciously" performed whenever one
adopts a corrigible belief.) What is under attack, or should be, is the notion
that if there were no such incorrigible beliefs (if, e.g., men had never
noticed their inner states, or learned to talk the language of appearing),
then we should be bereft of (i) knowledge about anything at all (even
"appearance") and, specifically, (ii) awareness of the really real. This attack
is a special case of a broader attack on the notion that there is an
hierarchical *ordo cognoscendi*, which is not simply a matter of the structure
of some given language at some given stage of the development of the race
but is, instead, a reflection of (or at least a clue to) some hierarchical *ordo
essendi* which is capable of being grasped by nonempirical methods. When

---

[16] The two dogmas which Quine has made notorious were the last gasps of the tradition which felt
such guarantees to be needed. Both dogmas attempted to buttress commonsensical inferences by
providing analyses of meanings which would "explain" our confidence in these inferences.

[17] *Sense and Sensibilia*, ch. 10.

the matter is put in these terms, it becomes clearer why an attack on the Given is an attack on ontology itself, as it existed during the Cartesian period. The attack on "naturally incorrigibly knowable objects" and on "mental particulars" are part of a general revolt against the notion that explanations and justifications of our talking, thinking, and valuing, as we do can be given in terms other than the now familiar psychological, sociological, cultural, and historical ones. The development of these new modes of explanation, as Comte and Dewey foresaw, is having the same effect upon philosophy as a discipline and a cultural form which earlier stages of scientific development had upon religion. The particular philosophical issues concerning mental particulars, incorrigibility, ideas as representations, and the like which I have been examining can be discussed in their own terms. But a full understanding of the changes which have made the possibility of ontology so dubious would require a much broader historical account of cultural change – an account on the Hegelian scale. I do not wish to suggest that Western ontology is a product of a few mistakes in the philosophy of language, or a few mistaken epistemological or methodological premises. (That would be like saying that Western religion is a result of a failure to understand that existence is not a predicate and that there can be no atemporal causes.) But I do wish to say that *a priori* "overcomings," or defenses, of ontology should be replaced by an attempt to go through the traditional "problems of ontology" one-by-one, examine the premises which generate the problems, and see whether there is any reason to believe these premises. The lasting value of the linguistic turn in philosophy, as I have argued elsewhere, is that it has begun such an attempt in a more systematic way[18] than has been attempted in earlier epochs. Although the analytical jobs being done by linguistic philosophers will certainly not be enough to let us understand what happened in history, it is equally certain that they are a necessary first step.

---

[18] Cf. *The Linguistic Turn: Recent Essays in Philosophical Method* (Chicago, 1967), pp. 32–3.

# CHAPTER 12

# Strawson's objectivity argument

In his recent book on Kant,[1] Strawson has offered a new and improved version of the central argument of the *Transcendental Deduction* – the argument that the possibility of experience somehow involves the possibility of experience of objects. This argument has a fair claim to be called the central argument of the *Critique* as a whole, since it is the argument which gives Kant's justification for breaking with the traditional Cartesian notion of a veil of perceptions which separates the mind from the world, and insisting that the world is, in some sense, given whenever experience is given. Strawson's account of this argument is an attempt to follow the lead Kant gives without getting involved in the "theory of synthesis" in terms of which Kant presents the *Deduction*. I think that this attempt is just what is needed in order to explicate Kant's insight, but I think also that Strawson has not entirely succeeded in disentangling the underlying "analytic" argument from the misguided Kantian picture of intuitions and concepts as distinguishable sorts of representations. In this chapter, I offer an exegesis of this passage in Strawson, and I suggest revisions of, and additions to, his arguments.[2]

Early in *The Bounds of Sense*, Strawson gives us the plot of the *Critique* in the form of six theses which Kant wishes to expound. I quote from this passage the two theses which are most clearly relevant to the *Transcendental Deduction*:

> that there must be such unity among the members of some temporally extended series of experiences as is required for the possibility of

---

[1] *The Bounds of Sense* (London, 1966). Unless otherwise specified, page references inserted in the text are to this book.

[2] I shall refrain from complicating matters by taking up Strawson's account of the *Refutation of Idealism*, even though the *Refutation* is also an argument for what Strawson calls "the objectivity thesis." I think that Strawson is right in treating the *Refutation* in the way he does – namely, as an addendum to the objectivity thesis which emphasizes the point that the notion of objectivity requires for its explication the notion of a spatio-temporal framework.

self-consciousness, or self-ascription of experiences, on the part of a subject of such experiences (the thesis of the "necessary unity of consciousness");

that experience must include awareness of objects which are distinguishable from experiences of them in the sense that judgements about these objects are judgements about what is the case irrespective of the actual occurrence of particular subjective experiences of them (the objectivity thesis). (p. 24)

On Strawson's account of the *Deduction*, it is (a) an argument for the objectivity thesis which starts from the thesis of the necessary unity of consciousness, and (b) an argument for the latter thesis on the basis of a definition of what counts as "experience" – *viz.*, the requirement that "particular contents of experience should be recognized as having some general character," a feature which Strawson also calls "the conceptualizability of experience" (p. 25). Putting (a) and (b) together, the *Deduction* is an answer to the question: "What features can we find to be necessarily involved in any coherent conception of experience solely in virtue of the fact that the particular items of which we become aware must fall under (be brought under) general concepts?" (p. 72). Strawson commits himself to presenting arguments showing that the use of concepts implies the possibility of self-consciousness and that self-consciousness implies experience of an objective world.

Strawson's proof of the objectivity thesis is cast in the form of an argument against the possibility of what he calls a "sense-datum experience." The first difficulty in interpreting Strawson's proof occurs in his description of this experience. Here it is:

No doubt, it might be said, the contents of a possible experience must be unified in some way and must be brought under concepts. But why should not the objects (accusatives) of awareness of such a consciousness be a succession of items such that there was no distinction to be drawn between the order and arrangement of the objects (and of their particular features and characteristics) and the order and arrangement of the subject's experiences of awareness of them – items, therefore, which would not be the topics of objective judgements in Kant's sense? Such objects might be of the sort which the earlier sense-datum theorists spoke of – red, round patches, brown oblongs, flashes, whistles, tickling sensations, smells. Certainly concepts, recognition, some span of memory would be necessary to a consciousness with any experience at all; and all these would involve one another. But why should the concepts not be simply such sensory quality concepts as figure in the early and limited sense-datum vocabulary? . . . It is quite conceivable that experience should have as its contents precisely the sort of essentially disconnected impressions we have been speaking of – impressions which neither require, nor permit of, being "united in the concept of an object" in the sense in which Kant understands this phrase. (pp. 98–9)

The puzzling thing about this description is that it is hard to see how there could be objects of awareness "such that there was no distinction to be drawn" between their order and arrangement and the order and arrangement of the subject's experiences of them. One would think that whether such a distinction was drawn or not depended upon whether the experiencer chose to draw it, and that it was not a matter determined by the objects themselves. For suppose I am confronted by brown oblongs and red round patches. If I know that my eyes are shut and that I am not being confronted with brown oblong physical objects nor round red ones (but instead, say, by after-images) then I shall not be tempted to distinguish between the way the oblongs are and the way they seem. If I don't know this, I shall probably go ahead and wonder whether I am seeing the putatively brown and oblong things as they really are. But there seems to be nothing about the oblongs or the patches which would, in Strawson's phrase, not *permit* of their being "united in the concept of an object," if I choose so to unite them. To put the point another way, what could be the nature of the "essential disconnection" which would dictate to me the inappropriateness of such unification? No matter how quickly and erratically the oblongs follow and are followed by the round patches, for example, I can still conceive of myself as watching the rapid movements of oblong and round pieces of wood – or, perhaps, as watching the rapid movements of square and oval pieces of wood which happen to look oblong and round due to the funny perspective.

Perhaps, then, what Strawson intends by a "sense-datum experience" is simply the experience of a man who does not have physical-object concepts in his conceptual repertoire. On this interpretation, the crucial proviso in the passage above is that the experiencer's concepts are limited to "such sensory quality concepts as figure in the early and limited sense-datum vocabulary." A subject who has only such concepts available will not have the concept of an object distinct from his own awareness, and thus will not be in a position to distinguish between the order and arrangement of objects and the order and arrangement of his experiences of objects. Let us call the experience of such a man a "sense-datum experience$_1$." If we are to show that a sense-datum experience$_1$ is impossible, we shall have to show that there is something incoherent about the conception of a man with so limited a conceptual repertoire.

But another interpretation of Strawson's intention is possible, one which does more justice to the notion of experience "such that there is no distinction to be drawn." On this interpretation, what Strawson has in mind is an experience such that, if a man, in his entire life, had only this sort of experience, he would never have been able to grasp physical-object concepts. As an example of what such experience would be like, we may take the auditory world Strawson describes in the "Sounds" chapter of *Individuals*. Strawson there says that unless there were, for example, a "master-sound" such that variations in its pitch were regularly correlated with what else was heard, one would not be able to formulate criteria for the re-identification of auditory particulars, and thus would not have the notion of an objective particular. Some systematic regularity such as this would have to be present in the experience of the inhabitant of such a world before he could formulate the notion of an object.[3]

Returning to our visual example of brown oblongs and round, red circles, then, we can think of Strawson as describing an experience in which these shapes and colors appear without any systematic correlation either with each other or with appearances of other sensory qualities. As long as this chaotic experience continued, we would not be able to formulate criteria for the re-identification of visual objects. But if at some point the proper sort of regularities did appear, and we then formulated such criteria and thereby added physical-object concepts to our conceptual repertoire, then later when the chaos reappeared we could (as we suggested above) use these concepts to think of ourselves as watching the erratic and swift movement of, say, pieces of wood. In other words, the sense-datum experience is not one which gives no purchase to physical-object concepts *once one has them*, but rather is one which, had one had no other sort of experience, would have left one unable to acquire them. What puzzled us originally about the passage quoted was that it seemed impossible to imagine a situation in which we couldn't apply physical-object concepts, and yet Strawson was describing an experience which he clearly thought *was* imaginable.[4] We now see that we can interpret "impressions which do

---

[3] We might be tempted to say here that a genius inhabiting an auditory world without such regularities could nevertheless *imagine* such regularities occurring, and then formulate criteria for re-identification of particulars in terms of these merely imaginary regularities. He would then have concepts which he would have no occasion to apply, except to imagined cases. In reply to this point, however, all we need say is that an imagined regularity would be as much a "part of his experience" as a "real" regularity.

[4] Cf. p. 109: "Each of us can perfectly well imagine a stretch of *his own* experience being such as the sense-datum theorist describes." (But see pp. 245–7 below, where I argue that Strawson should not have said this.)

not permit being united in the concept of an object" as "impressions which would not permit the formulation of criteria for re-identification of an object."

Let us call this second sort of experience a "sense-datum experience$_2$." If we think of Strawson as talking about a sense-datum experience$_2$, we must think of its "impossibility" in a restricted sense. What the argument for the objectivity thesis will show is not that we can never have such an experience, but only that we must have had another sort of experience first – *viz.*, an experience which *did* contain enough systematic regularities to give us a grasp of physical-object concepts. The impossibility in question will be the impossibility of having *only* this sort of experience. If a sense-datum experience$_1$ is impossible, and if all experience must be the experience of a person who has physical-object concepts, then it will necessarily be the case that not all our experience will have been a sense-datum experience$_2$.

As we shall see, it is the impossibility of a sense-datum experience$_1$ for which Strawson actually argues. I shall now examine this argument. After doing so, proposing modifications to it, and evaluating the strength of the modified argument, I shall come back to the notion of "sense-datum experience$_2$," criticize it, and take up the puzzling claim that we can, by *a priori* argument, demonstrate something about the order in which we must have had certain sorts of experiences.

Having inferred the thesis of the necessary unity of consciousness from the thesis of the conceptualizability of experience (an inference we shall examine in detail shortly), Strawson proceeds as follows toward the objectivity thesis:

> What then is implied by the potentiality of such an acknowledgement, by the potentiality – which must he present in every experience – of awareness of oneself as having it? The very minimum that is implied, Kant must reply, is precisely what the hypothesis of the purely sense-datum "experience" attempts to exclude. The minimum implied is that some at least of the concepts under which particular experienced items are recognized as falling should be such that the experiences themselves contain the basis for certain allied distinctions; individually, the distinction of a subjective component *within* a judgement of experience (as "it seems to me as if this is a heavy stone" is distinguishable within "this is a heavy stone"); collectively, the distinction between the subjective order and arrangement of a series of such experiences on the one hand the objective order and arrangement of the items of which they are experiences on the other. (p. 101)

Though he does not spell it out explicitly, what Strawson must be saying in this passage is that one would not know what an experience was if one did not know what a physical object was.[5] What unites the two notions is the seeming-versus-being distinction. In other words, Strawson is saying that if you don't know what the distinction is between seeming and being, you won't know what an experience is, whereas if you do know what this distinction is, you automatically know what a physical object is.[6] Therefore, only persons who can wield the concept of "physical object" are persons who can wield that of "experience," and since by the thesis of the necessary unity of consciousness all experiencers can wield the latter concept, all of them can wield the former. The inference is slightly clearer in the following passage:

> What is meant by the necessary self-reflexiveness of a possible experience in general could be otherwise expressed by saying that experience must be such as to provide room for the thought of experience itself. The point of the objectivity-condition is that it provides room for this thought. It provides room, on the one hand, for "Thus and so is how things objectively are" and, on the other, for "This is how things are experienced as being"; and it provides room for the second thought because it provides room for the first. (p. 107)

---

[5] Strawson has available an additional argument for this claim – the argument familiar from the "Persons" chapter of *Individuals* (London, 1959) – to the effect that you don't know what an experience is unless you know what a person is, and that a person must be thought of as something that has physical-object characteristics as well as "mental" characteristics. He introduces this additional argument in *The Bounds of Sense* at pp. 102–10 in terms of the distinction between empirical and transcendental self-consciousness. The point to bear in mind is that there are two *separate* arguments for the claim in question – the argument just cited from p. 101, which leaves the possibility open that one could know what an experience was if one did *not* have the notion of a person, but insists that *even so* our grasp of the notion of "experience" would presuppose our grasp of what a physical object was, and the argument which Strawson developed in "Persons." Strawson is certainly right in saying that Kant (rightly or wrongly) would prefer to get along without the latter argument, and would cling to the former.

[6] It might be objected at this point that one could grasp the contrast between "seems" and "is" even if one lacked the concept of physical object by making a distinction between veridical and nonveridical, trustworthy and untrustworthy, sense data, on the basis of the coherence or incoherence of some sense data with others. But what would it mean to say that a sense datum was nonveridical save that it did not properly represent the characteristics of some physical object? And how could we make sense of the notion that a given experience of something red was "untrustworthy" unless we have the notion of something which *is* red whether it seems that way or not? Without the latter notion, all that "sense datum which does not cohere with other sense data" can mean is "unfamiliar sense datum" and, as Bennett puts it, "to identify the hallucinatory with the unfamiliar is to abuse the ordinary sense of 'hallucinatory'." (Jonathan Bennett, *Kant's Analytic* [Cambridge, 1966], p. 34.) To put the point another way, we might imagine a sense-datum experiencer developing habits of expectation such that he expected the course of his sense data to reproduce certain frequent and familiar patterns and did not expect it to reproduce certain rare and "wild" patterns which it has occasionally followed in the past. But to develop such habits is not yet to have the concept of "seems."

The point that Strawson is making here is that you don't know what "experience" means if you don't know what "seems to me . . . " means, that you don't know what *that* means unless you know that something can seem to me to be $X$ and not be $X$, and that if you know that something can seem to me to be $X$ and not be $X$, you know what it is for something to be a physical object. So anybody who can say to himself: "This is the way it seems to me now" can also say to himself: "This may be how certain physical objects are now." The metaphor of "provides room for" is dispensable, and the argument boils down to what words you must be able to use if you are able to use certain other words. The central point is that you need to be able to use "is objectively there" if you are to be able to use "seems."

Clearly enough, everything now depends on whether Strawson can demonstrate the thesis of the necessary unity of consciousness, and thus show that every experiencer does understand what "seems" means. Before giving Strawson's argument for this thesis, however, we need to spend a moment examining the thesis itself. What is the "unity" referred to in the claim that "there must be such unity among the members of some temporally extended series of experiences as is required for the possibility of self-consciousness, or self-ascription of experiences"? In what sense do our experiences have to be "unified" in order for self-ascription to be possible? All we have to go on here is the notion of "disconnected impressions which do not require or permit of being unified in the concept of an object" which we discussed above. In that discussion, we concluded that the "disconnection" was a lack of the sort of systematic regularity of appearance which would permit criteria for the re-identification of objects to be formulated. So presumably the unity in question here is the existence of such systematic regularities as would permit the formulation of criteria for the use of the concept "my experience" or "seems to me that . . . ." What regularities might these be? Part of the answer is plain: they would, at a minimum, include those same regularities which were necessary for us to have acquired physical-object concepts. For the argument for the objectivity thesis was just that one had to have physical-object concepts in order to have the concept "seems to me that . . . ." Are there *other* regularities besides these which are needed? Strawson gives us no help here, and it is hard to imagine how the question might be answered. But (for the moment) we do not need to answer it, for when we turn to Strawson's argument for the necessary unity of consciousness, we find that reference to *unity* has dropped out of the conclusion; all that is argued for is "the potential acknowledgement of the experience as one's own." Before worrying further about "unity," let us examine the argument. It goes as follows:

> It was agreed at the outset that experience requires both particular intuitions and general concepts. There can be no experience at all which does not involve the recognition of particular items *as* being of such and such a general kind. It seems that it must be possible, even in the most fleeting and subjective of impressions, to distinguish a component of recognition, or judgement, which is not simply identical with, or wholly absorbed by, the particular item which is recognized, which forms the topic of judgement. Yet at the same time we seem forced to concede that there are particular subjective experiences (e.g., a momentary tickling sensation) of which the objects (accusatives) have no existence independently of the awareness of them. It is clear what Kant must regard as the way out of this difficulty. The way out is to acknowledge that the recognitional component, necessary to experience, can be present in experience only because of the *possibility* of referring different experiences to one identical subject of them all. Recognition implies the *potential* acknowledgement of the experience into which recognition necessarily enters as being one's own, as sharing with others this relation to the identical self. It is the fact that this potentiality is implicit in recognition which saves the recognitional component from absorption into the item recognized (and hence saves the character of the particular experience as an *experience*) even when that item cannot be conceived of as having an existence independent of the particular experience of it. (pp. 100–1)

The key to this argument is the notion of "recognition," and it behooves us to go slowly and to see how this notion is being used. The second sentence of the argument identifies the thesis that "experience requires both particular intuitions and general concepts" with the thesis that every experience "involves the recognition of particular items as being of such and such a general kind." This should give us pause, because of the implicit identification of an item recognized with an *intuition*. It is tempting, at least, to think of recognition as typified by such cases as recognizing a man to be Jones, or recognizing a white patch flashing through the woods as the tail of a deer. But these are acts of recognition which can be reported in a sentence, acts in which the "item recognized" has, prior to the recognition, already been brought under the concept signified by one of the words used – e.g., "man" in "This man is Jones." The recognition of an intuition as falling under a concept cannot be so reported, because no term can refer to the intuition prior to its conceptualization. So it seems clear that "recognition" is being used in a special way – a way which suggests that we can not only recognize that something which bears one description may bear another, but that something which bears no description may bear one.

This in turn suggests that we can somehow be *aware* of something – the intuition recognized – prior to being aware of it under any description, that we cognize it before we recognize it.

This latter suggestion is reinforced if we look at the next two sentences of the argument. The third sentence says that in every experience there is a recognitional component. Strawson in a later passage (p. 110) identifies "conceptual component" and "recognitional component," so it seems that this sentence reiterates that every experience involves both concepts and intuitions. But this sentence also tells us that we can "distinguish" this component as something not "absorbed" by the "item recognized." Here again we have the suggestion that there are two "distinguishable" components in each experience – so that we might be aware of one without the other. This suggestion is strengthened if we look at the next – the fourth – sentence, which is the crux of the argument and the most mysterious of its steps. This sentence tells us that although there should, in any experience, be these two distinguishable elements, it may happen that there are experiences whose "objects (accusatives)" (presumably the "items recognized") do not exist independently of the awareness of them. This claim would only conflict with the claim made in the third sentence if we somehow identified "the awareness of them" with the "recognitional component" and thus with the concept used in the experience. So Strawson must be identifying the contrast between intuition and concept first with the contrast between "item recognized" and "recognitional component," *and then with the contrast between "object of awareness" and "awareness."* He is identifying the role of the concept with the element of awareness in any experience.

Before puzzling over this identification, let us finish up our dissection of the argument by taking account of the solution of the "difficulty" created by the conflict between the third and the fourth sentences. The solution is that "the recognitional component can be present in experience only because of the *possibility* of referring different experiences to one identical subject of them all." This possibility "saves the recognitional component from absorption into the item recognized." Apparently, the idea is that only because we can be aware of ourselves being aware (that is, because we can acknowledge a given experience as *ours*) can we be aware. Further, this is the case because only by being aware of ourselves being aware do we distinguish the recognitional component (the awareness) from the item recognized (the object of awareness). The reasoning thus is:

(1) Experience requires the ability to discriminate between the recognitional component and the item recognized.

(2) The recognitional component is the awareness and the item recognized is the object of awareness.

(3) So experience requires the ability to discriminate between the awareness and the object of awareness.

(4) So experience requires the ability to be aware that we are aware.

(5) This ability explains how we can experience objects whose *esse* is *percipi* – even though in such experiences there is no distinction between the awareness and the object of awareness. We do so by adding on the awareness of our own awareness – thus producing a recognitional component as well as an item recognized. (Though the original awareness of the item is "absorbed" in the item, the awareness of the awareness isn't.)

There are numerous puzzles in this reasoning, notably a puzzle about why the *possibility* of being aware of our being aware should be enough to enable us to have experience of objects whose *esse* is *percipi*. (One would think that this possibility must be actualized.) But, in order not to get lost in the bushes, let us skip over all difficulties except the central one – the premise labelled (2) above, the assimilation of "concept" to "awareness." What would be required to make sense of this assimilation? Only, I think, the assumption that every experience can be reported in some such form as "This is the way I am experiencing this independently existing object," or "This is how this independently existing object seems to me," or "This is how I am aware of this independently existing object." It is only if all experiences are like this – if they all can be expressed by reports of how objects seem – that we can identify the "component of recognition" with the "awareness." If they are like this, they will divide up neatly into the item recognized *qua* independently existing object and the "component of recognition" *qua* my awareness of that object. I will always be aware of two things whenever I have an experience – the object itself as a sort of bare particular and myself as experiencing it as something of such and such a kind. Or, if I am not always aware of these two things, I always will be *able* to be aware of them, for they are there to be discriminated.

The trouble with the assumption that that is what experiences are like, however, is that this is what the argument as a whole was supposed to prove. So it cannot be assumed half-way along. We cannot show that every experience must be the experience of a person who has the concept of "experience" by assuming that all experiences come in the form "This is how I experience . . . ," nor by assuming that they *could* always come that way. What we have to do is show, on the basis of the single fact that experiences involve concepts – the thesis of the conceptualizability of experience – that no concept can be wielded if the concept "seems to me that . . . " cannot be (or, more nominalistically, that no words can be used if these words cannot be). As far as I can see, the argument of Strawson's which we have been analyzing gives us no help in this direction. Strawson has either begged the question or has buried his point beneath metaphors ("absorption," e.g.) which defy interpretation.

A further criticism of this argument is that it leads us back into the Kantian "theory of synthesis" which Strawson is attempting to avoid. As we have seen, explicating the argument seems to require us to take seriously the Kantian notion of intuition – the notion of something which we are aware of without being aware of it under any description. We cannot get along here with the notion of "impression" which was used in describing the sense-datum experience – a notion which was simply shorthand for "experience reportable using only concepts of sensory qualities." For here we are talking about any possible experience – including the experience described by the sense-datum theorist, in which all reports of experience are like "This is red" or "That is oblong." We are saying that even in the case of such experiences there is a distinction to be drawn between a "particular item" and a "general concept." But what is the "particular item" apart from its redness or its oblongness? We seem, as suggested above, to be saddled with awareness of bare particulars. I doubt that Strawson wishes such a consequence to follow, but I am unable to see how what he says can be interpreted otherwise.

Let us now look back over the ground we have covered. A sense-datum experience was defined as an experience in which only sensory-quality concepts were employed. The argument for the objectivity thesis was designed to show, starting from the premise of the necessary unity of consciousness, that a sense-datum experience was impossible. What it did show was that any experiencer who could use the concept "my experience" could also use physical-object concepts. So all that was required to show the impossibility of a sense-datum experience was to show that any experiencer could use the concept "my experience." The argument for the necessary unity of consciousness, it turned out, side-stepped the notion of "unity" altogether, and simply tried to establish the necessity for "the potential acknowledgement of the experience as one's own." We interpreted this latter phrase as meaning "grasping the concept 'my experience', or 'it seems to me that . . . '," thus making it fit the hole left open by the argument for the objectivity thesis. But because Strawson's argument for the necessity of grasping these concepts fails, this hole still seems open. So we do not yet have a way of backing up the objectivity thesis.

This ends, for the moment, my exegesis of Strawson. I want now to put forward an argument which, if successful, will do the job Strawson wants done, though not quite in the way he suggests. I do not think this argument for the objectivity thesis is conclusive, but sketching it will let us see more clearly what remains to be done if we want to continue along the path marked out by Strawson's reconstruction of Kant.

This argument goes directly from the thesis of the conceptualizability of experience to the impossibility of a sense-datum experience$_1$, bypassing the necessary unity of consciousness. A sense-datum experience$_1$ was an experience such that no concepts are used in it save those of sensory qualities. We can, I believe, show that no such experience is possible simply on the basis of an analysis of what it is to have such concepts. The argument is simply this: to use a concept is to be able to make a judgment, which involves having a thought expressible by a complete sentence; but if all one has are names for sensory qualities, one will not be able to construct sentences. In other words, if all one has in one's conceptual repertoire are such adjectives as "red," "hard," and "painful," then one does not yet have *anything* in one's conceptual repertoire. For one is not yet, lacking substantives, in a position to use these adjectives to form a judgment, and if one cannot form judgments, one does not possess concepts. In still other words, someone who has only the words "red," "hard," and "painful" in his vocabulary does not yet have any *words* in his vocabulary – even if he should call out "red" only when confronted with red objects, "hard" only when touching hard objects, etc. – any more than a parrot who could make only these sounds would be said to know the meanings of words. To know what "red" means – and thus to have the concept "red" – one must at least know what sort of thing can be red. So one must have physical-object concepts or concepts of such things as after-images or sensory states – substantival concepts.

If we accept this last point, then we may have shown that a sense-datum experience$_1$ is impossible, but we shall not yet have shown that physical-object concepts are required for experience to be possible. For the concept of a sensory state of the self, for example, is a candidate for playing the role of the needed substantival concept. Here, however, we need to remember Strawson's argument that one would not know what an experience was unless one knew what a physical object was. Can we use this argument to show that talking or thinking about anything "inner" (sensory state, sense impression, sense datum, sensation) which might be proposed as the only entities to be qualified by terms signifying sensory qualities will presuppose the grasp of the concept of the "outer"?

We said above that Strawson's argument for the objectivity thesis depended upon holding that you don't know what "experience" means if you don't know what "seems to me" means. This claim seems sound as long as we think of "experience" as meaning "experience of an object" – as long, roughly speaking, as we build the subject–object relation into our notion of something "inner." But further argument would be necessary to show that *all* concepts of "inner" states presupposed a grasp of this relation (that is, were tied to the notion of "seems," and so tied to the notion of "is objectively . . . "). Such argument would be to the effect that if one did not have the notion of "seems," one would not have the notion of self at all, and thus would have no notion of states of the self. A defender of Strawson might try to show, in other words, that the notion of "seems to me" was basic to one's notion of what it was to be a person, and that unless one thought of oneself as someone to whom objects appeared in such-and-such ways, one would not think of oneself as a *self* at all. Such an argument might be successful, but there is an alternative tactic which a defender of the objectivity thesis can employ. This is to appeal to the argument which Strawson presents in *Individuals*[7] – the argument that to have the concept of a "state of consciousness" one has to have the concept of the subject of such a state, and that one can have the latter concept (the concept of a person or a self) only if one can use physical-object concepts to distinguish one person from another. This is a quite independent argument, and it would serve equally well to complete the argument for the objectivity thesis (although it, unlike the former argument, would have no counterpart in the *Transcendental Deduction*).

To defend himself against either argument, the opponent of the objectivity thesis might insist that we could have a conceptual scheme which would enable us to think about states of the self without thinking about them *as* states of the self. Such an opponent might grant, that is, that someone who had no physical-object concepts would not have *our* concept of a state of the self, but could nonetheless grasp a concept which he applied just on those occasions when, e.g., we would apply the concept of "sensation of something red." The suggestion is that there might be terms in a solipsistic language which had the same extensions as terms signifying states of consciousness in our language, but not the same meanings, and that the use of these words would provide concepts which would make

---

[7] Cf. n. 5 above.

experience possible – but not an experience which satisfies the objectivity thesis. If the strategy embodied in this suggestion were successful, it would take the force not only out of both the Strawsonian arguments mentioned in the previous paragraph, but out of *any* which has the form: "The concept $X$ presupposes the concept $Y$, and therefore to experience $X$'s presupposes being able to experience $Y$'s." For in reply to any such argument, an opponent can grant that to experience $X$'s *as* $X$'s would require a grasp of the concept $Y$, but nevertheless insist that $X$'s may be experienced under another description, and that a grasp of the terms used in formulating this new description does not presuppose an ability to use the term "$Y$."

I think that the way of countering this strategy is to put the burden of proof on the opponent by requiring him to spell out what this new description would be, and to show that it could be part of a coherent language-game. In the present case, such a task would be more difficult than it may first appear. For the skeptic about the objectivity thesis will be required to show not merely that we could *react* to states of consciousness without having our concept of "state of consciousness" but also to show that such states could be *experienced* without this concept. "Experience" here must be taken in a sense concordant with Strawson's thesis of the "conceptualizability of experience" – that is, the thesis that experience requires both intuitions and concepts. Further, since our only test for relations of presupposal among concepts is whether a given word could be said to be properly used by someone who could not use some other word, to have a given concept must be identified with (or at least have as a necessary condition) the ability to use a given word, or a given group of words. Thus, nothing will be said to have experience which is not a language-user. Now to distinguish language-users from other entities, we must have some way of distinguishing the use of a language from other complicated ways of reacting to the environment. Formulating such a distinction is immensely difficult, but it seems safe to say that one constraint would be that a language must make possible such operations as justification, explanation, and self-correction. So the skeptic about the objectivity thesis, to make good his suggestion that experience is possible for beings who lack both physical-object concepts and "our" concept of selfhood, must describe the sort of inferences which can be performed in the new language he is suggesting. He must tell us what sorts of statements count as reasons for what other sorts of statements. It is therefore not enough for him to suggest that certain sounds would be uttered when and only when what we would call "a sensation of something red" occurs; he must also fill in enough details about inference-patterns to permit us to grasp the notion of a way of talking which can be satisfactorily translated neither into our ordinary discourse about states of consciousness nor into our ordinary discourse about physical objects.

I do not think it can be demonstrated that no such new language can be formulated. This is why no argument for the objectivity thesis can be clinching. A clinching argument could only be given if we had clear criteria for saying that a certain word could not be understood by a being whose vocabulary did not include a certain other word. To see the morass into which we can rapidly be led, consider the following (quasi-Russellian) move by the skeptic about the objectivity thesis: granted, he might say, that *our* words "red," "hard," and "painful" require the notions of physical objects or of states of consciousness for their use, nevertheless we can conceive of terms used when and only when the speaker is having what we should call "experiences of something red (or hard or painful)" as having a use in a language which contained, in addition, only the terms "resembles" and "is (spatiotemporally) next to," plus some logical constants. Such a language, our skeptic insists, permits counterparts of most of the inferences performed in our ordinary language. But now there arises (among others) the question: could a man who didn't know what a physical or a mental object was – who could not, in Strawson's phrase, re-identify particulars – know what "is (spatiotemporally) next to" meant? To answer this, we should have to decide whether this expression could be used by someone who could not use token-reflexives like "here" and "now," nor the notion of "the place where . . . is." There is certainly a case for saying that it could not be so used, but I do not see how the case could ever be made conclusive. All that we can do is put the burden of proof on the skeptic to spell out the inference-patterns which would provide a use. Until he does so, it is fair to characterize him in the terms in which Strawson characterizes the skeptic: one who "pretends to accept a conceptual scheme, but at the same time quietly rejects one of the conditions of its employment."[8]

It is now time to sum up what has been shown and to look back to problems which we deferred earlier. Have we shown that a sense-datum experience$_1$ is impossible? No. But we have shown that it is harder to describe such an experience than those who think it possible have imagined. We have confronted the man who thinks such an experience possible with the following choices: he must either (a) deny the thesis of

---

[8] *Individuals*, p. 35.

the conceptualizability of experience, or (b) deny that the ability to use certain words is a necessary condition of having certain concepts, or (c) explain how words signifying sensory qualities could have a use in a language which had no terms for re-identifiable particulars. If he chooses (a), he must explain what it would be like to have experience of something which was not experience of it *as* of such-and-such a sort. If he chooses (b), he must explain how we can experience something as of such-and-such a sort without *thinking* of it as of that sort, or else explain what it would be like to think without thinking in a language. If he chooses (c), he confronts the various difficulties we have rehearsed above.

We cannot here follow out the arguments that will ensue if our opponent chooses (a) or (b). Something more will be said about these possibilities in the concluding section of this chapter, but for the moment I shall only note once again that unless we both restrict the application of the term "experience" to language-users and restrict the concepts they can employ to those signified by words which they can use, we will have no basis whatever for offering transcendental arguments about the possibility of experience. Arguments of the Strawsonian type rest on considerations of which words can be understood independently of which other words. The relevance of these considerations vanishes if we admit the possibility of a being who could experience something as an $X$ but could not use the word "$X$" nor any equivalent expression.

Given, then, that a case has been made for the impossibility of a sense-datum experience$_1$, have we thereby made a case for saying that any "chaotic" sense-datum experience$_2$ must have been preceded by a "non-chaotic" experience (i.e., one which exhibited certain systematic regularities which would enable us to formulate criteria for the application of physical-object concepts)? The assumption behind the claim that such a relation of priority must hold was that a certain order must hold within experience before one could grasp physical-object terms like "stone" or "tree." But how could such order be experienced *as* an order by someone who had neither physical-object terms nor terms for sensory qualities? If our argument that having sensory-quality concepts presupposes having physical-object concepts is sound, we cannot now suggest that a person could formulate criteria for the application of the first physical-object concepts he acquires in antecedently understood, sensory-quality terms. But what other terms are there? To put the point more generally: the thesis of the conceptualizability of experience tells us that we must have *some* concepts in order to have *any* experience; so we cannot say that the *first* concepts we acquire are acquired only because we have had experiences of a certain type. Whatever the necessary conditions for acquiring our first concepts are, they will not include the fact that we have had certain experiences. Or, to put it in terms of language, we cannot explain language-acquisition on the basis of the infant's having had certain experiences. (Though we might, of course, explain it on the basis of the infant's sensory organs having been exposed to certain stimuli. And it doubtless is the case, as a matter of psychological fact, that unless these stimuli occurred in certain orderly and regular ways, language would not be acquired.)

These considerations make us see that the notion of a sense-datum experience$_2$ – the notion of "an experience which, if it had been the only sort of experience we had ever had, would not have permitted us to grasp physical-object concepts" – is incoherent. It is trivially true that if a sense-datum experience$_1$ is impossible for the reasons given above, then, for experience to be possible at all, the conditions which are necessary for the grasping of physical-object concepts must be fulfilled. The mistake comes in thinking that these conditions include the having of certain sorts of experience. To put the matter another way: it is a mistake to think that when we are, for example, aware of an auditory chaos we are duplicating the experience of the preconceptual infant. We cannot help applying some concepts (e.g., the concept "chaotic") to such a chaos – thinking of the chaos in some terms or other. But we cannot strip off the thoughts from the experience and thus recapture what the infant has. We cannot, to use Kantian terms, be aware of unsynthesized intuitions, nor imagine ourselves having unsynthesized intuitions. We can discover some conditions of the possibility of experience *a priori* (namely, the conditions which consist in having certain sorts of concepts at hand) and we can discover certain others *a posteriori* by psychophysiological inquiry (namely, the sorts of stimuli required). But we cannot get in between the concepts and the stimuli and describe a third set of conditions – e.g., the condition that intuitions display a certain "unity" or "order."

To reinforce this point, let us look once again at the contrast between an auditory chaos and an auditory experience which includes correlations with a master-sound. Earlier, we blithely said that the man who has only the former as his experience cannot formulate criteria for the use of the notion of "objective auditory particular," whereas the man who has the latter can. This suggests that the latter man is first aware of the master-sound and correlated sounds, and then, after performing some simple inductions, says to himself such things as "I'll call it 'misheard' if it doesn't sound the way it usually does when the master-sound is at that pitch."[9] But if our argument that one can't use sensory-quality terms before one uses physical-object terms was sound, he can't be aware of the master-sound or sounds correlated with it unless he *already* can make sense of the notion of objective auditory particulars which have pitches, are correlated with other such particulars, and the like. If this picture of antecedent awareness of (e.g.) pitches is wrong, what does the claim that experience must be of a certain sort in order to permit the formation of certain concepts come to? Simply this: in order to be correctly said to *have* a given concept one must have at some time or another *applied* it – used it in forming judgment (true or false) about some real or imagined entity. If a man's conceptual repertoire is so limited that the only sorts of judgments he can make are reports of observation or introspection, then it will necessarily be the case that if he has the concept "$X$," then he will have experienced something as $X$; he will, that is, have judged something or other (truly or falsely) to be $X$. This is not a remark about a psychological mechanism. It is not to say that he needed the experience of an $X$ in order to "abstract" the concept "$X$" from it. Rather, it is a remark about our criteria for crediting a man with the grasp of a concept. If we have no reason to think that a man has ever had the thought "that thing is red" or "this thing seems red to me," and if we think that judgments of the simple forms "that thing is . . ." or "this thing seems to me . . ." are the only sorts he can make, then we have no reason for thinking that he knows what "red" means.[10]

Thus, to say that the inhabitant of an auditory universe must have had sounds correlated with the pitches of a master-sound in his experience in order to have the concept of "objective auditory particular" is simply to say that he must have once had the thought "this sound always occurs when the master-sound has that pitch" in order to properly be said to have once had the thought "this is the same objective auditory particular as I heard ten minutes ago." It does not matter whether either thought is true; it does not even matter that the man is stone-deaf and his language-training is done by inserting electrodes in his brain. In the only relevant sense of "had in his experience" he will still have had the appropriate correlation in his experience. For purposes of describing the preconditions of grasping concepts, the distinction between "experiencing $X$" and "thinking one

---

[9] Cf. Bennett, *op. cit.*, pp. 34–6.

[10] But if he is equipped with lots of other concepts and so can make such judgments as "red is the normal color of barns," then the fact that he has not (being blind) made any judgments like "that thing is red" or "this thing seems red to me" will not prevent us from saying that he knows what "red" means and thus what redness is.

experiences $X$" collapses. Or, to use Kantian terms again, only the concepts and the judgments matter; the intuitions drop out.

We are now in a position to clear up two puzzles to which Bennett directs attention in his review of *The Bounds of Sense*. The first is that Strawson says that we can "perfectly well imagine" a stretch of our own experience being of the sense-datum sort, but that although "we can form such a picture," nevertheless the picture does not "contain in itself the materials for the conception of itself as experience" (p. 109). Bennett interprets this obscure metaphor as suggesting that Strawson thinks that a being must "actually *have* objective experience in order to have the thought of it, the thought (perhaps) of what it would be like to have such experience."[11] But if "actually have objective experience" means "must actually experience objects" in a strong sense in which a man with a functioning brain (stimulated by electrodes) but no functioning sense-organs (or a man whose life is one long hallucination), does *not* experience objects, then Strawson seems in no position to say this. On the other hand, if "actually have objective experience" simply has the weak meaning "think of one's experience as of objects," then the contrast between "objective experience" and "the thought of it" disappears. So there seems no satisfactory interpretation. The points made in the preceding paragraphs show, I think, why we should cease to look for one. It is just false that we can imagine to ourselves a sense-datum experience$_1$, because (roughly) we cannot imagine ourselves using adjectival terms without simultaneously using substantival terms. As to a sense-datum experience$_2$, the very argument which shows that physical-object concepts are necessary if one is to have experience shows that the notion of such an experience is incoherent. We could only imagine a sense-datum experience$_2$ if we could experience what the preconceptual infant experiences – but, by Strawson's own thesis of the conceptualizability of experience, the preconceptual infant doesn't experience anything.

The second puzzle which Bennett remarks on is that Strawson, by claiming that we can "perfectly well imagine a stretch of *his own* experience as being such as the sense-datum theorist describes," seems to be offering a "genetic" argument:

> When Strawson says that we "can perfectly well imagine" a pure hallucinatory stretch of experience, is he conceding that for thirty minutes this afternoon I might have and be aware of such a stretch? (If not, I am lost.)

---

[11] Jonathan Bennett, "Strawson on Kant," *Philosophical Review*, 77 (1968), p. 345.

If so, then the envisaged situation is this: from two until two-thirty I am aware of my sensory states; I therefore have (we concede) a strong concept of awareness-of [that is, awareness of something whose *esse* is not its *percipi*], and thus the concept of an object of awareness whose existence is not "to all intents and purposes" the same as my awareness of it. I have this latter concept throughout a period when I have nothing to which to apply it. Must not Strawson claim that I can have that concept at that time only because I have earlier been in a position to apply it? If not, then again his argument eludes me. But I think he would rest his argument on that claim: there is evidence in *Individuals* – especially in the thesis that a disembodied mind must be a *ci-devant* person – that Strawson really is prepared to argue genetically, basing philosophical conclusions on principles of the form "If *P*, then *Q* earlier"; which is certainly what he seems to do here. Perhaps he is entitled to, but the literature which argues that he is not deserves an answer.[12]

What has gone wrong here is suggested by Bennett's phrase "have a concept throughout a period when I have nothing to which to apply it," and by his interpreting "such as the sense-datum theorist describes" as "hallucinatory." As was argued at the outset of this chapter, we *cannot* picture to ourselves a stretch of experience to which we *could* not apply some physical-object concepts or other. All that "have nothing to which to apply it" can mean, then, is "have nothing to which we can apply it so as to produce a true judgment" – as, e.g., a man having hallucinations of elephants has nothing to which to apply the concept "elephant" so as to produce a true judgment. So as a result of trying to make sense of the impossible picture of an experience which is somehow recalcitrant to the imposition of physical-object concepts, Bennett winds up construing "sense-datum experience" as "hallucinatory experience." But this construal does not give Strawson what he wants – for hallucinatory experiences may be just as orderly and regular as perceptual experience. Further, it gives him something he does not (or at least should not) want – namely, the claim that you can only have hallucinations if you have previously had perceptions. This "genetic" claim is just not the sort of claim which can possibly result from an investigation of relations of presupposal between concepts.

The closest Strawson can (or should) come to a "genetic" argument is to argue that if we did not know what a perception was we would not know what a hallucination was. But even this claim is not a claim about temporal precedence of concept-acquisition. It is perfectly compatible with the objectivity argument as we have reformulated it that the concepts of

---

[12] *Ibid.*, p. 345.

"perception" and "hallucination" (and the concepts "entity whose *esse* is not *percipi*" and "entity whose *esse* is *percipi*") should be acquired *simultaneously*. The point of the objectivity argument is not to establish a genetic order, but to refute a claim about such an order – viz., the claim that we could have some other concepts before we had any physical-object concepts. This argument does not imply anything about the order in which experiences must come; rather, it warns us against taking seriously a bogus description of a putatively possible experience. It is unfortunate that Strawson should have obscured this point by his claim that we can "perfectly well imagine" a sense-datum experience.

There is still one last loose thread to be picked up – the topic of the "necessary unity of consciousness." We brushed this notion aside earlier by noting that Strawson's argument for the thesis that such a unity was necessary was actually an argument for the claim that one could not have experience if one lacked the concept of "seems to me" or "my experience." We then brushed this latter claim aside after arguing that Strawson had not given a satisfactory argument to support it. Returning now to the explication of "unity," we can see that the same sort of considerations which led us to call the notion of "sense-datum experience$_2$" incoherent should lead us to be suspicious of the notion of "unity." We said earlier that this unity presumably must include the sort of regularities reference to which is required to formulate criteria for the application of physical-object concepts, and perhaps some further regularities. But now we have seen that one could not be aware of the former regularities unless we *already* had physical-object concepts, and that this fact is implied by the objectivity thesis itself. It is tempting to put forward a parallel argument and say that if the thesis of the necessary unity of consciousness is true, then we could not be aware of any regularities unless we *already* had the concept of "seems to me" or of "my experience." But this will not quite work, since Strawson states the thesis of the necessary unity of consciousness not as the thesis that possession of these concepts is necessary in order to have experience but as the thesis that the unity which is "required" for the employment of these concepts should be present "among the members of some temporally extended series of experiences." The point is that the thought "I think" need not accompany all experiences, but that all experiences must be such that this thought *could* accompany them all. Here again, however, we face the puzzling question of asking what an experience would be like that *lacked* this unity. If we cannot answer this question, we cannot give any sense to the claim that certain regularities are required. And we cannot answer it, because it is no more possible to imagine an experience to which this thought could not be attached than it is to imagine an experience which cannot be subsumed under physical-object concepts.

It is a mistake to think that we can begin by imagining an experience which we might think possible and then go on to show by transcendental argumentation that it is not possible after all. If it is not possible, it is not imaginable either. But if it is not imaginable, then phrases like "must possess the requisite unity" or "must exhibit sufficient regularities" are of no use to us in stating what our transcendental arguments have shown. All that transcendental arguments – *a priori* arguments about what sort of experience is possible – can show is that if you have certain concepts you must have certain other concepts also. Let us call the claim that any experiencer must be able to use the concept "seems to me" or "my experience" the thesis that consciousness must be self-consciousness. To know whether this thesis is true, we must ask: is the notion of a being who has sensory-quality and physical-object concepts, but not the concept "seems to me" or "my experience," incoherent in the same way that the notion of a being who has only sensory-quality concepts proved to be incoherent? If it is, the incoherence is clearly far from obvious. No simple argument of the sort used for the objectivity thesis will do.

But this is not to say that a complex argument might not be offered. One can argue that just as an understanding of "seems" requires an understanding of "is," so an understanding of "is" requires an understanding of "seems." This would amount to saying that the notions of experience and of physical object are strictly correlative – each being unintelligible without the other. Not only would it be the case that, as Strawson says: "No one could be conscious of a temporally extended series of experiences as *his* unless he could be aware of them as yielding knowledge of a unified objective world, through which the series of experiences in question forms just one subjective or experiential route" (p. 27). But no one could have the notion of "a unified objective world" who did not have the notion of "one subjective or experiental route." What suggests that this might be the case is that to have the concept of a physical object is to have the notion of something that can be other than it seems. Thus, we cannot have the *general* concept "physical object" itself without having the concept "seems." But it may well seem as if we could have *particular* physical-object concepts like "stone" without the concept of "seeming to be a stone." If we had a multitude of such concepts, it would seem that we were having experience as of physical objects even if we did not understand the notion of "physical object" itself. But the difficulty with this suggestion is: what does it mean to say that "stone" is a "physical-object concept" if it is not a concept which can occur in a judgment such as "it seems to be a stone but it isn't"? Is it any more reasonable to call it a physical-object concept than to call it the concept of a sort of experience? To make this problem more concrete, suppose we have a man who has only the terms "stone," "hard," "soft," "heavy," "light," and the logical constants in his vocabulary. He calls hard and heavy things stones and no other things. Does it make sense to say that he is thinking about physical objects rather than about experiences? One is tempted to say that it does, simply because stones are physical objects. But this move settles nothing because what we are trying to decide is whether "stone" as he uses the word means what we mean by it. Suppose that the man in question in fact is never brought into contact with any stones, but that linguistic responses are induced in him by manipulations of his brain. In this case we might be tempted to say that "stone" is short in his vocabulary for "experience resembling experience of a stone," or "stony experience." But given that he does not have the concept of "experience," are we in any position to say *that*? It seems most reasonable to say that in his vocabulary "stone" is not short for anything except "something which is hard and heavy." But is it even short for that? Why not just for "hard and heavy"? Can there be a use of "something which" which is not short for "physical object which is"?

The drift of our reflections in the previous paragraph is as follows: the notion that we might have experience which employs general concepts without having the notion of experience itself rests on the notion that words like "stone" could occur in a coherent language-game which did not contain the notion of "seems," but it is not clear that in such a language-game "stone" would mean what it means to us. This doubt about whether it would mean the same may be linked up with Kant's notion that the notion of an object is the notion of something to which experiences are supposed to correspond.[13] If we do not have the notion of "experience," we do not, obviously, have *this* notion of "object." If "stone" is merely short for "hard and heavy," then clearly it provides no inkling of the notion of "what experiences should correspond to." Indeed, it is not clear that merely to use the term "stone" as an alternative to "hard and heavy" counts as playing a language-game at all. We should have the same misgivings here as we had with the case of the man who uses only sensory-quality concepts on the question of whether concepts are really being used. It looks as though to have a language-game one must not merely have, at a minimum,

---

[13] Cf. *Critique of Pure Reason*, A104.

substantives as well as adjectives, but one must be able to interpret the substantives as names of objects in the Kantian sense. If they cannot be so interpreted, then a sentence like "this stone is hard and heavy" does not seem to bear its usual sense. To put the point in another way, the "is" in "this stone is hard and heavy," if it does not contrast with "seems," appears to have no force. Instead of expressing a judgment, the sentence "this stone is hard and heavy" seems to express merely something like a habit of uttering the vocable "stone" when one utters the vocable "hard and heavy." If, in accord with Strawson's thesis of the conceptualizability of experience, the use of concepts (and thus the making of judgments) is essential to experience, then we have to say that the man who has no grip on the notion of "seems" lacks the means for making judgments, and thus lacks the use of concepts, and thus lacks experience.

The argument we have sketched says that only if we have the seems-is contrast, and therefore the basis of thinking about objects, do we have thought at all. Like Strawson's argument for the necessary unity of consciousness, ours starts from the thesis of the conceptualizability of experience. This latter thesis says that all experience "involves the recognition of particular items as of such and such a kind." The making of judgments thus requires *particulars* to be subsumed, and – to give the essence of the argument in a nutshell – *particularity requires objectivity.* That is: we cannot formulate judgments without words for particulars, and we cannot give a sense to these words which will keep their role distinct from words for universals if we do not have the notion of *object.* Putting the argument in this way, we can see that the thesis of the conceptualizability of experience, plus an examination of relations of presupposition between terms, produces both the objectivity thesis and the thesis that all consciousness is self-consciousness. The two theses are two sides of a single coin – the coin which is the relation of mutual presupposal between "is" and "seems." The skeptic about *either* thesis is the man who thinks that particulars could be subsumed under kinds (thus enabling thought, and thus experience$_1$ to exist) simply by the use of phrases like "this is $X$" or "something is $X$," "something $X$ish is happening" without calling upon the notions either of experience or of object. But, so our argument goes, when we ask how words like "this" or "something" could be given a use, we realize that we have nothing in mind save familiar examples of physical objects or of experiences. Without such examples to give the sense of "this particular" to the "this" or "something," the referents of these latter terms dissolve into mere collocations of universals ("hard and heavy," e.g.) rather than particulars subsumed under universals. The thesis of the conceptualizability of experience looks innocuous because it purports merely to explicate what it is to think – what it is to make judgments. But analysis seems to show that the very notion of making a judgment is bound up with the notion of there being objects to serve as the subjects of judgments. Is to make a judgment to subsume a particular under a universal? If so, then any judgment-making creature must distinguish between particulars and universals – that is, it must use certain words in the ways appropriate for words for particulars and other words in the ways appropriate for words for universals. It must distinguish between adjectives and substantives in its verbal habits. But what would it be to recognize this distinction – to give substantives a different linguistic role than adjectives – if not to have the concepts either of "physical object" or of "experience"?

It is these last two rhetorical questions to which our argument boils down. Thus, it boils down to a challenge to the skeptic to spell out the rules of a language-game which would either dispense with the classifying of particulars under universals or would involve the particular–universal distinction without including names for either physical objects or experiences. It is a challenge, in other words, to explain what sort of judgments could be made by a being who lacked both physical-object concepts and experience concepts. Whether the skeptic can meet this challenge is, once again, a question of whether he can show that a language could work which contained, e.g., only notions of sensory qualities, "next to," "resembles," and the logical constants. Without examining such proposals in detail, we cannot make the argument for the claim that all consciousness is self-consciousness any more conclusive than we were able to make the argument for the objectivity thesis. All that we have done is again to show that the task of the skeptic is more difficult than it first appears.[14]

---

[14] It should be noted, for the sake of completeness, that there is a shortcut to the thesis that any experiencer must have the concept "my experience" or "seems to me" – one which, if taken, will supply the missing premise for Strawson's form of the objectivity argument. This is to say, with Bennett, that although no argument could show that "a dog's visual field was 'nothing to' the dog," and thus no argument could show that all consciousness was self-consciousness, nevertheless self-consciousness "must accompany any conscious states which are to fall within the ambit of Kant's inquiry, for that inquiry excludes states which one could not know oneself to be in and which therefore cannot intelligibly be made a subject for speculation" (*Kant's Analytic*, p. 105). Strawson himself seems to toy with adopting this line (cf. *The Bounds of Sense*, pp. 28–9). It amounts to saying that although the possibility of self-consciousness is not a precondition of the possibility of experience, it is a precondition for the only sort of experience which interests Kant.

To place this alternative in dialectical space, we can enumerate four ways of getting to the objectivity thesis: (1) the way Strawson uses, which depends upon the claim that all consciousness is self-consciousness, but does not (I have argued) provide a satisfactory argument for the latter claim; (2) the way suggested at pp. 238–9 above, which does not depend upon the claim that all consciousness is self-consciousness; (3) the way which results from replacing Strawson's

Throughout the previous discussion, I have been insisting that *a priori* arguments about the conditions of possible experience cannot tell us anything about what intuitions must be like in order that they be subsumed under concepts, but can merely tell us about the sorts of thoughts one must have if one is to be able to have certain other thoughts. I have criticized Strawson for putting his case in a way which seems to resurrect the Kantian notion of unsynthesized intuitions which have internal characteristics which make them apt for certain sorts of synthesis. The tendency of my argument has thus been to widen (or at least to emphasize) the gap between Strawson's purely "analytic" approach and Kant's own approach via the "theory of synthesis." In this final section, I want to take up the question: why did not Kant himself draw upon the same sort of arguments as Strawson uses (e.g., the argument that to use "seems" you must be able to use "is")? Answering this question will, I think, open up the larger question of the relation between Kant's revolt against the Cartesian tradition in epistemology and the contemporary revolt carried on under the aegis of the *Philosophical Investigations*.

The Cartesian skeptic is the man who thinks that he might know all there was to know about his experience without knowing anything about anything else. To defeat him, we want to argue that you can't know about your experience without knowing about something else. Two moves are necessary to argue this: the first says that you have to have some concepts if you are to know about anything, including your own experience; the second says that the concepts which you must have if you are to know about your own experience presuppose the concept "physical object." The first move is expressed by the thesis of the conceptualizability of experience, and the second by the point that "seems to me" is intelligible only by contrast to "really is, and does not just seem." Both moves are aimed against the Cartesian's picture of the relation between knowledge and experience, which may be expressed as the notion that experience is self-luminescent. The Cartesian picture is of experiences as bits of mental content which are known not in virtue of any other mental contents,

unsatisfactory argument for this claim with the argument we have given in the last few pages and then continuing along Strawson's lines; (4) the way which results from using the Bennett gambit just described – i.e., restricting consideration to the experience of self-conscious beings – and then continuing along Strawson's lines.

On Bennett's claim that we know that dogs are conscious and that they are not self-conscious, all I have space to say here is that it seems to me very unclear *what* we say about dogs. The non-philosopher would not ordinarily describe them as "conscious" or as "having experience," and I do not know how to settle whether the sort of thing that he would say implies that he *should* so describe them.

but by virtue of their own natural "glow," by their being "before the eye of the mind." The major theme *common* to Kant's and Wittgenstein's revolts against Cartesianism is the claim that *all* our knowledge is, in Kant's phrase, discursive rather than intuitive – that is, that thought and the use of concepts are needed to achieve it. The major *difference* between these two revolts is that concepts are viewed in different ways. For Kant, a concept is a representation, a species of mental content, whereas for Wittgenstein, it is a skill, a skill at linguistic behavior – the ability to use a word.[15]

Kant was able to make the first move against Cartesianism, but was not able to make the second. For as long as concepts are discrete mental contents – representations – there is no clear way in which relations of presupposition between them can be discerned. It is only when the Wittgensteinian interpretation of concepts is adopted that we are able to give arguments for one concept presupposing another – arguments of the form: "No one who did not know how to use the word '. . .' would be said to know how to use the word '____'." Thus, Kant was able to say self-consciousness consisted in the use of concepts (instead of being, in Bennett's phrase, "an unanalyzable kind of glow which accompanies human but not canine mental states"[16]) but he was not able to go on to isolate the particular concepts which were necessary to self-consciousness. In particular, he was unable to show why the concept "physical object" was necessary for this. Instead, he could only speak vaguely about the unification of consciousness produced by the thought of an object in general, and about that thought as consisting in the unity of consciousness itself.[17]

---

[15] On concepts as a species of representations, see A320 = B377. There are, however, passages in Kant (especially in the *Deduction* in *A*) which construe concepts as rules. The clearest statement of this is at A106: "But a concept is always, as regards its form, something universal which serves as a rule." Robert Wolff, *Kant's Theory of Mental Activity* (Cambridge, MA, 1963), p. 70, says that "Concepts for Kant cease to be *things* (mental contents, objects of consciousness) and become *ways of doing things* (rules, forms of mental activity)," and claims that this shift "is an essential part of the argument of the *Critique*." I do not think, however, that either Kant or Wolff succeed in making clear what this shift amounts to, beyond the substitution of one unhelpful metaphor ("rule for unification of intuitions") for another ("object present to consciousness"). Passages like A106 do not lead anywhere unless we can make sense of the notion of "unity," and we cannot make sense of this until we can say something about what *un*unified intuitions are like; for reasons which Wolff himself (*Kant's Theory of Mental Activity*, p. 152n) states very clearly, Kant was never able to do this. In such passages, Kant was indeed groping for some better way of treating concepts than as the sort of abstract ideas which Berkeley had criticized; but he never found it. (See n. 20 below.)

[16] *Kant's Analytic*, p. 117.

[17] Cf. B137: "*Understanding* is, to use general terms, *the faculty of knowledge*. This knowledge consists in the determinate relation of given representations to an object; and an object is that in the concept of which the manifold of a given intuition is *united*. Now all unification of representations demands

The general answer to the question of why Kant was unable to make use of the fact that "seems to me" presupposes "is" (and vice versa, if our argument above for the thesis that all consciousness is self-consciousness was sound) is thus that he had no notion that points of epistemological interest could turn on the relations between the meanings of words. Indeed, if offered the support of Strawson's arguments, Kant would be suspicious of them because of their analytic character – the fact that they depend entirely upon connections between concepts, rather than on the connection between concepts and intuitions. Paradoxically enough, it was precisely because Kant did make the first move against Descartes that he was backed into a situation where he was unable to make the second. To see this point, we need to enlarge a bit more on the relation between Kant's version of the denial of the self-luminescence of experience and the Wittgenstein–Strawson version.

Kant's thesis of the conceptualizability of experience insists that we only get experience as a product of the synthesis of intuitions by concepts. The anti-Cartesian thrust of this thesis is that there is a species of mental contents which are not present to consciousness – viz., unsynthesized intuitions. This thesis introduces the notion of a whole class of mental contents of which we can never be conscious, and thereby separates the notion of "content of experience" from the notion of "mental content."[18] To say, as Kant did, that our mind could contain certain representations – the unsynthesized intuitions – which are nevertheless "nothing to us" until thought has taken place is to say that the mental is not known simply by virtue of being mental. To say this is to come very close to saying the sort of thing Wittgensteinian philosophers say, e.g., that a prelinguistic infant may be in pain without knowing that he is in pain, because he does not yet have the concept of pain. What prevents Kant from saying anything as clear or straightforward as that is that, instead of identifying, e.g., the concept "pain" with the use of the word "pain," he took the concept as

unity of consciousness in the synthesis of them. Consequently, it is the unity of consciousness that alone constitutes the relation of representations to an object." Cf. A105.

[18] As Sellars has recently pointed out, *Science and Metaphysics* (London, 1968), p. 10, the notion of "states of consciousness which are not apperceived" (what I am calling "mental content not present to consciousness") is present in Leibniz's theory of *petites perceptions*, but Leibniz, unlike Kant, "fails to nail down the point that the apperception of a representing involves a numerically distinct representing, i.e., a distinction between an apperceptive representing and the representing it apperceives." What is also new in Kant's claim is the notion that, as Sellars puts it, "there are broad classes of states of consciousness, *none* of the members of which are apperceived." Still more importantly, what is also new is the notion that it is only when *judgment* takes place – when a propositional attitude is assumed – that we get self-consciousness.

itself a sort of unconscious representation. To have a concept, for Kant, is to have yet another species of mental content – one which, like unsynthesized intuitions, is unconscious unless it is used in a judgment. (Unsynthesizing concepts, it seems, are as unconscious as synthesized intuitions.[19]) But this conception of what a concept is gives us no test for its presence, no reason infants lack the concept "pain," nor any reason to think that the infant does not make the appropriate judgment.

Thus, instead of offering a behavioristic test of the possession of concepts in the manner of Wittgenstein, Kant creates, as a result of his repudiation of the idea that mental entities are inevitably self-luminescent, two species of mental contents – concepts and intuitions – which are (a) modeled on experiences, on those full-fledged examples of "representations" which are full-fledged syntheses of intuitions in judgments, but yet are (b) objects of which we can never be conscious in isolation. The study of the relations between these two sorts of unapperceivable entities becomes the pseudo-subject of a pseudo-discipline, transcendental philosophy. The argument of the *Transcendental Deduction* (and of the *Refutation of Idealism*) is written within the context of this pseudo-discipline, and is thus written in terms of what would be required for intuitions to be synthesized, rather than in terms of what concepts are required given that certain other concepts are required. Kant tried to repudiate the "mental eye" picture of the mind which he had inherited from the Cartesians – the picture according to which all that it took to be known was to be mental, and in which it was puzzling how anything non-mental could be known – and tried to replace it by a picture of "mental synthesis." But this new picture gave him the notion that the platitudes which must be defended against the skeptic were *synthetic* truths, truths which were guaranteed by reference to the character of *intuitions* as well as by reference to the character of concepts. Now if we accept Kant's notion that such philosophically interesting, antiskeptical truths as the objectivity thesis are always going to be true by virtue of the character of intuitions as well as

---

[19] Kant does not say this in so many words, but a passage such as A68 = B93: "The only use which the understanding can make of these concepts is to judge by means of them," certainly suggests that concepts only turn up in consciousness when they are in judgments. Kant says in this same passage that "concepts rest on functions" and that by "function" he means the "unity of the act of bringing various representations under one common representation." This seems fairly close to saying that when a concept isn't doing its job of unifying, it can't be present to consciousness – and perhaps even close to saying that concepts don't exist when they're not doing this job. But Kant was in a permanent state of confusion on this subject due to his claim that we could *think* with concepts-without-intuitions even though we couldn't *know* with them (cf. Bxxvi, n., and the passages on unschematized categories).

by the character of concepts, we cannot be satisfied by the purely analytic arguments which Strawson attempts to offer for this thesis. For these are arguments which merely connect concept with other concepts – arguments which boil down to "You wouldn't know what was meant by '. . .' unless you knew what was meant by '___'." But, to turn the point around, if we do not think that there is such a thing as an appeal to the nature of intuitions which is not an appeal to the nature of the concepts under which intuitions are synthesized, we shall never be satisfied with the kinds of arguments for the objectivity thesis which Kant gives in the *Transcendental Deduction*. We shall never be satisfied that only that unification of intuitions which is the thought of an object is that unification of intuitions which is the unity of consciousness if all that we are told is that the two are equally unifications, and equally primitive. From Kant's point of view, the claim that Strawson's arguments are sufficient for the objectivity thesis betrays the central insight of the *Critique* – *viz.*, that truths which tell us about the nature of possible experience must be synthetic, and to be synthetic must make reference to something besides concepts.[20] From a Wittgensteinian point of view, however, Kant's insistence on the distinction between intuitions and concepts as two species of representations, is like the notion of "representation" itself, merely a relic of the "mental-eye" picture of the mind.

Thus, the form which Kant chose for his repudiation of the Cartesian view of our knowledge of the mental, determined the form of his argument for the objectivity thesis, and made it the unsatisfactory and inconclusive form which it is. We may generalize and perhaps clarify this point by sketching more fully the way in which Kant is a half-way point between Descartes and Wittgenstein. The tradition common to Descartes and Hume taught that the task of epistemology was to find a foundation for knowledge which was, so to speak, below the level of propositional attitudes – to decompose judgments into their component parts ("ideas") and to find in the connection between these parts the basis for knowledge (or, as in Hume, to find in the lack of connection between them the basis for skepticism). Kant went half-way toward overthrowing traditional

---

[20] The point that Kant's program is betrayed if we try to substitute purely analytical arguments for Kant's own appeals to the character of intuition is well made by Beck. Cf. *Studies in the Philosophy of Kant* (Indianapolis, 1965), pp. 116ff, where Beck argues that there is supposed to be an ostensive element in the arguments for the synthetic *a priori* principles: "Without intuition, the concepts are empty no matter how many *concepts* of intuition are given in them" (p. 117). See also Beck's discussion of the indefinability of the categories at pp. 84ff, and of "synthetic real definitions" at pp. 67ff.

epistemology, because he went half-way toward making the judgment the indecomposable unit of epistemological analysis. Wittgenstein went the rest of the way. When Kant said that "thoughts without content are empty, intuitions without concepts are blind,"[21] he took what might have been the first step toward saying that there are no such things as concepts and intuitions, other than as abstracted elements of judgments. He might, in other words, have gone on to conclude that an empty or a blind "representation" was not really a representation at all, and that only judgments were to count as such. If he had done this, he would have said that only one judgment could give support to another judgment, and that intuitions and concepts, as mere hypostatizations of the subject and the predicate terms (respectively) of judgments, did not contain epistemological authority which they could pass on to the judgment from which they had been abstracted. He would, thus, have approached the view of epistemology characteristic of the post-Wittgenstein era in analytic philosophy, according to which knowledge is not an introspectively detectable sort of glow which radiates from certain clear and distinct ideas, nor a result of a "fit" which is a property of successful syntheses of intuitions by concepts, but simply justified, true belief. On this view of knowledge, and of epistemology, we understand how knowledge is possible not by looking into the mind, but by looking at the behavior of the whole human being – specifically, that linguistic behavior which is the giving of reasons for beliefs.

Before this final series of steps could be taken, however, it was necessary to have provided alternative accounts of what intuitions and concepts are. It is not enough to say that they are hypostatizations of the subject and predicate terms of judgment – one wants an account of what it is to "have an intuition" or "to have a concept." It is the linguistic turn in philosophy which makes such accounts possible. By focusing on the utterance of statements, one can see intuitions (sensations) as internal, but noncognitive, states of the organism which are apt for the production (in organisms which have mastered a language) of certain assertions. To have a certain intuition, in other words, becomes analyzed as to be in a dispositional state – a state apt, given the fulfillment of certain other conditions, for making a certain assertion. To have an intuition is thus not to have a representation – not to be in, to use Kant's phrase, "immediate relation to an object" in a *symbolic* or cognitive way at all, but to be related to the object in, at most, a *causal* way. Turning to concepts, to have one of *them*

---

[21] A51 = B75.

is not to have a representation, but a skill – a mastery of a piece of vocabulary. To have a concept, in short, is to be disposed to behave in a certain way. With both concepts and intuitions thus analyzed into dispositions to linguistic behavior, the notion of "representation" itself seems to be left without work to do. The notion of a *Vorstellung* – something in the mind which stands in place of the object to be known – thus vanishes, and with it the notion of epistemology as the discipline which investigates the internal relations between *Vorstellungen*. Instead of treating experience as an arrangement of representations, and of considering the possibility of various sorts of experiences as a matter of what representations can be related to what others, we can now treat experience simply as "that which is reported by certain assertions" and the possibility of certain experiences as the possibility of certain assertions being made. To find necessary truths about experience thus becomes a matter not of appealing to the ineffable (as Kant was forced to do in appealing to the character of intuitions as well as the character of concepts), but of appealing to the conditions of certain assertions being made. To demonstrate a thesis such as the objectivity thesis is thus a matter of demonstrating that we cannot imagine an assertion about anything being made by a person who was not capable of making assertions about physical objects.

In the preceding paragraphs, I have attempted to flesh out the familiar notion that there are interesting parallels between Kant's Copernican revolution and the revolution in philosophical thought introduced by the later Wittgenstein, and at the same time to account in part for the differences. Both the comparison and the contrast may be summed up as follows. The tradition in philosophy inaugurated by Descartes was an attempt to overcome epistemological skepticism by finding metaphysical principles which would insure that the contents of our mind referred beyond themselves to physical objects (e.g., Descartes's divine guarantee of clear and distinct ideas, Leibniz's panpsychism, Spinoza's unity of the attributes of thought and extension in the One Substance). Kant transcended such "dogmatic" projects by seeing that the only way in which the reference was to be guaranteed was by showing that our very conception of what it was to be a mental content presupposed that there were physical objects – by showing that experience of the mental was possible only because experience of the physical was possible. He was the first to employ the strategy of saying that not any and every sort of experience which the skeptic might describe was a possible sort of experience. But unfortunately his conception of an "impossible experience" was explicated in terms of the notion of intuitions not being properly unified by concepts. To detect what was and what was not a possible experience thus became a matter of determining when intuitions were and were not so unified, a matter for which there were no criteria (and could be none, since ununified intuitions were ineffable). To save the Kantian program of showing the skeptic that the situation he described was unexperienceable, a clearer notion of "unexperienceable" had to be developed. It was left to the linguistic turn in philosophy to develop the explication of "unexperienceable" as "not such as to be expressible in a self-sustaining language-game (i.e., a language-game not parasitic on a wider language-game)." But this explication only becomes acceptable when the possession of intuitions and concepts is analyzed away into states apt for the production of linguistic behavior in the way we have described above. (For without this latter analysis, the skeptic can insist that there are possible experiences which are not expressible in language at all.) It is thus only when the last traces of the "mental eye" picture of the mind are eradicated that arguments such as Strawson's can be seen as sufficient against the skeptic. Kant made the first moves toward replacing that picture of the mind by a better one, but he was not able to go all the way. Consequently, he was not able to use the kind of argument which is available to Strawson.[22]

---

[22] I am grateful to Jonathan Bennett and to Richard Bernstein for extensive comments on the next-to-last draft of this chapter – comments which led me to make many changes.

# CHAPTER 13

# Verificationism and transcendental arguments

Many admirers of Wittgenstein's *Philosophical Investigations* and of Strawson's *Individuals* have taken the theme of both books to be an analysis of philosophical skepticism and their distinctive contribution to be a new way of criticizing the skeptic. This new way is summed up in a familiar passage from Strawson:

> He [the skeptic] pretends to accept a conceptual scheme, but at the same time quietly rejects one of the conditions of its employment Thus, his doubts are unreal, not simply because they are logically irresoluble doubts, but because they amount to the rejection of the whole conceptual scheme within which alone such doubts make sense.[1]

In an earlier period of analytic philosophy, the standard reply to the skeptic had been of the phenomenalistic Hume–Berkeley type. That is, the skeptic's suggestion that what were usually taken to be material objects or other persons might merely be the content of his own consciousness – his own representations – was met with the reply that to have such-and-such representations just *was* to be seeing a material object or another person. This if-you-can't-beat-him-join-him strategy, however, always (a) got shaky when "*was*" was questioned (did it mean "entailed"? "confirmed"?) and (b) had an unpleasant air of idealism about it, no matter how much it was claimed to be a "logical" rather than a "metaphysical" point. So when, on the heels of Austin's attack on "the ontology of the sensible manifold," Strawson revived the distinctively Kantian anti-idealist thesis that "inner experience requires outer experience," the shift in strategy was welcomed. Strawson's points about persons and material objects fitted together nicely with Wittgenstein's "private-language argument" to suggest that the skeptics' notion of a world of pure experience – a world containing nothing but representations – did not really make sense.

---

[1] P. F. Strawson, *Individuals* (London, 1959), p. 35.

For one wouldn't know what a representation was (nor could a representation exist) unless there were nonrepresentations – material objects and persons. The skeptic's conception of the world was thus revealed as *parasitic* on more conventional notions.

Recently, however, two articles have appeared which have seemed to undermine this neo-Kantian program. Both charge that the various "transcendental" arguments offered against the skeptic depend upon the tacit adoption of a dubious "verification principle." These articles – one by Judith Thomson on the private-language argument[2] and the other by Barry Stroud on various arguments of Strawson's and Shoemaker's[3] – make the point that these arguments all seem to be saying "In order for 'X' to have meaning there have to be criteria for identifying X's, and the skeptic cannot even talk about X's unless he accepts that these criteria are sound. Since these criteria are obviously satisfied, he cannot deny that there are X's." But, Thomson and Stroud rejoin,[4] the most that this sort of argument can show is that it must seem to us as if there are X's – not that there actually are X's. For purposes of giving "X" a place in the language-game, so to speak, apparent X's are as good as real X's. So, if all the "transcendentalist" has to go on is that "X" does have such a place, he will never get from there to the reality of X's. To mend his argument, the transcendentalist would need a principle which says that (as Stroud puts it, referring to the case of material objects) it is not possible "for all reidentification statements to be false even though they are asserted on the basis of the best criteria we ever have for reindentification"[5] – in short, a "verification principle."

I think that Thomson and Stroud have shown something very important – *viz.*, that no transcendental argument will be able to prove necessary existence (e.g., of material objects). Their point that appearance is as good as reality for giving meaning to terms seems to me decisive. But despite this, the kind of "parasitism" argument which is offered by Strawson and can plausibly be attributed to Wittgenstein survives intact. The reason is that a parasitism argument says to the skeptic: "If you merely say that all the reasons we have for thinking such-and-such's to exist or to be

---

[2] Thomson, "Private Languages," *American Philosophical Quarterly*, 1 (1964), pp. 20–31. This article has been reprinted in Stuart Hampshire, ed., *The Philosophy of Mind* (New York, 1966), pp. 116–43. I shall cite Thomson by reference to the pagination in this anthology.
[3] Stroud, "Transcendental Arguments," *Journal of Philosophy*, 65 (1968), pp. 241–56.
[4] Stroud, p. 255. Thomson does not make this point explicitly, but it follows naturally from what she says at p. 141.
[5] Stroud, p. 246.

impossible might be insufficient, you cannot be refuted. All that you have done then is to say that, in metaphysics as in physics, it is always possible for a better idea to come along which will give a better way of describing the world than in terms of what we thought must necessarily exist, or which will make it possible to recognize the existence of what we previously thought impossible. We can only catch you out if you purport to actually advance such a better idea. Then we may be able to show that your new way of describing the world would not be intelligible to someone who was not familiar with the old way." This line of argument is applied, in particular, to the "Cartesian" skeptic who says that everything that we now describe in terms of, e.g., persons and material objects, could be described in terms of experiences – in a "pure-experience" language. The force of "parasitism" arguments here is to show that we cannot in fact describe such a language (and thus, *a fortiori*, to show that we cannot describe a private language).[6] For the purposes of such arguments, it does not matter whether there are persons and material objects or whether we simply believe there are.

The point I want to make in this chapter, then, is that the only good "transcendental" argument is a "parasitism" argument. To develop this, I shall go over some things which Thomson and Stroud say and try to explain in more detail how the force of the antiskeptical arguments which they discuss can be preserved while admitting the point that there is no sound inference from the way we think or speak to truths about the possibility of experience or language. I shall begin with the more limited case of Thomson, who restricts herself to Malcolm's version of the private-language argument.

Thomson analyzes Malcolm's presentation of this argument into the following three steps:

> (1) . . . if a sign which a man uses is to count as a word in a language, his use of it must be governed by a rule – here specifically, if a sign which a man uses is to count as a kind-name in a language, his use of it must be governed by a rule of the following sort: You may call anything of a kind X "K," and you may not call anything "K" which is not of kind X. (2) If a sign which a man uses is to be governed by a rule of this sort it must be possible that he should call the thing a "K" thinking it is of the kind to be called a "K" and

---

[6] For the connection between the private-language argument and the possibility of a pure-experience language see John Turk Saunders and Donald F. Henze, *The Private-Language Problem* (New York, 1967). In a forthcoming paper called "Criteria and Necessity" ["Criteria and Necessity," *Noûs*, 7, 4 (1973), pp. 313–29], I have tried to capitalize on and highlight the connection which Saunders and Henze have drawn.

it not be . . . [(3)] There is no such thing as a man's thinking a thing is of the kind to be called "K" and it not being so unless it is logically possible that it be *found out* that it is not so.[7]

She points out rightly that the third – "verificationist" – premise is essential to the argument since "there must be something which rules it out that [one] should quite acceptably reply: Perhaps it can't be found out that my sensation is or is not of the required kind, but all the same it may be that it is."[8] Now let us construe "finding out" in (3) as what Thomson calls "weak finding out" – i.e., "confirming" rather than "conclusively verifying": only on such a construal, I should argue, does anything like the private-language argument emerge as plausible. Then to complete the argument we can add

(4) It is not to count as confirming or disconfirming that something is a K if our *only* reason for deciding that it is or is not is that a man is or is not inclined to call it a K, having as his sole reason that it is or is not similar to what he has previously called a K,

and derive the conclusion

(C) If the only logically possible way of confirming or disconfirming that something is a K is to find out whether a man is inclined to call it a K, having as his sole reason that he remembers that it is or is not similar to something which he has previously called a K, then "K" is not a word in his language.

What this argument comes down to is the claim that if all we "know" about K's is that there is a K if and only if a man believes there is, then we don't know *anything* about K's, not even that. To see the force of this, consider a man who occasionally utters "There is a K now," but cannot tell you what a K is; it is not, he says, a sensation nor a beetle nor anything else he can put a name to. It is just a K. To put it another way, nothing (except trivia like "There is a K now or *p*") follows from "There is a K now" and it follows nontrivially from nothing (to our knowledge). In this situation, Wittgensteinians want to say, "K" hasn't been given a meaning. To give it a meaning, all that we would need would be belief in a correlation of utterances of "K" with something – anything which would set up confirmation-relations between "There is a K now" and some other statements (other than logically entailed statements). But before such correlations are made, the man himself should not take himself to be

---

[7] Thomson, pp. 131–2.    [8] Thomson, p. 133.

describing something or reporting something when he says "There is a K now." Nor in fact would he. He would view himself as under some sort of compulsion, not as making a statement. The claim made in (4) is thus just a corollary of the slogan that meaning is use – where this slogan is spelled out as: a statement like "There is a K now" has to be taken to bear some non-trivial inferential relations before it has a place in the language-game. Seen from another angle, it is a corollary of the notion that "a great deal of stage-setting in the language is presupposed if the mere act of naming is to make sense."[9]

There is much that can be said against this argument, and to defend it and develop its full anti-Cartesian force would require more space than I have in this chapter.[10] I want to make only one point about it. Whatever else might be wrong with it, the principal objection which Thomson brings against the "verificationist" premise (3) does not work.

This objection is as follows:

> The principle, it will be remembered, was this: A sign "K" is not a kind-name in a man's language unless it is possible to find out whether or not a thing is K; and let us call this condition on a man's use of a sign "C." What we might then ask is: is "C" a kind-name in a language? Well, it is a kind-name in a man's language if it is possible to find out whether or not a sign in a given use does satisfy this condition. Does "K" in the preceding example [the example of a man who claims to be able to see that some things we call "black" have a distinctive color called "K"] satisfy it – over and above its seeming to its user that it does? Do "table" and "chair" satisfy

---

[9] Wittgenstein, *Philosophical Investigations* (3rd edn., New York, 1958), Part I, sec. 257. Note that an entirely adequate stage-setting would be provided if the man explained that K was a sort of sensation – for we know what sensations are and know that people are reliable reporters of them (even when a particular sort of sensation is not accompanied by a behavioral or environmental correlate). *Pace* the famous "private-diary" passage (*ibid.*, I, sec. 258), there is no difficulty in giving meaning to "E" once one has identified it as standing for, e.g., that funny sensation I had last Wednesday. All that is needed to give meaning to "sensation" is that some sensation reports should bear non-trivial inferential relations to some statements which are not sensation reports (statements about environment, behavior, brainwaves, or what you will). This condition does not have to be satisfied for each and every species of sensation, but only for the genus. The meaningfulness which "I am having a sort of sensation which I shall call 'e' " inherits from the correlations between other sensations and public events is passed along, so to speak, to "There is an E now." Thus, the condition specified in (4) – "our *only* reason . . . " – is no longer satisfied once a K is specified as a sensation. For we can have not only the fact that the man is inclined to say, "It seems similar to what I usually call 'K,' so I'll call it 'K' ", but all the reasons which make us take people's reports of their inner states as reliable.

[10] In particular, a defense of this argument would have to show that we could not describe a "pure-experience" language – one in which sensations, e.g., were correlated only with other sensations. I do not think that a knockdown argument can be given on this point, but I think that Saunders and Henze give a convincing presentation of the difficulties involved.

it – over and above its seeming to some non-sceptic that they do? . . . How should I find out whether or not they do – which is not merely to be a matter of asking myself whether or not it seems to me that they do?[11]

The question Thomson raises here is: why should we think that any established practice of confirming a statement S by reference to certain criteria having been fulfilled is a *sound* practice? And the answer is that it does not here matter whether it is or not. For instead of (3) we can substitute

(3') There is no such thing as a man's thinking a thing is of the kind to be called "K" and it's not being so unless some way of confirming that it is a K is accepted by him

and alter "the only logically possible way of confirming or disconfirming that something is a K" in (C) to "the only way accepted by a man of confirming or disconfirming that something is a K." We then get an argument which is just as good as the original (better, in fact, because it avoids Quinean doubts about the notion of "logical possibility"). This reformulated argument preserves the strength of the meaning-as-use principle explicated above while making clear that the verificationist does not have to say that any of the methods of confirmation which are built into familiar language-games should be good methods. All he has to say is that there has to be a situation which present practice would call "a man's having accepted a method of finding out whether something is a K" if there is to be a situation which present practice would call "a man's thinking a thing is of the kind *K* and its not being so." This brand of verificationism makes meaningfulness depend not upon a word–world connection, but upon connections between some bits of linguistic behavior and others.[12]

Summing up what I have been saying about Thomson, I conclude (1) that the verificationism she correctly discerns in the private-language argument is no more or less objectionable than the familiar Wittgensteinian claim that it does not make sense to suppose that a man might know the meaning of

---

[11] Thomson, pp. 141–2.
[12] Compare Neurath's notorious claim that as long as we have some protocols to endow non-protocols with meaning, it does not matter what the character of the protocols is. Specifically, it does not matter whether they are reports of the "given" or not. The step which Wittgenstein takes beyond Neurath is to remark that the protocols wouldn't be protocols, wouldn't themselves be meaningful, unless they had been caught up in a web of inferential relationships to other protocols and to non-protocols. The kind of verificationism common to Neurath and to the later Wittgenstein is, of course, of no use whatever in demarcating science from metaphysics or theology.

only one word, and (2) that the "what if we only believed that we had other ways of finding out, but did not really?" objection has no force against this sort of verificationism. I now go on from the particular case of the private-language argument to the general case sketched by Stroud.

Stroud argues that it not only takes a verificationist premise to complete transcendental arguments, but that invoking such a premise makes such arguments superfluous:

> The verification principle that the argument [Strawson's argument that we can know that objects continue to exist unperceived] rests on is: if the notion of objective particulars makes sense to us, then we can sometimes know certain conditions to be fulfilled, the fulfillment of which logically implies either that objects continue to exist unperceived or that they do not. The sceptic says that we can never justify our acceptance of the proposition that objects continue to exist unperceived, but now there is a direct and conclusive answer to him. If the sceptic's claim makes sense it must be false, since if that proposition could not be known to be true or known to be false it would make no sense. This follows from the truth of the verification principle. Without this principle Strawson's argument would have no force; but with this principle the sceptic is directly and conclusively refuted, and there is no further need to go through an indirect or transcendental argument to expose his mistakes.[13]

The first point I want to make about this is that it is not, as Stroud suggests,[14] a debatable matter whether such a verification principle might be true. It is obviously false. A principle which says that in order to make sense of talk about X's you have to be able to state certain criteria the fulfillment of which "logically implies" that X's exist would entail that everything that people had ever understood talk about and rationally believed in – witches, perturbations in the luminiferous ether, gods – would have to be incorporated in our ontology. For the criteria which witch-believers, e.g., used to identify witches were very frequently fulfilled. We cannot get out of this by saying that the criteria for there being witches turned out *not* to be fulfilled because eventually, in the eighteenth century or so, a better explanation of "witch"-phenomena was adopted. For broadening the meaning of "criterion" in this way would mean that we can never tell whether our criteria for anything are fulfilled; some better explanation of, e.g., "material object"-phenomena might always come along. Nor can we get out of it by saying that people never did talk "meaningfully" about witches or gods or the luminiferous ether. This is

---

[13] Stroud, p. 247.     [14] Stroud, p. 256.

an *ad hoc* dictum which twenty years of tinkering with the verifiability criterion failed to make good. As Stroud notes, this sort of verification principle is just the paradigm-case argument all over again,[15] and (as Chisholm[16] and others have argued) the latter argument would only work if we could somehow show that certain words could only be taught ostensively, and only by ostention of genuine examples of its referent. This latter claim should be the last which anyone impressed by Wittgenstein's remarks on meaning would want to make.

The second remark I want to make is that if transcendental arguments are, as by Stroud, defined as those which prove "that certain concepts are necessary for thought or experience,"[17] then the whole dialectical force of these arguments must be to show the "parasitism" of suggested alternative concepts. What would be the point of knowing, for example, that you have to think about material objects if you are going to think about anything at all, except to defeat the man who suggests a different "conceptual framework"? Transcendental arguments must be at *least* parasitism arguments, whether or not I am right in saying that they are at most parasitism arguments. But it would be strange if we could know *in advance* of someone's proposing an alternative conceptual framework that it too would be parasitic on the conventional one. No one would believe the claim that *any* new theory in physics would necessarily be such that it could never replace, but could at most supplement, our present theories. One would have to have an extraordinary faith in the difference between philosophy and science to think that things could be otherwise in metaphysics. So there is reason to suspect that the force behind any such claim will actually be arguments for the parasitical character of certain *particular* alternatives.

Thirdly, in the case of Stroud's clearest example of transcendental argument – Strawson on objective particulars – what we in fact find is just such arguments. There is no *general* argument in *Individuals* that we

---

[15] Stroud, p. 245.
[16] Cf. Roderick Chisholm, "Philosophers and Ordinary Language," *Philosophical Review*, 60 (1951), pp. 317–28.
[17] Stroud, p. 242. Later (pp. 251ff). Stroud suggests that this condition can be sharpened up by saying that transcendental arguments must find conditions for the possibility of language – because the skeptic could always get out of, e.g., a transcendental argument for "There are material objects" by denying that we understand talk about material objects but could not, on pain of self-referential absurdity, deny that there was language. I do not think that the absurdity would be greater in the second case, however. To make the skeptic say that we never understand what we mean by "table" seems to me as good a *reductio* as making him say that he is not using language when he asserts his skepticism.

cannot think without thinking about material objects; there are only arguments against particular suggestions about how we could avoid thinking about them. It must be admitted, however, that Strawson is misleading on this point. He says, in the context surrounding the passage quoted at the beginning of this chapter that it is absurd for the skeptic to suggest "that we do not really, or should not really, have conceptual schemes that we do not have; that we do not really, or should not really, mean what we think we mean, what we do mean." This is absurd, he says, because

> the whole process of reasoning only starts because the scheme is as it is; and we cannot change it even if we would. Finally, we may, if we choose, see the sceptic as offering for contemplation the sketch of an alternative scheme; and this is to see him as a revisionary metaphysician with whom we do not wish to quarrel, but whom we do not need to follow.[18]

These remarks are puzzling. In the first place, the fact that "the whole process of reasoning starts because the scheme is as it is" has no force; the same could be said about the process of reasoning gone through by the skeptic about witches. In the second place, Strawson seems to be going in two directions at once. On the one hand, he is saying that no revisionist metaphysics could possibly be a viable alternative because "we cannot change it even if we would." On the other hand, he seems to be saying that "revisionary" metaphysicians can just be ignored – that they are playing a different game. But this second strategy can hardly represent Strawson's real intention, for he goes on to spend the rest of the chapter explaining what is wrong with two revisionary efforts – the attempt to make "private particulars" basic and the attempt to make events or processes basic.[19] Further, these latter attempts are just what is required, and all Strawson has got, to show that "we cannot change it even if we would."

For a class of particulars to be "basic" is for it to be such that

> it would not be possible to make all the identifying references which we do make to particulars of other classes, unless we made identifying references to particulars of that class, whereas it would be possible to make all the

[18] *Individuals*, p. 35.

[19] To my mind, the contrast Strawson draws (but makes little use of) between descriptive and revisionary metaphysics is a false start. To describe our actual conceptual scheme will either be platitudinous or, in Wittgenstein's phrase, "assembling reminders for a particular purpose." What would the purpose be if not to put us on our guard against the revisionist? Suggesting that descriptive and revisionary metaphysics are distinct disciplines seems like suggesting that conservative and radical political thought are distinct disciplines.

identifying references we do make to particulars of that class without making identifying reference to particulars of other classes.[20]

If material objects are such a class, then *Aufbau*-philosophers who propose to construct bodies and persons out of "elementary experiences," and Whiteheadians who propose to construct them out of events, are just wrong. For if these revisionists are saying anything they are saying that thinking in terms of bodies and persons is optional.[21] Strawson's argument against "private particulars" (sensations, mental events, sense data) as possible candidates for basicness is crisp and simple; his argument against events is long and tenuous. Because I think the latter argument fails and has been adequately criticized in the literature,[22] I shall ignore it here. The former argument, however, seems to me the heart of what Strawson has to say in the first part of *Individuals*, and the basis for the general feeling that *something* important was shown there.

This former argument is built around the same point as is used in the "Persons" chapter of *Individuals*: the point that "the principles of individuation of such experiences essentially turn on the identities of the persons to whose histories they belong." To this, the *Aufbau*ist would presumably reply that this may be true for public discourse, for "identification" as agreement on reference between a speaker and a hearer – but that limiting the sense of "identify" in this way as Strawson does[23] stacks the cards. Each person can, he would go on, identify his own private experiences without thinking of himself as a person; he identifies his experiences first, and himself later, so to speak. To rebut this, Strawson needs to invoke some form of the private-language argument; he needs to be able to say, at least, that you cannot (as in the Cartesian tradition) identify one of your experiences just by having it, but that you have to know some language to identify it *as* an experience and that this language cannot be learned by someone who has not first or simultaneously learned what persons and their bodies are.

---

[20] *Ibid.*, pp. 38–9.

[21] One can, of course, take Goodman's line that the *Aufbau*ish efforts shouldn't be seen as resting on a claim of epistemological priority for their primitive notions, but as simply intellectually satisfying thought-experiments. (Cf. Nelson Goodman, "The Significance of *Der Logische Aufbau der Welt*," in P. A. Schilpp, ed., *The Philosophy of Rudolf Carnap* [La Salle, 1963], pp. 545–58.) It is questionable, however, whether anyone would have gone to the trouble of constructing such systems unless they had thought philosophical problems were thereby resolved, and hard to see how any such problems could be resolved unless epistemological priority were claimed.

[22] See especially J. M. E. Moravcsik, "Strawson and Ontological Priority," in R. J. Butler, ed., *Analytical Philosophy*, ii (Oxford, 1965), esp. pp. 114–19.

[23] Cf. *Individuals*, pp. 16, 45.

To come now quickly (and dogmatically) to a close: if I am right in saying that Strawson's only good transcendental argument for the "necessary" character of material object concepts boils down to the private-language argument, then we have some grounds for suspecting that there is really only *one* transcendental argument to worry about – that what looked like a general technique of argument which might be applied to anything is actually a single anti-Cartesian argument which keeps popping up in different guises. The target, in each case, is the same – the notion that we can start with knowing about nothing save our own experiences and go on from there. In theory, there is no reason why parasitism arguments should not work against many different revisionary schemes, including some that have nothing to do with Cartesianism. But in fact it is hard to think of examples. However, that may be, there can be no such thing as a *general* critique of the validity of transcendental arguments of the sort which Stroud attempts. They have to be criticized case by case; each charge of parasitism has to be evaluated on its own merits.

A last word about verificationism: the insight which lay behind the original (Peircian) verificationist notion that "you don't know what 'This is an X' means unless you know how to confirm it" may be explicated as the claim that to know meaning is to know inferential relationships. This insight has nothing to do with empiricism nor with phenomenalism. It needed, however, to be combined with the notion that knowledge is always conceptual ("intuitions without concepts are blind"), and the notion that to have a concept is to have the use of a word, before its anti-Cartesian force could be seen. When brought together with these latter notions it gave rise to the notion that you couldn't know about anything unless you could talk about quite a lot of different things. The Malcolmian formulation of the private-language argument, Strawson's arguments in both chapter 1 and chapter 3 of *Individuals*, and a great deal else that is central to contemporary metaphysics, thus does indeed, as Thomson and Stroud show, depend upon verificationism. But the sort of verificationism on which it depends is not obviously false, and is at any rate not the utterly implausible sort which Stroud suggests may be needed.[24]

---

[24] I am grateful to Aryeh Kosman for valuable comments.

CHAPTER 14

# Indeterminacy of translation and of truth

There are three theses connected with Quine's views about the indeterminacy of translation which should be clearly distinguished from one another. These are:

(1) A person's dispositions to accept sentences do not determine a unique interpretation of those sentences.[1]

(2) The notions of meaning, propositional attitudes, etc., do not possess the explanatory power often attributed to them by philosophers. (In particular, one cannot explain the truth of a sentence by saying it is "true by virtue of meaning," nor can one "explain why a person accepts a sentence by saying he accepts a proposition which the sentence expresses."[2])

(3) "Though linguistics is of course a part of the theory of nature, the indeterminacy of translation is not just inherited as a special case of the underdetermination of our theory of nature. It is parallel but additional."[3]

I doubt that (1) is still a subject of debate. Quine's opponents have by now been argued around to admitting that alternative systems of analytical hypotheses, producing non-equivalent translations, will predict dispositions to accept sentences equally well. (2) is a much more important, interesting, and controversial matter, and one which requires more argument than merely citing (1). The arguments for (2) consist mainly in exhibiting the poverty of the "explanations" provided by an appeal to the notions in question.[4]

---

[1] Gilbert Harman says that disagreement about (1) is the issue which separates Quine from his opponents. (Cf. "An Introduction to 'Translation and Meaning'," in D. Davidson and J. Hintikka, eds., *Words and Objections* [Dordrecht, 1969], p. 21).

[2] *Ibid.*, p. 15.

[3] Quine, "Reply to Chomsky," in *ibid.*, p. 303.

[4] Harman, in "Quine on Meaning and Existence, I," *Review of Metaphysics*, 21 (1967), pp. 124–51, does an admirable job of giving such arguments and of showing how Quine's hostility to the notions of "analyticity" and "proposition" should be taken as skepticism about the explanatory powers of these

(3) is often run together with (2). Thus, when replying to Chomsky's doubts about (3) Quine himself seems to merge the two theses by saying that grasping the difference between the general "under-determination of our theory of nature" and the special indeterminacy of translation will lead to "a change in prevalent attitudes toward meaning, idea, proposition," and that the difference escapes recognition "because of the uncritical persistence of old notions of meaning, idea, proposition."[5] The suggestion seems to be that accepting (2) should lead to accepting (3), or vice versa, or both.

I find this suggestion puzzling because I should want to accept (1) and (2) while rejecting (3). Quine's view that one could only deny (3) if one denied (2) in one's heart – if one was not yet quite free of the "old notions" – seems to me neither clear nor properly backed by argument. In the hope of clearing up the situation, I shall first examine Quine's explicit remarks in support of (3), and then go on to the analogy between translating number theory into set theory and translating the jungle language into English which Harman has developed and which Quine seems to endorse.[6]

## I   Quine's arguments for two distinct indeterminacies

In *Word and Object* and again in his reply to Chomsky, Quine explicitly takes up the question of whether the underdetermination of choice between theories in physics is different from the underdetermination of choice between translation manuals in linguistics. In *Word and Object*, after admitting that "we may meaningfully speak of the truth of a sentence only within the terms of some theory or conceptual scheme," he continues:

> May we conclude that translational synonymy at its worst is no worse off than truth in physics? To be thus reassured is to misjudge the parallel. In being able to speak of the truth of a sentence only within a more inclusive theory, one is not much hampered; for one is always working within some comfortably inclusive theory, however tentative. Truth is even overtly relative to language, in that, e.g., the form of words "Brutus killed Caesar" could by coincidence have unrelated uses in two languages; yet this again

notions rather than as a corollary of behaviorism or of "a taste for desert landscapes." I am much indebted to this article, and to conversations with Harman, for help in understanding Quine's position. Disagreements with some things Harman says will, however, emerge below.

[5] *Words and Objections*, p. 304.

[6] Harman, "An Introduction to 'Translation and Meaning'," *passim*, and Quine, "Reply to Harman," p. 296 (both in *Words and Objections*).

little hampers one's talk of truth, for one works within some language. In short, the parameters of truth stay conveniently fixed most of the time. Not so the analytical hypotheses that constitute the parameter of translation. We are always ready to wonder about the meaning of a foreigner's remark without reference to any one set of analytical hypotheses, indeed even in the absence of any; yet two sets of analytical hypotheses equally compatible with all linguistic behavior can give contrary answers, unless the remark is of one of the limited sorts that can be translated without recourse to analytical hypotheses.[7]

In reply to this, one might remark that we are always ready to wonder "What's it made of?" of any new stuff we come across. Are we then working within some comfortably inclusive theory? Perhaps we are; for the sake of argument, let us admit that the question is asked within the framework of chemical theory. The parameters we have in the back of our minds are the table of elements, standard tests for acids, etc. – and these "stay comfortably fixed." Is there anything similar for our question "What does the foreigner mean?" Well, there are the regulative principles Quine himself cites as used by linguists choosing between alternative translations. For example, "a premium is put on structural parallels: on correspondence between the parts of the native sentence, as segmented, and the parts of the English translation."[8] Again, "if a question were to arise over equating a short native locution to 'rabbit' and a long one to 'rabbit part' or vice versa they [the linguists] would favor the former course, arguing that the more conspicuously segregated wholes are likelier to bear the simpler terms."[9] One might add that there is the expectation that the foreigner will have a brief and convenient way of saying things like "*X* has the property *Y*," that he will be able to count, and so on. Roughly, just as we expect new things to be made out of the same sort of stuff as old things, we expect new languages to be made out of the same sort of components as old ones. Some of these expectations can be disappointed, but not all of them at once.

Quine does not think that there is a proper parallel between the parameters of chemical analysis and those we have just mentioned. This is indicated by his following up the remark just quoted about why we assign a short native locution to "rabbit" by saying "Such an implicit canon is all very well, unless mistaken for a substantive law of speech behavior." Following such a canon is "to impute our sense of linguistic analogy

[7] *Word and Object*, (Cambridge, MA, 1960), pp. 75–6.
[8] *Ibid.*, p. 75.     [9] *Ibid.*, p. 74.

unverifiably to the native mind."[10] This notion that we can separate the "canons" of our inquiry from the "laws" we discover (by reference to the unverifiability of the former) seems also to emerge in the following passage:

> Complete radical translation goes on, and analytical hypotheses are indispensable. Nor are they capricious; we have seen in outline how they are supported. May we not then say that in those very ways of thinking up and supporting the analytical hypotheses a sense *is* after all given to sameness of meaning of the expressions which those hypotheses equate? No. We could claim this only if no two conflicting sets of analytical hypotheses could be tied for first place on all theoretically accessible evidence. The indefinability of synonymy by reference to the methodology of analytical hypotheses is formally the same as the indefinability of truth by reference to scientific method.[11]

The trouble with this passage is that though earlier in *Word and Object* Quine has said that we cannot (*pace* Peirce) define truth-independent-of-any-particular-theory in terms of the limit of properly conducted scientific inquiry, he has also said that "It is rather when we turn back into the midst of an actually present theory, at least hypothetically accepted, that we can and do speak sensibly of this and that sentence as true."[12] He denies that this view commits him to a "relativistic" doctrine of truth since "Within our total evolving doctrine, we can judge truth as earnestly and absolutely as can be; subject to correction, but that goes without saying."[13] But what goes for truth generally should, one would think, go for truth about meanings. Further, what goes for the earnest and absolute use of "true" should go for the earnest and absolute use of "synonymous." "Same meaning" should have as much sense as "same makeup" – no more and no less. To make an invidious distinction here, we should have to show that there cannot be, e.g., two chemical theories which are "tied for first place on all theoretically accessible evidence."[14]

To put the point in another way, referring to the last sentence of the above quotation: "synonymous" is indeed not definable by reference to "the methodology of analytical hypotheses" if this latter term is meant to encompass the potential infinity of possible translation manuals in the same way as "scientific method" encompasses the potential infinity of all theories about anything. But if we narrow down the sense of "the

---

[10] *Ibid.*, p. 72.   [11] *Ibid.*, p. 75.   [12] *Ibid.*, p. 24.   [13] *Ibid.*, p. 25.
[14] Quine certainly does not think we can show anything of the sort. See *Words and Objections*, pp. 302–3, quoted below.

methodology of analytical hypotheses" to "those 'canons' by which we in fact choose between otherwise 'tied' manuals," then it is not at all clear that "synonymous" remains indefinable. The suggestion which Quine is concerned to refute in the passage quoted is that the noncapricious character or our resolution of "ties" is itself enough to give a sense to "same meaning"; the sentence about the two indefinabilities being "formally the same" is just not relevant to this suggestion.

At this point, however, it might be urged that I am forgetting thesis (2). If we rehabilitate "same meaning," surely we shall be rehabilitating "analytic"? Hasn't Quine's critique of the notion of analyticity shown what is wrong with the notion of "synonymous," and don't we now see that we must maintain (3) in order to maintain (2)? These questions can best be handled by reference to the distinction which Harman draws between "ordinary" meanings of "meaning" (and of "same meaning") and "meaning as conceived by certain linguistic philosophers."[15] Harman notes that there is a common and harmless use of "means the same" which gives no comfort to defenders of the analytic–synthetic distinction. In this sense, "in 1966 the sentence 'Lyndon Johnson has traveled to Vietnam' would be taken to mean the same . . . as the sentence 'The President of the United States has traveled to Vietnam.'"[16] Can we find an equally harmless sense which will cover translation between natural languages? Consider the following: $S$ (in $L$) and $S'$ (in $L'$) mean the same if and only if one is the most literal translation of the other among those currently canvassed. "Literal translation" here is to be explained by reference to the actual procedures of people in the business of translating between $L$ and $L'$. Such people will say, for example, that "The president of the French Republic is here" is a more literal translation of "Le Président de la République Française est ici" than "Pompidou is here" or "The President of France is here" – although all three English sentences "mean the same" in Harman's sense. When pressed for reasons, they will cite the usual behavioral facts and the sort of things which Quine calls the "canons" of linguistics.

---

[15] "Quine on Meaning and Existence, I," p. 127.
[16] *Ibid.*, p. 142. Harman explicates this sense of "means the same" by saying "two sentences mean the same if they are relatively obviously equivalent in truth-value by virtue of generally accepted principles" (p. 142) and "we say that one sentence means the same as . . . another if the two sentences are relatively obviously equivalent in truth-value, given shared-background information" (p. 135). I am doubtful about these explications (since they seem to lead to the claim that, e.g., any two simple theorems of Euclidean geometry mean the same); but there certainly is the sense Harman says there is, and I have no better explication to offer.

This sense of "same meaning" seems as "ordinary" as Harman's sense and as philosophically innocuous as the chemist's "same composition." The practice of conforming to various canons – those of linguistics or those of chemistry – gives a sense to "same." Once we see that this is where the sense comes from, we shall be prepared to agree with Quine that "appeal to meaning" will not "do any of the things these (linguistic) philosophers have wanted it to do for them,"[17] and thus be prepared to grant thesis (2). Specifically, reference to meaning, as so explicated, cannot explain the *possibility* of the practice of translation any more than reference to composition can explain the *possibility* of chemical analysis. If we say that French–English translation would be impossible unless certain sentences of the two languages meant the same, this will be as pointless (because as circular) as saying that chemical analysis would be impossible if things had no chemical composition, or that opium would be useless as a sedative if it had no dormitive power. Further, 'same meaning,' explicated by reference to the practices of linguists rather than used to explain them, gives no help to philosophers who wish to pick out the analytic sentences of English, or to explain truth by virtue of meaning.

So we may conclude that the "methodology of analytical hypotheses" *does* endow "same meaning" with a sense – a sense which does not weaken, and when properly explicated supports, thesis (2). But it may seem that we have missed Quine's point – for surely he is not talking of this ordinary and innocuous sense of "same meaning" which emerges from "the midst of an actually present theory," but of what Harman calls the "philosophical use of 'means the same'."[18] It is this latter use, presumably, which gives us the "old notions of meaning, idea, proposition" which are destroyed by thesis (3). This notion of a special philosophical sense of "meaning" suggests that we should take thesis (3) as saying something like: not only is the meaning$_1$ (ordinary sense) of a sentence as relative to a translation manual as the make-up of a rock is to a chemical theory, but its meaning$_2$ (technical, philosophical, sense) is indeterminate *also*.[19]

The trouble with this line of thought, however, comes when we try to pin down what "meaning$_2$" might be. We cannot just say that it is that sense of "meaning" in which *a priori* knowable truths *can* be explained as "true by virtue of meaning" and in which reference to meaning *does* genuinely explain the possibility of translation. The whole point is that there is no such sense. To exhibit the poverty of these "explanations," we must interpret "meaning" in its ordinary sense; we cannot say that, using

[17] *Ibid.*, p. 125.    [18] *Ibid.*, p. 142.    [19] I owe this suggestion to James Walters.

the sense of "meaning" in which these explanations are sound, they are unsound. We cannot say that in that sense of "meaning" in which translation is determinate, it is in fact indeterminate. Quine's talk of "old notions" and Harman's of a "philosophical use" suggest there are other ways of explaining what "meaning$_2$" is. They suggest that some philosophers have erected a genuine theory of entities called "meanings, ideas, or propositions" which are distinct from the "ordinary" entities referred to under these names (as distinct, perhaps, as the atoms of Bohr from the atoms of Democritus). To erect such a theory would be at least to say much *more* about these entities than simply that they are what explains, e.g., *a priori* knowledge and the possibility of translation. By suggesting the existence of such a theory, Quine and Harman suggest that we now have reason for thinking it a bad theory, and that these reasons are expressed by thesis (3). But there is no such theory.[20] There is nothing more to be said against the bad philosophical explanations in question than that they are empty or circular. There are no theoretically postulated entities which we can now show do not exist, and thus there is no "meaning$_2$" to be denied respectability, or to be discovered to be indeterminate after all.

Summing up what has been said about the last passage quoted from *Word and Object*, we can grant Quine the point that without the "ways of thinking up and supporting the analytical hypotheses" he mentions we should never have been able to employ even the vegetarian sense of "same meaning" suggested above. But, in spite of what Quine says in the passage quoted earlier, there is nothing culpable, nor philosophically misleading, about not having "any one set of analytical hypotheses" in mind when we "wonder about the meaning of the foreigner's remark." To say that there is would be like insisting that we need to have a hunch that the stuff at hand

---

[20] This is not to say that nothing corresponds to what Quine calls (cf. *Words and Objections*, p. 306) "the idea idea," and which he contrasts with "the serious externalization of empiricism: the shift of focus from ideas, which are subjective, to language, which is an intersubjective and social institution." But the idea idea is a habit of offering empty explanations, not a postulation of exotic entities. It lives on in such remarks as "Sentences are intentional because they are the expression of thoughts" and "We use words as we do because we have the concepts we have." These and similar pseudo-explanations are not to be dissolved by showing that there are no ideas (or thoughts, or concepts), but (in the matter of Wittgenstein's and Sellars' treatments of noninferential knowledge and "givenness") by showing how our knowledge of ideas, thoughts, and concepts depends upon our having language, and specifically language containing the terms "idea," "thought," etc. If there is anything here to be called a theory, it is a theory not about exotic entities but about a special sort of knowing. As I go on to suggest below, Quine's thesis (3) gets its most plausible interpretation if construed as an epistemological remark about the putatively "intuitive" knowledge of meanings.

is made out of some particular chemical element before we can sensibly ask "What is it made of?"

To return to an earlier point: can we make anything of the notion that there is "unverifiability" involved in the "canons" of linguistics of a sort not present in the "laws" of chemistry? Not, I think, without adopting a verificationism which is pretty close to what Quine repudiated in "Two Dogmas of Empiricism." The same holistic considerations which Quine there invoked against the notion that we can save analyticity by the use of the verification theory of meaning[21] count equally against the notion that we can save the regulative–constitutive (or heuristic–substantive, or canon–law, or made–found) distinction by an appeal to the distinction between what we would let be falsified and what we would not. The question of whether we find or impose the "linguistic universals" Chomsky speaks of is as unsatisfactory as the question of whether we find or impose the periodic table of elements. (For more on this point, see section III below.)

But if we drop verifiability as a red herring, perhaps we can catch a glimpse of what Quine is driving at. There is at least this difference between chemistry and linguistics: we can date the "discovery" of the periodic table, but not the "discovery" that people are more likely to report rabbits than rabbit-stages. We seem to have had the regulative principles of our linguistics with us always, whereas the principles that guide theory construction in chemistry have been built up by trial and error. Meanings (in the non-explanatory, vegetarian, sense) are as primordial a "posit" (to use another Quinean term) as are physical objects. The meaning of the foreign locution is what the bilingual knows and we don't, and doubtless men have talked about meanings as long as there have been bilinguals. The thought that *we* know what we mean, even if the witless barbarian does not, is doubtless equally old. Perhaps what Quine is pointing to when he notes that we wonder about the meaning of the foreigner's remark without having a set of analytical hypotheses in mind is simply that it is a bit odd to call what the bilingual knows (or what we know about ourselves) the result of applying a *theory*. Roughly speaking, what can be known non-inferentially ("intuitively") doesn't seem the sort of thing which there could be alternative theories about. Thus, when Quine picks out "the stubborn notion that we can tell intuitively which idea someone's sentence expresses, our sentence anyway, even when the intuition is irreducible

---

[21] Cf. *From a Logical Point of View* (Cambridge, MA, 1953), pp. 37ff.

to behavioral criteria"[22] as typifying the "uncritical persistence of old notions of meaning, idea, proposition," he may be getting at the heart of the matter. If so, the heart of the matter is this: the position Quine is criticizing thinks that discoveries about meaning are in principle exempt from the ordinary "underdetermination of our theory of nature," but Quine is insisting that they are subject to it. *The "parallel but additional" indeterminacy which according to thesis (3) afflicts translation is not an extra, second, indeterminacy, piled on top of the usual "underdetermination of our theory of nature," but is simply a matter of this latter underdetermination turning up where we did not expect to find it.*

The "special" indeterminacy of translation, on this view, turns out to be just one more case of the familiar Quinean point that theories go all the way down – that we cannot break our knowledge into the purely observational and nontheoretical on the one hand and the theoretical on the other. The man who says he's having a sensation of something red is, whether he knows it or not, working within the context of a theory – a psychological theory about the causes of human behavior which postulates the existence of things called "sensations" and specified conditions under which various sensations are had.[23] There could be alternative theories which denied the existence of sensations altogether, still other theories according to which he would be said to now be having some *other* sensation, and any of these theories might "tie for first place on all theoretically accessible evidence." The same sort of point goes for the man who says he is in pain, the man who says he sees a pig, and the man who says that when he said "*nolo episcopari*" he meant that he did not want to be a bishop. Non-inferential knowledge is always the result of the "internalization" of some theory or other, and so we cannot appeal to the existence of such knowledge for an exemption from the usual "under-determination of our theory of nature."

I want now to finish looking at Quine's arguments for thesis (3). I shall try to support the (somewhat strained) interpretation of (3) I have just suggested, by arguing that there is no better sense to be made out of what Quine says. In his reply to Chomsky, Quine claims that the parallel between physics and linguistics fails

> Essentially in this: theory in physics is an ultimate parameter. There is no legitimate first philosophy, higher or firmer than physics, to which to appeal over physicists' heads ... So we go on reasoning and affirming as best we

---

[22] *Words and Objections*, p. 304.
[23] Cf. Sellars's "myth of Jones" (Wilfrid Sellars, *Science, Perception, and Reality*, (London, 1963), pp. 183ff).

can within our ever under-determined and evolving theory of nature, the best one that we can muster at any one time; and it is usually redundant to cite the theory as parameter of our assertions, since no higher standard offers.[24]

This passage suggests that there *is* a "legitimate first philosophy, higher or firmer" than linguistics, to which to appeal over linguists' heads. But of course Quine cannot mean this: what would such a theory be? The only sort of thing to which we might be tempted to appeal over linguists' heads is the bilingual's translation, but Quine's whole point is that the bilingual is just one more theorist.[25] So the failure of parallel is presumably not that there is such an appeal, but that there is *thought* to be. Again, when Quine says that it is usually "redundant to cite the theory as parameter of our assertions" in physics, he may seem to be suggesting that in linguistics it is not so redundant; this suggestion seems to be the point of Harman's saying that "it makes no sense to speak of the translation of a single sentence of one language into a sentence of another language *apart from other transla-tions one would make*"[26] – apart, that is, from citing one's chosen transla-tion manual. But, *prima facie*, the redundancy is equally present; nobody expects or wants a French–English interpreter to continually remark that he is using Cassell's dictionary. So if there is a point to make about redundancy it may be merely that it would be no *more* redundant for the interpreter to cite his manual than it would be for a physicist to cite his theory. More specifically, the point must be that even if the interpreter has been bilingual since the age of three, it would *still* be in order for him to cite a manual.

So far I have been speaking as if I were offering an interpretation of thesis (3) – speaking as if Quine had simply formulated his point in a somewhat misleading way. But I now must admit that Quine continues his reply to Chomsky with a passage which completely resists the inter-pretation I have italicized above. After asserting what I have isolated as thesis (3), Quine continues:

> Thus, adopt for now my fully realistic attitude toward electrons and muons and curved space-time, thus falling in with the current theory of the world despite knowing that it is in principle methodologically underdetermined. Consider, from this realistic point of view, the totality of truths of nature, known and unknown, observable and unobservable, past and future. The point about indeterminacy of translation is that it withstands even this

---

[24] *Words and Objections*, p. 303.    [25] Cf. *Word and Object*, p. 74.
[26] "Quine on Meaning and Existence, I," p. 143.

truth, the whole truth about nature. This is what I mean by saying that, where indeterminacy of translation applies, there is no real question of right choice; there is no fact of the matter even to *within* the acknowledged underdetermination of a theory of nature.[27]

At first reading, this may seem to say simply that if you knew all about the elementary particles you would still have a free choice between "tied" translation manuals. So you would, but you would have the same choice between "tied" chemical and biological theories. There is nothing special about the case of linguistics. All that falling in with the current theory of physics does is to let you turn your back on "tied" theories of the ultimate constituents of matter. So perhaps when Quine says the "current theory of the world" he means not just physics in the narrow sense but the assemblage of all the disciplines – contemporary chemistry, contemporary biology, and so on. But then why not contemporary linguistics – the assemblage of currently accepted translation manuals plus whatever doctrine of "linguistic universals" these manuals may support? These manuals too are "part of the theory of nature," and presumably thus part of the "current theory of the world." As for "the totality of truths of nature," Quine seems to be saying that these range from statements about the distribution of particles to statements saying that so-and-so made the following sounds, but that when the man from Cassell's comes along and helpfully adds "and those sounds meant … " he is not tacking on another "truth of nature" but doing something quite different – not stating a fact at all.[28] But this claim does not give an argument for an "additional" indeterminacy; it just restates the point at issue.

As a last attempt at interpreting this passage, we might take the following line: there are no truths about meaning in the "totality of truths of nature" because there is no such thing as meaning (just as there are no truths about witches because there are no witches). This will not help, for the only sort of meaning which Quine wants to say does not exist is "meaning as conceived by certain linguistic philosophers."[29] In the "vegetarian" sense in which talking about "same meanings" is just shorthand for

---

[27] *Words and Objections*, p. 303.
[28] Since linguistic behavior is a datum of psychology, economics, sociology, intellectual history, and the like, presumably in all these fields "indeterminacy of translation" applies. Since we can trade off theories of what people believe and desire against theories of what their utterances mean, the special indeterminacy Quine attributes to translation will infect all fields in which humans *qua* believers and desirers are studied. This means that in the whole field of *Geisteswissenschaften* "there is no fact of the matter" in the way there are facts in the *Naturwissenschaften*. I find it hard to imagine Quine welcoming this result – but I cannot see how he might avoid it.
[29] "Quine on Meaning and Existence, I," p. 127.

talking about the currently accepted translations, Quine does not want to deny that there are meanings any more than he wants to deny that there are translations. Exploring this line just leads us back to the same old question: how can Quine grant that the linguists' analytical hypotheses are "not capricious" and also say that "where indeterminacy of translation applies . . . there is no fact of the matter"? What more does it take for there to be a "fact of the matter" than a rational procedure for reaching agreement about what to assert?

## II    The analogy with translating number theory into set theory

This concludes my discussion of Quine's explanations of and arguments for thesis (3). The mild "epistemological" interpretation I have suggested is all, as far as I can see, that the "additional" indeterminacy of translation comes to. Quine, certainly, would not agree. I think, however, that even if my interpretation were right, Quine would be making an important and philosophically fruitful point – a point over and above the even more important and fruitful one made in thesis (2). But we have not yet exhausted the alternatives to my interpretation. Harman has proposed that we explicate the claim that there is "no fact of the matter" by looking at the case of the various "translations" of number theory into set theory:

> For example, the sentence, "Three is a member of five" (which is assigned no truth-value by unreduced number theory), is translated by a true sentence under the von Neumann scheme and by a false sentence under the Zermelo scheme. Most philosophers would agree that it does not make sense to ask which general scheme for translating number theory into set theory is the correct scheme, although in certain contexts one or the other may be more convenient. In consequence it can make no sense to ask what is the correct translation of a particular sentence of number theory unless one asks *relative to some envisioned general scheme* for translating number theory into set theory.[30]

As a preliminary remark, we can note that the last sentence in this passage is a lame conclusion. Quine holds that "we may meaningfully speak of the truth of a sentence only within the terms of some theory of conceptual scheme"[31] for *all* sentences, not just those about which "it does not make sense to ask which general scheme . . . is the correct scheme." The important point is in the penultimate sentence; Harman is quite right in saying that most philosophers would agree that the question of correctness

---

[30] *Words and Objections*, p. 14.    [31] *Word and Object*, p. 75.

here makes no sense. But can Quineans go along with most philosophers on this point? Most philosophers would say that choosing between Zermelo and von Neumann was just a matter of choosing how we want to talk, not a matter of saying how the world is. But a Quinean must be more cautious about presupposing a clear-cut division between "language" and "theory."[32]

In the first place, the fact that number theory deals with abstract entities makes no difference – for Quine, numbers, sets, and the relations between them are on a methodological par with molecules, atoms, and the relations between them.[33] In the second place, there seems no clear reason for saying that Zermelo and von Neumann are offering *translations*; why not say that they are offering different hypotheses about what numbers are? We cannot, consistently with Quine's principles, argue that Zermelo is offering a translation rather than discovering a fact simply on the ground that there is no way except momentary convenience or idiosyncratic taste to decide between him and von Neumann. If this were enough, two equipollent theories in physics would count as alternative "translations" of (alternative "conceptual shorthand" for) the observational data – an instrumentalist result which would be repellent to Quine's scientific realism. (In any case, such a move would so broaden the meaning of "translation" as to make the term useless.) Consider the hypothesis that every atom contains just three times as many elementary particles as the current theory says it does, but that the "extra" particles neatly cancel out each other's effects. Do we have here merely a different way of speaking, or rather a foolish factual claim? Isn't the whole point of Quine's attack on the dogmas just that this last question is not a useful one to ask? The proper Quinean attitude towards Zermelo and von Neumann should be simply that it is not important which theory we choose, not that there is nothing to be right or wrong about. Quineans should have the same attitude, it seems to me, to the fact that, as Quine says, "In the French construction 'ne ... rien' you can translate 'rien' into English as 'anything' or as 'nothing' at will, and then accommodate your choice by translating 'ne' as 'not' or by construing it as pleonastic."[34]

What we have in the von Neumann–Zermelo case is a conflict between our verificationist intuitions[35] and our sympathy with Quine's attack on

---

[32] Cf., e.g., *The Ways of Paradox* (New York, 1966), pp. 123ff, and *Words and Objections*, pp. 308ff.

[33] Cf. Smart, "Quine's Philosophy of Science," in *Words and Objections*, p. 5.

[34] *Ontological Relativity* (New York, 1969) p. 30.

[35] Cf. Paul Benacerraf, "What Numbers Could Not Be," *Philosophical Review*, 74 (1965), p. 58: "In awaiting enlightenment on the true identity of 3 we are not awaiting a proof of some deep

the analytic–synthetic distinction. We want to say that there is no matter of fact in dispute, but we have to say something about the appearance of a dispute. What is there to say except that the dispute is "just about language" or "merely verbal," or "a matter of style" rather than "content"? But how can we justify saying these sorts of things given Quine's attack on the analytic–synthetic and language–theory distinctions? There are two ways in which we might hope to get out of this trap. The first is to deny that there are numbers; Quine suggests this move, and Benacerraf has explicitly adopted it.[36] This looks like an escape because now instead of saying that the disagreement was "merely verbal" we can say that there was a real disagreement about entities which were thought to exist but didn't. (Thus, disagreements about witches between schools of demonologists were not "verbal" disagreements, but they were not disagreements about matters of fact either; they were, so to speak, disagreements about matters of putative fact.) This tactic looks less promising, however, when we find Quine advising us not to "discriminate between elimination and explication" and not to take seriously, e.g., the question "Is physicalism a repudiation of mental objects after all, or a theory of them?"[37]

But further, and more to our purpose, there does not seem to be any move we can make about translation which will parallel denying that there are numbers. We can say that there are no meanings, but (even apart from the distinctions between senses of "meaning" made above) this is not to the point. In the case of sets and numbers, the former will do the work of the latter. In the case of witches, talk about neuroses and hallucinations will do the work done by demonology. In the case of physicalism, talk of brain-states may do the work done by talk of mental entities. But what would it mean to say that English sentences will do the work done by native sentences? In any sense in which this might be intelligible, we knew it before we started translating. The translation manuals we come up with do not let us talk about one thing instead of talking about something else.

---

theorem . . . We do not know what a proof of that *could* look like. The notion of 'correct account' is breaking loose from its moorings if we admit of the possible existence of unjustifiable but correct answers to questions such as this."

[36] Cf. *Ontological Relativity*, p. 45; *Word and Object*, pp. 262ff; and Benacerraf, *op. cit.*, pp. 73, 70–1. Benacerraf's move, however, seems to depend upon the claim that "there is a difference between *asserting* that 3 is the set of all triplets and *identifying* 3 with that set, which last is what might be done in the context of some explication . . . The difference lies in that, normally, one who identifies 3 with some particular set does so for the purpose of presenting some theory and does not claim that he has *discovered* which object 3 really is" (*ibid.*, pp. 67–8). This distinction between explication and discovery, and between assertion and identification, is just as suspicious, from a Quinean point of view, as Carnap's internal–external distinction.

[37] *Word and Object*, p. 265.

Rather, their function is to help us explain the natives' actions by helping us identify the natives' beliefs and desires. Translation between natural languages is just not very much like either explicating number theory or explaining away mental events or witches. There are no objects to be identified with other objects, except in the trivial sense in which we identify the meaning of one sentence with that of another sentence. But in *this* sense of "meaning" talk of meanings never did any explanatory work anyway, so we cannot speak of some other thing now doing the same work.[38]

Our first attempt to escape from the trap created by verificationist intuitions on the one hand and the denial of the language–theory distinction on the other hand led nowhere. Let us now try a second. The problem was that we wanted to say that Zermelo and von Neumann had a "merely verbal" disagreement, but that Quine's position seemed to let us give this phrase no sense. We may have been too hasty. Harman tells us that Quine's "account of translation provides the basis of an account of verbal disagreement."[39] He notes that an epistemological conservatism leads us to adopt the "identity scheme" (when our neighbor says "rabbit" he means "rabbit") for speakers of our own language, but that we override this conservatism when "a relatively obvious modification of the identity translation" will result in our attributing similar beliefs to our neighbor and to ourselves. "If so," he says, one will accept the modified translation scheme and take the apparent disagreement in belief to be "merely verbal." In general, there is no real (underlying) distinction between a difference in view and a difference in meaning. But if the disagreement is systematic to a degree sufficient to override our conservative commitment to the identity scheme, then we call it a difference in meaning; otherwise we call it a difference in belief.[40] So we can call the difference between von Neumann and Zermelo merely verbal if we can find some systematic way of transforming what the one says into what the other says by proclaiming that they use some words differently – e.g., that when Zermelo says "unit set whose sole

---

[38] To put the point another way: there is indeterminacy in explication (of, e.g., number theory by set theory) in explanation (of, e.g., macrostructure by microstructure) and in translation (of, e.g., French by English) – but it looks like the same old indeterminacy in all three cases. It is just the fact that there are a potentially infinite number of mappings of (1) set-theoretical statements onto number-theoretical statements, (2) micro-structural statements onto macrostructural statements, (3) English speech dispositions onto French speech dispositions, which will be "tied" if we disregard simplicity, familiarity, convenience, charm (and entrenchment – see section III below).

[39] "Quine on Meaning and Existence, I," p. 148.    [40] *Loc. cit.*

member is $n$-$1$" he means what von Neumann means when he says "set of all preceding numbers," and so on.

This may work, but will it give us what we need? The notion of "merely verbal" is never going to mark off, e.g., philosophy of mathematics from physics, nor will any considerations of simplicity or obviousness of transformation. One can envisage wild set-theoretical schemes for "translating" number theory which would not go over in any simple way into either von Neumann's or Zermelo's scheme. One can envisage alternative physical theories (elves vs. gremlins, for instance) where avoiding the identity translation would be fairly easy. In any case, we shall hardly be able to say that the linguist who translates "Gavagai" as "rabbit" and the one who translates it as "rabbit-stage" disagree merely verbally. For, as Quine has emphasized, there will be very complicated and unobvious shifts all over the language (in the treatment of identity, quantifiers, etc.) which will separate their respective translation manuals.

So there seems no way out of the trap we described above – no way to express, consistently with Quinean principles, our sense that there is no matter of fact to be right or wrong about in the case of "translating" number theory into set theory. But suppose there were. Suppose that there is an intuition of absence of "matter of fact" in this case which has nothing to do with the notion of "merely verbal disagreement." Suppose this latter notion has been just a red herring. Still, how do we transfer this intuition to the case of translating the native's language? There are (let us say) no rational procedures for preferring von Neumann to Zermelo or vice versa; preferences here are (we somehow know) arational. But there just *are* rational procedures for preferring the "rabbit" manual to the "rabbit-stage" manual, *viz.*, those which led Quine to call our choice of analytical hypotheses "non-capricious." There is nothing in the number theory case to correspond to, e.g., the principle that "the more conspicuously segregated wholes are likelier to bear the simple terms." The latter expresses our hunch about what people are likely to do; we have, as it happens, no hunches about what numbers are likely to be.

## III   Entrenchment

To sum up: there are two things wrong with the analogy Harman offers. The first is that it is difficult, within Quine's system, to back up our intuition that in the number theory case there is no such thing as correctness. But even if we bate this point, there remains a second: the disanalogy introduced by the presence of "implicit canons" guiding our choice of analytical hypotheses for translation and the absence of such canons in the number theory case. Thus, analysis of the analogy brings us back around again to a question discussed in section I: we will only be able to get rid of this disanalogy if we can make good on the notion that such "canons" somehow do not count – because, for instance, they are "un-verifiable." I argued briefly above that Quine's holism made it difficult for him to state a distinction between "implicit canons" and "substantive laws." I shall conclude the chapter by spelling out this difficulty more fully, in order to bring out a more general dilemma in which Quine is caught.

Consider the principle that "the more conspicuously segregated wholes are likelier to bear the simpler terms." Suppose we grant that what counts as conspicuous segregation is relative to the language into which we are translating. This amounts to granting that we can only explain what conspicuousness of segregation is by enumeration – by putting rabbits on one list and rabbit-stages, parts of the Great Rabbit, instantiations of rabbithood, etc., on another. In short, no real generality is introduced by our principle about conspicuous segregation; all it says is that the terms used in our translation should be as familiar as possible – that the natives should, *ceteris paribus*, be construed as saying as banal things as we do. Let us go further and grant that the same is true for all the "linguistic universals" we might come up with. In each case, the "discovery" of such universals will be a matter of preserving banality and avoiding quaintness – just as the "discovery" that speakers of different languages tend to share the same beliefs is a matter of applying the principle of charity. The need to preserve banality may sometimes yield to the need to ascribe true beliefs, and conversely. But what counts as a false belief or a quaint expression will always be a matter of what *we* believe and what *we* say.

Does the provincialism of linguistic universals give Quine what he wants – the nonrational character of our procedures for choosing between translation manuals? No, not unless the provincialism of projecting "green," or of assuming that Saturnian sodium will produce the same spectrographic lines as terrestrial sodium, shows the nonrationality of botany and astronomy. Goodman's point that deciding on the rationality of an inductive inference requires attending to the degree of entrenchment of the predicates used lends no aid or comfort to the notion that what we used to think constitutive is really regulative, or that what we call "rational" really is not, or that what we thought we found we actually imposed. But Goodman's point is the general principle of which our need to resort to enumeration to define "conspicuous segregation" is merely a special case. The general principle is, roughly, the policy of trying to fit things into what we think of as natural kinds; linguistic universals are just one sort of natural kind. What separates both linguistics and chemistry from the case of number theory is that in the latter the notion of "entrenchment," and thus that of "natural kind," seems to find no foothold.

To show that the linguists' "implicit canons" do not count as grounding a rational policy – that they are not merely special cases of our general policy of projecting the entrenched – we should have to show that they were unrevisable in the light of future inquiry in some stronger way than the policy of, e.g., projecting "green" and not "grue" is unrevisable. We can imagine revising the latter policy after the Day of Changing Colors; can we imagine revising the linguists' "canons"? I cannot suggest a situation in which we would revise them, but for that matter I cannot suggest a situation in which we would abandon the principle of non-contradiction or the relativity of simultaneity. In general, Quineans should not have to meet this sort of challenge. Quine's attack on traditional notions of "necessity" does not depend on saying that we can always describe a situation in which it would be rational to give up any given claim; the point is rather that we cannot explain the difference between the cases where our imagination succeeds and the cases in which it fails by attributing to the latter a special sort of necessity – "logical," "mathematical," "metaphysical," or what you will.[41] But if we cannot so explain the difference, we cannot explain it by the regulative–constitutive (or "canon"–"law") distinction either. Quine has argued, as part of his defense of thesis (2), that when we fail to imagine how we could rationally come to give up a belief we all now share, we cannot conclude that we have come upon a new sort of truth – e.g., truth by virtue of meaning. But the same sort of argument should show that we cannot conclude that we have come upon a new sort of declarative sentence – one which expresses a resolve rather than a description of the world. In the case of the linguists' canons, Quine seems to treat unverifiability (i.e., unimaginability of revision) as signaling absence of truth-value. But if he is going to do this, he should do it across the board. If he does, plenty of physics, chemistry, and philosophy will turn out to be devoid of truth-value.

If my argument is sound, the dilemma facing Quine is this: he should either give up the notion of "objective matter of fact" all along the line, or reinstate it in linguistics. On the first alternative, he can say that the notion

---

[41] Cf. Quine's "On Necessary Truth" (in *The Ways of Paradox*, pp. 48–56), especially the concluding paragraph.

of "being about the world," which the positivists used to explicate both "analytic" and "meaningless," was as empty as these latter notions themselves, and cannot survive in their absence. On the second alternative, he can say that the linguists discover "substantive laws" just as the chemists do, remarking merely that these discoveries are likely to hold few surprises. On the first alternative, we emphasize the similarity of all inquiry to the Zermelo–von Neumann case; we emphasize the potential infinity of mappings which (if we disregard entrenchment) would remain "tied" under any given constraints. On the second alternative, we emphasize the difference between inquiry, in which respect for entrenchment gives us a criterion of rationality, and the Zermelo–von Neumann case, in which the notion of entrenchment does not apply. So far in this chapter I have been suggesting the second, but either alternative would make sense. The first has the advantage of emphasizing the revolutionary character of the Hegelianism which Quine picked up from Dewey, and which both men put to good use in their *Aufhebung* of standard empiricist distinctions. The second has the advantages which always attach to conservatism. All I have argued here is that we cannot go between the horns in the way suggested by Quine's defense of thesis (3).[42]

---

[42] I am grateful to Tyler Burge and Milton Fisk for helpful suggestions and criticisms.

CHAPTER 15

# Dennett on awareness

D. C. Dennett's *Content and Consciousness* is an extraordinarily interesting
and original book, and one which will raise the level of current discussion
in the philosophy of mind. In this note, however, I should like to criticize
one central thesis of the book – that puzzles in the philosophy of mind,
and notably those about incorrigible knowledge, can only be cleared up by
"an analysis of phenomena at the sub-personal level."[1] This thesis seems to
me dead wrong, and I hope to show, by an analysis of what Dennett says
about direct awareness and about incorrigibility, that the revival of
Putnam's notion of "functional state" (on which Dennett depends heavily
in his defense of the thesis) is not a profitable strategy.

Dennett's thesis is, roughly, that only by opening up the person (who
has been treated as a sealed "black box" in traditional philosophy of mind)
and saying something about his internal "functional organization" can we
make the distinctions we need. I want to begin to cast doubt on this by
taking up what Dennett says about the need to distinguish two senses of
awareness. He regards such a distinction as the beginning of wisdom in
this area of philosophy, and I think he is right. But I also think he makes
the distinction in the wrong way.

The two senses of awareness Dennett distinguishes are as follows:

(1)   $A$ is aware$_1$ that $p$ at time $t$ if and only if $p$ is the content of the input
      state of $A$'s "speech center" at time $t$.
(2)   $A$ is aware$_2$ that $p$ at time $t$ if and only if $p$ is the content of an internal
      event in $A$ at time $t$ that is effective in directing current behavior.[2]

---

[1] Dennett, *Content and Consciousness* (New York, 1969), p. 131. Cf. p. 101. I am grateful for Professor
Dennett's comments on an earlier draft of this note, and also to Gilbert Harman.
[2] *Ibid.*, p. 118. For Dennett's use of the notion of "content," see pp. 76ff. I do not think that Dennett
ever makes this notion really clear or useful (see below, pp. 296ff) But his way of using it is suggested
by his saying that "Assigning content to an event must be relating the event to a particular verbal
expression" (p. 82) and that "The ideal picture, then, is of content being ascribed to structures, events
and states in the brain on the basis of a determination of origins in stimulation and eventual

290

One way in which Dennett wants us to apply this distinction is to separate the way in which dogs are aware of bones from the way in which we are.[3] But one would think that the distinction in question could be made in a way that has become familiar – simply by distinguishing between the kind of awareness that goes along with linguistic behavior from the kind that can exist in nonlanguage users. Thus, one might think that one could get along with the distinction between

(3)  $A$ is aware$_3$ that $p$ at time $t$ if and only if he understands, and at $t$ would, *ceteris paribus*, assent to, "$p$" or some translation thereof.

(4)  $A$ is aware$_4$ that $p$ at time $t$ if and only if his nonlinguistic behavior is such as would be expected of people who would assent to "$p$" or some translation thereof.[4]

Now I do think that this latter distinction suffices, and in what follows I want to show that nothing is gained by doing things Dennett's way. I have three points to make. In the first place, the distinction between what we have and what dogs have has nothing to do with the distinction between "what one can report directly, infallibly, and without speculation or inference . . . and what serves, or is relied upon, to direct behavioral responses."[5] In the second place, the notion of "what one can report directly, infallibly, and without speculation or inference" combines, to no good purpose, the two quite distinct notions of "non-inferential" and "incorrigible." In the third place, neither of these latter notions is explicated by

appropriate behavioral effects, such ascriptions being essentially a heuristic overlay on the extensional theory rather than intervening variables of the theory" (p. 80).

[3]  Cf. *Ibid.*, p. 119. On the importance of preventing the inner life of dogs from serving as an objection to Kantian arguments about conditions of possible experience, see Jonathan Bennett, *Kant's Analytic* (Cambridge, 1966), p. 105, and my "Strawson's Objectivity Argument," *Review of Metaphysics*, 24, 2 (1970), p. 235n [Chapter 12 in this volume, p. 251n]. But the utility in distinguishing between senses of awareness, of course, stretches further. Anything resembling Sellars's "psychological nominalism" (the doctrine that all awareness of anything is a "linguistic affair") is going to involve making such a distinction to allow for babies and animals. See also Fred Dretske's admirably careful and detailed demarcation of "non-epistemic" from "epistemic" seeing (in *Seeing and Knowing* [New York, 1969]).

[4]  My (4) is of course as vague as Dennett's (2), but the vagueness matches the vagueness of our criteria for deciding what, e.g., a given dog believes at a given time. Also, as Gilbert Harman has pointed out to me, Dennett wants to say that the driver who is engrossed in conversation was not aware$_1$ of passing cars (Dennett's example at *op. cit.*, p. 116), but the driver might well be aware$_3$ of them. However: (a) I do not see how Dennett would justify the claim that "There is a car passing me now" was *not* at the input-stage of the driver's speech center, given that he would assent to this if asked; (b) I take it that mismatches between the case of the driver and the case of the dog should be settled by reference to the dog, for the philosophical importance of Dennett's distinction to appear.

[5]  Dennett, *op. cit.*, p. 118.

developing what Dennett calls the notion of "'speech center' in the functional or logical sense."[6]

In tying in awareness with the ability to make introspective reports, Dennett relies upon the point that the two "quite different sorts of features of situations that govern our talk of awareness" are (1) "our dependence on awareness of things for manoeuvering in our environment" and (2) "our ability to make introspective reports."[7] But why are *introspective* reports the key to the sort of awareness humans have? Consider a man who didn't grasp terms like "aware of," "consciousness," "mind," "thought," "sensation," etc., but had the usual range of vocabulary for talking about the external world. You ask him why he dodged and he says that there was a tree in the way, so you conclude that he experienced the tree *qua* tree. Similarly, if he replies that it was because he saw a twelve-foot live oak, or the totem of his tribe, in the way. Is he "introspecting" when he answers such a question? Why should we say so? One introspects only one's mental states; knowing non-inferentially that one has a fast pulse or a fluttering stomach is not introspection (but rather kinaesthetic sensation), just because these are physical states. Saying there is a tree in the way is reporting a physical situation. Should we say that since "being aware of as" *is* a mental state, and since he is telling us (indirectly) what he was aware of as, introspection must somehow be involved, even though he doesn't know what a mental state, nor introspection, is? This seems pretty tenuous, but suppose we allow it; suppose we allow, in other words, that our "Rylean ancestors" (as Sellars[8] calls them) were capable of introspection. On such a view, however, introspection will not be an *incorrigible* faculty. For if all an introspector comes up with are things like "there was a tree in the way," what is it that he is supposed to know incorrigibly? Shall we say that he has incorrigible knowledge of a mental state but "can't express it"? Why should we not say this of a dog? If we make incorrigibility into a mystical property of an organism's inner state rather than a feature of our reception of his utterances, the only reason we shall have for denying such a property to the brutes will be their lack of a language – but if this is what is involved, then we might as well use the distinction between (3) and (4) instead of the distinction between (1) and (2) in the first place.

I conclude that Dennett has run together a feature of humans (their being aware of things *as*) which is simply a product of their ability to talk,

---

[6] *Ibid.*, p. 118n.    [7] *Ibid.*, pp. 115–16.
[8] Cf. Sellars, *Science, Perception and Reality* (London, 1963), p. 178.

with another feature (being able to make incorrigible reports) which is a product of their talking in a certain special way (about their own minds). Coming now to my second point, I want to suggest that he runs these two together because he identifies the latter with a third feature of humans, their ability to make non-inferential reports. By way of putting this in context, it is perhaps useful to remark that the fundamental difference between Dennett's line and the one that I am taking is that he thinks that to understand incorrigibility you have to look inside the person whereas I think that you have to look outside, to what I have called an "heuristic rule" and "a feature of our reception of utterances." Very crudely, Dennett takes incorrigibility to be a matter of nature (the way the knower is *an sich*) and I take it to be a matter of social practise (the way other people treat the knower).[9] Because one will not find anything to call "incorrigibility" on the inside of the person, one *must*, if one takes Dennett's line, identify incorrigibility with the only remotely relevant thing one *can* find – namely, direct connections. We thus revitalize the old notion that only incorrigible knowledge is direct (non-inferential) knowledge, a notion which comes from the Cartesian picture of the mental as the only sort of thing which the eye of the mind gets to see, and which brings in its wake epistemological skepticism and the theory of "unconscious inference." When the Cartesian tradition asked "How is that no error is possible?" it answered "Because of an analogue of direct perception under ideal conditions – *viz.*, the perception by the eye of the mind of entities in the inner theatre." When Dennett asks the same question, he replies "Because of an analogue of direct transmission of messages":

> The speech center part of our machine does not examine or analyze its input in order to determine its qualities or even its similarities and dissimilarities with other inputs, but rather produces English sentences as *expressions* of its input. The infallibility, barring verbal slips of the "reports" of the analyzer output, is due to the criterion of identity for such output states. What makes an output the output it is is what it goes on to produce in the speech center, barring correctible speech center errors, so an output is precisely what it is "taken to be" by the speech center regardless of its qualities and characteristics in any physical realization.[10]

On the Cartesian picture, the line of mental sight's being clear ensures freedom from error; on Dennett's picture, so to speak, the telephone line's being clear ensures it. But now we must remember that all this stuff about

---

[9] For more on this contrast, see my "Intuition" in P. Edwards (ed.), *The Encyclopedia of Philosophy* (New York, 1967).
[10] Dennett, *op. cit.*, p. 110.

"centers" and "lines" is metaphorical, for we are concerned with functional entities and connections and not physical ones. So what does the "direct-ness" come to? Simply, as Dennett says, to "the criterion of identity for such output states." The analyzer's output is whatever the speech center's output is, barring slips. But now consider the following dilemma: either (a) nothing is relevant to the truth of "the analyzer's output was $X$" save whether the speech center's output was $X$ (barring slips), or (b) other considerations are relevant. If we think of the machine as a physical set-up, we *must* choose (b). For then we can draw a line between the hardware that counts as "analyzer" and that which counts as "speech center" and look to see whether what goes on at the dividing line is the sort of event whose "content" is $X$, quite independently of what the speech center says. It is only if we think of the set-up "functionally" that (a) might make sense. But what does it mean to think of it "functionally"? If we abstract from the line separating the hardware, we abstract also from the analyzer vs. speech center distinction. The trouble is that in hardware terms "directness" just does not produce infallibility, whereas in non-hardware terms "directness" makes no sense.

So we are left with (b). Other considerations than what the speech center says are relevant to whether the analyzer's output is $X$, but neverthe-less the "criterion of identity" of the latter is what the speech center says. All this can mean is that we let the latter override all other considerations, just as we let a person's contemporaneous beliefs about his mental states override every other consideration bearing on the nature of those states. But if to assert this criterion of identity is merely to say that we in fact do override in this way, what light has been gained on the nature or ground of incorrigible knowledge? We are no longer saying that it is rational so to override because of something called "directness," we are just saying that we override. To note, as Dennett does in the quotation above, that the speech center does not "examine or analyze its input" is irrelevant to whether we adopt such a practise about overriding. (Consider the heuristic rule that the Constitution is what the Supreme Court says it is; we have good and sufficient reasons for insisting that lower courts adopt this rule and attribute infallibility to the Supreme Court, but they do not include the claim that the Supreme Court does not "examine or analyze" the Constitution but rather simply "expresses" it.) Nothing about the wiring of the machine helps tell us whether we *should* adopt such a practise for some given machine. We might, given enough experience with a particular machine, have good reasons for doing so. But, once again, we should have to tell a very complicated story about why this would be the best decision.

We cannot, for example, take a short-cut by saying that whenever we find the weight of other evidence about analyzer output bearing against the speech center's report we shall decide that the speech center made a slip. (Consider the claim that to understand how it is that the Scriptures are infallible we need to see that any apparent false prediction made in Scripture simply results from a misinterpretation.)

So much, then, for "directness" or "expression" as explication of incorrigibility. Coming now to my third point, I want to bring what has just been said to bear on Dennett's definition of "aware₁." This definition stands or falls with the notion of "'speech center' in the functional or logical sense." Suppose we assume that a distinction between analyzer and speech center can be drawn for any mechanism we are interested in. How do we draw it? What criteria do we bring to bear on any given physical set-up to fix what Dennett calls "the awareness line"?[11] At a minimum, we should need to distinguish between where "analysis" was going on and where mere "expression" was going on. Both analysis and expression, however, may be equally complicated input–output functions; so complexity is no help. A computer which translates Russian texts into English is presumably analyzing, but an output device which translates binary into alphanumeric is presumably merely expressing; so an appeal to the distinction between "computing" and "coding" is no help. Nor can we use the notion that the analyzer comes to an end when it produces an event which "has the same content" as the eventual output in English of the speech center. For this notion of "same content" is just a matter of there being some function which maps the event onto some English sentence. How do we know whether it is a function which offers an "analysis" or one which is simply "expressive"? This just rephrases the question of whether we are at the awareness line, or still inside the analyzer, or by now inside the speech center. There just is *no* natural way of making this distinction; it can only be made *ad hoc* and whimsically. The reason is that "speech center"

---

[11] *Op. cit.*, p. 122. Dennett says here that in the case of a manufactured machine this "conceptual" line could presumably be matched by a "neat physical line," though there might be difficulties about doing so in the brain. The reverse is probably the case. The brain's speech center *can* be localized, more or less, but in manufactured machines – especially general-purpose computers programed to first calculate a result and then, in the same registers, compute how to express the result in English – it usually cannot. The line in such machines can be drawn in dozens of equally plausible places, and it is as plausible to draw it temporally as spatially. But would it really matter to the notion of "direct awareness" if cerebral localization had proved impossible? And does it matter to this notion that the so-called "discovery of a speech center" in one of the cerebral hemispheres is not (as it would have to be for Dennett's purposes) the discovery of a line between analysis and expression, but simply of an apparatus necessary for linguistic but not for non-linguistic behavior?

(unlike, say, "valve lifter"[12]) is an immensely abstract concept – as abstract and difficult to pin down as the distinction between, e.g., "saying something different" and "saying the same thing in different ways" (and for just the same reasons). We should not be bemused into thinking that we can look into a machine and see where its speech center is, in the same way as we might look and see where its valve lifter is. What counts as "speech" is a far more arbitrary matter than what counts as a "valve" – and "speech center" shares in this arbitrariness.

I conclude that the functional sense of "speech center" is just too loose a notion to throw any light on the nature of human awareness. In particular, it is not going to help us understand "direct knowledge" nor "incorrigibility." But I believe that one can account for the attractiveness of the notion by going back for a moment to the notion of "content." If one thinks of the analyzer just as "that which culminates in an event which has the same content as what is said," then one will naturally think of the analyzer as the analogue of the mind. For the mind is what culminates in thoughts, and the obvious example of something which "has the same content" as an English sentence is just the "thought behind it." Dennett's analyzer outputs (or speech center inputs) are, in fact, just thoughts under another name. All that we know about them ("functionally" speaking) is that they are the sorts of inner states which, *ceteris paribus*, give rise to certain utterances, and that they share the intentional properties of those utterances (they can be about $X$, be mistaken, etc.). But that, as Sellars has pointed out, is just what we know about the nature of thoughts.[13] The reason it seems at first blush that talk about speech center inputs might give us the key to an understanding of incorrigibility and directness is that thoughts are paradigms of what can be directly and incorrigibly known. So things which are just like thoughts except in name look as if they must necessarily be knowable in the same way. Since analyzer outputs, unlike thoughts, sound as if they ought to be physically locatable (at least in principle), it seems as if we were now explaining the slightly fishy (thoughts) by reference to the scientifically respectable (analyzer inputs). But in fact analyzer outputs are not (for the reasons given in the previous paragraph) physically locatable, any more than thoughts are locatable by reference to the pineal gland.

---

[12] For the use of "valve lifter" as a paradigm of a functional concept, see Jerry Fodor, "Explanations in Psychology" in *Philosophy in America* (ed. by Max Black), Ithaca 1965, and William Kalke, "What Is Wrong with Fodor and Putnam's Functionalism," *Noûs* 3 (1969), pp. 83–94.

[13] Cf. Sellars, *op. cit.*, pp. 186ff.

I can point to the moral of this examination of Dennett on awareness by generalizing what I have just been saying about the notion of "content." All that the ascription of "content" to brain-events comes to is the notion that some states in the causal chain that leads up to the production of verbal utterances may themselves be thought of as inner replicas of those utterances – thus, in Dennett's words, the analyzer output is "a *report* of sorts itself."[14] Such mentalizing of the brain is, as Dennett remarks, an invaluable heuristic device for physiologists,[15] but taken as an *explanation* of how the brain works (much less of how it is that, e.g., reports of the mental are incorrigible) it is just the old "analogy of a community of correspondents." This analogy, Dennett rightly says, is "of all the common analogies used to describe the brain ... the most far-fetched and least useful."[16] I think that Dennett ignores his own strictures against this analogy (or, rather, fails to see that he is himself using it) because he thinks that ascribing content to brain-events is essential to his program of treating what appear to be names of mental entities ("pain," "thought") as non-referring expressions.[17] Dennett thinks that if we do not have such mental entities we shall still need to explain the existence of such truths as that "people just *can* tell what they are thinking," and that "what they report are their thoughts." He thinks that nothing except recourse to the brain "functionally construed" – i.e., to the "sub-personal" level of explanation – will give us such explanations.[18] But, if what I have been saying is right, the only sort of explanations that emerge from the sub-personal level are the same sort as those which Cartesianism offered – unfruitful metaphors which treat inner states of the person (the mind as inner eye, the analyzer-as-reporter) as capable of the same sort of things (perception, assertion) as the person himself. Truths of the sort Dennett mentions are explicable without going beneath the skin – simply by telling a story about how men came to develop the language and the habits they did.

My conclusion, then, is that we should not try to straighten out the philosophical troubles which were created by one set of metaphors and analogies (the Cartesian ones) by inventing a new set. The "remarkable and fruitful analogy" (in Dennett's words[19]) between logical states of a

---

[14] Dennett, *op. cit.*, p. 110.    [15] *Ibid.*, p. 79.    [16] *Ibid.*, p. 87.
[17] Cf. *ibid.*, pp. 96, 113, 14ff. This program seems to me essentially the same as Ryle's and to be subject to the usual criticisms leveled against Ryle, and in particular those made by Cornman (James W. Cornman, *Metaphysics, Reference and Language* [New Haven, 1966]). The need for such a drastic move as saying that "thought" does not refer is, I think, obviated by Sellars's treatment of thoughts as quasitheoretical entities.
[18] Cf. *ibid.*, p. 113.    [19] *Ibid.*, p. 102.

Turing machine and mental states of a human being is, like the familiar Cartesian analogies, a result of mentalizing the physical – an exercise which whether carried out regionally (as in Dennett and Putnam) or globally (as in panpsychist metaphysics) is just too easy to be of any real help.[20]

[20] The same sort of mentalizing is at work, I believe, in the Chomsky–Fodor notion of tacit knowledge (of, e.g., rules of language). The "brain as community of correspondents" view is, in fact, defended by Fodor in "The Appeal to Tacit Knowledge in Psychological Explanation" (*Journal of Philosophy*, 65 (1968), pp. 627–40). For what seems to me a decisive reply to Fodor, see Thomas Nagel, "The Boundaries of Inner Space," *Journal of Philosophy*, 66 (1969), pp. 452–8; see also Nagel's and Harman's contributions to Sidney Hook, ed., *Language and Philosophy* (New York, 1969). The Chomsky–Fodor stretching of the term "knowledge" (and, more generally, of the term "mental process") seems to come to no more than expectation that physiological processes correlated with paradigm referents of these terms will turn out to resemble those correlated with fringe referents. Such resemblances may exist, and if found they would probably modify our mentalistic concepts by interweaving physiological with the present behavioral criteria. But no light is shed on present problems in epistemology or philosophy of mind by the statement of such an expectation.

# CHAPTER 16

# Functionalism, machines, and incorrigibility

In a well-known paper published in 1960, Hilary Putnam put forward an analogy between the logical states of Turing machines and the mental states of human beings, and offered an explanation of how the "privacy" of the mental could be matched in a machine.* In subsequent papers by Putnam and various other philosophers, the notion that mental states are functional states has been taken as a new alternative to traditional theories of mind (dualism, behaviorism, materialism, etc.). I shall argue that the notion of "functional state" cannot help to clarify that of "mental state" unless something like Putnam's interpretation of the "privacy" of states of a machine can be accepted, and I shall go on to claim that nothing like this interpretation is going to work. I think, however, that the point Putnam makes in his 1961 paper against traditional "theories of mind" is sound and important, and can be clarified by being disentangled from talk of "functionalism."

It is hard to find in the recent literature an exact characterization of what a "functional" state is. We may, however, begin with Jerry Fodor, who says that common-sense psychological theories that do not pry into physiological mechanisms postulate inner states (beliefs, desires, etc.) which purport to account for behavior, and that "the characterization of these states is purely functional since we know about them only what role they play in the production of behavior."[1] Such states sound much like old-fashioned Rylean dispositions to behave, but presumably the difference is that Rylean behaviorists dreamed of an explicit definition of "the belief that $p$" in terms of movements of the body, sounds emitted, etc., whereas functionalists recognize that implicit definition must replace explicit and

---

* "Minds and Machines," in Sidney Hook, ed., *Dimensions of Mind* (New York 1960), pp. 138–64. Parenthetical page references in the text will be to this article, unless otherwise noted.

[1] "Explanations in Psychology," in Max Black, ed., *Philosophy in America* (Ithaca, 1965), p. 174.

that reference to other inner states (desires, other beliefs, etc.) must enter into an explanation of what such phrases mean.[2]

To say that men have mental as well as physical states, then, will be to say, uncontroversially, that a theory postulating such "internal" states works. If this is all there is to be said about the mind, then indeed functionalism takes away traditional puzzles about materialism versus dualism – for the utility of such a theory will never lead us to wonder whether the states postulated might exist in some realm of being other than the routine physical realm. But if this is all that mental states are, it is hard to see why there ever were greater puzzles about the relation between the body and the mind than about the relation between the body and its diseases, or between Newtonian particles and their inertia and mass. More generally, if all it takes to be a functional state is to be (a) unobservable ("inner"),[3] (b) not capable of being characterized without reference to other unobservables, and (c) capable of alternative "physical realizations," practically anything you can mention will have lots of functional states. Condition (c) will be satisfied by anything, for example, which can be thought of as having a microstructure that might conceivably be different, even though its macroscopic behavior, and the common-sense theory used to explain that behavior, remain the same.

I suspect that the notion of mental states as functional states would have had little attraction if it had not been tied up, in Putnam's original article, with the notion of the "logical state" of a Turing machine. As Kalke has pointed out in a very acute critical treatment of Putnam and Fodor, any state of any machine can be viewed as a functional state if one describes the "function" and the "realization" in the right way.[4] In the next few pages, I shall simply be drawing corollaries of Kalke's point and applying them to some particular features of Putnam's presentation.

You know what logical state a Turing machine is in if you can calculate as a function of its input (a) its output, (b) where it will go for its next

---

[2] I am grateful to Gilbert Harman for this way of explaining the difference between, e.g., Ryle and Putnam.

[3] It is hard to see what an "internal" or "inner" state is except a state that cannot be "sensed" to occur at a given moment by observing the entity in question. It cannot just mean "under the surface" or "beneath the skin," for the physical realizations of functional states (e.g., brain-processes) which are discovered in what Fodor calls "phase two" theories are not themselves "inner" states. So I think that "unobservable" is a fair gloss on "internal," given the standard proviso that observability is relative to theory and circumstances.

[4] William Kalke, "What Is Wrong with Fodor and Putnam's Functionalism," *Noûs*, 3, (1 1969), pp. 83–94.

input, (c) from what part of the program it will get its next instruction.[5] You know its logical state, that is, when you know those among its dispositions to behave which can be inferred from examining its program (its "machine table," as Putnam calls it). It has other dispositions to behave that are not logical states: among these are the disposition of a certain flip-flop to go on if and only if another flip-flop is on, the same flip-flop's disposition to fuse when the voltage gets too high, the disposition of the console to collapse when kicked, etc. The logical states are among, but of course do not exhaust, its "functional" states. For having a collapsible console is a functional state in the sense delimited above. The collapsibility is not observable, cannot be characterized except by reference to other unobservables (pressure, e.g.), and can be physically realized in plastic, copper, cardboard, etc. Yet, *relative to the program in question*, collapsibility is not a "logical" state.

Why does it seem – as it surely does – that a logical state of a machine is more like a person's mental state than, say, the collapsibility of its console? Mainly, I think, because we think of the Turing machine as *computing*, of computing as a mental operation, and of the dispositions described in its program as those which account for its computational capacity.[6] In the case of an automatic oil refinery, we are less likely to take any of the behavioral dispositions inferable from its program as analogous to mental states. But we may, if we think of the refinery as *deciding* when to flush out a tank, *calculating* the degree of impurity of the crude, etc., rather than simply as *refining*. The trouble is, however, that, in the spirit of our animist ancestors, we can project this mentalism too easily onto anything. How clever of the amoeba to wiggle away, realizing that the hot water will harm it! How sensible of the console to collapse when kicked hard enough, instead of obstinately resisting! We can carve out any chunk of the universe, treat it as a probabilistic automaton[7] by writing up a description of its behavior in the form of a program, and describe its activity in terms

---

[5] This is a rough account of "logical state." For the full account, see Putnam, "Minds and Machines," pp. 140–1.

[6] Consider a Turing machine that had only one logical state – describable roughly as "reproduce on the 'output tape' whatever comes in on the 'input tape,' and then go on to the next square on the 'input tape'." Such a Turing machine – an automatic-feed mimeograph machine, for instance – would be in a perfectly good logical state, but if this were the only sort of Turing machine we had yet imagined the analogy Putnam suggests would fall flat. It is the fact that certain complex Turing machines can be made to do certain particular kinds of things which gives the analogy what attractiveness it has.

[7] Cf. Putnam, "Psychological Predicates," in W. H. Capitan and D. D. Merrill, eds., *Art, Mind, and Religion* (Pittsburgh, 1966), pp. 42–3, for a generalization of the notion of "Turing machine" into that of "probabilistic automaton" and the remark that "everything is a probabilistic automaton under *some* Description." (Putnam defines a "Description" of a system $S$ as "any true statement to the effect

like "computing," "deciding," "trying," "choosing," "preferring," etc. Its logical states will then seem much like mental states (especially if we "complicate" the chunk by splitting up its behavior into lots of discrete bits, thus producing a program that is very difficult to read).

The important point to note is that the notion of "logical state" is capable of just as wide application as that of "functional state." It is not as if there were just one program, or "machine table" per machine, and not as if those chunks of the universe called "machines" in ordinary language were relevantly different from anything else. At the level of abstraction at which Putnam is formulating the definition of "logical state," anything you like is at any time in as many logical states as there are distinct programs you have the patience to write. So it is not that there is something special about computers, a grasp of which enables us to understand our own mentalistic discourse better. The analogy between people and computers will appear only when we bring psychological language to bear on the computers – where "psychological language" is defined by enumeration, giving specific examples of what counts as a psychological predicate (e.g., "belief," "desire," etc.). To say that computers have quasi-mental states whereas refineries and amoebas don't is merely to say that psychological language is more useful for talking about the former than about the latter – but this is not because of anything "internal" to the machine, but simply because it is designed to behave in more characteristically human ways than are refineries or amoebas.

To see more clearly how thin is the analogy between logical states and mental states, consider the three features that Putnam lists as distinguishing "logical and mental states respectively from structural and physical ones":

(1)    The functional organization (problem solving, thinking) of the human being or machine can be described in terms of the sequences of mental or logical states respectively (and the accompanying verbalizations), without reference to the nature of the "physical realization" of these states.

(2)    The states seem intimately connected with *verbalization*.

(3)    In the case of rational thought (or computing) the "program" which determines which states follow which, etc., is open to rational criticism (p. 149).

that $S$ possesses distinct states $S_1, S_2, \ldots, S_n$ which are related to one another and to the motor outputs and sensory inputs by the transition probabilities given in such-and-such a Machine Table.")

(1) does not locate a significant analogy; for it is trivially true that, for any given description of anything that can be construed as "behaving," its functional organization can be described in terms of "functional states" in the sense given above without reference to the "physical realization" of those latter states. Logical states do not differ from other functional states in respect to alternative modes of realization; and digestion, e.g., is not a mental state simply because enzymes other than pepsin might do the job. All that (1) does is to make us note that a given description of an entity's "function" (computing, collapsing, fusing, refining) will, together with a given way of chopping up its behavior, suggest a way of describing that behavior in terms of a program.

Does "verbalization" help out here, and can (2) prop up (1)? It all depends on what we call "verbalization," and whether we can get a characterization of this notion that does not have to he explicated by the notion of "mental." If we hook up recorded messages to our oil refinery so that it makes noises like "I've just decided to flush tank number nine" at appropriate moments, should this count as verbalization? When the console squeaks and shows cracks just before buckling under repeated kicks, is it "verbalizing" (in its own language, so to speak) its intention to give way? The trouble is, once again, that practically anything can be thought of as "verbalizing" (as saying something rather than just making noises) given the right animistic "set." Any functional states will "seem intimately connected with verbalization" just as long as we provide "mentalistic" characterizations of those states and extend our "mentalizing" to interpret as "nonnatural" meanings what would ordinarily be called "natural" meanings.[8] The quotes Putnam puts around "verbalization" point to the need to adopt the appropriate animism for Turing machines' inscriptions on tapes; a similar effort of imagination will produce the same results for any chunk of the universe. To make something out of the analogy, we would have to show that animism is somehow better founded in the case of inscriptions on tape than in the case of the console's squeaks: but what would such a foundation look like here?

Coming now to (3), in what sense is a program "open to rational criticism"? Presumably the sort of thing Putnam has in mind here is that one may remark about either a man or a computer that its way of solving a mathematical problem was inefficient. But this sort of remark can be made of anything that is viewed as employing means to effect an end – and

---

[8] I borrow this terminology from H. P. Grice, "Meaning," *Philosophical Review*, 66, 3 (1957), pp. 377–88.

anything that does any significant amount of "behaving" may be so viewed. For any program that one writes for any chunk of the universe, one can imagine another program that would have been more or less efficient.

To sum up, none of the features Putnam mentions gives us anything logical that mental states have in common and that they do not share with other functional states. Since the functional–structural distinction by itself sheds no light on what it is to be mental, and since anything functionally described may (with more or less strain) be mentalistically described, the analogy between logical states and mental states seems unlikely to help us shake off hopes or fears of psychophysical dualism. In a previous article,[9] I have urged that this dualism would not have been intelligible if we had had merely such relatively long-term items as beliefs, desires, moods, intentions, and the like to cope with. I argued there that it was occurrent, datable thoughts, and sense impressions – mental *events* as opposed to mental features – which made dualism plausible, and that the peculiarity of these events was that they were, uniquely, the topic of incorrigible beliefs. On the strength of this point, I suggest that privacy *qua* incorrigibility is the test case for the ability of "functionalism" to help us see through traditional puzzles about the relation between mind and body. I think this suggestion is buttressed by the fact that both Putnam and D. C. Dennett (who has recently developed the suggestions offered by Putnam's early article in considerable detail[10]) spend a great deal of time reconstructing the notion of "privacy" for machines, and that this reconstruction is practically the only point at which the actual makeup of the machine becomes relevant to their discussion. I turn now, therefore, to examination of two quotations which summarize their respective analyses of incorrigibility:

> If the machine prints "Vacuum tube 312 has failed" when vacuum tube 312 is in fact functioning, the mistake may be due to a miscomputation (in the course of "reading" and "interpreting" the input tape) or to an incorrect signal from a sense organ. On the other hand, if the machine prints: "I am in state A," and it does this simply because its machine table contains the

---

[9] Cf. "Incorrigibility as the Mark of the Mental," *Journal of Philosophy*, 67, 12 (1970), pp. 399–424, pp. 406ff [Chapter 8 in the present volume, pp. 154ff]. In the present chapter I shall not bother to distinguish the various senses of "incorrigibility" I distinguished there, but shall ask the reader to refer to that paper for a defense of the claim that incorrigibility is a respectable notion which can be used to help mark off the mental from the physical.

[10] *Content and Consciousness* (New York, 1969), ch. 5. Reviewed in *Journal of Philosophy*, 69 (1972), pp. 220–4.

instruction: *Print "I am in state A" when in state A,* then the question of a miscomputation cannot arise. Even if some accident causes the printing mechanism to print: "I am in state A" when the machine is *not* in state A, there was not a "miscomputation" (only, so to speak, a "verbal slip") (Putnam, p. 148).

Human beings have some capacity for the monitoring of internal *physical* states such as fevers, and computers can have similar monitoring devices for their own physical states, but when either makes a report of such internal physical conditions, the question of how these are *ascertained* makes perfect sense, and can be answered by giving a succession of states through which the system passes in order to ascertain its physical condition. But when the state reported is a logical or functionally individuated state, the task of ascertaining, monitoring or examining drops out of the reporting process (Dennett, p. 103).

Two points of analogy between mental states and logical states are offered: (1) it makes no sense to suggest about a report of either that a mistake (as opposed to a verbal slip) was made; (2) it makes no sense to ask how either was ascertained by the man or machine who has them. The first point is crucial, but the second is, I think, a red herring. I shall concentrate first on "ascertaining" in order to clear the ground for a discussion of "mistakes."

Why does it make sense to ask how a man ascertains that he has a fever, but not how he ascertains that he has a pain? Surely in both cases it is reasonable for the man to reply "I just know" or "I can feel it" or "I know what a fever (pain) is like." In both cases, in short, knowledge may be noninferential (unless we invoke an unverifiable theory of "unconscious inferences"). Is the point then that one *could* have inferred that one had a fever, but could *not* have inferred that one was in pain? Well, what of the man who says "I'm not quite sure what pain feels like, but I certainly wouldn't want to have that feeling again, and other people tell me that being burned is always painful, so I guess it was pain that I felt"? Why is he not making an inference?[11] Perhaps, then, the notion of "states through which the system passes" is not to be explicated by reference to the notion of inference. Perhaps it is a matter of physical states. But this will not work either. Even if we could adopt some standard way of individuating physical

---

[11] The same point holds for a machine's knowledge of its logical states. One can program a machine to print "I am in state A" when in state A, but one can also program a machine to *find out* that it is in state A. A theory-constructing machine could, for example, watch its own inputs and outputs for a while and conclude that whenever it had been in state B and came upon input X it went into state A and stayed there until it came upon input Y. It could then argue inductively that it must now be in state A. *Pace* the last sentence of the quotation from Dennett, "the task of ascertaining . . ." may or may not "drop out of the reporting process."

states, we have no idea whether a human being goes through more of them in answering the question "Do you have a fever?" than in answering "Are you in pain?"

Putnam attempts to clarify the notion of "ascertaining" by saying that "the 'verbal report' ("I am in state A" or "I am in pain") issues directly from the state it 'reports'" (145–6). This latter notion, in turn, is explicated by Dennett, who says that "The report issues directly from the state it reports in that the machine is in state A only if it reports it is in state A" (103). But this will not do. Consider a panel on the console which sometimes lights up to read "The danger sign is on." The danger sign will be on only if the machine reports that the danger sign is on, but its being on is not a logical state of the machine. Further, if this is what we mean by "issuing directly," then we have no reason to say that pain-reports issue directly from pains, for one can be in pain without reporting it (and even, in pre-linguistic children, without knowing that one is).

What Putnam needs to explicate "issues directly" is some relation that could not possibly hold between flip-flop 72 being on and the machine's printing out "Flip-flop 72 is on" but will always hold between the machine's being disposed to print out "I am in state A" and its actually printing it out. But what could such a relation be? If the physical set-up of the machine is such that it always prints "Flip-flop 72 is on" whenever it is on, it seems reasonable to say that whenever it is on it is disposed so to print. Why should this disposition not count as "issuing directly" in a report just as much as the disposition to print "I am in state A"? I suspect that Putnam would say that it is part of the meaning of "issues directly" that only logical states can issue directly in reports, and that physical states cannot. Thus, we find him saying elsewhere that

> "Flip-flop 72 is on" may be correctly (reasonably) uttered only when the robot "knows" that flip-flop 72 is on – i.e., only when it can *conclude* that flip-flop 72 is on from empirically established theory together with such observation statements as its conditioning may prompt it to utter, or as it may hear other robots utter.[12]

But this just begs the question. What we want to know is why it doesn't count as knowledge (but only, so to speak, as a sort of reflex movement) if the machine is just wired up to print "Flip-flop 72 is on" whenever it is on (rather than using internal sensors, theory construction, and the rest, to

[12] "Robots: Machines or Artificially Created Life?," *Journal of Philosophy*, 61, 21 (1964), pp. 668–91, p. 671; hereafter referred to as "Robots."

"ascertain" that it is on). We cannot say that the former case fails to be knowledge simply because the machine cannot give reasons for its claim, for that would rule out "direct" knowledge of its logical states as well. All we can say is that logical states are somehow suited to be the kind of thing that is knowable without evidence, but physical states are not. But we will say *that* only if we have already accepted the analogy between mental states and logical states – an analogy which we wanted to support by showing that logical states can be known in a way in which physical states cannot. We have gone around in a circle.

I think, however, that this whole question about "issuing directly" as opposed to "ascertaining" is merely a result of Putnam's having run together the notion of direct (noninferential) knowledge and the notion of incorrigible knowledge. The real difference between pains and fevers, from an epistemological point of view, is not a matter of evidence or inference, but just that you can be mistaken in thinking you have a fever but not in thinking that you have a pain. That is why we call the one physical and the other mental. What Putnam needs to do is to show that machines can have incorrigible knowledge of their logical states but not of their physical states. So let us come now to the point labeled (1) above – the point that a machine can make "verbal slips" but not "mistakes" about its logical states, but can make both about its physical states. What does this verbal slip/mistake distinction come to? In human beings, it is explicated by reference to locutions like "When I said *S* I wasn't lying, but yet I didn't believe *S*; I *meant* to say something different." What would it be for a machine to say something different from what it believed? What are the tests for what a machine believes at a given time, other than what it prints out? We might suggest: what it would have printed out if something hadn't gone wrong with the printing mechanism. But this assumes a distinction between the printing mechanism and the "central processor" which may not exist. (Consider a computer such as Babbage's original "analytical engine," whose processing registers are made out of gears with numbers printed on them, numbers visible to the operator. Here there can be no separation between, so to speak, what the machine thinks and what it says.) We cannot explicate the slip/mistake distinction for machines by reference to the physical set-up of the machine any more than we can do it for humans by reference to different sets of nerves.[13]

---

[13] To see this latter point, note that if we diagnosed a report as a slip of the tongue because the state of certain efferent nerves did not correspond to the state of certain "central" nerves in the usual way,

It is tempting, perhaps, to think that we can distinguish between the machine's beliefs and its utterances by distinguishing between its program and its performance and thus between "programming errors" and "machine errors." But these distinctions presuppose that we do not have to infer the machine's program from its performance, but have the program available in advance. If we do, then we can give one sort of criticism of the program (by reference to the ends for which the program was written) and another sort of criticism of the hardware (by reference to whether it actually does what the program prescribes). This gives us a distinction between two ways of going wrong, to be sure, but what does it have in common with the distinction between mistakes and slips? There is nothing connected with a human being analogous to having his program available in advance – but suppose there were. What would such a document tell us? Not what the man would do – for he might make slips. Not what he was "built" to do – for this could cover making slips as well as making mistakes. Perhaps his stream of consciousness for all his life? But why should *that* be the analogue of the machine's program? Why indeed, unless we had *already* decided that logical states were analogous to mental states? We cannot get any independent support for the latter analogy by focusing on the mistake/slip distinction. We can give sense to this distinction (for machines) only if we have adopted the analogy first.

Once again, we have gone around in a circle. Once again, we need to remember that the "program" of a machine (or a man) can be written at any level of abstraction we wish. For example, we can write a program for a man which treats him as a stimulus-response mechanism or we can write a program that uses intentional terms; the former program will see many distinct sorts of input (many topologically distinguishable sorts of inscriptions) where the latter sees only one (the word "man," say). For a machine (as Kalke points out)[14] we can write a program in "engineering" terms or, at the other extreme, in FORTRAN terms. Here again, what counts as many different inputs in the first program may count as only one in the second. Just as the number of distinguishable inputs (and outputs) will differ, so the number and kind of distinct logical states that the machine may be in will differ. The point is that all these programs are equally programs, and all the logical states read off from them equally *logical* states. But only if we

our diagnosis could be overruled by the man in question saying (and behaving in a way consistent with saying) "No, I meant exactly what I said."

[14] Cf. *op. cit.*, p. 88. Kalke rightly remarks that even the "engineering" program is still "functional" rather than "physical," since it too allows of being realized in lots of different ways.

choose just the right program – the FORTRAN program for the machine and the intentional for the man, say – will we be able to make the sort of analogy we were struggling for in the last paragraph (between "slips" and "machine errors" on the one hand and "mistakes" and "programming errors" on the other). This should make us see that what analogy there is is not between mental states and logical states *an sich*, but between programs that divide up the environment into roughly the same number and kinds of inputs and which also divide up the behavior of the pro-gramed entity (man or machine) into roughly the same number and kinds of outputs. Given two chunks of the universe of approximately equal complexity (relative to some given level of abstraction) and given some level of abstraction at which the environment and behavior of each chunk can be described in the same terms, these two chunks will be found to have analogous states. Specifically, if one of them is assumed to have mental states, the other can reasonably be said, *ceteris paribus*, to have mental states. Our ability to "mentalize" anything we like, referred to above, is just a corollary of Kalke's point that "nearly any two physical-chemical systems could be considered functionally isomorphic under some description fixing the behavior and boundary of each."[15]

Does all this mean that all analogies between men and machines are necessarily made rather than found? That no interesting empirical similar-ities might be discovered? Certainly not. Once we *fix* on a given level of abstraction, we can then go on to find lots of "real" similarities and differences. For example, suppose we have decided (as we naturally would) to describe a machine that took in and put out sentences of English in terms of the same "intentional" program we would use for a humanoid organism that did the same thing. We could then *find out* whether, e.g., it made slips of the tongue as well as mistakes, or just mistakes, or neither. We could see whether it said things like, or paraphrasable as, "Sorry, I didn't say what I meant" at appropriate times and backed up these remarks with appropriate behavior. No light on the nature of verbal slips would be shed by a discovery that the machine made verbal slips – because our criteria for "slip" would be the same old familiar criteria. (But then why should we expect such light to be shed?)

---

[15] *Op. cit.*, p. 91. The point Kalke makes here is also made in a wider context by R. C. Buck, "On the Logic of General Behavior Systems Theory," in Herbert Feigl and Michael Scriven, eds., *Minnesota Studies in the Philosophy of Science*, 1 (Minneapolis, 1956), pp. 223–38. I think that much of the excitement generated by the slogan "let's study and build computers in order to find out about the mind!" vanishes when this point is appreciated – although the possibility of learning about the *brain* by studying and building computers survives intact.

So far, in considering Putnam's claims that machines can be incorrigible about their logical states we have merely considered how we might clarify the slip–mistake distinction. Let us now face the question about incorrigibility head on. Consider a logical state characterizable, in part, as "if you get X as an input, print Y; also print 'I am in state A' and then shift into state C." Suppose the machines gets X, prints Z, also prints "I am in state A," and then shifts into C. Was it in state A? If we say that it was, then we must (on Putnam's view) say that printing Z was a "slip." If we say that it was not, but was instead in state B (a state such that if it gets X it prints Z, also prints "I am in state B," and then shifts into C), then we must say that printing "I am in state A" was a "slip." How could we possibly tell which to say? How could it matter? But what does "incorrigibility" come to if we cannot use the machine's own reports to decide this sort of case? In an analogous case for human beings – e.g., "I'm frantic with hunger and can think of no reason not to eat it" accompanied by not eating it – we still take the report of hunger as incorrigible (putting insincerity and ignorance of the language to one side, as we have been tacitly putting it to one side for the machine). We do so in the human case because, roughly, we have found it to be a fruitful heuristic rule that when first-person contemporaneous reports of certain states conflict with other evidence about the presence of those states, the former should override the latter.[16] If, with respect to a very sophisticated machine, we found that certain states played roles in its behavioral economy very close to those which being frantically hungry, thinking of Vienna, etc., played in ours, then (given that the machine reported on such states and reported making no inferences to such reports) we might decide to extend the same heuristic rule to the machine's reports of those states. But if we then found that the simplest and most fruitful explanations of the machine's behavior involved overriding these reports, we should cease to apply this rule.[17] If we so ceased, we could then say either that the machine seemed to have no mental states or that the machine didn't seem to have incorrigible knowledge of its mental states. The latter remark would be paradoxical, but it would be a natural

---

[16] If we ask which states these are, we can reply "the mental ones," but this is not an answer that gives us an explanation or justification of the rule, for "mental" just means "the sort of state people are incorrigible about." (I try to defend this latter claim in "Incorrigibility as the Mark of the Mental" referred to above.)

[17] Genuine doubt about whether or not to apply such a rule would be possible, of course, only if the states in question were describable in much more complex "multi-tracked" ways than we have just used to describe "state A." Suppose the description of state A given above were completed simply by "If you don't get X as input, turn yourself off." Inquiry about the worth of the machine's self-reports would then find no foothold.

way of expressing a modification of our concept of "mental" which might be induced by coming across machines of the sort described. The important point is just that in deciding whether a given functional state is mental we have nothing better to go on than (a) whether it plays a role analogous to that of some mental states in humans, and (b) whether it seems best to apply the above-mentioned heuristic rule to reports of it. The two criteria are distinct, and may conflict. Putnam goes from the assumption that certain machine states can fulfill the first criterion to the claim that, provided knowledge of them is "noninferential," the second will be fulfilled also. But why should it be?

Summing up what has been said so far: (1) there is no *prima facie* analogy between logical states in general and mental states in general, but only between those logical states which are inferable from programs written at the "right" level of abstraction and applied to machines whose performance is antecedently described in mentalistic terms; (2) the more restricted analogy cannot be strengthened by pointing to the noninferential character of reports of the chosen logical states; (3) even if the right level of abstraction were chosen, the mentalistic description were adopted, and "noninferentiality" were assumed, it would still be an open empirical question whether any given such state of any given machine was incorrigibly knowable by that machine. So we may answer the question "Do machines have privileged access to their own states?" by saying "We can describe machines that do, but machines said to have such access must satisfy the same sort of criteria that human beings who claim such knowledge must satisfy." Once again, no illumination is shed on either mentality or privacy by considering machines. If the machine is simple enough, the analogy seems merely whimsical. If it is complicated enough so that the analogy appears to have "foundation," it is *so* complicated that the analogy comes down to saying "Anything that displays all the relevant behavior of a human in a given mental state might as well, *ceteris paribus*, be said to be in that state" – an entirely uninteresting remark.

The main negative point I wished to make in this chapter has now been supported as well as I can support it. Before concluding with some positive remarks about Putnam's approach, however, I should like to look for a moment at Putnam's "alternative" account of privacy in machines. In a paper subsequent to "Minds and Machines," after noting that "evincing" is too simple a model for reconstructing the notion of privacy, Putnam goes on as follows:

> If he [a robot] is in the appropriate internal state for red, but knows on the basis of cross-inductions from certain other cases that what he "sees" is not

really red, he will say "it *looks* red, but it isn't really red." Thus he will have a distinction between the physical reality and the visual appearance, just as we do. But the robot will never say "that looks as if it looked red, but it doesn't really look red." That is, there is no notion in the robot-English of an *appearance of an appearance of red*, any more than there is in English. Moreover, the reason is the same: that any state which cannot be discriminated from "looks-red" *counts* as "looks-red" (under normal conditions of linguistic proficiency, absence of confusion, etc.). What this illustrates, of course, is that the "incorrigibility" of statements of the form "that looks red" is to be explained by an elucidation of the logical features of such discourse, and not by the metaphor of "direct" access. ("Robots," pp. 65–6)

There are various things wrong with this tactic. In the first place, one does not have the notion of a visual appearance if one merely has the notion of "looks red, but is not." A visual appearance is something mental, but on Putnam's account one could have the notion of "looks red, but is not" without having any notion of mentality – for this notion will merely be a paraphrase of "I'm disposed to say that this is red, but there are counter-vailing considerations."[18] In the second place, it is no help to say that anything that cannot be discriminated from "looks-red" counts as "looks-red," for "cannot be discriminated" is so vague that it would be equally true to say that anything that cannot be discriminated from "red" counts as "red." Putnam's point about "no appearance of an appearance" comes down to: the program is set up so that the machine does not recognize anything as counterevidence to "I am disposed to say that this is red." But this shows nothing about incorrigibility, for a simpler machine might have been programed to recognize nothing as counterevidence to "This is red." So the claim will have to be: machines are incorrigible when they report their own dispositions. But we have just finished showing what is wrong with this claim. In the third place, talk about "the logical features of such discourse" is merely a pre-Quinean way of referring to the existence of such heuristic rules as that discussed above: the rule that nothing is to count as overriding certain reports. But once we ask whether this rule should be applied to the machine's report that "it looks red," we realize that, we must distinguish two cases: (a) nothing is relevant to the question whether it looks red to the machine save whether the machine says "it looks red"; (b) there are other criteria for its looking red to the

---

[18] For details on the difference between this "hesitant to say" sense of "looks" and the sense in which one's "looks like" reports say something about one's mental state, see Wilfrid Sellars, *Science, Perception, and Reality* (London, 1963), pp. 140–53 (and compare pp. 190ff).

machine – e.g., what the machine goes on to do about the red-looking thing, what else the machine says, etc. On (a), our attribution of incorrigibility to the machine would be as trivial and as whimsical as attributing incorrigibility to a phonograph which plays a record saying "I am now playing a phonograph record." On (b), there is a serious question whether to ascribe incorrigibility, but we should have to tell a much longer story than Putnam tells to know whether to ascribe it or not.

I conclude from this look at Putnam's more sophisticated account of privacy in machines that neither "evincing" (what Putnam in this later passage scornfully calls the "metaphor of 'direct' access") nor endowing the machine with the "looks like" vocabulary help us see what privacy is and why machines might have it. But, once again, I see no reason to deny that machines could have it. The point is rather that to ascribe it to them we should have to endow them with the full complexity of linguistic and other behavior with which humans are endowed, and then ascribe it to them on the same grounds as those on which we apply it to humans. In short, I want to grant Putnam's point that it would not be irrational (but would be a matter of "decision") to grant civil rights to robots, but contest his point that reviewing considerations for and against so doing leads to greater clarity about ordinary mentalistic discourse and greater understanding of what is wrong with dualism, materialism, epiphenomenalism, etc.

Despite all these criticisms of Putnam, I think that he is quite right in the conclusion of his 1960 article:

> The moral, I believe, is quite clear: it is no longer possible to believe that the mind-body problem is a genuine theoretical problem, or that a "solution" to it would shed the slightest light on the world in which we live. For it is quite clear that no grown man in his right mind would take the problem of the "identity" or "non-identity" of logical and structural states in a machine at all seriously – not because the answer is obvious, but because it is obviously of no importance *what* the answer is. But if the so-called "mind-body problem" is nothing but a different realization of the same set of logical and linguistic issues, then it must be just as empty and just as verbal. (p. 164)

I suggest that the reason why nobody would take the problem of "identity" seriously here is that no one imagines there could be any explanatory power gained by reference to the logical states of the machine which might not be had by reference to its structural states. It is not a matter of a problem we once thought to be genuine having been revealed as "linguistic," but rather of its having been solved by empirical means. Nobody thinks, in other words, that we would be less able to predict and control the behavior of the machine if we described it in only "hardware" terms. If we want to know what it's going to do, we feel, we can always ask the man who built it. The reason Cartesian dualism was so popular for so long was simply that nobody was at all sure whether we might not lose some explanatory power if we had nothing but physiology to go on – and the reason Cartesian dualism is so unpopular nowadays is not because of any application of the powerful methods of modern analytic philosophy, but simply because we keep reading in *Life* and *The Scientific American* about cerebral localization, the production of any desired emotion, thought, or sense impression by the insertion of electrodes, and the like. These results make us think that if we knew enough physiology we could forget about common-sense ways of accounting for the behavior of our friends and relations. Given this notion, the question about identity is indeed pretty silly – we become materialists without being identity theorists. Because we suspect that common-sense psychological theory is a dispensable crutch, we look at all theories about the relation between mental and physical entities (identity or nonidentity, causal relations vs. parallelism) as just about as tiresome as theories about the "relations" between astrological and astronomical entities, or demons and germs, or unicorns and narwhals. If we understand materialism as an Identity Theory, then, as Putnam says, "*Of course* materialism is false; but is so *trivially* false that no materialist should be bothered" ("Robots," 690). If we understand materialism as a possible *replacement* for common sense, then it is obviously true, but, equally obviously, it does not conflict with whatever dualism is built into common sense. It is so obviously true that no ordinary-language philosopher should be bothered.

We could, of course, all be misled by recent fragmentary successes in cerebral localization. Perhaps in the end we shall never come up with anything like so neat or handy a way of accounting for behavior in physiological terms as what we now have in terms of beliefs and desires. Perhaps it will become clear that we shall never come up with any way at all, handy or unhandy. If physiology lets us down, then dualism will be back among us with redoubled strength – no matter how many anti-Cartesian conceptual analyses we perform. Functionalism will then be no better than logical behaviorism in putting down dualists. Just as it took modern science to make us atheists – despite all the clever conceptual analyses of the ancient skeptics – it will take physiology to make us materialists. If physiology doesn't work, all the analogies between beliefs and habits, beliefs and valve lifters, beliefs and logical states, will fall flat.

If what I have been saying is right, then we should not say, as Fodor, for example, does, that "functional analysis" is indispensable no matter how good physiology gets. Fodor summarizes his view as follows:

> Explanation in psychology consists of a functional analysis and a mechanistic analysis: a phase one theory and a determination of which model of the theory the nervous system of the organism represents. Neither aspect of the explanation is dispensable ... To put it succinctly, a complete psychological explanation requires more than an account of what the neurological circuitry is; it requires also an account of what such circuitry does. This second sort of account is given in terms of the familiar constructs of psychology: drives, motives, strategies, and so forth.[19]

The suggestion that such an account *must* be given in these terms is not argued for, and, if it is not, then we have no argument for the "indispensability" of the functional, and no reason to agree with Putnam that it is because the "notion of functional organization" has been overlooked that "discussions in the philosophy of mind are often curiously unsatisfying."[20] The illumination gained from the comparison of logical states to mental states is genuine, but it comes from an appeal to our growing empirical knowledge about how men work and about how to build humanoid machines, not from an appeal to a philosophical notion which is, I have been arguing, too thin and abstract to help us.[21]

---

[19] Fodor, *op. cit.*, p. 177. Note that Fodor does not include thoughts and sense impressions in the list of things that we should still have to talk about, and that in general it would be much more difficult to treat these as "functions" than to so treat desires and beliefs. Yet, as I tried to show in "Incorrigibility as the Mark of the Mental," occurrent thoughts and sense impressions are our paradigms of the mental.

[20] Putnam, "The Mental Life of Some Machines," in Hector-Neri Castañeda, ed., *Intentionality, Minds, and Perception* (Detroit, 1967), p. 200.

[21] I discuss the topic of "functionalism" and its analysis of "awareness" also in "Dennett on Awareness," forthcoming in *Philosophical Studies* [*Philosophical Studies*, 23, 3 (1972), pp. 153–62; Chapter 15 in this volume]. I am grateful to Gilbert Harman and George Pitcher for helpful comments and suggestions.

# Index of names